Good Housekeeping's

Cooking for Company

First published in Great Britain 1970
© The National Magazine Co. Ltd
Reprinted 1972

Line drawings by Yvonne Skargon

Colour photographs facing pages 97 and 144,
and on back jacket, Anthony Blake; facing
page 145, Frank Coppins; facing page 208,
John Street; all other colour photographs by
Michael Boys. Black and white photographs
by Michael Leale

ISBN 0 85223 002 8

Printed in Great Britain by
Fletcher & Son Ltd, Norwich
and bound by Richard Clay
(The Chaucer Press) Ltd, Bungay, Suffolk.
Set in Monotype Baskerville and Univers.

Good Housekeeping's

Cooking for Company

EBURY PRESS · LONDON

Foreword

Parties of all sorts, from a grand wedding buffet to an informal 'Wine and Pâté' evening, can prove great fun and enormously rewarding. It makes all the difference, however, if you are well prepared and – especially in the case of the more formal occasions – if you have a reasonably detailed blueprint to follow.

In this book, written by Shirley Green, we have brought to bear all the Good Housekeeping Institute expertise, and we offer ideas and advice on running a great variety of parties, from impromptu to grand. Entertaining is of course much less formal than it used to be, but we include the know-how for those gatherings where some traditional formality is still essential. The menus, the cookery countdowns and the information about catering and shopping are supplied by the famous Good Housekeeping Institute, where all the recipes have been tried and tested by a team of experts headed by Margaret Coombes. This book will, we hope, lend you confidence to give parties for your friends without suffering either sleepless nights or days of slavish preparation.

Finally, we should like to remind you of Good Housekeeping Institute's unique after-service. If you have any cookery enquiry, just write to the address given below, and we shall be pleased to do all we can to help.

CAROL MACARTNEY
Principal

Good Housekeeping Institute,
Chestergate House,
Vauxhall Bridge Road,
London, S.W.1.

Contents

Contents, continued

List of Colour Plates

Acknowledgement
Our thanks are due to the following firms for the loan of accessories used in the black and white photographs in this book: Craftsman Potters Association of Great Britain Ltd.; Wilson & Gill; Heal and Son Ltd.; Robert Jackson and Co. Ltd.; Liberty & Co. Ltd.; Josiah Wedgwood & Sons Ltd.

1
Menu Planning, Shopping and Preparation

MENU STRATEGY

Good marriages may be made in heaven, but good menus are made with ordinary mortal toil. No hostess gets by on inspiration alone – or if she thinks she does, it's only because her mind has learnt to cope automatically with the groundwork.

Be Realistic

To begin with, accept your limitations, as regards both cooking ability and circumstances. Unless you're lucky enough to have competent help, include only one course that's going to need serious on-the-spot concentration. Try to start off with something like pâté, for instance, so that you can enjoy a pre-dinner drink with your guests and need vanish only at the last minute to get the toast ready. Or if the weather's cold, serve a piping hot soup that you've prepared in advance, and simply heat it up at the last moment. Plan for a sweet that's simple, too. It's impossible to predict how long the main course of a meal is going to take, and you don't want to have to sit through it in agonies, oblivious to the conversation and wondering whether something's boiled dry or burned to a cinder. Obvious dishes to avoid, unless you're sublimely confident of your skills and timing, are anything potentially hit-or-miss like a hot soufflé, or anything fried. Otherwise your meal will be punctuated with mysterious pauses that will have your guests every bit as worried as you are.

For the inexperienced cook, who lives in terror of last-minute disasters, the simplest solution is to choose as the main course a casserole, which can be entirely prepared in advance. Potatoes baked in their jackets could make a foolproof accompaniment, and as vegetables would be an integral part of the casserole, there'd be no need to worry about what was happening to them. (You could offer a simple salad as a separate course.) Unless precision timing is your *forte*, it's always best to choose vegetables that can tick over happily for a few minutes while your guests catch up with them. Why sit wondering if the sprouts have gone soggy and yellow, when French beans, peas or carrots would have done just as well? And never risk trying out something new. If you want to branch out into more exciting fields, have a full 'dress rehearsal' with your family the weekend before.

Balance and Variety

Always plan a menu that has plenty of variety. If you start with a quiche, follow with steak and kidney pud, and then expect your guests to eat apple pie, you'll stun them with the sheer preponderance of starch. And if you start with game pâté, follow with coq au vin, and then serve marrons glacés, the cumulative richness will destroy both digestive systems and friendships. These are all fairly obvious points, but texture is something that can more easily be overlooked. A menu of egg mayonnaise, followed by kidneys in wine with fluffy mashed potatoes, followed by a fruit fool or sorbet, would provide a fair variety of flavours – but the overall effect would be slushy and lacking in 'bite'. The general principle is that a 'wet' course should precede a 'dry' one, or vice versa. A crisp fried main dish, preceded by a soup, and followed by a creamy sweet, would be a reasonable combination.

If you think your menu is running the risk of imbalance, it's often possible to retrieve the

7

situation with a simple gimmick. Serve a crisp green salad with macaroni cheese, croûtons with a cream soup, pastry fleurons with ragoût, and each dish immediately picks up interest. Conversely, serve a sauce with something that's dry, or add a side-plate of tomato salad – and the palate is immediately refreshed.

Flavour obviously needs considering, because too much food that's bland in taste is merely dull, whereas too much that's piquant is just impossible to eat. This is why a sharp Hollandaise sauce is served with turbot, and a lemon sauce with a steamed sponge pudding. And in reverse, it's why cream goes with a tart-flavoured apple pie, or rice is always served with curry.

Appearance is another vital factor, and one that can easily be improved by a moderate use of garnishes. A steak with chipped potatoes looks far more appetising if set off with a sprig of watercress and a grilled tomato, and any really anaemic-looking combination – creamed fish with marrow and potatoes, for instance – desperately needs a small sprig of parsley and perhaps some coralline pepper to make it look something more than a penance.

What to Serve to Whom

Now that imported foods are so much more readily available, the time of the year needn't dictate your menu planning to such a degree. Nevertheless, it's foolish not to make use of foods that are in season, because they'll not only be cheaper, but in prime condition. Where you do need to consider the seasons is in the planning of hot and cold dishes, and to a certain extent, in the quantities you serve, because most people are capable of tucking into larger helpings during the cold winter months. But even this distinction is becoming blurred with the more widespread use of central heating.

Consider the individual tastes of your guests, and don't risk serving curry, tripe, or any other fairly specialized taste, without checking first that they're going to like it. And be considerate to them in other less obvious ways. If you know one of your guests is likely to be shy and inexperienced, don't serve something that needs to be eaten with blasé defiance of conventional table manners. There's no sadder sight than a young girl furtively chopping her spaghetti with her fork, or pecking miserably at the spare ribs and leaving the best part of them. And similarly, don't serve foods that need specialized cutlery unless you possess it – or are on exceptionally relaxed and easy terms with your guests. It's difficult enough making a frontal attack on corn on the cob without being deprived of the cob spears to hold it by. Lobsters present tortuous problems without special lobster forks, and the thought of trying to hold down a hot escargot shell while it's swimming in garlic butter makes the mind boggle.

How Many Courses?

Whittling down the menu to three courses has become common practice nowadays, even at the most formal luncheons and dinner parties. People have come to accept that most hostesses cope single-handed, and have the sense to prefer a simple meal, well cooked and well served, to an over-ambitious one with a hostess red-faced and flustered. A generously-filled cheeseboard can provide an easy extra course, but must offer variety to cater for all tastes. Not everyone likes ripe Camembert and runny Brie – or that smelly goat cheese you discovered while on holiday. Serve some 'safe' English cheese, too, offering the choice of mild cheeses like Wensleydale and Caerphilly for people who like their flavours bland, robust cheese like Stilton for people who like their flavours strong, and either Cheddar, Cheshire or Red Leicester, to cover 'in-between' possibilities. To make the cheeseboard look more exciting, include one of the more unusual Continental cheeses, say the Danish Havarti or French Fromage de Monsieur – or perhaps the fairly new English Ilchester cheese. Fruit, carefully selected and washed to look refreshing, can form the final effortless course, that needs only a good cup of coffee (or two) to round off the meal to perfection. This is the theory – and you'll know it's worked when you've been able to relax and enjoy yourself almost as much as your guests.

SHOPPING

Only a fool would rush into shopping without a comprehensive list, but it takes more than method to make sure of getting good ingredients. It takes charm – the long-standing kind of charm that establishes friendly relations with local shopkeepers.

Buying the Meat

Most vital ally is your butcher, and there are two ways to get the best out of him. First is to throw yourself on his mercy, but show eagerness to learn. He'll find this refreshing, after people who buy routine chops and joints with a disinterested air. Second is to learn a little about meat, and amaze him by asking for something knowledgeably. This will earn his admiration and put him properly on his mettle. And always let him know when you're entertaining, so that he'll make that extra effort to do you proud.

Neither of these approaches can work unless you give him advance warning of what you need. It's no good asking for a crown of lamb on the spur of the moment. Any good butcher is an artist, and would like two to three days to prepare it properly – which isn't much when you consider he's got to persuade two best ends of lamb to form a perfect circle. If you want any unusual cut of meat – say veal knuckles for osso buco – give a week's notice if possible, because it will have to be specially ordered. And give notice even, of more standard requirements. If you want to serve beef, for instance, let your butcher know a week in advance so he can see that it's really well-hung.

And don't look dubious if it has a rather tired appearance when you collect it. That's how it should look (those bright red juicy-looking joints are often too fresh to be tender). The same applies to steaks, particularly for quantities, because no butcher is likely to have eight 6-ounce steaks on the off-chance. Give advance notice, too, of anything you want boned and rolled that wouldn't normally be prepared in that way, such as shoulder of lamb; two or three days should be adequate in this case. And finally, always be prepared to take your butcher's advice. If you ask for a fillet steak and he recommends some good Scotch rump he's had hanging for about a fortnight, take his word that it's a better buy. He's nothing to gain by losing your custom – and you've everything to gain by having the help of an expert.

Shopping for Fish

Get on good terms with your local fishmonger, too. He'll be equally relieved to find someone who thinks in terms of more than cod, plaice, and coley for the cat. A large fishmonger will keep about twenty varieties of fish as standard, but if you give a couple of days' notice, almost everything that's in season can be available. Smaller fishmongers will probably need advance notice for scallops, lobster or fresh mussels and out-of-the-ordinary fish. And irrespective of the shop's size, oysters will always need ordering. If you give the exact time you want to collect them (this should be as late on the day as possible), the fishmonger will have them all ready, open and waiting. For special occasions, it's worth insisting on the more expensive English oysters. These have a roundish shell, and a whiter meat and better flavour than the Portuguese type.

Contrary to the appearance of meat, which can be deceptive, when fish is good it looks good, too. The flesh is firm, the silvery scales sparkle, the eyes are bright and bulging, and any markings are bright. One test of freshness is to press the fish with your finger, and see if it retains (which it shouldn't) the impression. But few of us are brave enough to risk a fishmonger's displeasure: his tongue can be as sharp as his proverbial wife's. Your simplest guide is the smell and freshness of his shop as a

9

whole. It will smell 'fishy' of course, but this should be in a pleasant rather than an offensive way. Another guide is to note the number of deliveries. Even with the wonders of modern refrigeration, a shop that takes deliveries only twice a week can't hope to provide fish in peak condition every day. The violent temperature changes involved in taking it in and out of the fridge are inevitably harmful, and though the fish won't be 'off' (you'd smell it if it was) it will be just 'all right' – which isn't really good enough when guests are expected. In the absence of a fishmonger who takes daily deliveries (he, by the way, has the disadvantage that he runs low on stocks towards the end of the day), you can always plan your entertaining on delivery days.

Unlike the butcher, the fishmonger doesn't normally need advance warning of any filleting or gutting that's needed, because he always performs these tasks with incredible skill and speed on the spot. He doesn't always do them automatically, though. He may not clean herrings, for instance, because so many people buy them for their cats, but if asked, he will willingly do so – plus the following, at no extra charge: fillet fish of most kinds, especially flat fish; skin sole (dark side only or both sides if requested); skin plaice on the dark side – but only if requested; bone herrings; scale fish; open shell-fish; crack lobster claws; slice smoked salmon. In some shops he will even dress crab – that is, if you ask him very, very nicely.

The Grocery List

Grocers are less vital personal allies, because most groceries are sold ready-packed nowadays and many articles are standardized. But a skilled and knowledgeable tradesman is worth tracking down all the same. There are still things like bacon and cheese (for a glossary of cheese types and how to choose them, see Part IV) on which it's good to get advice, and it's always reassuring to be able to discuss the relative merits of butters or tea-blends with someone. Fortunately most groceries needed for entertaining can be bought well in advance, or stocked as part of your regular stores (see Part IV again for store-cupboard reminders

and check lists). It's best to cut on-the-day-shopping down to a minimum, and certainly to buy all the tiny extras – salted nuts, crisps, cocktail biscuits, olives, pearl onions and baby gherkins – as much as a week beforehand, so you've one minor worry completely off your mind.

Fruit and Vegetables

Greengrocers are worth cultivating (and no pun is intended) not so much because the range and quality of their goods is likely to vary enormously, but because the quality of the assistants and their attitudes towards you may differ. A good manager will probably have an interested staff, who may even be prepared to order things in for you specially. This can be a real boon if for instance you want to make a tomato salad and need the large flavour-full Provençal versions rather than the firm, round English type. They'll also let you know whether the melon you've chosen really will be ripe enough for eating tomorrow – a service no supermarket can offer, however clean and plentiful the produce. There, you are thrown upon your own expertise, though if you know what to look for, it's true you'll probably find it more cheaply.

Even with your trusty tradesman, to order fruit and vegetables by telephone is a risky way of going about things. It's only human for him to sell the best of his goods to the customers who come and seek them out.

Although root vegetables, potatoes, apples and citrus fruits can be bought well in advance, most green vegetables and all soft fruits deteriorate rapidly and beyond all recovery. (Anyone who's been faced with a yellowed bunch of watercress or a punnet of mouldy strawberries will know just how rapidly.) Although ideally it's best to buy perishables on the day you entertain, it's probably best for your peace of mind to buy the day before. It's easy to take things for granted, and then find that something as obvious and mundane as a white cabbage can't be got for love nor money, or that last week's glut of gooseberries has vanished from the scene. This way, you've still time to hunt around, or to fill in unexpected gaps with alternatives.

PREPARATION
Ordering and Hiring

Order wines and spirits well in advance, and if you think you're likely to run short of glasses, arrange for your off-licence to lend you some. If you've bought your drinks there, this should be a free service, but otherwise, it's worth a small hiring charge. If you're not sure how much drink people are likely to get through, consult Chapter 8 on Wines, or Part IV on Catering Quantities. One way to make sure you don't run out is to arrange drinks on a sale-or-return basis, so you only have to pay for the bottles that actually get opened.

Decide if you need to hire anything other than glasses. Your local Classified Directory probably lists one or two hire firms, who'll be able to supply anything from dining-chairs and china to record players and tape-recorders. Listed under 'flooring contractors', you may find a firm that hires out strip-flooring sections – a good idea if you're expecting frantic dancing and have a fitted carpet that can't be rolled back.

Remember to leave a note for your milkman, ordering extra milk and cream if you're likely to need it. And if your garden's devoid of blooms, place an order with your local florist.

Get Ahead with the Cooking

Now you can settle down to worrying about the cooking, and how you'll ever manage it all in time. Most sensible way is to do as much as possible in advance – and it's surprising just how much can be 'got out of the way', even if you haven't got a freezer in which to cache it.

If you're making a pie, whether it's sweet or savoury, you can cook the contents the day before. You can make the pastry, too, and keep it in a cool place overnight until you need to roll it out. Flan pastry cases can be cooked 'blind' the day before, and stored in a tin overnight, to be quickly refreshed in the oven the next day. Rice or pasta can be pre-cooked too, and re-heated by being plunged into boiling water for 5 minutes. Mousse can be made the evening before if you're not going to set it in the fridge; praline, too, can be made in advance and stored in an airtight jar. Fresh fruit salad actually prefers to be made the evening before, so that it can soak in the white wine or whatever else you've added. Meringues can be made a whole week in advance, for storing till they're ready to have their fresh cream added.

Soups can be easily made in readiness; this is an ideal way to get one whole course settled and off your mind. Another is to pre-prepare the entire main course. This is quite possible with a casserole, which would only need a thorough heat-through on the night.

But it's vegetables that take the time – and vegetables that need to be fresh and not soaked overnight in water. Simple way round this is to wash and prepare vegetables like sprouts, cabbage, carrots and mushrooms and place them in individual plastic bags, which must be sealed and put in the fridge. Potatoes will just have to soak overnight in water. Salad ingredients can be washed, dried and stored in individual sealed plastic bags, too, and put in the fridge or a cool larder. Salad dressings can also be made the day before, but they'll need shaking well before you serve them. Mayonnaise is worth getting out of the way in advance, and the dressing for a shellfish cocktail, too.

Garnishes, too, need preparing in advance wherever possible. Finally, check the salt and pepper and write yourself a note to make mustard. And if they're going to be wanted, make butter pats and put them in the refrigerator. Check that the iceboxes are full.

2
Setting the Scene

Getting a room ready for company depends largely on the numbers you're expecting. Here, though we assume a fairly major invasion, most of the suggestions hold good for small groups, too, and can easily be scaled down to size.

Clearing the Decks

Begin by nominating a room (or the garage) and use it as a store for non-essential furniture, fragile treasures, or anything you think needs 'tidying away'. This isn't meant to imply that guests are light-fingered – quite the opposite, they're likely to be ham-fisted – but mortified with embarrassment if they manage to break anything. Spare them in advance (but of course don't overdo it). The art is to shed enough items for the free circulation of guests, without leaving your home looking bleak and unwelcoming. Remember that guests usually arrive in clusters, and take ages actually getting *in* and *out*. If that low hall table can serve no purpose but to bark their shins, consider moving it. And certainly take off any ornament, vulnerably poised at coat-end height. A low arrangement of dried flowers in an unbreakable container will look just as attractive, and if it does manage to get swished over, there'll be no water to spill.

Keep traffic lanes clear up the stairs and on landings, because though *you* know where to expect the odd ornament or whatnot, guests won't. Try to organize separate coat rooms for men and women. This will cut down on bathroom usage, because women will be able to make last-minute inspections of hair and make-up in 'ladies only' privacy. Ideally, donate your own bedroom to the ladies, because the dressing-table facilities will be good, and if you're a really dedicated hostess, sweep your own make-up paraphernalia into one of the drawers. Then set the top afresh with make-up tissues, cotton-wool balls, hair lacquer and a refreshing cologne stick with a near-by waste-bin to take any débris. And add an ashtray, on the basis that there'll always be someone bad-mannered enough to smoke in your bedroom. For a final thoughtful touch, fill a small dish with emergency repair items like needles, cottons, a brown silk for laddered tights, scissors, safety pins and so on.

Moving to the bathroom, clear it of all but your most essential needs, and add a generous supply of guest towels and guest soaps. Check that the medicine cabinet is well-stocked, especially with pick-me-ups for guests who have made merry too wholeheartedly. And while we're looking on the gloomy side, remove any mats that have ever been known to slip.

The Party Room

That leaves the room where it's All Going to Happen. Best way to ensure freedom of movement is to divide it into three self-contained areas – one for serving drinks, one for sitting and talking, and one for eating. Obviously, if you have a separate dining-room, you've only two areas to worry about. Organize a proper bar against the far wall, so that there's plenty of surrounding space where people can – and probably will – congregate. A bar can easily be improvised; for example, a wallpaper-pasting trestle table covered with a floor-length cloth provides a handsome version. Concentrate seating closely at the other end of the room, so there's floor-space left free in the middle for comfortable to-ing and fro-ing, or possibly dancing. This compact arrangement of chairs will also make sure that no-one gets left out in the conversational cold – though if you can possibly manage it, include a coffee table or two in the group. Drinks set on the ground invariably get knocked over, and ashtrays that perch on the arms of easy chairs lose their contents once someone sits down heavily. Don't worry too much about inadequate seating. No one can expect you to have enough arm-chairs for everybody, and most men will sit quite happily on dining-chairs (so will women, if they're being careful of their dresses), and take them to the table, if necessary.

For evening occasions, especially in winter, lighting is a vital ingredient of successful enter-taining. Many of your guests may be meeting for the first time, and a harsh, unsympathetic glare can turn introduction-time into an ordeal for those who are in the least shy, whereas soft, subtle lighting will help break the ice. So keep the centre light-fitting switched firmly off, and either rely on subdued wall lighting, or strategically placed table-lamps. This will create an atmosphere of relaxation and inti-macy, and can also underline your separate room areas. At the dining-table itself, for in-stance, if you're not dining by candlelight, a pendant light fitting can contain the table-top in its own pool of privacy. This can be a bless-ing if you're stacking dirty dishes on to a side-table, sideboard or trolley, because the unlovely remains can recede gracefully into the gloom. But the pendant must hang low – a rise-and-fall unit is the surest way of finding the right height, because it goes up and down as easily as a roller blind. Usual height to aim for is eighteen inches from the table-top, so that there's no risk of dazzling guests – their faces will get thrown into a flattering shadow, but food will be clearly seen.

Another essential ingredient for relaxing the atmosphere is music (and the Teenage section of Chapter 5 suggests several ways of providing it) though unless it's meant for dancing to, it must be kept at background level. It must also be continuous, because even people who haven't noticed it playing will *hear* the silence when it stops. Tape or cassette recorders need the least attention, but as the finer points of sound pro-duction won't be appreciated, avoid using any expensive stereo equipment and treasured records, which could easily get damaged. Choosing the music must be a purely personal matter, but as a rough guide, it needs to be relaxing but not hypnotically sleepy, or your

party will never get off the ground. And it must certainly never be so restless as to inter-fere with the thought processes and make conversation difficult to follow.

If you're going to supply cigarettes and cigars for your guests (a generous, but by no means expected gesture), buy in advance so that you've got the chore out of the way, but don't open packets of cigarettes until about half an hour before your guests are due. It's sur-prising how quickly they lose their flavour and freshness. And certainly buy as many, if not more, filter cigarettes than plain ones, because they're increasingly popular nowadays, with men as well as women. When you do open the cigarettes, don't put them all in a cigarette box, which easily gets overlooked in a crowded room, but distribute them around in wine glasses – the ideal containers, provided they're reasonably stable. Put some matches handy for your guests' convenience, and scatter ashtrays profusely for your home's safety. Don't offer the cigars around until after the meal – remembering that women sometimes smoke them, too!

All this is going to lead to a chokingly smoky atmosphere, so air the room thoroughly before-hand, but also make sure it stays warm enough for women guests in sleeveless/backless dresses. A small fan-heater is useful to boost up the temperature at the last minute. Then keep track of how smoky the room's getting (a scented candle can be helpful – but not in a room where food has to be served), and *ask* if people would like the window opened/fire turned up, so no-one suffers in polite silence from snug but stale or clear but freezing air.

Finally, note the telephone numbers of your local all-night taxi services and keep them in a safe place. Someone's sure to miss the last bus – or drink too much to be able to drive home.

LAYING THE TABLE

This is one of the pleasanter pre-tasks of enter-taining, because the results are immediately satisfying and rewarding, But whether the setting is formal or informal, don't overdo it. China, cutlery and glasses provide a lot of detail in themselves, and too much decoration can look fussy.

Formal place setting

Cutlery on Parade

Rules for arranging cutlery may be less strict nowadays, but they're still very much in existence. Knives (blades pointing inwards) and spoons always go on the right, whereas forks always go on the left. Exceptions are the dessert spoon and fork in neat alignment across the top (spoon handle to the right; fork handle to the left) and fruit knife if it's needed (handle to the right). However, the dessert fork and spoon and fruit knife can just as correctly go to the sides, and it's simply a matter of how much room you can afford: the more you build out the setting sideways, the more widely you have to space the chairs. But even if you've plenty of space, don't sprawl out your cutlery. Keep all items as close together as possible without actually touching. This produces a much tidier result, especially if all handles are lined up a consistent half-inch from the edge of the table. The oft-quoted advice 'start at the outside and work your way inwards' should come out right with a properly laid table, which is doubtless why the rules have survived. For instance, a menu of soup, followed by fish, then the main meat course, and finally the dessert, should have a left-to-right place setting as follows: fish fork; meat fork; space for plate; bread knife; meat knife; fish knife; soup spoon. Dessert spoon and fork above the plate-gap would get logically left to the end by any inexperienced guest who religiously worked his or her way inwards. Only possibility for error lies with the bread knife, theoretically the last knife

to be used, but one that is needed throughout the meal. Perhaps this is why it's increasingly common to find the bread knife placed vertically across the side plate – that, and the fact that it's a very good way of anchoring a springy linen napkin into position. Most people's 'eye' is sufficiently 'well in' to do all these things automatically, but the principle of a place setting is that it should form a neat square, with the inside knife and fork about nine inches apart, and the dessert spoon and fork about nine inches from the table edge. The theory is also that all people are right-handed; left-handed guests will have to do some quick re-jigging – but they'll be adept at this after a lifetime's practice.

Most cutlery manufacturers seem to sell seven-piece place settings now, consisting of two knife sizes, two fork sizes, and dessert spoon, soup spoon and teaspoon. This would cover the place setting described above, with the exception of the fish knife and fork, which people are expected to buy separately, it seems. The same is true of steak knives – 'extras' well worth investing in, because the psychological effect of a really sharp knife goes half-way towards convincing people the meat is tender. Most hostesses can manage with these few basics (and considering some cutlery services number as many as five hundred individual items, we're all getting off lightly).

The Glasses

The glass situation has simplified considerably, also, and people usually prefer to choose a few sizes from a suite, but to buy more of them. A workable minimum is to use two sizes of stemmed wine glasses, which will cover everything from wine to fruit juice in the large size, and everything from short cocktails to liqueurs in the small. Then all you need is a set of chunky tumblers for spirits, long cocktails or soft drinks, and the obligatory (it deserves it) balloon glass for brandy. Even if you're only serving one wine with a meal, it adds extra glamour to set two glasses, and offer iced or Perrier water in the second – usually very welcome. At a *very* formal affair, or an informal one if you've brought wines back from holiday and want to give a dinner-cum-wine-tasting, arrange the glasses in a straight line across the top of the cutlery in their order of use. Start from the right with the sherry glass, for instance and finish with the port glass at the left, so that the last glass sits just above the meat knife. For a single wine glass, anywhere above the right-hand cutlery will do, and it's a matter of what balances and pleases the eye best.

And now for the Real Skill

Assuming all these essentials, the creative side of table-setting is more or less confined to the choice of (crisply laundered, please) tablecloth – or whatever surface you prefer – napkins, centre-piece, and candles and flower-arrangements if there's room. The effect already sounds cluttered, but the art lies in making your visual impact simply.

Contrary to general belief, formal settings need the simplest table treatment of all, because the essentials can't help but be extra elaborate. Meals of several courses are going to need more in the way of cutlery, china, serving dishes and glasses, and may well need extras like finger bowls, too. What's more, all these items will probably be more decorative than usual. The glasses may be intricately cut crystal, the china may well have a richly coloured or

lacy gold border, and the cutlery, even if it isn't solid silver, will probably attract more attention than everyday stainless steel. That's why the traditional damask cloth, with its discreetly matching napkins, is as valid today as in any other century. With its fine texture, it has a subtle self-pattern that increases the sense of richness and decoration, without setting up in strident competition. And though it may sound corny, there is no more glamorous sight, space permitting, than one, two or even three silver candelabra. This isn't as opulent as it sounds, since cutlery manufactuers have realised the demand for beautiful but reasonably priced tableware and have started making convincing silver-plated versions of Georgian candelabra and cutlery. With plain white candles (coloured only if there's definite point to their being so), once the silver is shining and the crystal sparkling, it only needs flowers to complete the scene.

More about flowers comes later, but obviously if you already have some colour on the table, your arrangement must relate, either by blending or contrasting. Otherwise, it's best to make a bold colour statement, like filling a large low bowl with deep red roses, and carrying it home by using deep red candles. Or for a softer, more relaxed effect, sit a single red rose-

Buffet setting

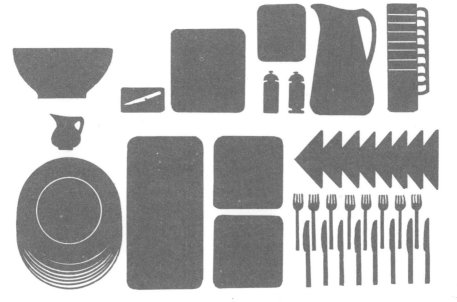

bud (set out at the last possible moment, so it doesn't get a chance to wilt) alongside each damask napkin on the side plate. Never introduce a colour and leave it stranded; always relate it to your scheme as a whole.

Improvisation

If this formal setting sounds terrifyingly grand, it's possible to achieve equally appealing results from much humbler beginnings. If for a start, you're minus a large enough table, a whitewood trestle table (or two pushed together for a really large crowd) need only cost a few pounds. What's more, it can in future double as an improvised bar, buffet-table, or barbecue table, and will fold flat against the garage wall until it is needed again. Cheap but sumptuous tablecloth could be any plain cotton sheet, preferably a pastel-coloured one, topped by a white cotton-laced bedspread. This would look soft and romantic (meantime covering the trestle-legs), and with its old-fashioned prettiness, could lend itself to the Victorian idea of trailing strands of ivy the length of the table-top. Any undersheet in the pink/mauve/blue/green range could have a fruit bowl centre piece piled high with purple grapes, and perhaps a small sprig of grapes hanging from each wine glass. Then white or matching candles could stand on white saucers, with wreaths of ivy round each base, to disguise the 'ordinary' holders. Any undersheet in the hotter yellow/orange ranges could have the same trails of ivy, but a centre-piece of flowers in related shades. A low bowl of yellow roses for instance, or vari-shaded gerberas or button chrysanthemums. And if finger-bowls are being used, make the most of this heaven-sent opportunity to delight your guests. Nip flowers off at their heads (it's worth being ruthless) and float a single up-turned flower-face in every finger-bowl.

Informal Glitter and Colour

Informal gatherings offer rather more scope, because the relaxed atmosphere encourages improvisation, and fiascos will meet with hilarity rather than disapproval.

One glittering but easy-to-achieve table-setting, that only costs the price of paper doilys and a small aerosol of paint, looks stun-ning on any coloured or white-lacquered table – or any plain tablecloth, come to that. Using gold or silver doilys, let one large one form each place mat. Sit a medium-sized doily to the left, and put the side-plate on top, so the lacy edge shows all round. Then cut out the centres from more medium doilys (very small sizes aren't manufactured), and place top right, to take a wine glass apiece. Centre decoration is equally simple, and sits on one large doily. Find an old plate (no-one will notice if it's chipped or cracked) and spray with gold or silver paint – whichever matches your doilys. Then make a plate-size frill by halving and then pleating large doilys, and a smaller frill by halving and pleating medium doilys. Sit one on top of the other, and clamp firmly into position on the plate with a large and chunky candle – which *should* match your table for full visual impact.

For an even more glittering effect, that's particularly good for parties or buffets, cover your table all over with aluminium kitchen foil, moulding it firmly round the table edges. If you want to be on the safe side, secure it with sticky tape, too. Then regardless of the time of year, dig out all your gold and silver Christmas tree baubles. For a buffet centre-piece, if you're lucky enough to have a glass cake-stand, fill each tier with the baubles till they cover the entire surfaces, haphazardly clustering them together. Alternatively, fill any glass bowl with them – a goldfish bowl would be ideal, if you happen to have one unoccupied. To carry home the theme, sit one large bauble in every empty wine glass – people can transfer it to their side-plate when their glasses get filled. Finally, have plenty of candles to accentuate the brilliance. Fill disposable foil baking trays with ordinary squat night-lights, and mass them tightly together to make a solid area that comes alive with light.

Style and Imagination

Above all, feel free to mix formal and informal ingredients. Any style that's followed through too precisely becomes stiff and unpredictable, and it's the unexpected touches that give individual flair. The grand table setting described at the beginning of the section should logically have a 'grand' flower arrangement, elaborately constructed of 'dignified' florist-shop flowers like carnations and gladioli. But simple garden flowers, like daisies or sweet peas, casually plonked in a china or pottery jug, could surprise everything to life like a breath of fresh air. Conversely, an informal table-setting, with bare scrubbed pine table-top, pewter-coloured pottery, and black and white paper napkins, could become dramatic and exciting with one magnificent silver candelabra.

Always try to see your table-setting ingredients with fresh, as opposed to familiar eyes. A black and white gingham tablecloth, for instance, spells barbecues and informal buffets at first glance, and would certainly look fresh and pretty in these circumstances. But re-appraise those restrained geometric checks, and the restricted but striking black/white contrast. Imagine it set with plain white bone china, classically simple rummer-type glasses, silver cutlery, and a flower-arrangement of white gardenias in a low silver bowl, and you'll understand how easily formal/informal distinctions can and should blur.

As far as flowers go, they're far too fresh and natural to take kindly to rules, and fortunately, elaborate arrangements are fast going out of fashion – taking their rigid theories of mass,

Informal place setting

line and composition with them. Even vases have become practically obsolete, and anything attractive that can hold water can hold flowers today.

The simplest and most stunning approach for any occasion is to mass flowers tightly over a large area, dispensing with leaves altogether, so that a really positive impact is made. The nearest traditional way to do this is in a shallow bowl, studded thickly all over with the tallest flowers in the centre, the shortest at the sides, to form a perfect half-sphere. This does involve precision-cutting and all the paraphernalia of chicken wire, florist's 'foam' or pin-holders to secure each individual stem, and unless the bowl is fairly large or the table fairly small, the result can get lost in acres of tablecloth. The modern – for want of a better word – way is to bring in the biggest baking tin from the kitchen and fill it almost to the top with water. Then buy a vast quantity of any simple but brightly coloured flower that blends or contrasts with your existing colours – say flame-orange tulips. Break them off just below the heads, and fit them into the tin as closely as is possible without actually crushing them. This may sound brutal, and does reduce the flowers to mere design-elements, but the effect is as natural as a close-growing cluster of crocuses or daffodils, that have far more beauty *en masse* than dotted about the grass individually.

If this sounds too inflexible an approach, consider a small wicker basket or bowl, with another bowl inside to hold water, completely filled with nasturtiums that jostle for position in a natural way. Or for a more formal occasion use a vegetable dish or tureen that matches the rest of your china, and fill it to the brim with roses or gardenias. For smaller tables, imagine flowers in an egg-cup, perhaps one to each guest; in a glass jelly mould; in a dead-plain circular glass ashtray. Think in terms of shapely objects, like an old-fashioned teapot, or perhaps prettiest of all, a curvaceous gravy-boat. If your table's too tiny to take flowers at all, consider buying a glass candle-holder that has a small posy base, especially for flowers. Or make a small wreath of flowers or leaves to go round the base of the candle and/or the base of any existing holder.

3
Presenting the Food

Except for Very Important Occasions, no one's going to expect you to have matching sets of everything. In fact, minus the glamour of a damask cloth, gleaming silver and glittering crystal, the uniform perfection of a complete dinner service can be boring. Nowadays, dishes can be chosen more spontaneously – or even improvised – and the result is a much wider scope for serving food simply and sympathetically.

Dishes and Containers with an Air

If you're going to need your soup bowls for the dessert as well, don't count on managing to get them washed up between courses: you may of course, but the anxiety will probably show. Instead, serve any thick 'peasant' soup in crude pottery bowls, or if it's not too thick to drink, in pottery mugs – omitting the soup spoons this time, so that people don't dither indecisively before starting. If you don't have enough side-plates for salad as well as a roll, sit individual salads in wooden bowls, or in white petal-shaped rice bowls, or even in small white-ribbed soufflé dishes. If you've already used up – or simply don't have – any dessert plates, remember that any cool, summery sweets, from strawberry fool to sorbet, look even cooler served in a large wine goblet or champagne glass. It doesn't even matter if the glasses don't match, as long as they hold roughly the same quantities, because they'll all share the common factor of translucence.

Use to the full any oven-to-tableware you possess, or invest in some if you're going to entertain at all often. In the first place, it saves on washing up, but it also spares you those agonizing moments of trying to transfer food intact from cooking pot to serving dish. And it also ensures that food arrives piping hot to the table, in a sensible, simple and unfussy manner. With few exceptions (noticeably roasts), food always looks its best like this. There's no more appetising way to serve a casserole, for instance, than in the cheap and traditional brown earthenware pot it was cooked in. If your wrists are strong, you may prefer impressively weighty cast-iron, and if you crave colour, there's no beating enamelled cooking-ware. But a word of caution, that goes for china too: unless you've pre-planned your pattern and colour requirements carefully, it's safest to stick to all-white. It's a very flattering colour for food (as, surprisingly, is black), and it's always simpler to introduce colour in details, than to try to reduce it when it's part of your essentials. Of course, if your oven-to-tableware covers everything from plates to matching coffee-cups, then the problem is simplified. Another exception to the rule of serving straight to the table is any large whole fish, such as salmon. A long, slender fish dish, anything up to three feet long, is indispensable. It's not such an extravagance, either, since you can make it double for hors d'oeuvre, salads or even pâtisseries.

Don't be Hidebound

Take the opportunity, or make it, to show off the pretty dishes you've gathered by the way; whether you fell in love with them in a junk shop, or they survived from your mother's old dinner service. Bring out that oval meat dish or gravy boat with stand. Most old china acquires a mellow quality, and even when the patterns of individual pieces don't match, there's usually a relationship of mood and tone that lends especial charm to a modern table. What's more, if you've played safe with all-white basics, you'll need such dishes for the individual interest they provide. Wash up that pewter dish or platter while you're about it, and imagine it holding a sizzling hot pizza, or a bunch of purple grapes on a cool bed of leaves. Gently sponge that old wicker basket or bowl, and use it for handing round hot crusty rolls, wrapped in a coarse linen napkin. In summer, particularly, rinse any large glass bowl (even an ovenglass mixing bowl), part-fill with crushed ice for the sheer luxury of it, and fill to the brim with delectable fresh fruit.

Don't be afraid to raid the kitchen for utensils you usually dismiss as just useful. That well-scrubbed wooden chopping board would look very handsome set out with cheese, and could take pride of place on a side table until needed. Even better, if you're lucky enough to have one, would be a marble pastry slab – though guests would have to move to it, rather than it to them. If it's too big to cover with cheese without spending a fortune, you can always pad out with an attractive garnish of lettuce leaves/watercress/tomatoes. Re-appraise that large jar, whether china, glass or earthenware, and imagine it filled with leafy-topped celery. Or if you haven't got one, use a

large-sized glass storage jar – even though it does say pasta on the side. Finally, turf the eggs out of that contented-looking pottery hen box, and fill it with peppermints to hand round after the meal. So long as originality never slips into gimmickry, the pleasant end matters more than the 'correct' means today.

To Garnish or Not?

Provided they don't become too involved, garnishes are an appealing way of livening up dishes that may be delicious, but look uninspiring. Strictly speaking, dumplings are a garnish to boiled beef, and Yorkshire pud to roast. But most of us think of garnishes first as forms of decorating, as edible accompaniments second. This attitude has led to some highly indigestible travesties, such as elaborately sculptured raw turnip, or baroque-piped borders of (ugh) cold mashed potato. Remember, however, that in the first place, plenty of dishes look good just as they come, and don't need any last-minute interference: you haven't *got* to do something to prove you've taken the trouble. In the second place, no garnish should be anything other than a natural accessory to the food that it's served with. Although it may not always *get* eaten, like the lettuce under the shrimp cocktail, it should always be able to be eaten, and pleasurably.

Never smother a dish with the garnish, but keep it comparatively small, and to the edges rather than in the centre of the dish as a general rule. Prepare any complicated garnish well in advance, because it can take almost hours longer than you bargained for. Since hot food usually demands a hot garnish that has to be prepared on the spot, always stick to something simple and speedy, or the dish may be luke-warm by the time you get round to serving it. Even when a dish desperately needs colour, confine yourself to adding one, two or at the most (and even this is doubtful) three forms of garnish. And don't under-estimate the value of garnishes in terms of texture. Any appropriately garnished smooth dish, from a ragoût or mince that's enlivened by a crisp crescent shape of pastry, to an ice-cream with a crunchy fan-shaped wafer, will prove the point.

Simple but Eye-catching

Soups, as much as anything, benefit from a good garnish. A creamed soup can easily look insipid, but float a few leaves of watercress across the top at the last minute, or lightly sprinkle with chopped parsley, chopped chives, or finely chopped hard-boiled egg, and it becomes interesting to the eye. An obvious but rarely used garnishing approach is to add a handful of cooked peas to a pea soup, a little chopped ham to ham and pea soup, chopped tender celery leaves to a celery soup, and so on. (Incidentally, a handful of cooked peas scattered at the last minute on top of a casserole works visual wonders.) Any thin soup – and of course, minestrone – appreciates the addition of pasta, whether in noodle, shell or mini-initial form, though be sure to add it half an hour before serving, so it'll be thoroughly cooked. And don't forget the grated Parmesan or dry Gruyère – proof that a good garnish should add flavour as well. Most wintry soups (French onion soup springs immediately to mind) are improved by croûtons. And if you're confident your guests like garlic (don't waste time on them if they don't!), slice and toast some garlic bread, to cast on the surface.

Salad and Fruit Garnishes

Most main dishes derive interest from salad-type garnishes, though these can often be very simple. Even for the grandest occasion, a silver salver of rare roast beef needs nothing more than a sprig or two of watercress, and a sizzling steak is quite happy with a single crisp, fresh lettuce leaf. Radishes, tomatoes, cucumbers, sticks of celery with tender young top-leaves – all look delectably refreshing in their own right. But if you have the time and inclination, there are some enchanting things that can be done with them.

Fruit can make an obvious and attractive garnish, not only for sweets but for savouries, too. Lemon is the traditional garnish for fish, because it counteracts any oiliness, and it's usually finely sliced and overlapped to form a garland round any whole fish on a serving dish. These mere ornamental slivers (remember to supply squeezable chunks as well) can be made

extra-decorative if you're prepared to invest in a 'canelle' knife. Use this to peel top-to-bottom strips from your lemon (orange or cucumber for that matter), so that when it's cut into slices, it has a ready-patterned edge.

All good garnishes are so inseparably a part of the food they accompany that they fall naturally into Parts II and III, where many more ideas can be found.

Serving the First Course

The serving of food is far more informal nowadays. Usually, the hostess lingers with her guests till the last minute, steadying her nerves with a *single* drink, and then leading them to the table, where the first course is already set out, with a warmed roll waiting on each side plate, to avoid the time-wasting business of cutting and offering bread. Obviously, this can only work with cold starters like pâté, avocado pear, artichoke and so on, that won't spoil while they're waiting. But provided you have a smoothly-running trolley, or just a sensible tray, no one's going to be scandalised if you bring in individually served hot starters. Some first courses will get yowls of appreciation (or silent approval, depending on the degree of formality) if they make their entrance as a whole. Elaborately arranged *hors d'oeuvre* of course are meant to be admired intact. A platter piled high with crisp-fried whitebait, or a bowl filled to the brim with steaming mussels, makes far more impact *en masse*. And it would be a pity to slice into any Quiche Lorraine without an audience. But in all these cases, with the exception of the *hors d'oeuvre*, the hostess must relieve her guests of the responsibility of helping themselves.

If you want to make the proceedings fairly formal, stand up at the end of a course and start removing used plates. Although serving from the left is universally accepted, removing is split down the middle, and can be either from the left or the right. It really doesn't matter which, so long as you are consistent. This isn't senseless etiquette: once people realise the system's in operation, they'll avoid any abrupt movements in the expected directions. If you don't make a point of standing up before you start to clear away plates, people may start handing them up the table to you before you know where you are.

The Main Course

Unless you have properly trained help, it's senseless to attempt formality in serving the main course. General practice is for the hostess to serve the main dish individually, either handing plates round the table, or taking them round herself (to ladies first). But vegetables and sauces generally get left as free-for-all, with guests helping themselves to the various dishes. A systematic round-the-table approach is too much to hope for here, so both the host and hostess must watch carefully to see that no one's been overlooked, but is too shy to say so. When space and dishes permit, it may help to have more than one dish of gravy, mint sauce and so on.

Difficult-to-serve main courses – such as whole fish, bird or joint of meat – should be tackled by the host, who should then hand round the plates. Guaranteed to stimulate table-talk *and* ensure civilized-looking slices, would be an electric carver (now that households are smaller, many men have lost the old-fashioned art of carving). Also invaluable would be a heated tray on a side-table, because second helpings are welcome at the most formal gatherings if the numbers make it practical, and it's a blessing to be able to keep plates warm for the hot courses.

Pudding, Cheese

Most cold puddings, like starters, are simplest served individually. This way you can guarantee they'll look attractive in advance, whereas the last people served from a sherry trifle, for instance, are often faced by a sorry mess. Hot puddings should be served by the hostess, and at this stage of the meal, if the gathering's small enough, she should enquire after the state of each individual helping before serving a standard portion. Many people will want to skip this course, and should never be pressed against their will.

Cheese, especially if the cheese-board's large,

can be the host's prerogative, but if it's small enough to circulate freely, guests can help themselves. Always offer French bread as well as biscuits, because many people prefer it with soft or especially strong cheeses.

Coffee, Wine

With coffee we are back in the domain of the hostess. At formal gatherings it should be served away from the table, in the comfort of the sitting-room. And though the 'ladies' are no longer obliged to 'withdraw', it's a natural break for them to go upstairs and repair their make-up if they want to. The hostess should ascertain exactly how each guest wants his or her coffee, and hand the filled cups. Then the host can take over the duties of offering liqueurs, cigarettes and cigars, and the conversation can continue. This formula is equally suitable for less formal occasions, though it depends on personal tastes and circumstances.

Throughout the meal, the host should attend to the wine, pouring a little from each fresh bottle into his own glass, to make sure no small pieces of cork reach the guests. He should serve the wine from the right (which is how at-table coffee should be served), either working his way straight round the table, or more formally, working clockwise round the table, starting with the lady guest of honour on his right, and going from lady to lady, then completing another full circle to fill up the men's glasses. From then onwards, it's simply a matter of topping up glasses in the same way, rather than waiting for them to get empty.

4
Taking to the Air

Considering our climate, American-style bar-becues are probably rash enterprises, but they're on their way to becoming as popular as that other hazardous national pastime, the English picnic. And certainly, if you have to get soaked in a sudden downpour, it helps to be eating sizzling hot sausage instead of a cold slab of veal and ham pie. The main snag of course is the cost of equipment, especially when you know it's going to lie idle for all but a few nights of summer. This makes it even more essential to concentrate your spending on a good-quality basic unit. Otherwise, you can pay a lot for sophistications that you never use.

Top priority must be size. Any barbecue that's too small will have no variation of heat zones – and it's these that make for flexible cooking. Mini-barbecues are obviously the cheapest, but they're gimmicks more than any-thing, and will limit you to sausage-and-bacon-type fare for small numbers only. As a rough guide, it takes a barbecue grid diameter of at least eighteen inches to cook enough food for eight people in one go. For open garden or hillside sites, it's wise to buy a barbecue with a windshield, and it's always worth choosing one that offers some control over the position-ing of the grid. And a *rôtisserie* spit is certainly

useful, though by no means essential. These are usually sold as optional extras, but make sure you buy one that's battery-operated for easy turning.

Blue-print for a Home-made Barbecue

If you're not prepared to spend money on such a seasonal extravagance, you can always build your own barbecue. This needn't be as ambi-tious as it sounds, and the barbecue described and illustrated below is simple enough for a teenager to tackle. What's more, it can earn its keep the year round by doubling as a place for safe and tidy bonfires. All you need is a piece of flat ground, about 2 feet 3 inches by 4 feet (but see below); 106 bricks; 1 by 1 cwt bag of brick-laying mortar mix; 2 metal scraper-type door-mats (or a couple of oven shelves, if you can spare them); a piece of small-guage chicken wire, slightly larger than your door-mat or oven-shelf; and a trowel or small household shovel. If possible, use old bricks obtained from a demolition contractor (making sure he's cleaned off the mortar first), because these will be ready-weathered to blend more

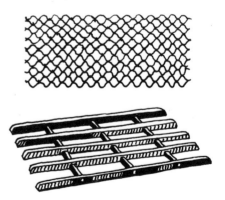

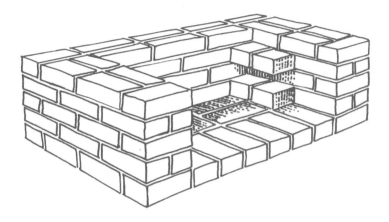

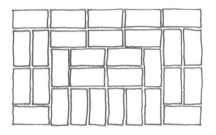

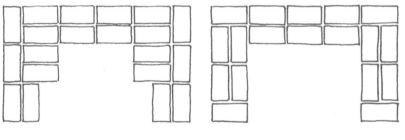

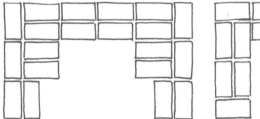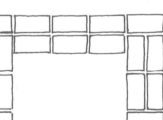

naturally into their surroundings. Get your mortar-mix from a builder's merchant, and your metal door-mats and chicken wire from any large ironmongers. And if this already sounds ominously like hard work, you can save time by doing without the mortar, and simply stacking your bricks into position; disadvantage of this short cut is that too much rough treatment will bring your barbecue down like a house of cards. On the other hand, you can dismantle it for winter, or move it about if you want to change your barbecue scene.

Before you begin building, choose your site with care. It must be far enough away from the house not to be a fire hazard, but near enough to make kitchen reinforcements practical. It's no fun tripping through semi-darkness with a tray full of glasses. The shelter of some vegetation is ideal, but if you intend to use your barbecue for the more intensive heat of bonfires too, keep it far enough away from plants to avoid singeing. If you don't have the natural shelter of trees or shrubs, invest in a wind-break of Norfolk reeding, because those summer 'breezes' often have nasty nip in them. Or go to town on a festive atmosphere, with a canvas shelter, that will ward off rain too.

To begin building, first stamp on your site-soil until it's packed hard and flat. Prepare your mortar-mix according to the instructions on the bag – and mix it only a little bit at a time unless you want a rock garden, too. Ideally, you need a small area of concrete or paving to mix it on, but if this isn't handy, use a piece of hardboard, smooth side up. Using your trowel or shovel, spread a thin layer of mortar over your site. Lay your first course of bricks as shown in figure 1, and fill the gaps between the bricks. Spread your next layer thinly over the area needed for your second course (figure 2), and follow similarly, with courses 3, 4, and 5, keeping rigidly to the arrangement of bricks shown – this is essential for the overall strength of the structure. Finally, bend the chicken wire over one of your scraper mats or oven shelves, and rest it on the lower protruding bricks, to form the bed for your charcoal. Then rest your other mat or shelf on the upper protruding bricks, to form your grid for cooking on – and your barbecue is complete.

What to Burn

Next step is to stock yourself up with fuel. Charcoal or charcoal briquettes are sold by many coal merchants, ironmongers or hardware departments of large stores, and a couple of 7-lb. bags will give you an ample fire for 4 hours. To ensure the fire gets off to a good start, arrange some Metafuel firelighters before adding the charcoal – and to make sure it doesn't come to a damp end, have something like a metal dustbin-lid handy to keep out the rain. Once charcoal turns to sludge, it's difficult to get rid of. Other cooking essentials are old leather gloves for handling the spit, etc; metal tongs for turning the food; long-handled forks; pastry brushes or spoons for basting; plenty of aluminium foil for wrapping certain foods in; a damp cloth for cleaning fingers; and a thick roll of newspapers or a pair of bellows for fanning the fire if it turns reluctant.

Table and Tools

Essentials for serving the food are a table, on which to set other than straight-from-the-grid food. It helps if this has some cheap and cheerful cloth – perhaps of brightly coloured paper or crisp black and white gingham. Stack plates for self-service – it doesn't matter if they're a motley crew of second-best and remnants – though if you're taking your barbecues seriously, brash and brilliant enamel ones would help the mood along. Obviously it's simplest if most food can be eaten by hand, in which case, don't forget a vast communual finger bowl and plenty of paper napkins, but otherwise bring out the kitchen cutlery. Again, for enthusiasts, it's worth buying a set of wooden-handled steak knives and forks. This is one case where plastic cutlery won't do (as anyone who's tried to cut meat with airline cutlery will know). And for atmosphere, candles in storm shades – preferably the kind that can be spiked into the earth – or lanterns hanging from branches, can be lit as the moon rises in (you hope) a cloudless sky.

Getting the Fire Ready

Now you're ready for blast-off – but temper enthusiasm with caution, because all barbe-

Soup and Salad party: p. 82

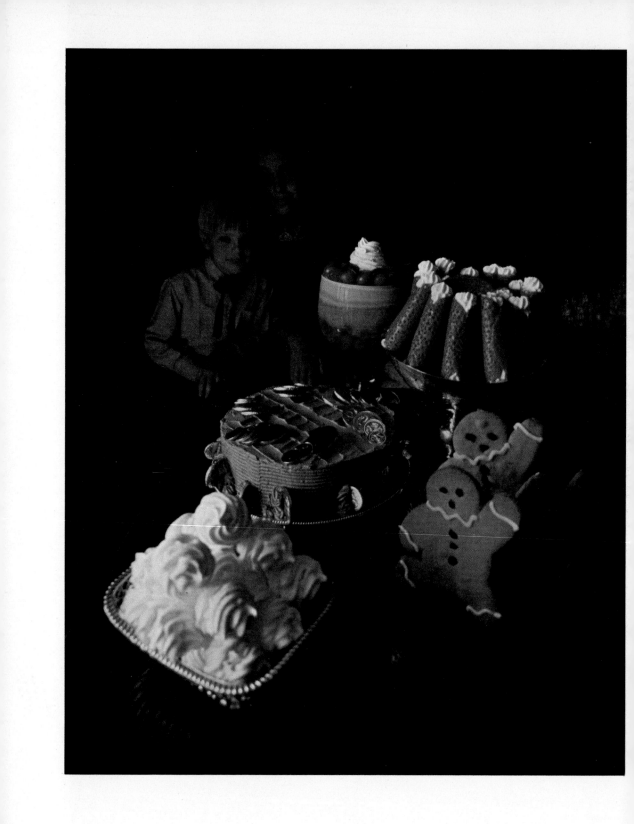

cues, bought or built, need careful handling. The idea is to maintain the charcoal at red-glow point throughout, and there must never, ever be any flames. Begin by piling the charcoal about 2–3 inches high over the firelighters, or, for a large joint which needs a slower, more controlled heat, spread the charcoal in a single 1-inch layer. About half an hour before you want to start cooking, light the firelighters, because it will take this long for the charcoal to burn through evenly. To keep the charcoal at the right stage, always feed fresh charcoal on gradually, by pushing a ring of fuel from the outer edge of the fire into the centre. This should be done regularly in small quantities – large amounts are not only wasteful, but reduce the heat. And never throw charcoal directly on top of the fire, or flames will leap up in an alarming fashion. (From all these do's and don'ts, you will see it's obviously a good idea to have a private barbecue first, so that you and your equipment can get fully acquainted.)

Organization

When you feel confident enough to invite your friends round, don't get over-ambitious and invite them all at once, and don't get involved in cooking too many things at once. For a start it gets expensive, because outdoor appetites are always large, but it also gets difficult to organize the cooking without long and tedious waits in between. One simple way to maintain a continuous pipe-line of food is to cheat outright, and have some pre-prepared dish keeping hot over a candle-heater. A vast casserole, for instance, could precede or follow the barbecue food, according to how the cooking's going. This would certainly solve the problem at barbecues where the grid isn't big enough to cook all the food at one sitting. And it would leave you free to concentrate on one other dish.

Cooking Meat, Poultry, Fish

If you're feeling affluent, and want to serve 'big juicy steaks', these should be seasoned and brushed over with oil, before being placed directly on the greased grid. They'll take the usual time for grilling, as will chops – which should be treated in the same way, but

skewered if necessary to keep them in good shape. Gammon and pineapple could make a slightly cheaper barbecue dish, though this should be cooked in a flat baking tin, to stop the juices from escaping. Add the pineapple rings when the gammon's almost cooked, so they just have time to go golden, and if you can manage it, fry some eggs in a heavy frying pan at the last minute, using the dripping from the gammon. An easy way to pad out this, and most barbecue foods, is to empty a giant-sized can of baked beans into a heavy old saucepan, and heat through.

Barbecued chicken is a traditional, and with today's prices, quite a cheap dish to make, but to roast the bird whole, you'll definitely need a spit. Otherwise, cut the chicken up into joints and place directly on the greased grid. In both cases, brush the poultry over with oil or bacon fat before cooking, and brush it frequently throughout, with dripping that's perhaps had a chopped clove of garlic added for extra flavour. Don't attempt to cook anything but a tender chicken that's meant for frying, and always serve it with a barbecue sauce (of which more details in Part II, where full barbecue recipes and timings are given).

A very good-looking and equally cheap barbecue dish could be kebabs, because with these it's possible to make a little meat go a long way. And if the meat has to be less than

25

Party for the Five-to-Eleven-year-olds: p. 108

top quality, it can be marinated overnight, to ensure tenderness and flavour. Allowing one skewer to each guest, spike tender, lean pieces of steak or lamb, and intersperse with bacon rolls, mushrooms and tomatoes, for instance. But the permutations are endless, and kidneys, sausages, chicken livers, olives, pineapple chunks and baby onions can all make a contribution, though it's best to keep each kebab down to say four complementary ingredients. Once the pieces are securely skewered, brush over with oil and cook on a greased grid, remembering to turn once or twice.

Last but not least, don't forget fish, especially reasonable but tasty ones like herring and mackerel, that are small enough to be wrapped in aluminium foil and cooked whole. Fish steaks and fillets are best wrapped in aluminium foil, with a knob of butter, to prevent them from breaking up. Have masses of lemon-halves ready for squeezing over them. And serve not chips, but jacket potatoes with everything, smothered in butter or cottage cheese with chopped chives.

Salad and Etceteras

Be ready with lashings of salad to refresh the palate. Both salad and dressing can be pre-prepared: keep the salad in the salad compartment of the fridge till the evening. It's a good idea to set out several bowls of ingredients, with the dressing separate, and let guests mix their own salad. This way, the dressing gets freshly added, and there's no risk of the salad going soggy while it waits. Plenty of cheeses, butter and more French bread than you can possibly imagine will be eaten, are essential to round off this kind of feast – which should be washed down throughout with something cool and refreshing, like soft punch or an ice-cold lager. And if the evening turns chilly, forget your Southern States pretensions and serve a good old English nightcap like hot, thick soup.

Picnic Preamble

Picnics are supposed to be treats and not punishments, but anyone with childhood memories of marauding wasps and sand-gritty

sandwiches can be excused for fighting shy of them. And today's horror-version of people squatting by parked cars, chomping on stodge as the lorries roll by, doesn't inspire much more confidence. Nevertheless, picnics *can* be enchanting, even elegant, affairs, what's more, they're occasions where everything, bar possibly the weather, is slanted in your favour. You can prepare everything peacefully in advance. You know your guests are as determined to enjoy themselves as any charabanc outing. You know (but try not to bank on it) that the informal atmosphere will make light of minor disasters.

Quick convenience picnics aside, don't get stuck in the sandwich rut. Even if you're short of preparation time, they're really no quicker than cooking sausages, making salad, and getting together butter, cheese and crusty French bread – though they do avoid the paraphernalia of plates, cutlery, condiments and napkins at the eating end. Where sandwiches are essential, the least you can do is make sure the bread is fairly thin and the contents moist and thick. And if you're using sliced bread for speed, cut off the all-too-rubbery crusts. Packed in polythene bags, wrapped in aluminium foil or stacked in air-tight plastic boxes, the freshness of such sandwiches will stay sealed in, and they'll make a succulent meal in the most snatched of situations.

The Versatile Vacuum Flask

But presuming your picnic is from choice and not necessity, it's worth making full use of that inexpensive and neglected invention – the vacuum flask. Perhaps we've failed to see its potential because we started off by using it for milk-included tea, one of the few failure-stories in vacuum flask history. For sceptics who think a picnic can't be civilized, imagine one that starts off with iced Gazpacho or Vichyssoise (from the familiar tall flask), follows on with a hot beef casserole (from a wide-necked food flask), and finishes off with a chilled fresh fruit salad (from another wide-necked flask). All accompanied by a dry rosé, deliciously chilled with an ice cube per glass from whichever flask happens to be vacant. Coffee has never been such a problem as tea, and manages to taste fairly true when milk is included. And milk on its own tastes fine, though ideally, it should either be poured in boiling or pre-chilled, to rule out any risk of curdling. It's always best to fill the flask to the top, because any space left is going to contain air and give scope for temperature changes. Remember that hot things shouldn't be kept more than 8 hours in a vacuum flask.

Other Aids

For anyone feeling the first signs of picnic addiction, there are several more sophistications on the market, which cost a few pounds, but give years of service. Cheapest is the insulated bag that's been around for years. This looks like an ordinary lightweight zip-bag, but it's insulated with glass fibre to keep the contents cool (or warm if anyone wants that) for a few hours. As with vacuum flasks, it helps if there's no space left for air to circulate in, and newspapers can easily be added to fill any gaps.

But an insulated bag can only keep the outside temperature at bay for a few hours, and for a picnic that has to be packed further in advance, a cold-safe is the next, if slightly more expensive, step up the scale. A box rather than a bag, with polstyrene-insulated walls of rigid polythene and a snap-tight lid, it can keep things either cold or hot for up to a day. Temperature is maintained by sachets, either fixed in the lid or loose for distributing among the contents, that need pre-freezing or pre-heating before packing. But for the ultimate in keep-it-cool luxury, you can't beat the portable fridge that runs off small gas cylinders.

Plan — even for Picnics

For food that needs its freshness sealed in but isn't too vulnerable, like cheeses or salad ingredients, have masses of small polythene bags handy. For semi-vulnerable items, like open-fruit flans, quiches and pizzas, use air-tight cake tins and remember to keep them upright. For totally vulnerable items, like cream, soufflés, jellies and trifles, use screw-top jars or self-sealing plastic containers, setting jellies and trifles directly into them. And help yourself by choosing foods that are happy to travel. Hard-boiled eggs and Scotch eggs are obvious examples, but better still are savoury pies, patties and fruit pies, all of which can be cooked the day before – in fact should be, to give them time to get firm. If you feel you're overdoing the pastry content, then consider cold cooked chicken pieces or lamb cutlets in egg and bread-crumbs. And take plenty of fresh fruit for light relief.

According to Henry James, a picnic should be 'not so good as to fail of amusing disorder, nor yet so bad as to defeat the proper function of repasts'. In other words, no one's going to throw a tantrum if someone puts his foot in the butter, but everyone's going to get short-tempered if you forget the corkscrew. The only way for a picnic to appear carefree and spontaneous is for you to sit down and make a list.

Make sure you've got stacks of paper napkins (a damp facecloth in plastic bag would be rather nice, too) and while you're at it, why not paper plates and a tablecloth. Organize plenty of glasses. (If you're afraid they'll get broken, take Woolworth tumblers, which are perfectly plain and unobjectionable. Or unbreakable plastic tumblers, unless you've an aversion to them.) And gather together enough kitchen cutlery, not forgetting one good sharp knife, carefully wrapped to get there safely. Bring a roll of kitchen paper for mopping-up operations, plus the full battery of salt, pepper, sugar, tubes of mustard, and a screw-top container full of salad dressing. If you're dealing with large numbers for tea or coffee, beg, buy or borrow a small bottled gas picnic stove or a spirit burner, and don't forget the matches or the tin of dried milk. And if you've planned on eating anything canned, don't forget the can-opener. And in case the fields aren't as parched and sun-baked as they ought to be, bring a large rug or groundsheet for dry and clean sitting. Finally, bring a large paper or plastic bag to hold all the aftermath, and keep the Keep Britain Tidy Group happy.

5
Specially for Children – up to and including Teenagers

Anything involving children needs planning like a battle – because left to their own devices, that's what you could end up with. It doesn't get easier as toddlers turn to teenagers, either. It just gets different, and you exchange a few exhausting hours of on-the-scene supervision for several behind-the-scene hours of wishing you could go to bed.

Basic Guide-lines

Golden rule for successful parties is to segregate the age groups. It's very tempting, if you have children with birthdays in the same month or even week, to try to kill two birds with one stone. But apart from the fact that children are possessive about birthdays, a year or two's difference to you is a generation gap to them. Games can fall flat on their face by being too sophisticated for the four-year-olds but too babyish for the school-age five-year-olds. On the whole, it's best to steel yourself to separate occasions.

Another golden rule is to remember that all children, at least until they near their teens, are very conservative about food. Stick to food that's easily recognizable, and don't fight the losing battle of trying to improve their tastes. Accept that children the world over *prefer* gooey canned fruit to the delectable real thing. And unless you're truly dedicated, don't waste time over mouth-watering éclairs or gâteaux. Young children, especially, will be just as happy with corny old cup cakes or miniature chocolate Swiss rolls.

Final golden rule is pad out rich, sweet foods with plenty of appetizing savouries. These seem to be much more popular nowadays, and even sandwiches disappear with ease. One word of warning based on personal experience: if

you're thinking of piling a dish with differently filled sandwiches, each identified with a flag on a cocktail stick, watch that no young wag switches them around – it's definitely one of the nastier experiences of life to bite into a banana sandwich when you were expecting a cream cheese one.

The Pre-school Set

Under-fives tire quickly, so it's best to see the party ends before the tears begin. About two hours is quite long enough, and it's essential to send written invitations to the mothers, stating the times clearly, so that they can come and collect their children. Very young or shy children may not like being separated from their mothers, so let mothers come, too, if they want to. It's not such a bad idea, anyway, because it means more adults to help organize the games. But even with plenty of help, it's best not to be too ambitious with the number of young guests invited, as crowds, even of contemporaries, can intimidate small children.

Games for this age group could well include Oranges and Lemons, Ring-a-Ring-of-Roses, Musical Parcel (but make the parcel easy to unwrap), and Here We Go Round The Mulberry Bush. Try to slow down the tempo between energetic and excitable games, perhaps by telling a story, singing nursery rhymes together, or watching television, if the party coincides with a regular children's favourite. (Watch out for this by the way. Missing a weekly TV treat could cancel out the pleasure of the party.)

Make absolutely sure that everyone 'wins' something. This is fairly good advice right up to the ten-year-olds, though as the age-group rises it gets more difficult to 'justify' the extra prizes. A simple way out of this, which makes sure every hot and happy hand goes home with something to clutch, is to sit a gift beside each tea-party plate. Especially with under-fives, this needn't be expensive, and can be anything from a small ball or crayon to a colouring book. Better still if it's a giant-size lollipop, because this will make the table look pretty too.

Table-setting for this age-group should be kept bright, simple – and above all practical. Easiest and most sensible way to achieve all these ends at once, is to invest in disposable paper tableware. This comes in plain bright colours for older children, with animal and nursery-favourite patterns for younger ones, and of course, seasonal patterns for Christmas. Not just the tablecloth, but napkins, cups and plates are available in matching sets – and best of all, some of the tablecloths incorporate a layer of plastic between the top and bottom sheets of paper, so that your polished table is safe from spills. However, a sheet of polythene, fastened over to the underside of the table with Sellotape, will provide the same protection under an ordinary paper cloth. If you use the complete range of paper items together, you'll find no other decoration is needed beyond the food itself, with the candle-topped cake as centre-piece, and the colourfully wrapped gifts on each side plate.

The actual food for under-fives should not be too rich, and sweet things could easily be restricted to the birthday cake (an iced sponge cake rather than the traditional marzipanned-and-iced fruit cake), chocolate finger biscuits, jelly, canned fruit and ice-cream. Don't underestimate the swing in favour of savouries. Even the smallest guests will demolish cocktail sausages, potato crisps and sandwiches. Familiar fillings such as scrambled eggs, cheese spread and tomato usually seem to be top of the pops, but keep sandwiches tiny, triangular, and minus the crusts. If all the items are small and easy to tackle, you can then keep cutlery to an absolute minimum. It's best if only teaspoons are needed, because even the youngest child should be able to manage that. And it's best to confine drinks to orange and lemon squash, as opposed to the fizzy versions, and of course, to have plenty of milk at hand. Mean-while, back in the kitchen, be prepared with small plastic or greaseproof bags. Many children won't have room left for their piece of birthday cake, so wrap it up and they can take it home.

Two Years On

Moving to the *five-to-seven*-year-olds, the food and drink situation stays much the same, but games and table-settings can get a little more adventurous and the party can last a good hour longer. By now, the children will probably arrive under their own steam, but – especially in winter – check that mothers know the scheduled finishing time, and confirm by telephone if possible that the small individual who insists that he's allowed home on his own is telling the truth, and not just trying his wings for the first time. Or better still, organize a lift for him or her, as the case may be, with another collecting Mum.

This age-group gives scope for rougher and noisier games like Blind-Man's-Buff (which would have terrified them two years previously) Musical Chairs, Musical Parcel (tightly wrapped this time), Hunt the Thimble, I Spy (a nerve-soother for the mother in charge), and Fanning the Balloon Race. In fact, anything to do with balloons will be entrancing to the five-to-sevens, who will have overcome their fear of the 'squeaky' noise and tendency to burst. One sure way to make yourself the most popular Mum in the neighbourhood is to give them all a balloon to carry home – but hide these in a separate room to ensure survival. As this is an appreciative age-group, it's worth making the most of your opportunities. Delight them with an indoor firework display – just Sparklers on their own will bring 'oohs' and 'aahs' of delight. Another two years and the magic will be gone. They'll want squibs and bangers to thrill their ears and not their eyes. This is the time for Punch and Judy shows too – while they're at the post-timid but pre-blasé stage. Even so, keep a watchful eye on the youngest of your guests for possible signs of distress. (More details of this in the 'Help!' section at the end of the chapter.)

With prizes, increase the scope to include

mas, and are available with non-seasonable motifs. And although by this time, young guests will be able to cope more successfully with cutlery, it's worth investing in some sets of plastic versions. They'll be lighter for small wrists to lift, it won't matter if they get lost, and they're sure to come highly coloured. It's not really important what colour at this stage, because with under-sevens, the more colours the merrier, and you must quell your own good taste.

Fun, Games – and Noise

Grin-and-bear-it time comes with the *seven-to-nine*-year-olds. This is the boisterous age, and all you can do is make sure Dad doesn't slink off and leave you to it. That, and be sure to have plenty of games in hand, so that as soon as one begins to go dangerously off the rails, you can bring it to a brisk close and pitch straight into a new one. Again, it's best to intersperse the rough with the more restful games, though by this age it's for your sake more than theirs. Still popular will be games like Blind-Man's-Buff, Musical Chairs, and for a quiet period, Musical Parcel (this time with enough knots and sticky tape to defeat Houdini.)

But do bring in some slightly more sophisticated games like Pinning the Tail on the Donkey and Wrong-Hand Drawing. And if the party starts to lag, have a Hunt the Present Game. Have your clues written on cards well in advance (in printed letters for clarity), and by means of the clues (plus some unobtrusive help if necessary), let each child find his or her present. To make this more exciting, it's worth giving them the run of more than the party room. After all, you can lock up those rooms you particularly want private – including the room where the party-tea is laid! If you're lucky enough to be giving an all-girl party, remember that this is the age for the dressing-up craze. Providing you can rout out the raw materials for this pastime, it can be one of the most successful, least taxing, and longest-lasting party-game in existence. This is also the age most likely to respond to professional entertainment of the conjuror, magician and ventriloquist type. A little younger, and it would all

things that can be shown off at school. Again, these can be very inexpensive items like coloured pencils, felt pens, novelty-shaped rubbers or pencil sharpeners. For girls, embroidered hankies, simple headbands and slides will probably be popular.

Again, paper tableware would seem the best and brightest bet for this age-group, but place settings can be made that little bit more individual. One impact-maker is to write the names of each guest on his/her balloon (simplest method is with a thick felt pen once the balloon is blown up) and tie them to the back of each respective chair. It's best to tie the balloon with a fairly short string, because unless you're blessed with a strong upward current of air, the balloon will droop sadly, though of course, if it's a summer out-of-doors party, the balloons *might* oblige by bobbing about above the chairs. Equally pretty idea for an outdoors place setting is to tie a paper windmill to the back of each chair, where with luck, it will whirr away throughout the mealtime. Or if you've a fairly large garden and a very windy day a small kite for the back of each chair would be delightful. Both indoors and outdoors, it's worth adding crackers to each place setting, because they're far too great a success to be confined to Christ-

go over their heads: a little older, and they'll feel they've seen it all on television. But again, more of the professionals in the 'Help' section at the end.

Table-settings are worth a little more trouble, too, because detail will now be appreciated, as well as immediate impact. Even if you don't want to move away from the practical advantages of paper-ware, choose a plain tablecloth for a change and add the interest with individual touches. Fiddly but worthwhile idea is to make a miniature maypole and sit it in the middle of the table, with coloured streamers-plus-presents attached, leading to everyone's side-plate. Especially for girls, pop a paper flower on each side-plate (again for taking home), and make a small garland of paper flowers to sit round the cake in the centre. (As this could get expensive, it's worth learning how to make flowers yourself from lengths of coloured tissue.) Or mark out individual place settings by sticking on a star-shape with a metallic sticky tape that comes in several gleaming colours. A central star can take the birthday cake, and if you haven't run out of either tape or patience, make a smaller star to take each glass. Unbreakable plastic tumblers are sensible here, come in attractive smoky colours, and are almost indistinguishable from the real thing. If your guests have been regulars for the past few years, they'll appreciate these signs that their advanced years are now being recognized.

Food and drink can get more ambitious for the seven-to-nines, with the traditional birthday cake appearing, and individual trifles in waxed petal-dishes. 'Grown-up' cakes like chocolate éclairs and meringues will now reward the extra effort, and bridge rolls, instead of easy-to-manage sandwiches, become practical. This is in addition, of course, to the usual sausages, crisps, jelly, ice-cream, etc., as anyone acquainted with a nine-year-old appetite will know without telling. Drinks can finally start swinging a little, too, with the fizzy versions of orange and lemon, perhaps some Cokes, milk shakes, or even fruit cup with bits of fruit floating on top. And whatever's being drunk, for some unfathomable reason, straws seem to increase the enjoyment.

The In-betweens

Nine-to-twelves make up a difficult-to-assess age group, because some children will be growing up more rapidly than others. Also, the sexes will be regarding each other with mutual contempt/suspicion/interest for the first time, and former camaraderie will be forgotten. It's impossible to know whether to carry on with party games or to venture into the teenage field of music and dancing. Safest thing is to cover both eventualities, and play the party by ear. Have plenty of more sophisticated party games ready, like Charades, Consequences, The Memory Game, Sardines, Never Say No, and Murder, but at the same time, try to have a record-player and plenty of pop records to hand. Then if supervised games aren't going down too well, you can leave the children to chat or perhaps start dancing. At all costs, don't disappear from the scene altogether. That's the thin end of a wedge that your children will try to drive home once they become fully-fledged teenagers. Stick around to make sure that game of Sardines doesn't turn into too much giggling in cupboards. You were young once yourself – and that's as good a reason as any for keeping your eye on events!

Table-setting can obviously be more grown-up now, and a buffet arrangement will not only seem sophisticated to the guests, but will also save you a lot of work. As well as the usual bridge roll and sausage type savouries, start introducing bits of cheese on cocktail sticks. Scotch eggs and individual pork pies. This is the age-group when appetites are really getting into full swing, and simple hot food is well worth the effort. If you confine yourself to things like jacket potatoes with a cheese filling, mushroom, and bacon rolls, hot sausage rolls, hot fish fingers – all in prodigious quantities – you can't go wrong. Provide drinks like ginger beer, Cokes and fruit cups, all of which look alcoholic without actually being so. And though by this stage, presents need only be meted out to actual winners of games, you are still dealing with *children*, who are your responsibility. If any child has a long walk home ahead of him or her, where possible try to offer a lift – or at least make sure you have the parent's consent to let him go it alone.

Almost Grown-up

Teenage parties are very little different from adult parties – except that the alcoholic content is probably nil. Success depends almost entirely on atmosphere, music and conversation – and as the latter ingredient is the least predictable among this shy-for-all-their-bravado age group, you must ensure the other two ingredients are there, to encourage the third. Have plenty of pop records (but as you've already a teenager in the house – is it likely you haven't?!) and don't bother about the quality. Don't lend from your own well-polished collection, unless you're prepared for your favourites to come back scratched, and don't ask them to play their records too quietly. Teenage music needs volume, and you'll have to crave the neighbours' indulgence just the once, if the authentic discothèque atmosphere is to be created.

Again, a buffet is the best idea, set out in a very sophisticated way. So long as your buffet table is set well away from the main dancing area, some presentable, if not the very best, china will be appreciated. As glasses are likely to get taken into the dancing area, it's best to make them as cheap and cheerful as possible, so that breakages won't be too much of a disaster. And to cut down on washing up, try to identify them in some way so they can be kept track of and used continually throughout the evening. Ideal solution here, because they stick to everything, including glasses, are paper party badges, available from most large stationers. Let the table 'cloth' be fairly dramatic – with even a touch of gimmickry. Aluminium foil from the kitchen, for instance, makes a strikingly glittering background for food, and sheets of coloured tissue are effective, but watch that your coloured lights don't neutralize their brilliance.

Food served can now include more 'cocktail' type accessories, and items like vol-au-vents and open sandwiches can appear alongside the bridge and sausage rolls. The same sort of hot foods as suggested for the ten-to-twelves will be equally suitable, and bringing them in will give you a chance to see how things are going.

Whether or not you serve any alcohol is a matter for your own judgment. With older teenagers, a not-too-potent fruit cup could be served, or perhaps a little cider – but *not* vintage cider, which can knock the most seasoned adult drinker silly. If you're afraid of seeming strait-laced, consult your own teenager about what the current form is. However, don't take his/her word for gospel – and don't let yourself be talked into serving anything you disapprove of.

The same is true about supervision. Obviously, you're going to cast a damper on the party if you stick around, and you'll extinguish it completely if you try to 'organize' them into anything. But don't let your children pressurize you into going out for the evening, regardless of what other parents are supposed to do on such occasions. If the guests know you're still in the house, albeit discreetly and probably uncomfortably tucked away in the kitchen or bedroom, you'll have a sobering effect on the potentially wild high jinks. Ideal compromise is to welcome the guests at the door. This needn't, in fact shouldn't, be formally done. Just let them in, take their coats, and head them for the party room. Then they know you're around.

Definitely have a prescribed ending time for the party. Relax this slightly if the party is obviously still in full swing, but be ruthless with any stragglers who are going to grow up into those adult guests every hostess knows and dreads. Even at this late age, try to see that they go home together in groups, or manage to get lifts. Some teenagers may well be driving their parents' cars. This chilling thought alone should give you the courage to resist pleas for serving anything other than the mildest and most moderate quantities of alcohol.

Safety First

A word on preparing children's party rooms: particularly with younger ones, clear away obvious breakables like ornaments and table lamps. Move out as much furniture as possible and push the rest to the walls, so that there's room to play games. If at all possible, have the party-table set out in a separate room. It's not fair to ask excited children to be careful, but it's a tragedy for all concerned if the food goes flying. If it's not possible, push the table to the far end of one wall, separate it from the rest of the room with a row of dining chairs – and make whatever's behind them strictly taboo. Then at tea-time, all you'll have to do is pull out the table and position the chairs. And distribute plenty of generous-sized ashtrays – regardless of whether you approve or not of young people smoking. If they're going to, they're going to, so you may as well spare your floor and furniture furtive burns.

If you're considering a professional entertainer (see 'Help!' below) find out in advance what his requirements are. He may need space set aside for him and a free table-top.

For older children, keeping the buffet table at the far end of the room is a must, so that plenty of room's left free for dancing. And talking of dancing, it makes sense to roll up the carpet where possible, because it's going to get plenty of scuffing, if not spilt drinks.

If you don't have central heating, make absolutely sure that fireguards are well-fitted to fires – in such a way that a passing jolt won't dislodge them. It's worth remembering that even radiators can get very hot, and with very young children are perhaps worth fencing in.

HELP !
Party Games

If you've forgotten all your party games, get a book from your local library and read them up well in advance. Or if you've left things too late, ask the advice of your child's teacher when you collect him/her from school — she'll be versed in what's currently popular. For addresses/telephone numbers of services mentioned here, consult Good Housekeeping's booklet, *Aids to Entertaining*, price 10p.

Music, Records

If you're stumped on how to provide a guaranteed flow of music for Musical Chairs/Parcel, consider hiring a barrel organ, because the sound can be turned on and off as easily as a tap. A leading firm for carnival novelties operates a comprehensive hire service, though out-of-London costs are increased by transport charges. It supplies everything from pretty paper lanterns to please the girls, to hideous face-masks to delight the boys, as well as a free

catalogue, where every page is packed with inspiration for cheap take-home gifts.

If you're worried you'll run out of pop records for teenage parties, or would simply like to offer something different, hire a juke box from a firm of juke box distributors. Again, out-of-London areas get more expensive, but charge covers installation, and the records – fifty in all with one hundred selections – always include the top thirty.

Getting a Group

If you're feeling really ambitious, and your neighbours are tolerant, why not hire a live pop group? Make sure you've got a house large enough to take it (i.e. with a far-flung room to retreat to), because it only takes three innocuous-looking youngsters with amplifiers to let all aural hell loose. Obviously, a well-known group will be expensive – but at deafeningly close quarters, a cheap semi-professional group can sound near enough to current idols to pass party muster. If your local paper doesn't carry their ads, you could advertise there yourself, or ask at a local guitar shop. Or you could look through, or advertise in, a musical trade paper such as *Melody Maker*.

Professional Entertainers

If you want a Punch and Judy show, conjuror, ventriloquist or magician, again, watch the small ads in your local paper, or advertise yourself. Be prepared for travel expenses to cost extra, and for Punch and Judy shows to be up to twice as expensive (they take two operators!). For under-sevens, book only a half-hour show, at any age, an hour should be ample. Again, if your local paper comes up with nothing, try the national trade paper for artistes, *The Stage*.

If party-time makes you feel frail, one way to ensure a lengthy respite is to organize a film show. Under-fives will be too young to appreciate what's going on, but from five-up-to-tens cartoons will be well, if not uproariously, received. Films can be hired from various film libraries, but if possible see the film or films through first, to make sure the material is suitable for your age-group.

6
A Wedding in the Family

Pre-wedding nerves are usually associated with the bride, but it's the poor bride's Mum who really deserves the sympathy. She's the one faced with the formidable task of organization, and if you find yourself in this happy but fraught situation, your only hope for keeping family life sane is to prepare well in advance.

The Guest List

Thrash out with the bride-and-groom-to-be how many guests need inviting – and then stick to the decision. 'Small' weddings have a way of snowballing into something grand, and this can place a great strain on the average family's finances. In addition to providing the reception – which is what this chapter is chiefly concerned with – the bride's parents also have to foot the bill for the stationery, any press announcements, the cake, photographers, flowers for the church, and cars to the church. And although every mother wants this to be the biggest and best day in her daughter's life, it's a mistake to get over-ambitious and take on more than can be coped with — especially if there are other daughters following on. It's better to have a simple and informal occasion, that may not follow the etiquette books exactly, than one which is 'correct' in every detail, but becomes an ordeal.

The Cake

First move must be the cake, because this needs baking far enough in advance for the traditionally rich mixture to mature. Even for a small wedding, it's worth making a fairly large cake, because it will provide a scene-stealing focal point at the reception, and probably get immortalized in wedding photos. Any tier left intact can be kept for the first wedding anniversary – or even the first christening. And all the people who couldn't be invited or couldn't come, can be sent a small 'finger' through the post. This isn't obligatory, but it's a lovely old custom, and an inexpensive way of letting people know they weren't forgotten. If you want to make the cake yourself (many people order it from their favourite baker, or from the caterers who may be handling the reception,) it must be baked at least one month, preferably two, before the wedding day. Part III gives the recipe, tells you how to organize the tiers, and gives detailed instructions on how to add the royal icing. But allow plenty of time, because you'll probably only be able to manage one tier at a time. If you're confident about your cake-making, but dubious about your icing skills, your baker will almost certainly be willing to add the icing and decorations. This seems a sensible compromise, because professional icing standards are hard to attain. And it *is* worth tackling the cake yourself, if only to hear the awed whisper 'the bride's mother made it' go round the reception like wildfire.

R.S.V.P.

Next move is to send out the invitations. For a fairly large number, where it's difficult to assess how many will accept, send them six weeks ahead, but for a smaller wedding, three to four weeks should be enough. Surprisingly, for this lazy age, people still react to the R.S.V.P., and replies should start pouring back within two or three days. These advance tactics are essential, because you'll need to alert caterers (or yourself) about the numbers expected at the reception, and then work out how much per head you can afford to spend on them.

What Kind of Reception

Planning the reception depends not only on the numbers and finances, but also on the time of the wedding. A fairly early morning wedding will only need a buffet reception of cocktail-type savouries, either with the luxury of champagne throughout, or with sherry or cocktails, plus champagne for the toasts only. But a late morning wedding will leave you with a hungry-for-lunch horde on your hands, and a complete buffet or sit-down meal becomes essential. In this case, you could welcome the guests with sherry or a cocktail, serve red or white wine with the meal, and save the champagne for the toasts – or again, serve champagne throughout. For champagne throughout, allow half a bottle to each guest; for toasts only, remember each bottle will fill eight champagne glasses. An afternoon wedding will need no more than a few cocktail savouries, plus some cakes, with champagne only. But whatever the time of day, the champagne needn't be vintage, and guests need only be offered enough to put them in celebration mood, because people who've drunk too much look ugly anywhere – but ugliest of all at a wedding-party. And though most people remember to serve soft drinks, it's amazing how many forget that guests may be dying for a cup of coffee in the morning, or a good old cup (or two or three) of tea in the afternoon.

At an Hotel

Hotel receptions are the most painless, but also the most expensive way of giving a reception, though there's usually a wide price range, with several menus to choose from, both buffet or sit-down. If you're afraid it sounds too impersonal, there are several ways in which you can influence the arrangements, and there's no reason why you shouldn't get an estimate on a menu of your own planning. Check whether flowers are included or not, because these can be expensive extras, and specify how you'd like them. And make sure well in advance that you like the room they're offering you. Sometimes even the most elegant hotel has a 'reception' room that looks like a down-at-heel cinema. For a sit-down meal, make

yourself responsible for the seating arrangements. Whether in a hotel or at home, there's a recognized 'top-table' seating plan that runs (from left to right, facing) as follows:

Usher/Bridesmaid/Groom's Father/Bride's Mother/Groom/Bride/Bride's Father/Groom's Mother/Best Man/Chief Bridesmaid, but arrange other guests as you would for any dinner party, trying to mix them up in a way that will stimulate conversation, but making sure that any shy people are near someone they know. Put your plan down on paper, and take it (with name cards that can be printed, typed or handwritten) to the hotel manager the day before, so they'll be ready and waiting when you arrive. And don't be afraid to 'interfere' with the placing of the hotel tables. For a small-to-medium reception of under fifty, a good way to arrange the tables is in a square or rectangle, with the guests sitting on the outside only, facing inwards. This way, everyone gets a good view of what's going on, without offering anyone else a view of their back.

In a Hired Hall

Hiring a hall or room, and then hiring a firm of caterers, is another way to tackle a reception. Again, everything must be checked in advance, and caterers (hotels, too, for that matter) are most safely chosen on personal recommendation. They'll have the same variety of tariffs as a hotel, but may not work out much cheaper overall, because it's the labour rather than the accommodation costs that are high.

At Home

Probably the most enjoyable reception is the one that's given at home. If you don't feel you can cope with the large-scale catering, get in an outside firm and leave the worrying to them. They'll provide the food, the drink (on a sale or return basis), the china, cutlery, tablecloths, tables and chairs if necessary, and of course, waitresses and kitchen staff. What's more, they'll clear up all the chaos afterwards.

If you don't want to trust your luck to hotels or caterers (though most of them are worthy specialists in their fields), you can prepare your own buffet reception at home. Part II gives detailed menus for a wedding buffet as grand as any that a hotel could provide, but practical enough to be managed in your own kitchen. Obviously it helps to have some assistance, be it a friendly neighbour who lends a hand all round, or someone hired for the day to keep the washing-up in check. But you'll almost certainly need to hire some equipment, either from hire-firms, or perhaps from a hotel. Cutlery, china, champagne buckets, silver candelabra, trestle-tables and chairs are likely items, though whoever supplies your drinks will supply your glasses free of charge. Plenty of chairs are essential, because too much standing makes people tired and irritable, especially during 'lulls' – while the bride is changing, for instance.

Basically, the room should be arranged as for any buffet, with the food table at one end, 'bar' at the other, and chairs kept clear of the centre to allow free circulation. The wedding cake should be given pride of place, either in the centre of the buffet table, or on a small table of its own. But the tablecloths must be white, and paper napkins the silver-on-white wedding versions that most stationers stock. Flowers can afford to be more formal and elaborate than for usual buffet situations, making full use of height to give them importance. Unless you are fairly talented, it's worth ordering arrangements from the local florist for this very special occasion, perhaps linking them with the bridal bouquet in some way, or sticking to traditional but beautiful all-white flowers.

Even with a serve-yourself buffet, older relatives will appreciate some help, and someone must keep an attentive eye on people's glasses. As you yourself will be circulating among the guests, arrange for the bridesmaids and ushers to do any fetching or carrying where necessary. Leave the supervision of drinks to the best man, who may well call on the father of the bride or groom, or some close friends, to help him out. Seat children together, round their own table if space permits; if you're short of chairs, simply sit them on cushions in a corner, and let them eat picnic-fashion. And if you don't want children (only hypocrites would deny that they can sometimes be a nuisance at grown up occasions), be brave enough not to invite them in the first place.

If lack of space seems to rule out an at-home reception (a reasonable-size room can manage 25 people, a large one up to 50), consider – provided it's a summer wedding – a marquee. Most caterers can supply and erect them, or you can hire them direct from marquee manufacturers or hire firms, who will also come and put them up. Then, even if the rain thunders down on the canvas, the atmosphere inside will stay gay and festive.

Guests – Before and After

A marquee solves the problem of space during the reception, but not before, and after. Some guests will live too far away to travel to and from the wedding in one day, and may come down the previous day. You are *not* expected to put them up, because you've got enough on your plate already – and your daughter is going to need the bathroom almost entirely to herself. If you know they can't afford full board at a hotel, you can compromise by offering them meals, so they can book bed and breakfast only. But be quite brazen about feeding them out of cans and on cold meat and salad, because this is no time for cookery demonstrations. Remember that they'll have to vacate their hotel rooms by midday, so will probably want to leave their luggage with you before the wedding. What's more, they'll almost certainly want to change their clothes before travelling back, which means it would be an extra kindness to put a bedroom at their disposal after the reception. But with luck, some kind neighbour may be able to put them up, and this is the happiest solution all round. Guests who travel down the day of the wedding, and then don't have time to get themselves back, are a different proposition and far more welcome, because they'll stave off the awful sense of anti-climax that sets in once the wedding's over.

If the reception's been held outside the home, many guests will automatically drift back with you, either to see the presents or just to have a chat. You're under no obligation to provide them with a meal, though tea or coffee with biscuits, or an alcoholic drink, is usually a hospitable and gratefully received gesture. After an hour or so, they'll either drift off, or suggest having a meal out. This is an especially good idea, with or without overnight guests to entertain, because an evening of nothing after such a hectic day is depressing rather than relaxing, however tired you are. But now that the wedding's over, it's every man for himself, and you can't be expected to foot the bill.

Meeting Problems Half-way

Books on wedding etiquette are legion, and your local library will doubtless have one or two that will help you through the wilderness of what is right and what is wrong. It's easy to pooh-pooh etiquette, yet the big occasions in family life deserve to be celebrated with some ceremony. But the really practical hints often get left out of the books. What happens if it's belting down with rain, for instance? Usually the bride manages to get rushed back and forth under the only available umbrella – but guests are in their finery, too. A dash of a few yards

in a downpour can destroy a hair-do or ruin a hat, and the only solution is to be prepared. Make an advance arrangement with a hotel or hire firm, so that if the previous day is unpromising, you have two or three large umbrellas delivered. These can be manned by the best man and/or ushers, in a romantically dashing fashion that will turn the disastrous weather into a pleasant adventure.

Parking is another problem that should be foreseen, and if you think it could prove troublesome, get in touch with your local Police station. They'll be only too happy to help, because they'll want to keep traffic moving easily through the streets and avoid the double-parking that causes jams. If it's necessary, they'll even section off parts of the road for your use alone, and a pound or two to a Police charity afterwards won't be construed as bribery! For really large weddings, where cars will be converging from all sides and probably getting lost, the AA will put up signs to help them reach their destination as quickly as possible.

Finally, cutting the cake mustn't be a problem, because all eyes (and doubtless a camera) will be on the bride as she does it. If you're making the cake yourself, the simplest way to avoid unseemly struggles is to cut a large slice from the bottom tier of the cake before you decorate it, and re-cut the same slice when the cake is coated with icing but before the piping's done. This way, the bride only has to slice through the surface decoration – and the fraud is invisible to the casual observer. Bought cakes have an even more cunning solution, where the bride only needs to cut either side of a silver ribbon for a perfect slice to be pulled out immediately. But this is all the work that's expected of her, and someone else sets to cutting up the large wedge, and serving dainty fingers of cake to the guests.

7
Giving a Cocktail Party

Cocktail parties have been 'going out of fashion' for so long now, and surviving, that it looks as if they're here to stay. One very good reason for their tenacious hold on life is that they offer a fairly cheap way of entertaining large numbers of people without the need to get involved in serious cooking. Another is that they've been adapted to meet today's no-staff-and-not-much money situation. Gone are the vast gatherings of remote acquaintances, desperately trying to outdo one another with witty small-talk, while the cocktail shaker rattles in the background. Nowadays, unless a professional barman is hired, so that cocktails can be mixed quickly enough to keep pace with demand, very few cocktails proper are served, and those that are usually get mixed in the glasses. Also, gatherings tend to be smaller, and to include friends rather than acquaintances, so that the parties truly become enjoyable.

Any really ambitious cocktail party needs professional help, and the United Kingdom Bartender's Guild will always try to trace a fully-trained bartender in your area. Don't rely on your local pub, because the fall in demand for cocktails means experienced men are hard to find. This is why most cocktail parties have simplified their scope, and it's become perfectly acceptable to offer a choice of only two cocktails, with sherry as a third alternative, whisky as a possible fourth, and plenty of fruit juices, soft drinks – and soda for people who want to make a little liquor go a long way. Part IV of this book gives recipes for various cocktails, but among the most popular are the gin-based Dry Martini and the Champagne Cocktail. These make a suitably contrasting pair for any party, and have the added advantage that both can be mixed in advance if large numbers are expected. A more unusual, but increasingly popular pair of cocktails could be the rum-based Daiquiri, which even the most vehement rum-haters seem to love, and the Campari/sweet vermouth-based Americano, that can be made long or short, according to how much soda you add. These are deliciously refreshing drinks, ideal for any hot summer evening, and the acidy-lime flavour of the one is perfectly balanced by the sweeter taste of the other.

Variations on the Theme
Simpler forms of cocktail parties are quite in order, but should be described as such. Make it quite clear on the invitation that you're giving a sherry party, or a champagne-cocktail party, etc., so that friends who don't happen to like your particular choice have the opportunity of refusing. For a sherry party, provide medium and dry sherry as a must, but to be on the safe side, have a bottle of sweet sherry handy, too. Sherry is the perfect pre-dinner drink, and not too expensive, so this kind of party has much to recommend it. Both the medium and dry sherry should be served slightly chilled, but the sweet sherry should be served at room temperature. Champagne-cocktail parties aren't anything like as expensive as they sound, and have a glamorous enough image to bring your friends flocking round. It only takes one tablespoonful of brandy to each cocktail, and if you don't want to go to the expense of non-vintage champagne (it's certainly not worth wasting vintage), you can substitute any dry sparkling white wine.

The Invitations
Most cocktail parties last from one to a maximum of two hours (quite long enough to shift from aching foot to aching foot), and it's essential to send out formal invitations, letting people know exactly where they stand as regards time. The idea of a cocktail party is to have a get-together that leaves people free to go off and enjoy the rest of the evening elsewhere.

Organizing Drinks and Glasses

During the drinking time available, count on serving an average of four drinks per person. This may not sound much, but the aim is to stimulate guests into conversation and not stun them out of it. Also, you can always bank on a quota of people who are practically teetotal. Women rarely consume as much alcohol, as men, and they'll probably form half of your numbers – which is why it's essential, at every type of cocktail party, to have plenty of fruit juices and soft drinks available. For a large cocktail party, the only way to be safe with your quantities, and not shamefacedly sorry, is to arrange to get your drinks from your off-licence on a sale or return basis. And it's worth getting glasses from the same source, as these are usually lent free if your order is large enough, and second to running out of drink, the worst disaster that can befall you is running out of clean glasses.

As a rough guide on alcoholic quantities; with spirits, reckon on getting 32 nips per bottle for use as basic cocktail ingredients, but only 16 to 20 nips per bottle if taken 'long', with soda, ginger ale, tonic and ice, etc. With sherry, expect to get 10–12 glasses from each bottle, and with champagne for use in champagne cocktails, expect a safe 10 helpings and a possible 12. With tomato juice, a one-pint can should provide 4–6 glasses – and a large lump of ice in the top will make it go further. Obviously, these estimates depend on the use of appropriate-sized glasses. Informality about what glass goes with what drink has made life much easier, but for a sherry party, it's worth organizing a supply of sherry glasses, and champagne glasses would give an especial sense of occasion to a champagne-cocktail party. Otherwise, it's simplest to cut down requirements to two basic shapes and sizes: a small-to-medium stemmed wine glass for cocktails, and a flat-based tumbler for spirits, long cocktails and soft drinks.

What to Eat?

Food is a smaller but equally vital factor in the success of any cocktail party, because drinking on an empty stomach ceases to be pleasurable as soon as the first drink hits home. As people are going to be holding a glass in one hand and probably a cigarette in the other, bite-size items that can be popped straight into the mouth are essential. This explains why canapés, in some form or other, are the most widely served of cocktail savouries. Their main disadvantage is that they take a fair amount of preparation. However, it's possible to simplify the process by using a ready-made base, such as a small plain cheese (as opposed to cheese-flavoured) biscuit, water biscuit, or brown or white bread, which should be fried or toasted, or rye or pumpernickel bread used 'straight', or small shapes of pastry, which can be made two or three days beforehand and stored in air-tight tins till needed. The savoury butters *need* to be made a few hours beforehand, and some of the more ornate garnishes can be prepared in advance.

Equally suitable for cocktail parties are the usual savouries, such as cocktail sausages, cheese straws, cocktail onions, olives, gherkins and salted nuts. Savoury dips surrounded by plenty of small, dry biscuits, breadsticks, potato crisps, celery and carrot sticks, all help to off-set the effects of alcohol in an easily digested way. But if it's at all possible, every cocktail party gets a tremendous lift if something hot can be served half-way through. Recipes for various savouries are included in Part IV. As regards quantities of food, it's as well to allow 6 small savouries to each guest. Again, this doesn't sound much, but some people will be saving their appetites, others will be on a diet, and no one will be looking on your party as a substitute for a meal.

All preparations for the party room, from the setting up of the bar, to the hunting of taxi-hire numbers, are dealt with in Chapter II. The only procedure exclusive to the cocktail scene is that food should be set out attractively on trays and dishes and distributed liberally around the room. If it's left on the same table as the drinks, people tend to gather round the bar, and the party stagnates before it has time to begin. Remember, circulation of people is essential to a cocktail party, where it's the art of civilized conversation that counts, not the mere scoffing and quaffing of food and drink.

8
Keeping a Clear Head on Wines

If wine were made compulsory – a bottle per head per day – the world would probably be a much happier and more humane place. That's why it's a tragedy we've managed to surround it with so much phoney mystique. Wine only exists to give pleasure to people, but many are afraid to order a bottle in case they betray a lack of *expertise*, when all they really need to know is what they like and what they don't like. It's true there are rules – but these are natural rather than academic. It's fairly safe to say that anyone who's tried drinking burgundy with Dover sole or port with pizza won't have liked it, and won't try the same combination again. Nevertheless, wine's a fascinating subject, and a little knowledge is well worth acquiring, so long as it doesn't become the little learning that's a dangerous thing. There's nothing more dreary than the wine snob who thinks he knows so much, but doesn't know enough just to sit back quietly and enjoy what he's drinking.

The Basic Rules are just Commonsense

It's generally accepted that dry wines should come before sweeter ones, and the light before the full-bodied ones, for the very good reason that the reverse order turns the dry wine bitter and the light wine insipid. Equally reasonably, it makes sense to serve a dry white wine with fish and white meats, rather than to obliterate their delicate flavour with the richer, heavier reds, whereas red meats and game *need* this stronger company. And sweet desserts need sweet wine for a partner, because a dry one will taste sharp and acrid by contrast. At rigidly formal functions, there may be as many as seven or eight courses, with a different wine for each course. But at home, even the most formal occasion usually contents itself with two wines for the savoury courses and one sweet wine for dessert. And the average dinner-party gets by very happily with one wine only – the one that's appropriate to the main course.

These are the general principles, but for anyone interested in getting down to particulars, there follows a run-through of what wines go with what. (Don't forget that Part IV gives a descriptive reference list of wines, and also tells you how to use them in cooking.)

Before the Meal

For pre-dinner drinks, otherwise known as apéritifs, it's pretty much a matter of anything goes. But if you're serving good food and wine, it's a pity to blunt people's appreciation by serving strong cocktails or straight spirits. Americans may knock themselves insensible with dry martinis or whiskies before a meal, but anyone who's eaten Great American Dream Food will understand why. And incredible as it may seem, they're probably going to sober up during the meal by drinking coffee or even *milk* throughout! Meanwhile, back in civilization, it's better to offer dry or medium sherry (not a sweet one, because it won't stimulate the appetite – this goes for all sweet wines and vermouths), a dry Madeira, dry white port, sparkling wine, Portuguese vinho verde and the dry vermouths, all of which go well with simple 'nibbles' like nuts, crisps, biscuits and olives. And if you're going in for the complication of canapés, offer an ordinary red wine or rosé with strongly-flavoured salami, anchovies, game-pâté versions.

During the Meal

With mixed *hors d'oeuvre* which tend to be spicy, oily and/or vinegary, either carry on with the dry or medium sherry, or serve one of the cheaper red or white wines – a young Beaujolais, for instance. With smoked salmon, smoked trout or eel, again a glass of apéritif sherry will be suitable, possibly preferable to light white wine. The same goes for avocado pears, artichokes or asparagus. With oysters, however, have Chablis, dry Champagne or Muscadet, and with potted shrimps, try any light, dry white wine. With *soups*, no one's going to look askance if you serve nothing at all. Piping hot soups should never be served with a chilled wine: if the soup is flavoured with sherry, Madeira or Marsala, it's pleasant to match it with a glass of the same wine. *For fish, and plainly cooked chicken, pork and other white meats*, serve any of the drier white wines, whether still or sparkling. But fresh salmon or lobster deserve one of the fuller bodied and usually pricier white Burgundies, going up the price scale to the final extravagance of a Montrachet. *For beef, lamb, mutton or ham*, serve any of the red wines of Bordeaux or Burgundy, or any similar ones from Spain or Portugal. But where rich and/or fatty foods like *duck, goose and game* are concerned, it takes a robust red wine of the Rhône or one of the fuller white wines from the Rhineland to act as a counterbalance. A red Bordeaux goes well with 'lighter' unhung game birds, but for grouse or other game that's been hung, you can't beat a good, gutsy Burgundy. Gamey meat like venison, wild boar and hare is usually served with a strong dark red wine, but surprisingly, it's equally delicious with one of the fuller hocks, especially those from the Palatinate. With *puddings and desserts*, indulge your sweet tooth to the full with a rich Sauternes, a Spätlese or Auslese hock, or one of the sweeter Champagnes. But with any iced pudding or ice-cream, don't waste good wine on a palate that will be too chilled to notice it. Dessert fruits (with the exception of pineapple) and fruit salads, like the heavier dessert wines like port, the sweeter sherries and Madeiras. Wine with *cheese* is largely a matter of personal taste, because, especially with the milder cheeses, almost any type is compatible. Red wine, robust and dry, goes very well with stronger-flavoured cheeses, but many people prefer to stick to the traditional port.

Exceptions and Special Cases

All this is fine as far as it goes, but there are several special cases. Sometimes the whole character of a dish can be changed by the sauce or stuffing that goes with it – for example, suprême of chicken in a bland cream sauce would call for the usual light white or rosé wine, but the far richer coq au vin, cooked in red wine and flamed in brandy, would absolutely clamour for a full red wine. Wherever food has been cooked in wine or beer, the general rule is to serve the same for drinking. Serve a full-flavoured Burgundy with beef cooked in Burgundy, for instance, and serve beer with any braises or casseroles that have had beer included. Eggs for a first course, whether aspic, mayonnaise or *en cocotte*, need no special consideration, but will take extra kindly to a light white wine. For omelette as a main dish at a simple lunch, a red *vin ordinaire* makes good company. But for a formal occasion, when say a cheese or fish soufflé is being served, a good white Burgundy or a mellow hock is more in keeping.

Some foods aren't supposed to go with wine, and it's true that anything in which vinegar predominates ruins wine's flavour. The acids in pineapple, grapefruit, oranges and lemons have the same effect, but other ingredients can modify this reaction. A salad, for instance, tossed in French dressing made with wine or herb vinegar, plus oil to smooth it and a little sugar, will be quite friendly towards a robust red or white wine. But other taboos seem to be based on snobbery as much as anything. Just because alcohol is prohibitively priced in India (as well as prohibited by religion), it gets vetoed here when *curries* are served. True, the flavours are too fierce to waste a good wine on, and too heavy to take a red one, but there's no reason why people shouldn't drink a dry white wine if they want to. A light lager seems to be a semi-accepted compromise, and it has to be admitted that for a real thirst-quencher, there's nothing to beat basic tap water. *Chinese food* comes up against this same arbitrary veto, though heaven knows why, when the Chinese themselves drink rice wine, brandy or whisky throughout a meal, punctuating it with shouts of *'yum sing'* – literal translation 'to the bottom'. But as Chinese food consists of so many varied delicate flavours, a dry white wine or a light lager is probably the pleasantest accompaniment for Western palates. Certainly any *well-spiced* dish that makes maximum demands on the palate calls for 'guzzle-wines' as the rugged *ordinaires* have been called. Strongly flavoured pizzas, paellas and pastas are good examples, and it doesn't matter whether you choose red or white wine, though traditionally Chianti goes with pizza, and Spaniards usually drink red wine with paella, despite its seafood bias.

Shopping for Wine

But none of this helps decide *how* to buy a wine, because there are far too many variables involved in the making. The type of grape, the country of origin, the aspect of the vineyard, the method of wine-making, the weather in any given year – all influence what ends up in the bottle. This means that, as with any form of shopping, your best bet is to choose a reliable retailer and place your trust in him. A good wine merchant will be a genuine expert, with nothing to gain from pulling the wool over your eyes – just a reputation to lose. First of all, don't be intimidated by the wine lists, because they're fairly easy to find your way around, the wines of a kind being grouped together. First among the table wines are the Bordeaux, listed under reds (called claret in English) and whites, and the Burgundies, also listed under reds and whites. Other French wines are listed under their regions, such as Rhône and Loire, with Champagne standing alone. The hocks (Rhine wines), the Moselles and the Alsatian wines are listed under those headings. The Italian wines (of which Chianti is only one example) and the table wines of Hungary, Yugoslavia, Portugal, Spain and so on are listed under the country of origin. Sparkling wines other than Champagne often get listed together, regardless of region, and so do the pink (rosé) wines.

Wines within each category start with the cheapest, and there are still some very drinkable ones at not very much over fifty pence – though an extra ten pence or so can well be worth it. Most of the moderately-priced wines, and many of the finer ones, are shipped in bulk and bottled here. Anything that's château-bottled or domaine-bottled will be dearer, because it costs more to ship bottles, and also the wines often have a scarcity value that puts the price up still higher. The detailed naming of individual wines is given in the chart in Part IV, but for rough guidance, here are some recognized good vintage years:

Red Bordeaux: 1952, 53, 55, 57, 59, 61, 62, 64, 66.
White Bordeaux: 1959, 61, 62, 64, 66.
Red Burgundy: 1953, 55, 57, 59, 61, 62, 64, 66.
White Burgundy: 1955, 57, 59, 61, 62, 63, 64, 66.
Rhenish (Hocks, Moselles, Steinwein, Alsatian): 1959, 61, 62, 64, 66.

All these wines are good for drinking now, though some of them, for instance the best of the clarets and red Burgundies, may not reach their peak for a few years. However, it's always best to enjoy them too soon rather than too late. But this vintage table *can* only be a rough guide, because some superb wine gets produced in the poorer years, while some quite ordinary stuff can come out of the good ones.

Champagne shippers (like port shippers) decide whether a particular year is good enough to be called a vintage year, and then put the date on their labels. Because champagne changes character after several years in the bottle, it's best to pick a comparatively recent year. Non-vintage champagne, a non-dated combination of the new wine with stocks of the previous year or years, is very good value – provided it comes from one of the dozen or so leading shippers. Sherry, because of the way it is made, has no vintage years.

Keeping the Cost Down

So far as price goes, obviously a wine isn't 'cheaper' just because it's lower in price – it also has to be a good honest wine in its own price range. In these matters, it's worth taking the good wine merchant's advice. But there are several other ways of cutting down your wine bills. Some wine merchants and department stores offer a discount on an order for a dozen mixed bottles of wine, and a slightly higher discount on a dozen of the same wine. Some also offer free delivery to any address in England, Scotland and Wales when the order is not less than a dozen bottles. Of course, it's always worth shopping around for recognized brands of sherry and spirits at reduced prices, perhaps when a reliable department store is holding its half-yearly sale.

For a party, when good old 'plonk' is all that's needed, it's often cheaper to buy *vin ordinaire* in larger containers, like the half-gallon size (the equivalent of three bottles), the gallon and the five-gallon size. Alternatively, you may be able to obtain wine in a cask-like 1-gallon container fitted with an inner 'skin' and a tap; with this, any wine not used up at once will keep in good condition for a time.

Membership of a wine club can also provide wines that, quality for quality, are cheaper than you'd get through a retail outlet. But there's always an annual club subscription, and this has to be offset against your saving. Some of these clubs spring from the getting together of wine-lovers, but others are organized by wine merchants as a promotional service to customers. Some of them – the Wine and Food Society, for instance – don't sell wine but simply organize tastings. Others sell wine by sending their lists of selected wines to members. It's a system that can cut down overheads and mean cheaper wine, but it suffers from the disadvantage of all mail-order set-ups – you don't see the goods until you've bought them. Obviously it's best to be careful, and a club run or backed by a reliable wine merchant is the safest way to go about it. Otherwise, unless you've friends who are already members, ask about facilities for sampling wines before joining.

A way of enjoying the finer wines of life without paying too dearly for them is to buy them early for 'laying down'. This way you can get a good vintage year that will have scarcity value when it's ready for drinking. Some wine merchants will store these wines for you in ideal conditions, though they won't usually bother for less than a dozen bottles. What's more, by sampling their own stocks of the same wine, they'll be able to tell you when yours is coming up to its mature best.

Your Domestic 'Cellar'

Most people can find room for their own mini-cellar, perhaps in a hall cupboard or tucked away under the stairs. Basically, what stored wines want is stillness, a peaceful out-of-the-way place where they're not going to get shaken. They also need a steady temperature that's cool, but not as cold as a fridge. And they want comparative darkness, and should certainly be kept away from direct light. So that the corks don't shrink and dry, they need to lie horizontally, and for safety, they should be stored label upwards in firm racks or 'bins'. Never 'bin' a bottle if the wine is oozing out through the cork, and use up as quickly as possible any stored bottle that shows signs of 'weeping'.

With the exception of Beaujolais, all red wines benefit from being stored for two or three months, and this is the minimum time for resting old sedimented wines that have been disturbed in transit from the wine merchant to your home. But plenty of wines gain nothing, and may even deteriorate, by being stored. These include Champagne, most whites, rosés and light reds. In fact, the cheaper wines and most branded wines are sold ready to drink at once.

Serving Wine

For your own satisfaction, but especially when guests are coming, it's worth knowing the simple and commonsense rules for serving wine. To begin with, you don't 'have' to decant a wine. The object of the exercise is to separate the wine from its lees, and with a red wine, to let it 'take the air' as well. If a wine has a very heavy sediment, it's obviously safest to decant it, pouring steadily but not quickly, and being ready to stop the moment any muddiness appears. But this condition is usually found only with older and more expensive wines;

generally, so long as a bottle has stood for half an hour or so before serving, gentle handling and careful pouring should be enough to ensure that every glass is clear. Just as it's never essential to decant wine, it's equally never harmful, so it can really boil down to whether or not you boast a beautiful decanter.

All white wines should be served chilled but not iced – half an hour in the fridge is quite long enough. An ice bucket on the table isn't enough, though, and should only be used to stop the wine's temperature rising in the heat of the room. Red wines are best served at room temperature, but 'room temperature' can vary in these days of erratic central heating, and it's wisest to let them stand for a couple of hours in a 'comfort zone' of around 65 °F. They should never be heated up violently, because they lose character and never recover it. Uncork the bottles an hour or so before serving, because contact with air improves the taste and bouquet of red wine in some secret and mysterious way. Some people prefer to serve cheap red wine chilled, presumably on the basis that there's not much taste or bouquet to be coaxed out of it.

Theoretically, glasses for wine should be clear, colourless and fine, preferably with a bowl that narrows towards the rim to hold in the wine's perfume. Certainly it seems a crime to serve wine in a coloured glass, when the richness of red and the golden subleties of white wine look so rewarding. But though many people consider stemmed glasses essential (even if they're only the perfectly acceptable Woolworth's versions), there's a growing tendency to serve ordinary 'plonk' in ordinary old tumblers. Wine snobs can throw up their hands in horror, but they're used across the breadth and depth of France, and it's really only the finer wines, with a bouquet worth trapping, that need cosseting in any special way.

Type of glass best suited to various wines, as shown in a recent Wine and Food Society diary. Left to right: brandy; sherry; port; claret or burgundy; champagne, modern; hock, Moselle, Alsace; champagne flute; hock, old style.

9
Streamlining the Work

Entertaining just isn't worth it if you're going to get yourself into a frenzy and make the whole family suffer for it before and after. Everyone gets a bit twitchy on an occasion of any formality, and no amount of sophisticated equipment, or even help in the kitchen, is going to rule out those pre-doorbell butterflies. But if you know the mechanics of the evening are going to run smoothly, you're half-way towards one of those successes when food, wine, company and conversation 'gel' into an almost magical whole.

Having the right equipment doesn't mean being armed with a battery of gadgets. It can be as basic as having a cooker with enough rings on top, or a fridge that, as well as everyday supplies, can pack away a consommé, salad ingredients, a mousse, and still have room for a couple of bottles of wine. Pop-up toasters are fairly standard items, too, but without them it's easy to burn the toast for the 'trouble-free' pâté when your mind's on the main course. It's no great problem to do a fresh supply, but it is hard to dispel the charcoal-smell that sneaks out of the kitchen and hovers mockingly over the dining-table for the rest of the meal.

Mixers and Blenders

Electric mixers aren't commonplace yet, but whether you go the whole hog with a large table-top machine or stick with a small hand-held version, you'll find you've bought a reliable slave that's worth its weight in gold. Some types can do rubbing in for shortcrust pastry and fruit cakes (provided the fat's at room temperature); do the creaming for Victoria sandwiches and Madeira-type cakes, and for steamed or baked puddings. Most can do the whisking for fatless sponges like Swiss rolls, for meringue egg whites and for soufflés and mousses, as well as for hot drinks and sauces. And most can make icings or (with the beaters in the saucepan) cream vegetables like potatoes and swedes.

Obviously, the more expensive mixers have the greater abilities, and the same applies to blenders, that can either attach to mixers or live independently. These can purée fresh, canned or frozen fruit, make fruit fools and ice-cream mixtures, and purée vegetables for soups. They can reduce fruit or vegetables to juice for drinks – or, less radically, merely chop them for salads and so on. They'll chop or grind nuts for you, produce all kinds of crumbs, from bread to biscuit to cake, and blend all custard and packet desserts, packet cake mixes and milk shakes, as well as managing dips, sandwich fillings and pâtés. They'll make mint, apple and horseradish sauces, French dressing and, better still, mayonnaise. But best of all, they'll retrieve that agonizing situation when you realize your sauce has gone lumpy, by beating it back to smooth perfection.

Cooker Plusses

If your cooker's big enough for everyday, but sadly limited on special occasions, consider supplementing it with some extras. An infrared grill, for instance, may take 10 minutes to heat up, but can then manage chops or steaks in double-quick time. Use it in a well ventilated kitchen though, as you'll find the frying fumes overpowering. An electric fast-fryer can cope with deep-frying fish, fritters and chips quickly enough to leave only an imperceptible gap in your hostess-at-table duties. Again, it takes a few minutes to heat up (while the first course is being eaten, perhaps), but the actual frying time is only 3 minutes.

If your cooker's too mini to make sense, but has to live in a mini-kitchen that can accommodate nothing larger, you can boost your cooking potential with work-top or table-top extras. Rather flashy at first sight, but really a very useful item, is a small spit-roaster. This obviously offers chicken-off-the-spit and kebab possibilities, but also has grilling facilities and two fast-boiling rings — which Parkinson's law would quickly make use of.

Serving and Re-serving

But your troubles don't end when you've managed to cook the food. You've got to get it to the table while it's still sizzling hot, because guests take a while to help themselves, and you can't shout 'Hurry up, it's getting cold' at them as you can with your family. The best way to ensure smooth, speedy and hot service is to invest in a heated trolley, with a warming compartment for plates and fitted serving dishes on top. The only snag (apart from price, of course!), is that it looks rather ugly, and doesn't do much to hide its hotel-catering-industry roots. Much cheaper, and much less obtrusive, is an electrically heated hotplate or tray, that can sit quietly on a side-table, and keep everything hot till it's needed. Some even have built-in 'hot-spots', to keep casserole or coffee-pot at an extra high temperature. But most attractive and cheapest way of all is to buy one of the cauldron-casseroles on night-light stands. These are perfect for one-dish courses, like paella, and make a major contribution to the general party atmosphere, especially if the lighting's dim.

With or without ways of keeping food hot, some kind of trolley is an asset, preferably with easy-running orbital castors instead of the old-fashioned jerky kind. Constant back-and-forth-trips to the kitchen have a disrupting effect on any meal, and also make guests worried as to whether or not they should be helping. A trolley is vital enough when you're trying to carry in hot dishes, but even more so when you're carrying out the unlovely remains.

From Carving to Washing Up

For the man of the house (and for you, too, if you don't like to watch your well-cooked creations being massacred!), an electric carving knife produces elegant slices, not only off joints and poultry, but from bread as well, when wielded by even the most naturally ham-fisted of males. And for yourself, so that the after-

math doesn't seem so daunting, persuade him to buy you a washing-up machine. Some people don't think they're worth the trouble of loading up, and this may be true where minute quantities of washing-up are concerned, but after entertaining, a minute quantity's one thing you can be sure you won't have.

Coffee-time

However you like this most personal of drinks, organize some easy-to-cope-with equipment for serving larger-than-usual numbers. Waiting an eternity for coffee to drip through a filter, and then having to go through the process again to have enough, can make an irritating end to a well-run meal. Automatic electric percolators, or ordinary top-of-the-stove versions, solve the problem for many, and some electric versions are handsome enough to sit 'perking' on the table. For Cona addicts, guests can sit and watch their own fragrant brew being made, in just nine-and-a-half-minutes flat from the time the water boils. Plug-in electric models are the latest, but for extra mobility, and with barbecues in mind, you can't beat the non-electric Cona with a small spirit lamp.

The Bountiful Freezer

But the best piece of hostess equipment any women can have is a home freezer. Freezers are usually associated with farmers' wives, beset with gluts of plums on the trees or gooseberries on the bushes, and quite capable of hacking up meat carcases into chops and joints. This is enough to put off the average cook, especially since most freezer recipe-books seem to harp on stews and meatballs – not very scintillating dishes to look forward to.

No-one seems to point out that you can pour all your effort into a fabulous fresh salmon pâté, chicken Marengo, quiche, or a fricassee of veal, and enjoy the results at leisure much later on. It's always disenchanting to see the labours of an entire morning demolished in a few minutes flat, leaving you with a stack of dirty dishes to wash. And if you're going to toil around the shops gathering the myriad ingredients needed for a terrine, to say nothing of a cassoulet, it makes sense to make them on a large scale, with the future in mind. If you've spent ages making an Espagnole sauce (simmer for 40 minutes is just a *part* of it!), you may as well reap the benefit of your efforts ten-fold! If you're making a Bolognaise sauce, why not produce enough for mountains of spaghetti to come?

Most casseroles and meat dishes will keep at their best for two months (but reckon on only about one month for liver pâtés) soups, stocks and sauces for four, cakes and pies for six months. But generally speaking, uncooked foods last longer, so if you're given a duck and can't be bothered to cook it, you can freeze it and keep it in mind for your next dinner party.

Some foods don't take kindly to freezing, like mayonnaise which curdles, boiled potatoes which go mealy, and anything with a cream or milk base, from custard pies to sauces. And some foods are more difficult to freeze than others. Eggs will crack if frozen whole, for instance, and need to be beaten up with a little salt or sugar for success.

There are rules, of course, and the most vital is cleanliness throughout, because though bacteria quieten down in arctic-freezer conditions, they whizz into activity as soon as thawing out begins. Paradoxically, thawing is often best done in the middle of the fridge: it may take longer, but the end product has a better flavour. All food packages *must* be labelled with a description and date, or chaos will come, and you'll find you're about to serve up an apple pie for a main course instead of the steak and kidney pie you expected. Worse still, you'll probably throw perfectly good food away lest it has passed its safety margin.

If you're making a jumbo-sized terrine, cut it into meal-size pieces before freezing. Otherwise, you'll have to spend a day or more thawing out the whole – and another day or so eating it all up, because foods like terrine shouldn't really be thawed and then refrozen. If you're in danger of running out of containers, line them with foil first. Then, when the contents are deep-frozen and solid, you can take out the foil 'package', and put the original container back where it came from. Above all, experiment with thawing out times. Be warned by the sad true tale of the woman who made a vast fricassee of veal for her son's twenty-first birthday, froze it in an equally vast fish kettle, took it out to thaw on the morning of the Great Day, and was still desperately chipping at the edges when the last hungry guests departed.

Mastering the arts of home freezing fully is the only way to get the best from a very expensive item of equipment. Part IV gives a chart of more detailed information, and for people who want to go into the matter even more fully, *Choosing and Using a Home Freezer*, by the Good Housekeeping Institute, cost 10p plus a large stamped-addressed envelope.

Convenience Foods

The phrase has a grim ring about it, but only hypocrites would pretend they used such things only as last-minute stop-gaps. Just once in a while, it makes a change to do some lazy entertaining – and see who, if anyone, spots the difference. People will if you're undiscriminating in your choice, but given a little craft and guile, you'll have the conscience-pricking pleasure of receiving compliments on your cooking. Open a can of lobster bisque, for instance, swirling some extra cream into each individual bowl just before serving, and you'll have a very convincing starter. Canned consommé, vichyssoise, or any of the more expensive soups will escape detection, especially if given a last-minute garnish.

Make use of frozen vegetables, particularly in winter, but give them at least as much consideration as you would do fresh. They *are* tasteless when they're plonked straight from the saucepan into the serving dish, but salt, pepper and a small knob of butter will work minor wonders. And do follow the cooking instructions, because these can be critical in keeping or killing flavours. Canned vegetables have been given a very bad name by starchy processed peas, but many, like baby carrots and French beans, can be very good if seasoned and served well.

Everyone's familiar with canned fruit, either from Sunday high teas or children's birthday parties. Some, like peaches, bear little resemblance to the original, but are quite likeable in their own right. Others, particularly raspberries, loganberries, and mandarin oranges, are surprisingly authentic, and less cloyingly sweet than most others. Frozen fruits are more authentic in flavour, but less convincing in looks – strawberries in particular look depressingly slimy. The best way to use them is in a fruit mousse, fool or sorbet, so that the genuine taste is there, but the looks get obliterated.

Frozen foods come into their own a lot more with main courses. Fish is a particularly good buy, because it's cheap and clean, and the little it lacks in flavour can be made up for with the sauce you'd probably be putting on it anyway. Frozen steak-and-kidney pie and chicken-and-ham pies are fabulous, though expensive, and as good as most people can make. But frozen pastry is the biggest success story of them all, particularly the flaky type. It seems horrifying at first, when pastry's so cheap and easy to make, but any qualms vanish once you realize it's *better* than anything you and your rolling pin could produce. Equally humiliating are many of the Marks & Spencer food products. Their frozen steak and kidney puds are so 'home-made' they turn making your own into a rather pointless gesture.

Canned foods can provide a very good basis for main dishes, too. Imagine a Burgundy-style casserole based on a canned pheasant, or a Deep South dish of glazed ham with peaches, both from cans. Turn to the recipes in Part III if you want to do more than imagine them. They're fairly expensive, it's true, but convenience foods are meant to be convenient, and there's no especial reason why they should also be cheap. The secret of using them successfully lies in not slapping them down on the table just as the manufacturers made them, but using them as a basis for your personal interpretation.

Help, Voluntary or Paid

Helpers, whether family or hired, are not necessarily the godsend they sound. The result depends largely on you – because you're responsible for directing such talents as they may have. Be wary of the idea if you're someone who usually likes to be left alone in your kitchen.

People who can't delegate at the actual moment of crisis can still benefit from before or after help. Someone to come and clean up the house in the morning, for instance, will leave you free to worry about cooking alone. Or someone to come and demolish the mountains of washing-up after may be more welcome than anything else. Depending on the willingness and talents of your children, you can easily set them to making garnishes in advance or preparing vegetables – though this is likely to be less popular.

Professional helpers should be able to work on their own initiative, though the only sure way of finding one that can is personal recommendation. Ideally, they'll be able to take control completely, and leave you free to relax with your guests. But unless you're confident of their abilities, you'll worry far more than if you were coping yourself.

Without doubt, the best of all helpers is the kindly next-door neighbour, who knows you and your cooking well enough to be able to work side by side with you. Under these circumstances, you can tackle more ambitious menus that need constant attention, secure in the knowledge that someone will be looking after the sauces and adjusting the temperatures so that all is well. (But of course, you'll have to do the same for her some time!)

Dip and Spread Party: p. 81

PART TWO

1
Gala Buffet Parties

INFORMAL BUFFET PARTY IN THE GARDEN FOR 30

The Menu

Pâté Niblets

Swedish Chicken salad
Salmon Patties
Potato Salad Loaf
Paddy's Salad
French Dressing

Oven-crisped Vienna Loaves   Butter

Gooseberry Soufflé
Strawberry Kebabs
Cream-filled Sponge Drops

Coffee (black and white)

The Wines

Serve an apéritif if you wish; otherwise we suggest a choice of white wines that will please and refresh from start to finish of the party. For instance, sparkling hock or Moselle; Alsatian Sylvaner or Traminer; of French wines, a dry Vouvray (Loire) or a Meursault (Burgundy).

Have also soft drinks or a fruit cup.

Plans

Even though it's informal, the planning for a large party like this should start some weeks ahead, and the written invitations need to be sent out at least a fortnight in advance. When in doubt, make a list – of the guests, the menu, the cutlery, crockery, accessories, food and wine to be ordered, and the day you want each item to arrive. You'll probably need more plates, glasses, knives and forks, ashtrays and cruets than you possess, but it may well be possible to borrow the extras from indulgent friends – as long as you've invited them, of course.

When you get around to planning the layout of a garden party buffet, make the most of having more space than usual. Resist the temptation to range everything on one big table: this only result in lines of faintly irritated guests – particularly those heading for the sweets section who are having to queue right through the Salmon Patties for the second time around. Far better to set up three or four different-sized smaller tables, keeping them all close to the house; one of the larger ones can hold the apéritif bits and pieces, another the main-course foods, with plates, baskets of cutlery and piles of large paper napkins, while a smaller table can hold the salads, dressings, butter and breads. The dessert table, on which you'll also want to serve coffee later on, is best placed nearest of all to the house. (You will of course have plans for alternative arrangements in the house if the weather should let you down.)

Unless you're going to be very grand and hire some help, you'll need to recruit two or three willing and able helpers other than your husband. Make sure they all know in advance exactly what their particular tasks are, so that you don't have to keep briefing them once the party's in full swing; two men, at least, will be vitally needed as wine waiters – people are often oddly shy about helping themselves to drinks. Wait until most of the guests have arrived and are sipping their first glass of sherry before you serve the main course, and leave the sweets in a cool place until just before they're to be eaten.

Pie and Patty Party: p. 77

Shopping and Preparation

Amounts: Apart from basic store-cupboard items and the ingredients for the individual recipes which follow, you will need 6 Vienna loaves, 2 lb. butter for spreading, icing sugar for strawberries, condiments.

The Day Before: Roast the chickens for the salad, cook the rice, 3 Potato Salad Loaves and the Sponge Drops from the recipes given. Buy, wash and dry the salad ingredients and store them in separate plastic bags in the refrigerator or a cool larder.

Have all tableware and glasses polished, stacked and covered with a cloth, ready to lay out – whether indoors or outside.

Complete any major house-cleaning and furniture re-arrangement you want to make.

Early on the Party Day: Make the 4 soufflés, but do not decorate them. Make the Salmon Patties and French Dressing, as in the recipes which follow. Carve the chickens, cover them and leave aside for finishing the dish later.

Later in the Afternoon: Lay the table or tables, complete the floral and other décor arrangements, crisp the loaves and make up the other recipes which follow:

Pâté Niblets

1 lb. pâté (bought or home-made)	4 oz. butter
1 large sandwich loaf	Parsley, snipped small

Oven temperature: hot (425 °F, mark 7).

Cream the pâté in a bowl until smooth and of piping consistency. Cut 15 thin slices from the loaf and remove the crusts; cut each slice into 4 squares. Melt the butter and use about a third of it to brush the baking sheets which will take the bread slices. Arrange the bread on the baking sheets. Brush the slices with the remaining butter and bake the slices just above the centre of the oven for about 15 minutes, until golden-brown and crisp on each side. Allow to cool, then pipe some pâté on to each piece with a forcing bag and large star vegetable nozzle. Top each piece with snips of parsley.

Salmon Patties

1 lb. plain flour	2 egg yolks
Salt and pepper	2 oz. butter for sauce
Cayenne	2 oz. flour for sauce
8 oz. butter	1 pint milk
8 oz. Cheddar cheese grated	3 7-oz. cans of salmon
	1 egg, beaten

Oven temperature: hot (425 °F, mark 7).

Make cheese pastry with the first six ingredients, plus water to mix. Make up a white sauce with 2 oz. butter and 2 oz. flour, milk and seasoning. Drain the salmon, remove the skin and bones, flake it and add it to the sauce, stirring with a fork. Roll out the pastry $\frac{1}{8}$ inch thick and stamp it with fluted cutters into 30 3-inch rounds, 30 2$\frac{1}{2}$-inch rounds and 30 1$\frac{1}{2}$-inch rounds. Line 2$\frac{1}{2}$-inch brioche tins with the largest rounds. Almost fill the lined tins with salmon mixture. Brush the edges of the pastry liners with beaten egg and place the 2$\frac{1}{2}$-inch lids in position; brush these with egg, too. Put the 1$\frac{1}{2}$-inch rounds on top for decoration and brush these with egg. Make a hole in the centre of each patty with a fine skewer and bake in the centre of the oven for about 30 minutes. Cool 5–10 minutes before easing out of the tins.

Swedish Chicken Salad

1$\frac{1}{2}$ lb. long-grain rice	1$\frac{1}{4}$ pints double cream
4 3$\frac{1}{2}$-lb. oven-ready chickens, roasted	1$\frac{1}{4}$ pints home-made or lemon mayonnaise
4 green eating apples	1 level tbsp. curry powder
4 red eating apples	Salt and pepper
6 bananas	
Lemon juice	

Cook, drain and cool the rice. When the chickens are cold, carve them into slices and cut into strips. Core the apples and slice them thinly. Peel and thickly slice the bananas. Dredge both apples and bananas with lemon juice at once. Whip the cream to mayonnaise consistency and lightly fold it into the mayonnaise; add the curry powder. Fold in the chicken, apple and banana, add more lemon juice and season to taste. Pile the mixture on a bed of rice, or mix the rice with the chicken.

Potato Salad Loaf

1½ lb. potatoes, peeled and diced	1 small onion, skinned and grated or finely chopped
6 oz. ham roll, sliced	
2 level tsps. powdered gelatine	1 level tsp. chopped chives or parsley
1 tbsp. water	Salt and pepper
3 tbsps. salad cream	1 hard-boiled egg to garnish
3 gherkins or olives, chopped	

Line a loaf tin measuring 8½ by 4½ inches with greaseproof paper, letting the paper extend about 2 inches above the rim.

Cook the potatoes in boiling salted water for about 10 minutes, until they are tender but not mushy; drain them and rinse in cold water. Line the tin with slices of ham roll and dice the remainder of the meat. Put the gelatine and water in a small bowl and stand it over a pan of hot water, stirring until the gelatine is dissolved. Mix the gelatine with the salad cream and pour over the potatoes. Add the gherkins or olives, the onion and the chives or parsley and season to taste; mix well. Place half the mixture in the ham-lined tin. Cover with a few slices of the diced ham roll, and then pile in the remaining potato mixture. Smooth the top of the loaf carefully, fold the paper over it and chill it in the refrigerator. Just before serving, unfold the paper, invert the tin on to a serving dish and remove the paper. Garnish the dish with slices of hard-boiled egg. (Serves 8–10.)

Paddy's Salad

4 large or 8 small lettuces	2 bunches of radishes, topped and tailed
1 large or 2 small cucumbers, sliced	4 bunches of watercress, trimmed
1 green sweet pepper and 1 red sweet pepper, seeded and thinly sliced	1–2 bunches of spring onions, chopped
	Sprigs of parsley, snipped

Use large platters or round trays for the salad. On each make a bed of torn lettuce leaves. On top of these, lay circles of overlapping cucumber slices, pepper and radishes. The outermost circle should be a collar of watercress. Scatter snippings of spring onions and parsley over the platters. These quantities should make enough salad for 30 people.

Note. You can dress some of the salads, and leave others plain.

French Dressing

2 cloves of garlic, skinned, or a little skinned and chopped onion or chives	1 level tsp. salt
	3 level tsps. continental mustard
	1 level tbsp. celery seeds
Freshly ground black pepper	5 tbsps. tarragon or thyme vinegar
5 level tsps. caster sugar	10 tbsps. cor noil

Crush the garlic, if used; place the garlic, onion or chives with the pepper, sugar, salt, mustard and celery seeds in a screw-topped jar. Add the vinegar and then the oil, put the lid on the jar firmly and shake the jar thoroughly until the mixture is well blended. (Makes ½ pint approx.)

Gooseberry Soufflé

1 lb. gooseberries, topped and tailed	Green colouring
	¼ pint single cream
4 large eggs, separated	¼ pint double cream
	Poached gooseberries to decorate
4 oz. caster sugar	
1 tbsp. orange liqueur	Sugar for gooseberries
½ oz. powdered gelatine	A little whipped cream, chilled, to decorate

Prepare a 7-inch (or 2-pint) straight-sided soufflé dish with a paper or foil collar.

Cook the gooseberries with 2 tbsps. water until they are soft, then sieve them to make ½ pint purée. Whisk the egg yolks and sugar over hot water until they are thick and pale. Add the gooseberry purée and continue to whisk until the mixture begins to thicken; remove from the heat. Place 2 tbsps. water and the orange liqueur in a small basin, sprinkle the gelatine over and place the basin over hot water. Stir until the gelatine has dissolved, then stir it into the gooseberry custard and add enough green colouring to make the mixture look a little darker than you want it. Leave aside to cool, whisking it occasionally.

Meanwhile, whisk the 2 creams together until they are of the same consistency as the gooseberry mixture. Lightly fold the whipped cream into the gooseberry mixture. Whisk the egg whites until stiff but not dry and fold them lightly into the purée. Turn the whole mixture carefully into the prepared soufflé dish, place a clean 1-lb. jam jar in centre and leave to set.

To serve, pour a little hot water into the jam jar and ease it out carefully. Fill the cavity with the well-drained and sweetened poached gooseberries. Ease the paper band off with a warm knife. Decorate the dessert with rosettes of whipped cream. (Serves 8.)

Strawberry Kebabs

4 lb. well-shaped strawberries	Cocktail sticks
	Icing sugar

Spear the hulled strawberries on cocktail sticks and arrange in a decorative pattern on plates, surrounded by cream-filled sponge drops. Have sugar dredgers filled with icing sugar.

Cream-filled Sponge Drops

3 oz. caster sugar	¼ pint single cream
3 large eggs	¼ pint double cream
Vanilla essence	Caster sugar to sweeten,
3 oz. plain flour	if wished

Oven temperature: hot (425 °F, mark 7).

Grease a baking sheet or line it with non-stick vegetable parchment.

Whisk the sugar and eggs together until really thick and creamy; add a few drops of vanilla essence. Sift in the flour, folding in a little at a time. Spoon the mixture into a forcing bag fitted with a ½-inch plain nozzle. Pipe small drops well apart on the prepared baking sheet. Bake towards the top of the oven for 7–10 minutes, until evenly but lightly browned. Use a palette knife to lift on to a wire rack to cool; store in an airtight tin. Just before serving, whip together the lightly sweetened single and double cream until the mixture just holds its shape; sandwich the drops in pairs, like opened oysters. (Makes 20 pairs.)

THE GRAND BUFFET FOR A WEDDING PARTY OF 30

The Menu

Melon Slices with Lemon

Rare Roast Sirloin   Tomato Guardsmen
Chicken, Orange and Banana Salad
Crumbed Lamb Cutlets
Pork Galantine
Cucumber Chartreuse   Jellied Beetroot Ring
Party Green Salad
Jacket Potatoes   Garlic Bread

Lemon-Berry Mousse   Ginger Cups
Hazelnut Meringue Gâteau

Coffee

The Wines

These can be special, but they needn't necessarily all be expensive – keep the champers for the toasts and cake-cutting, and brief the ushers to make sure that everyone's glass is filled to the bubbly brim when those moments arrive. If you'd like to serve bubbly wine throughout, there's quite a selection of good ones, from various countries, which cost much less than champagne; Sparkling Schloss Rheingarten is a delicious example. You might like to give your guests a sparkling wine instead of sherry as an apéritif, and then follow up with red and white wines to go with the meal. These can well be *ordinaires*, like those by Peter Dominic or Nicolas, but if you want something more select, the reds could include a light claret like Château Dassault 1962 or Château-Pitres 1964; for the white, an Alsatian Traminer or a good white Burgundy. With the sweets, you'll want some sweeter wines: a Château d'Yquem is splendid but expensive, and there are lots of very good Sauternes and Graves. Or you could, of course, serve champagne throughout the reception and keep the corks popping merrily all the way.

First Plans

This is the biggest of all the 'do's', and nobody needs to be told how much planning it needs. If you follow through our suggested routine, and if you're a fairly experienced cook, you could manage it single-handed, but it makes the whole operation so much less of a mammoth task if you can recruit a couple of friends or relatives to help – particularly as you'll have to be away at the wedding itself during the last crucial stages of preparation.

For this occasion with a capital 'O', it's best to hire all the glass, cutlery and china, so that everything matches and can all be delivered together. Check it over when it arrives, to make sure nothing's missing, then forget about it all until the day before the wedding, when you can unpack, wash and polish. The same firm that supplies the china could probably also include those invaluable floor-length white table cloths, and your local stationer should have the masses of silver-printed paper napkins that you'll need. Set out all the cutlery, china and glasses on the eve of the wedding (it takes longer than you think), and cover overnight with more white cloths or tissue paper. Order all the other outside items well in advance – more than a month for the cake, and at least a fortnight for the wines. And stock up with more-than-usual quantities of all basic store-cupboard items, quite apart from the ingredients for the recipes. The actual timing that you use for our step-by-step cooking plan will of course depend on the time of the wedding, so adjust it to fit your own schedule. And if the worst comes to the worst and you *are* doing the whole thing single-handed, surely a house-bound neighbour would let you use her oven for the potato-baking – and keep an eye on them while you're at the ceremony. This copes with the last big cooking problem, for you can dress the salad and crisp the garlic bread the moment you get back – the guests will be busy enough with apéritifs and the melon wedges for the first 15–20 minutes.

Detailed Arrangements

Two or three Days Before: Make the meringue layers for the Hazelnut Meringue Gâteau;

make mayonnaise from the egg yolks. Make the Ginger Cups and store in an airtight tin. Make chocolate curls for the Lemon-Berry Mousse. *The Day Before:* Roast the sirloin and the chickens and store in a cold place. Cook the rice for the chicken dish. Coat the Lamb Cutlets and store in the refrigerator. Make and finish the Pork Galantine. Make the Beetroot Ring and Cucumber Chartreuse and leave to set. Make the Lemon-Berry Mousse up to and including the raspberry layer. Toast the hazelnuts. Prepare all the salad items, putting them into plastic bags in the fridge.

The Day of the Wedding, early on: Hard-boil the eggs for the 'Guardsmen'. Butter and wrap the Garlic Bread ready for the oven. Cook the Lamb Cutlets. Scrub the potatoes. Make the filling for and assemble the Meringue Gâteau, but do not pipe the cream. Cut some lemon wedges and keep in a plastic bag.

3 hours before the Reception: Whip the cream for the Lemon-Berry Mousse, decorate and keep in a cool place. Pipe the cream on the Gâteau and keep in a cool place. Turn out and garnish the Jellied Rings. Slice the Beef and assemble the platter. Slice the Galantine. Cut melon slices and keep in a plastic bag. Arrange the green salad.

At the Last Convenient Time: Rub the Jacket Potatoes with fat and salt and bake in a hot oven (425 °F, mark 7); they'll take about an hour, but won't spoil by keeping if you lower the heat. Fill the Ginger Cups. Arrange the savoury dishes and melon and cover with a cloth or plastic film. Dress the Party Green Salad. Crisp the Garlic Bread.

Coffee: To make enough for 30 demi-tasses you'll need 14 oz. fresh coffee and 8 pints of water. The coffee can be made in advance in a large saucepan, strained and re-heated.

Note: Most of the following dishes are shown in the colour picture facing p. 72.

Rare Roast Sirloin with Tomato Guardsmen

5 lb. contre-filet (eye of the sirloin)	Small hard-boiled eggs
	Black olives
Tomatoes	

Oven temperature: hot (425 °F, mark 7).

Ask your butcher to tie the joint into a neat shape. Place in a roasting tin and cook for 15 minutes per lb. plus 15 minutes over or, if a medium roast is preferred, allow 20 minutes per lb. plus 20 minutes over. Leave in the refrigerator or other cool place until about an hour before it is required. Slice thinly, fold each slice and arrange on a narrow dish on each side of the 'Guardsmen'. To mount the 'Guardsmen': use cocktail sticks and impale on each a tomato (stem-side down), then a hard-boiled egg, and top with an olive.

Chicken, Orange and Banana Salad

2 3½-lb. oven-ready chickens, roasted	¾ pint home-made orange mayonnaise
1 lb. long-grain rice	French dressing
6 large bananas	Chopped parsley
6 oranges	Toasted flaked almonds

When the chickens are cold, carve them into slices and then into strips; keep in a cool place. Cook the rice in salted water in the usual way, drain and cool. Peel and slice the bananas. Peel the oranges and divide into segments free of pith. Add any orange juice to the mayonnaise, with the grated rind of 2 oranges. Marinade the banana in French dressing, and add enough dressing to the rice to moisten well. Finish the salad; fold the dark chicken meat, half the banana and half the orange into the rice; add enough well-seasoned mayonnaise to taste, and pile on to a lettuce-lined serving platter. Arrange the chicken breast on the rice, and the remaining fruit round the edge. Coat the chicken breast with more mayonnaise and garnish with chopped parsley and toasted flaked almonds. (Serves 10.)

Crumbed Lamb Cutlets

20 lamb cutlets, trimmed	4 oz. onion, skinned
1 lb. fresh white breadcrumbs	A few sprigs of parsley
	Thinly pared rind of 2 lemons
½ lb. streaky bacon, rinded and cooked until crisp	Salt and pepper
	4 eggs
	8 oz. white cooking fat

Oven temperature: fairly hot (400 °F, mark 6).

Prepare the cutlets. While making the breadcrumbs in an electric blender, feed in the bacon, onion, parsley, lemon rind and seasoning; turn the mixture on to a plate. Break the eggs into a shallow bowl and beat lightly. Dip each cutlet in egg, then into the crumbs, pressing the crumbs well in. Chill. Melt the fat in 2 roasting tins and add the cutlets, turning them in the fat so that both sides are covered. Bake for about 45 minutes, until the meat is tender, drain and cool on kitchen paper. Add the frills before serving. (Serves 10.)

Pork Galantine

1 lb. pork	Summer savory
1 lb. lean ham	Salt and pepper
2 oz. onion, skinned	Thinly cut rashers of back bacon, rinded
¼ pint thick white sauce	Vinegar
1 large egg	Aspic jelly and sliced radish for garnish
Dried rosemary	

Put the pork, ham and onion through the mincer twice. Blend with the white sauce, egg, herbs and seasonings to taste. Shape into a roll. Flour a boiling cloth and lay the rinded rashers of bacon overlapping each other over the cloth, the length of the roll. Place the pork roll over the rashers, reshape it in the cloth, then secure the join and ends tightly. Boil gently in water to cover, to which a little vinegar and salt have been added, for 2½ hours; turn the roll occasionally. Drain, leaving the roll under a weight to cool. Remove the cloth. Glaze the roll with aspic and garnish with radish, or serve sliced. (Serves 10.)

Cucumber Chartreuse

2 lime jelly tablets	Green colouring
1–1½ pints hot water	1 lb. cucumber, peeled and diced
½ pint cider vinegar	Small tomatoes
1 level tbsp. sugar	

Break up 2 lime jelly tablets and put in a 2-pint measure. Make up to 1½ pints with hot water and stir until the jelly has dissolved. Add the cider vinegar, the sugar and a few drops of green colouring and leave to cool until of the consistency of unbeaten egg white. Fold in the cucumber; when it is evenly suspended, pour the mixture into a 3-pint ring jelly mould. Unmould, and fill centre with tomatoes. (Serves 15.)

Jellied Beetroot Ring

Prepare as for the Chartreuse, but use 2 raspberry jelly tablets, ½ pint red wine vinegar and 1 lb. cooked and diced beetroot. When it is unmoulded for serving, put a long-stemmed glass in the centre to hold horseradish dip. Try using Lawry's packet horseradish dip-mix, folded through soured cream. (Serves 15.)

Party Green Salad

Wash 5 lettuces, 3 bunches of watercress, 6 heads of chicory and 3 cartons of mustard-and-cress. Trim if necessary, and keep in plastic bags in a cool place. Halve 3 green peppers, discard the seeds, slice very thinly, and keep in a plastic bag. To assemble, roughly break up the lettuce to use as a bed. Thinly slice the chicory and arrange, with the other ingredients, in groups or rings. Then snip some parsley and chives over all. Just before serving, moisten with French dressing. (Serves 30.)

The French dressing can be made in advance. Measure 1¼ level tsps. each of salt and dry mustard, freshly ground pepper, 1 level tsp. sugar, ¼ pint vinegar and ½–¾ pint oil into a lidded container. Shake vigorously.

Garlic Bread

Oven temperature: warm (325 °F, mark 3).

For each French loaf allow ½ lb. butter and 2 cloves of garlic, skinned and crushed. Cream the butter with the garlic. Cut the loaves into thick slices, leaving a 'hinge'. Spread garlic butter between the slices and wrap the loaf loosely in kitchen foil. Place in the oven and heat for 15 minutes. Raise the temperature to hot (450 °F, mark 8), folding back the foil, for a further 10 minutes to crisp the bread.

Lemon-berry Mousse

6 large eggs, separated
10 oz. caster sugar
12 tbsps. lemon juice
Grated rind of 3 lemons
5 level tsps. powdered gelatine
6 tbsps. water

For the Topping
2 lb. frozen raspberries, thawed
4 level tsps. powdered gelatine
2 tbsps. water
Sugar
¾ pint double cream and ¼ pint single cream (or 1 pint whipping cream)
An 8-oz. pkt. of plain covering chocolate

Put the egg yolks and sugar into a large bowl and use a rotary whisk or hand-held electric mixer to cream them until thick and creamy. Gradually whisk in the lemon juice, 1 tbsp. at a time. Fold in the lemon rind and the gelatine, dissolved in the water in the usual way. When the mixture is just showing signs of setting, quickly and evenly fold in the stiffly beaten egg whites. Spoon into one really large serving bowl or 2 small bowls and chill.

Sieve the raspberries for the topping or purée them in an electric blender, if available. Stir in the gelatine, dissolved in the water in the usual way, and adjust the sweetness to taste. Pour over the lemon mixture. When set, cover with a layer of whipped cream and top with chocolate curls. (Serves 12.)

Chocolate Curls: Holding a small, sharp knife at an angle of about 45°, slowly work (away from yourself) along the flat side of the block of chocolate until a curl forms; put the curls on to non-stick paper. Repeat until this is no longer practical, then coarsely grate the remainder. (Serves 12.)

Ginger Cups

2 oz. butter
2 oz. caster sugar
2 level tbsps. golden syrup
2 oz. plain flour
½ level tsp. ground ginger
1 tsp. brandy
Grated rind of ½ a lemon

For the Filling
½ pint double or whipping cream
2 oz. stem ginger

Melt the butter with the sugar and golden syrup. Remove from the heat and beat in the flour, ginger, brandy and lemon rind. Cool for about 2 minutes. Place 3 or 5 tsps. of the mixture, well apart, on a baking sheet lined with non-stick parchment paper. Bake in rotation towards the top of the oven for 7–10 minutes, until deep golden-brown. Meanwhile butter the base of some jam jars. Remove from the oven. As the mixture begins to firm, lift with a palette knife and drape each one over the base of the buttered jam jar. When set, remove and store in an airtight tin. Fill just before serving: whip the cream; chop most of the ginger and fold in. Divide between the ginger cases and decorate each with a slice of ginger. (Makes 12.)

Hazelnut Meringue Gâteau

8 egg whites	1 lb. caster sugar

For the Filling

4 oz caster sugar	4 oz. hazelnuts, toasted
3 egg yolks	1 tbsp. sherry
¼ pint milk, warmed	½ pint double cream
½ lb. butter	

Oven temperature : lowest possible setting.

Draw 2 10-inch circles on baking sheets lined with non-stick parchment paper. Stiffly whisk the egg whites, add half the sugar and whisk again until really stiff. Fold in the remaining sugar. Use half the mixture to fill each circle, drawing the meringue out to the edge in each case. Dry in the oven, set for about 3 hours, until crisp and firm. Cool, remove the paper, and parcel the discs in kitchen foil for a day or two, until required.

On the party day, cream the sugar and egg yolks until pale and creamy; add the warm milk. Return the mixture to the saucepan or double boiler and cook over a low heat until the mixture thickens and well coats the back of a spoon – don't boil. Cream the butter until fluffy and gradually beat in the cool but not cold egg mixture. Continue to beat to a light consistency. Grind or mince all but 12 hazelnuts. Stir into the butter filling, with the sherry, and use to sandwich the meringue discs together. An hour before serving, whip the cream until it holds its shape, but do not over-whisk. Use a large star vegetable nozzle to pipe 12 whirls of cream on the gâteau and top each with a hazelnut. Keep in a cool place until just before serving. (Serves 12.)

GALA BUFFET FOR 30

The Menu

Prawns Mornay
Onion Quiche   Cheese Pastries

Roast Turkey with Nut and Apricot Stuffing
Ham Cornets
Salmon and Asparagus Mousse
Cole Slaw with Dressed Tomatoes
Waldorf Salad
French Bread and Butter

Chocolate Cream Gâteau
Tropical Fruit Salad   Strawberry Cloud

The Drinks

At the beginning of the party, you'll probably want to give your guests dry or medium sherry or a ready-mixed cocktail, but if you're serving wine right through the meal, this could easily double as the apéritif, too. Choose your wines from among the inexpensive ranges of *ordinaires* on the market: Nicolas have one in litre bottles. But there's enough of a choice to suit most tastes. For this buffet, try the medium-sweet white Chassepré, the young red Canteval, the stronger, more full-bodied red Vieux Ceps and the dry but fresh Sciatino rosé, which should be served slightly chilled.

Basic Plans

Designed as a winter evening party, this gala buffet could transfer without structural changes to any other time of the year – though it would be a pity to waste so much ingenious plotting of winter-restricted ingredients in the summer. Even with a helper, the menu is frankly ambitious, so working wives had better plan it for a Saturday night, starting at about 8 o'clock, so they've time to convince themselves that all is well. Depending on how gala the event, either borrow extra cutlery, china, etc., from neighbours, or free yourself of the worry altogether by hiring extra tableware. This will save time (but not money) and give you the satisfaction of seeing everything match in an impressive way.

To prevent queues and traffic jams, lay one main table with the cold savoury foods, plus plates, knives, forks and napkins in separate piles. Distribute the cheese pastries and other 'smalls' in bowls around the room. Keep the desserts out of the way on a separate tray or trolley till they're needed, and on another trolley, table or sideboard assemble all the drinking paraphernalia. Have someone with a good pouring arm constantly in attendance behind this 'bar', to save guests the embarrassment of wondering whether or not to help themselves.

Schedule

A Week in Advance: Order the turkey from the butcher and ask him to bone and deliver it the day before the party – not forgetting bones and giblets for the stock. Place orders with the green-grocer, baker and milkman for delivery on the day before or the morning of the party, and buy in the store-cupboard things in the normal course of shopping.

2 Days Before: Make the flan cases for the Onion Quiche, bake them 'blind' and store them when cool in an airtight tin. Bake the cakes for the Chocolate Cream Gâteau and store for filling and icing on the day of the party; make the chocolate squares for the Gâteau. Make plenty of mayonnaise, too.

1 Day Before: Stuff and cook the turkey. Make the Salmon-and-Asparagus Mousse, but do not turn out. Prepare the ingredients for Cole Slaw, but keep separate. Store them all, covered, in a cold place, preferably the refrigerator.

The Day of the Party: Mix and dress the Cole Slaw and make the Waldorf Salad. Make the Strawberry Cloud and the Fruit Salad. During the afternoon get your husband to slice the turkey (an electric knife is a joy). Make and stuff the Ham Cornets. Arrange on the platters and slip them into large plastic bags. Slice and fry the onions ready for the Quiche. Other hints for spreading the tasks are given with the individual recipes, where necessary.

Amounts: If you are starting with a hot dish – that is, the Prawns Mornay or the Onion Quiche – reckon that everyone will want a portion. Of the cheese savouries we've suggested, you may like to make only one kind – enough, perhaps, for two per person. Again, a choice of three sweets is appealing if you can manage it, but it's hard to forecast which will be a favourites. So calculate on two of each dessert, or your own permutation.

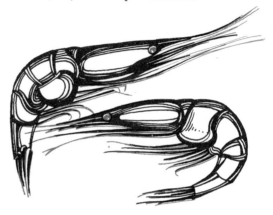

Prawns Mornay

2 oz. butter	8 oz. frozen prawns
2 oz. flour	defrosted
Salt	4 oz. Cheddar cheese,
Freshly ground	grated
pepper	Parsley and lemon
1 pint milk	

Oven temperature: moderate (350 °F, mark 4).

Make a roux with the butter and flour and add salt and pepper. Add the milk, stirring continuously, bring to the boil and simmer gently. Stir in the prawns and 2 oz. of the cheese and simmer for a further 5 minutes. Divide the mixture between 6 natural scallop shells and sprinkle with the remaining cheese. Put the shells on a baking tray, supporting each other, and heat in the oven for 20–30 minutes, until bubbly. Garnish with chopped parsley and serve a lemon wedge on each shell. (Serves 6.)
Note. The sauce can be made early in the day. Re-heat it before adding the prawns.

Onion Quiche

12 oz. shortcrust pastry (12 oz. plain flour, etc.)	4 eggs
	2 oz. flour
	¾ pint milk
4 oz. butter	Salt and pepper
2 lb. onions, skinned and sliced	2 cans of anchovies
	Stoned black olives

Oven temperature : fairly hot (400 °F, mark 6).

Make up the pastry in the usual way and use to line 2 plain 8-inch flan rings placed on baking sheets. Bake 'blind' for about 20 minutes. Melt the butter in a frying-pan and fry the onions till soft, taking care not to brown them. Divide the onions between the flans. Beat together the eggs, flour, milk, salt and pepper, then pour over the onions. Arrange the anchovies on top in a criss-cross pattern and place a black olive in each space. Bake in a moderate oven (350 °F, mark 4) for 20–30 minutes, until set. (Serves 12.)

Cheese Dartois

6 oz. Cheddar cheese, grated	1 lb. chilled or frozen puff pastry (made-up weight)
1 egg	
Pepper	Beaten egg for glaze
French mustard	

Oven temperature : hot (425 °F, mark 7).

Blend the cheese with the egg and season with pepper and mustard. Roll out the pastry very thinly on a lightly floured surface to a rectangle 16 by 12 inches; trim the edges. Cut down the centre lengthwise, then cut each piece in two, crosswise, to give 4 equal pieces. Place 2 pieces on a baking sheet and spread (but not right to the edge) with the cheese mixture. Cover with the second portions of pastry. Press lightly and seal the edges, then brush with beaten egg. Mark into fingers, but not right through the pastry. Bake towards the top of the oven for about 25 minutes, until puffed up, crisp and golden-brown. Cut into fingers while still warm. (Makes about 20.)

Note. These savouries are nicest served hot. Make in the morning and in the evening warm through for 5–10 minutes in a fairly hot oven (400 °F, mark 6).

Cheese Medallions

6 oz. butter	Salt and paprika
8 oz. Samsoe cheese, grated	4 oz. plain flour
	Cress or paprika to garnish (optional)
1 egg yolk	

Oven temperature : fairly hot (400 °F, mark 6).

Beat 4 oz. butter until creamy; gradually add 4 oz. cheese, the egg yolk, salt and paprika to taste. Work in the flour. When well blended, wrap the dough and put in a cold place for about 1 hour. Knead lightly, if on the firm side, and roll out on a floured surface to ⅛–¼ inch thickness. Stamp into rounds with a 1-inch plain cutter and place on greased baking sheets. Bake for about 10 minutes, until beginning to colour. Cool on a wire rack, handling with care. Pair up with a little filling made by creaming the remaining 2 oz. butter and gradually beating in 4 oz. grated cheese. (Makes about 20 pairs.)

Note. Make the cheese discs and store for a day to two in an airtight tin. Make the filling at the same time, but beat it again before sandwiching the discs on the morning of the party.

Curried Cheese Horns

3 oz. margarine or butter	A little water
	Chutney
6 oz. plain flour	3 pkts. (3 oz. each)
Salt and pepper	of full-fat soft cheese
3 oz. Cheddar cheese, finely grated	Milk
	Curry powder
A little beaten egg	

Oven temperature : fairly hot (400 °F, mark 6).

Rub the fat into the flour. Add a pinch of salt and mix in the Cheddar cheese. Add a little egg and water, stirring until the ingredients bind together, then with one hand collect the dough together and knead very lightly till smooth. Put on a floured surface and roll into a rectangle 12 by 16 inches and about ⅛ inch thick. Trim if necessary. Brush the pastry with eggs and cut into ½-inch strips, widthwise. Wind round cream horn cases, about half-way up the length of the cases. Place on baking sheets and bake for about 10 minutes, until golden-brown. Cool for a few minutes, turn gently and remove the pastry from the tins. Cool on a wire rack. To serve, place a little chutney in the base of each horn, then, using a small star vegetable nozzle, pipe in the filling (see below).

Filling: Beat the soft cheese with sufficient milk to give light piping consistency; season with curry powder, salt and pepper to taste. (Makes about 32.)

Note. Make the horn cases one or two days before. 'Refresh' in the oven on the day, cool and fill.

Roast Stuffed Turkey

A 10-lb. boned turkey (14 lb. approx. before boning)	8 oz. dried apricots, sliced
12 oz. fresh bread-crumbs	8 oz. hazelnuts, chopped or ground
2 tbsps. chopped parsley	Salt
2 medium-sized onion, chopped	Freshly ground pepper
	3 eggs, lightly beaten
	Stock to bind
	4 oz. lard or dripping

Oven temperature: Very hot (450 °F, mark 8).

Get your butcher to bone the turkey for you, and ask for the bones for stock. In a large bowl mix together the breadcrumbs, parsley, onions, apricots, hazelnuts, salt and pepper. Pour in the beaten eggs and mix, then add enough stock to bind together. Push the leg meat into the cavity of the turkey, then stuff the cavity. Thread a large bodkin or trussing needle with fine string or thread and sew up all the open ends of the turkey; push into shape. Weigh, and place in a deep roasting tin. Melt the lard in a small pan and pour over the turkey. Sprinkle with salt. Roast for 3–3¼ hours. Remove from the oven, lift on to a clean tray and leave till cold. Unpick the string. (Serves 30.)

Ham Cornets

3 level tsps. powdered gelatine	½ pint mayonnaise
4 tbsps. water	1 lb. cooked ham, thinly cut into 16 slices
2 19-oz. cans of new potatoes, drained	Chopped chives

Dissolve the gelatine in water as directed on the packet. Dice the potatoes. Measure the mayonnaise into a bowl. Add 2 tbsps. of it to the dissolved gelatine, then pour the gelatine into the remaining mayonnaise, mix well and pour over the diced potatoes. Leave until set. Meanwhile roll the ham slices round cream horn tins to shape. Remove the tins, spoon in the potato mixture and sprinkle with chopped chives. Set in a cool place for 5 minutes. Arrange on the turkey platter. (Makes 16.)

Waldorf Salad

1½ lb. each of red eating apples and green eating apples, cored and thinly sliced	8 oz. walnut halves
	2 heads of celery, chopped
	¾ pint French dressing
Lemon juice	Watercress

Mix the red and green apples together in a bowl and sprinkle well with lemon juice. Chop all but 8 of the walnut halves and mix with the apple. Add the celery, mix well, pour on the French dressing and mix again. Turn into a serving dish. Decorate with a few slices of red apple and the remaining walnut halves and arrange watercress round the edge of the dish. (Serves 18.)

Cole Slaw

1 white cabbage, finely shredded (3 lb.)	18 small tomatoes, skinned
2 green peppers, seeded	Mint sprigs
2 bunches of radishes	Salt and freshly ground pepper

For the Cole Slaw Dressing

2–5 fl. oz. cartons of soured cream	Freshly ground pepper
½ pint mayonnaise	4 level tbsps. Burgess cream and horse-radish
Salt	

Place the shredded cabbage in a large bowl. Finely slice the green peppers and radishes and mix with the cabbage. Pour on the dressing and mix very thoroughly. Arrange in a serving dish. Place the tomatoes in the centre in rows of 3, with mint sprigs between the tomatoes in the centre row. Season with salt and freshly ground black pepper. (Serves 18.)

To make the dressing, put all the ingredients in a bowl and mix very thoroughly.

Salmon and Asparagus Mousse

2 level tbsps. aspic jelly crystals	Salt and pepper
1 pint water	1 tbsp. cider vinegar
1 oz. butter	3 eggs, separated
1 oz. flour	2 7½-oz. cans of salmon
½ pint milk	1½ level tbsps. powdered gelatine
¼ level tsp. dry mustard	¼ pint double cream
A pinch of cayenne pepper	An 8-oz. pkt. of frozen asparagus, cooked and cooled

If you decide to serve this mousse you will need to make two. And you should not attempt it unless you have an electric blender.

Make up the aspic jelly with the water as directed on the packet. Leave till beginning to set, then pour a little into an 8¼-inch spring-release cake tin fitted with a plain base. Use the jelly to coat the sides of the tin and place in the refrigerator to set. When the lining is set, pour more aspic jelly into the tin till it is ¼ inch deep. Leave to set thoroughly. Meanwhile put the butter, flour, milk and seasonings into the electric blender goblet and blend for 15 seconds. Turn into a pan, bring to the boil and cook for 3 minutes. Beat in the vinegar, then the egg yolks. Return the mixture to the heat and cook without boiling for a few minutes. Drain the juice from the salmon and discard. Add the fish to the sauce and check the seasoning. Put 6 tbsps. liquid aspic jelly in a small basin or cup, sprinkle in the gelatine and stand the cup in a little hot water until the gelatine is dissolved; add to the salmon mixture. Pour half into the goblet and blend for about 30 seconds, till smooth. Turn into a bowl and repeat with the remainder. Leave till just on the point of setting. Fold in the lightly whipped cream, followed by the whisked egg whites. Spoon into the tin. When set, arrange the asparagus spears on top. Spoon the remaining aspic jelly over and leave for about 1 hour to set. To unmould, hold a warm cloth round the

sides, release the clip and remove the ring. Warm the base and slide the mousse on to a serving plate. (Serves 8.)

Strawberry Cloud

1 lb. frozen strawberries thawed	3 tbsps. water
	1 tbsp. lemon juice
3 eggs, separated	1 tbsp. strawberry liqueur (optional)
4 oz. caster sugar	¼ pint double cream
½ oz. powdered gelatine	Ratafias

Put the thawed berries through a fine plastic sieve. In a large, deep bowl whisk together the egg yolks and sugar until thick, pale and creamy. Gradually whisk in the sieved fruit. Dissolve the gelatine in the water, as directed on the packet. Stir into the egg yolk mixture, together with the lemon juice and liqueur. When this mixture shows signs of setting, fold in the stiffly whisked egg whites. When evenly mixed, turn into a 6-inch (1½–1¾ pint) collared soufflé dish (or use a 2½-pint glass serving bowl). Chill until set. Decorate with whirls of whipped cream and ratafias. (Serves 6.)

Note. Equally delicious made with frozen raspberries.

Tropical Fruit Salad

8 oranges	6 oz. sugar
2 20-oz. cans of lychees	Juice of 1 lemon
	½ oz. flaked almonds, toasted
1 15-oz. can of guavas	

Cut the skin and pith from the oranges and discard. Cut the flesh into slices and place all but 18 slices in the base of a shallow serving dish. Drain the juice from the lychees and guavas and put in a saucepan, with the sugar and lemon juice; dissolve the sugar, then boil rapidly till reduced to a thick syrup. Meanwhile arrange the guavas in the centre of the dish and the lychees round the edge, with the remaining orange slices laid over the top. Glaze with the thickened syrup and sprinkle flaked almonds in the centre; chill. Serve with cream. (Serves 8.)

Chocolate Cream Gâteau

5 oz. plain flour	4 tbsps. orange liqueur
1 oz. cornflour	1 pint double cream
1 oz. cocoa	½ lb. special moulding
6 large eggs	chocolate (see note)
8 oz. caster sugar	Icing sugar
3 oz. butter, melted	

Oven temperature: fairly hot (375 °F, mark 5).

Grease and line 2 9-inch straight-sided sandwich tins.

Sift together the flour, cornflour and cocoa. Put the eggs and sugar in a large, deep bowl over a saucepan of hot water and whisk with an electric hand mixer or rotary whisk until the mixture is very pale and thick enough to form a trail. Remove from the heat and continue to whisk at intervals until cool. Sift in some of the flour and fold in the rest with a metal spoon, together with the melted butter (cooled but still flowing). Continue until all the flour is incorporated. Divide the mixture between the tins and bake for about 30 minutes; turn out carefully and cool on a wire rack.

Make the chocolate squares (see directions).

Put one cake on a serving plate and sprinkle the surface with 2 tbsps. orange liqueur. Whip the cream until light and fluffy – it should just hold its shape. Spread half the cream over the cake and place the second cake on top. Sprinkle with the remainder of the liqueur. Melt the chocolate in a small basin over hot water (including any scraps left from making chocolate squares), cool slightly and pour over the top of the cake. Smooth with a knife, allowing a little chocolate to drip down the cake sides. When set, decorate with the remaining whipped cream and the chocolate squares. Dredge with icing sugar. (Serves 8.)

Chocolate Squares: Melt about half the chocolate and spread in a thin skin over non-stick paper. When nearly set, cut 1½-inch squares, using a sharp knife. Leave until firm.

Note. Block chocolate is suitable, but still better is special moulding and covering chocolate which does not finger-mark and retains its gloss.

2
Dinner Parties, Intimate or Grand

As a formal meal for entertaining, the Dinner Party still reigns supreme. Few enough people really like eating and drinking a lot at lunch-time, and anyway the evening is the only clear leisure space that most of us have free. But all this does mean that, if you're the hostess, the preparations have to be sandwiched in beside an outside job, or beside all the normal time-consuming business of running a house and family; all too frequently you've only just seen the bare feet of the last child disappearing up the stairs as the door-bell chimes with the first guest. So it's more important than anything else that you know exactly what you're letting yourself in for, and that you get everything planned and organized well in advance. Fortunately, if you give dinner parties often enough, this soon becomes a habit.

With an informal dinner for a couple of friends, the invitation usually slips out casually two or three days beforehand, but a formal dinner party needs much more notice given – a fortnight isn't too much. The invitation needn't be in writing – a phone call is quite definite enough; and you can at the same time take the opportunity of finding out your proposed guests' likes or dislikes, so that you and they don't have to share the embarrassment when you carefully serve them something they hate.

There's nothing cowardly about sticking, to a simple, well-cooked three-course meal. The higher you try to fly with complicated and elaborate dishes, the greater will be your fall if they come unstuck; the same applies to new dishes – new to you, anyway – so if you must serve them, practise first on your husband or a long-suffering friend. There's no reason why the three-course format should restrict your range: your individual dishes can be exciting, and you can fill out with some special cheeses and choice fresh fruit. One golden rule to stick to is balance: *don't* follow pastry with pastry, or one rich dish with another, and *do* play a heavy main course down with a light starter and sweet on either side. Chapter 1, Part I hammers home the rules in rather more detail. The six menus we've chosen here are all well-balanced, and comparatively easy to plan and to prepare. They each follow the same basic pattern, so that you can ring the changes by slotting in any speciality recipe of your own, or by using one from the recipe section of this book.

Decide on your menu not less than a week before the dinner party. This gives you lots of time to make a plan of action – extra groceries needed, wine to be ordered, and flowers, not only for the dining table, but also for the other rooms, and to make sure that tablecloth and napkins are clean and crisp; spread all the preparations out over several days, and you'll hardly notice them – but keep track of things with a list! It's also invaluable to make a step-by-step list of the final cooking of the meal – times and all. This saves last-minute 'what to do next' havering, which all too easily results in nothing being completed at all.

Make your zero hour for 'everything under control' *not* the very minute the guests are due to arrive, but one hour beforehand. By this time, the table should be reassuringly laid with its freshly polished glass and silver, its flowers and table napkins, the choice of apéritifs set out in another room, with bowls of crisps, salted nuts and olives, and the food baking and bubbling safely in oven and pot. You should now have time to lose that sweaty-browed look and, more important still, to relax a little, so that you can genuinely *welcome* your guests, drink the first glass of sherry with them, and generally contribute something other than the food to the evening. If you're using one of the menus here, the dishes won't need much attention between courses, so you will be free to concentrate on your guests.

The second golden rule for a good dinner party – apart from balance – is consistent hospitality. Anticipation should be kept at peak level for as long as possible, and the downward cadence towards departure time, when it comes, should be imperceptible. If you've been clever, you won't have over-fed your guests – too much food is as inhospitable as too little – so they'll still be able to do justice to coffee and little dishes of petits fours, sugared almonds, liqueur chocolates and chocolate peppermint creams. Then, just before they leave, you could give them an alcoholic nightcap, such as a stirrup cup, whisky-and-soda, light glass of wine – or even a cup of tea. (You won't of course, force alcohol on the drivers in the party.)

MENU 1
Dressed Avocado Pears

Farmhouse Chicken Pie
Puffed Potatoes   Green Beans
Baked Mushrooms

Orange-Praline Mousse

The Wines
A white Burgundy or a crisp, fresh Sancerre from the Loire, chilled, but not too much, could be drunk right through the meal.

Note for Beginners
This is a particularly suitable dinner-party menu for the young and fairly inexperienced cook. The whole main course can be left alone in the oven to finish cooking, both while the avocado pears are being prepared and while they're being eaten. They can be served in the simplest way – and it's really the best way, too – just halved, with a choice of two dressings,

tomato vinaigrette and garlic cream. Use the avocados as a centrepiece, and after the first course, replace them by a bowl or basket of fresh fruit.

Advance Preparations: Cook the chicken and bacon, make the forcemeat balls and the sauce the day before. Prepare the shortcrust pastry to the rubbed-in stage and keep it in a cool place ready for mixing and rolling out next day. Make the praline for the mousse and store in an airtight tin or jar. Prepare the dressings for the avocados. Make the mousse overnight, unless you're setting it in the refrigerator, in which case it is better to make it on the morning of the party.

On the Day: Cover the chicken pie filling with pastry, using a pie funnel. We cunningly cut an oval in the centre of the pastry, which lifts off to make cutting the pie at table simpler. Potatoes can be peeled in the morning (or overnight), then cooked and turned into a shallow buttered oven-to-table dish and put into the oven alongside the pie. Even-sized mushrooms (wiped, not washed, and de-stalked) go into the oven on a baking sheet, with a knob of butter and some seasoning on each, to cook for the final 20 minutes or so.

Dressed Avocado Pears
(See colour picture facing p. 216)

3 avocado pears   Garlic cream dressing
Tomato vinaigrette

Cut open the avocado pears, using a stainless knife, and make a deep cut through the flesh up to the stone, entirely encircling the fruit. Separate the halves by gently revolving in opposite directions. Discard the stone. Brush the cut surface with lemon juice. Arrange as a centrepiece, with a choice of dressings. (Serves 6.)

Tomato Vinaigrette: In a container with a tight-fitting lid shake together ¼ pint oil, ⅛ pint red wine vinegar, ¼ level tsp. salt, freshly ground pepper, ¼ level tsp. dry mustard, ½ level tsp. caster sugar and ½ level tbsp. tomato ketchup.

Garlic Cream Dressing: In a container with a tight-fitting lid, shake together ⅛ pint garlic vinegar, ¼ pint single cream, ½ level tsp. salt, freshly ground pepper, 1 clove garlic, crushed, ¼ level tsp. caster sugar and 1 tbsp. chopped parsley.

Note. Each of these dressings is sufficient for six people. If you make them a day ahead, shake well just before serving.

Farmhouse Chicken Pie

2 2½-lb. chickens, oven-ready weight thawed	6 peppercorns
	1 lb. back bacon in a piece, rinded
½ a lemon	1 tbsp. corn oil
1 bay leaf	1 oz. butter
Salt	Forcemeat balls
For the Sauce	
3 oz. butter	½ pint double cream
3 oz. flour	Salt and pepper
1½ pints chicken stock	12 oz. shortcrust pastry (12 oz. plain flour)
2 tsps. lemon juice	Milk

Oven temperature: fairly hot (400 °F, mark 6).

Place the chickens with the giblets in a saucepan and half-cover with water. Add the lemon, bay leaf, salt and peppercorns, bring to the boil, cover and simmer for 1 hour. Cut the bacon into ½-inch cubes and fry in the oil and butter for 20 minutes, remove from the pan. Fry the forcemeat balls (see below) in the same fat until brown. Make a roux for the sauce with the butter and flour and slowly add the 1½ pints hot chicken stock. Add the lemon juice, remove from the heat, stir in the cream and season to taste. Divide the chicken flesh into largish pieces and mix with the cubed bacon and the sauce. Spoon into a shallow 5-pint ovenproof dish and add the forcemeat balls. Use the pastry to cover the dish and brush the pie with milk. Mark the centre with an oval shape and cut almost through the pastry. Decorate with pastry leaves. Bake for 30 minutes, reduce the heat to moderate (350 °F, mark 4) and cook for a further 45 minutes. (Serves 6.)

Forcemeat Balls: Mix together 6 oz. fresh white breadcrumbs, 1 large onion, chopped, 3 level tsps. dried sage, 2 oz. butter, melted, 1 egg, beaten, and seasoning to taste. Shape the mixture into 12 balls.

Puffed Potatoes

3 lb. old potatoes, peeled	2 oz. butter
	1 large egg
1 small onion, finely chopped	A little hot milk
	Salt, pepper, nutmeg

Boil the potatoes, drain well and then sieve them. Sauté the onion in 1 oz. butter until soft but not coloured. Add to the potatoes, with 1 oz. butter, the egg and enough milk to give a light but stiff 'cream' consistency after thorough beating. Season well with salt, pepper and grated nutmeg.

Pile into a well-buttered soufflé-type dish. Place in the oven alongside the chicken pie, so that both are ready together. The puffed potatoes should be golden-brown. (Serves 6.)

Orange-praline Mousse

4 oz. cube sugar	1½ pints milk
2 large juicy oranges	1 oz. powdered gelatine
6 egg yolks	6 egg whites
2 level tsps. cornflour	Praline (see below)
For the Decoration	
Fresh orange segments	Whipped cream
	Sponge drops

Rub the sugar lumps over the skin of the oranges to extract the zest. Squeeze 1½–2 oranges to give 6 tbsps. juice. Beat the egg yolks and blend with the cornflour. Scald the milk, with the sugar lumps added, pour on to egg yolks, stirring, return to the pan and cook without boiling until thickened. Add the gelatine, dissolved in the fruit juice in the usual way, stir well and leave until cool and on the point of setting. Quickly and evenly fold in the stiffly beaten egg whites and half the praline. Turn the mixture into an 8¼-inch spring-release cake tin fitted with a loose base; leave to set in the refrigerator. Turn out carefully on to a flat serving plate and decorate with orange segments (cut from extra oranges), whipped cream, sponge drops and the remainder of the praline. (Serves 6.)

Praline: Dissolve 4 oz. caster sugar in a pan over a low heat. Raise the heat and continue until golden-brown. Quickly turn out on to a greased baking sheet and when cold, crush finely.

MENU 2

Lobster with Brandy Mayonnaise

Osso Buco   Saffron Rice
Chicory and Watercress Salad

Glazed Apple Flans

The Wine

A dry Orvieto or white Chianti will not only complement this classic Italian main course, but will also go well with the lobster.

Planning

This is a sophisticated menu which you'll probably prefer to use at a weekend dinner-party, as the Osso Buco takes quite a time to prepare and cook and it's best served straight from the oven. (If you're unfamiliar with this dish, it's a delicious Italian stew of veal on the bones, with the marrow in them, and it's traditionally eaten with saffron rice, cooked risotto style in chicken broth.) The chicory and watercress salad makes a nice fresh palate-cleanser – especially if its dressing is made with red wine vinegar, which also turns the chicory slightly pink; 4 heads of chicory and 3 bunches of watercress will make a reasonable helping each for half a dozen people. The apple flans need glazing under the grill just before serving. It doesn't matter if this makes a slight pause between courses.

Advance Preparation: Make the mayonnaise for the lobster and cook the apples for the dessert the day before. The flan pastry cases can be baked blind, stored in a tin and refreshed in the oven the following day.

On the Day: In the morning prepare meat and vegetables for the Osso Buco (if not done the day before), ready for slow cooking later on. You can cook the saffron rice a shortish time in advance, put it in a wide but shallow ovenproof dish, cover with foil and leave in the bottom of a slow oven for an hour, without fear of it drying out. Prepare the lobster – frozen or canned – shortly before dinner. Refresh the flan cases; add the warm apple purée, the soured cream and the Demerara sugar as late as possible.

Osso Buco

3 lb. shin of veal (6 pieces)	1½ level tbsps. flour
	¾ pint stock
Salt and pepper	1 lb. tomatoes, skinned
3 oz. butter	and quartered
1 medium-sized onion, chopped	A pinch of dried rosemary
2 carrots, thinly sliced	3 tbsps. chopped parsley
	1 small clove of garlic,
2 sticks of celery, thinly sliced	skinned and finely chopped
¼ pint dry white wine	Grated rind of 1 lemon

Oven temperature: moderate (350 °F, mark 4).

Ask your butcher to saw the veal into 6 slices 1½–2 inches thick. Season with salt and pepper. Melt the butter in a saucepan large enough to take the veal in one layer, brown the veal, then put it aside. If necessary, add a little more butter before gently frying the onion, carrot and celery until they are just beginning to brown. Pour off the excess fat, return the meat to the pan and add the wine; cover and cook gently for 1 hour. Transfer the meat to a large shallow casserole.

Blend the flour with a little stock to a smooth paste and stir in the remainder of the stock. Pour round the veal, add the tomato and rosemary, cover and continue to cook gently in the oven for a further 1 hour, until the meat is tender. Sprinkle with the parsley, garlic and lemon rind mixed (Serves 6.)

Glazed Apple Flans

(See colour picture facing p. 193)

4 oz. plain flour	2 oz. butter, at normal
A pinch of salt	temperature
2 oz. caster sugar	2 egg yolks

For the Filling and Decoration

1½ lb. cooking apples, peeled, cored and sliced	4 oz. sugar
	A scant ¼ pint water
	2 5-fl.-oz. cartons of
2 level tsps. ground cinnamon	soured cream
	5 oz. Demerara sugar

Oven temperature: fairly hot (375 °F., mark 5).

Sift the flour and salt on to a pastry board, or better still a marble slab. Make a well in the centre and into it put the sugar, butter and egg yolks. Using the finger-tips of one hand, pinch and work the sugar, butter and egg yolks together until blended. Gradually work in all the flour and knead lightly until smooth. Put the paste in a cool place for at least 1 hour, then roll out thinly on a lightly floured surface and use to line 6 loose-based, 4-inch fluted French pastry tins. Bake blind for about 15 minutes, until light golden-brown; cool on a wire rack. Meanwhile gently cook the apples with the cinnamon, sugar and water. Before the apples go mushy, put aside 12 slices for decoration and cook the remainder until broken down. Divide the apple pulp between the pastry cases and top with soured cream and sugar. Place under a hot grill until the sugar caramelizes. Decorate it with apple slices. Preferably serve at once. (Makes 6.)

Saffron Rice

3 oz. butter	1 chicken stock cube
1 small onion, chopped	1 pint hot water
12 oz. long-grain rice	1 pkt. saffron powder (1.9 grains)

Melt 2 oz. butter in a large frying-pan, add the onion and rice and stir until beginning to brown. Dissolve the crumbled stock cube in the water, stir into the rice and bring to the boil. Stir in the saffron powder and continue to boil gently, stirring occasionally, until the rice is tender and all the liquid is absorbed – about 25 minutes. It may be necessary during the cooking to add a little more hot water. Add the remaining 1 oz. butter to the cooked rice. Turn the rice gently until the butter has melted and transfer it to an oven-to-table dish. If necessary, cover it and keep hot in the oven (at lowest setting) for 1 hour. (Serves 6.)

MENU 3

Lettuce and Onion Soup
Cheese Straw Stooks

Roast Loin of Pork   Fantail Potatoes
Spinach, Broccoli or Ratatouille
Red-currant-and-Port Preserve

Grape Delight

The Wine

A fragrant, full hock or an Alsatian Traminer would be excellent with the loin of pork.

Planning

A conventional Sunday roasting joint, made rich and unconventional by its filling and accessories. The flavours of the sweet-cure bacon and leaf-sage permeate right through the meat, and make a rather exotic blend with the ratatouille (if you chose that as vegetable) and the potatoes, which are oven-glazed with cheese. You should be able to buy the red-currant-and-port preserve quite easily, but it will look home-preserved if you tip it into a small fluted dish with a silver spoon for serving. For the soup, a tureen and ladle aren't necessary unless you particularly want to use them; individual bowls, warmed first and brought in on a pretty tray, will do just as well.

Advance Preparation: You can make the soup a day ahead, though with an electric blender it can be done the day of the party, since it won't take long. Cheese straws, piled into stooks, can be made ahead and refreshed in the oven before serving. Make the chocolate curls for the sweet. You can also prepare the pork ready for the oven and keep it in a cool place.

On the Day: There's plenty of time to concentrate on your table setting with this menu. Potatoes, prepared reasonably early on (or overnight) go into the oven with the pork. If you choose ratatouille as a second vegetable, remember there's a frozen one on the market; you need two packets for 6 servings. Grapes, yoghourt and chocolate curls make the quick dessert that can be assembled in individual glasses shortly before the guests arrive.

Lettuce and Onion Soup

2 oz. butter	2 pints chicken stock
1 large onion, skinned and finely chopped	Salt and pepper
	A 2.75-fl. oz. carton of double cream
1 large lettuce, finely shredded	Cheese straws as accompaniment

Heat the butter in a saucepan, add the onion and fry gently until soft, being careful not to allow it to colour. Add the lettuce and cook in the butter for a few minutes, then add the stock and seasoning. Bring to the boil, cover and simmer for 5–7 minutes. Place half the mixture in an electric blender, blend until smooth, turn into a bowl and repeat with the remaining mixture. Return it all to the saucepan, bring to the boil, remove from the heat and gradually add the cream, stirring all the time. Serve hot, with cheese straws. (Serves 6.)

Note. When making soup a day ahead, proceed up to and including the blending.

Roast Loin of Pork

(See colour picture facing p. 169)

2½ lb. loin of pork (boned weight)	12 fresh or dried sage leaves
½ lb. sweet-cure back rashers, rinded	Oil
	Salt

Oven temperature: fairly hot (375 °F, mark 5).

Ask your butcher to score the pork rind deeply and evenly. Place the meat on a flat surface, fat side down, and cut the flesh to open it out a little. Lay the bacon rashers over the flesh and then place the sage leaves at intervals. Roll up carefully, secure firmly with string, parcel fashion, and place in a roasting tin. Rub the rind thoroughly with oil and salt. Roast in the centre of the oven for 30–35 minutes per lb. stuffed weight, plus 30 minutes over. Remove the string, place the meat on a serving dish and return it to the oven, reduced in temperature to cool (300 °F, mark 1–2). Drain off all but 1 tbsp. of the fat. To make the gravy, stir in 2 level tsps. flour, cook for a few minutes, then gradually add about ½ pint stock or vegetable water. Check the seasoning, bring to the boil and simmer for a few minutes. (Serves 6.)

Fantail Potatoes

(See colour picture facing p. 169)

6 even-sized oval potatoes (4–6 oz. each)	Salt and pepper
	2 oz. Cheddar cheese, grated
2 oz. butter	

(Oven temperature: fairly hot (375 °F, mark 5).

Peel the potatoes. (At this stage they may be left covered with water to which a slice of lemon has been added; drain well before using.) Cut each potato into thin slices, but not quite through to the base. Place in a roasting tin, sliced side uppermost, dot with butter and sprinkle with salt and pepper. Cook above the joint for 30 minutes, basting occasionally. Remove from the oven, sprinkle each potato with grated cheese and return to the oven for a further 30 minutes, until crisp, golden and cooked through. (Serves 6.)

Grape Delight

(See colour picture facing p. 192)

2 10-oz. cans of grapes	2 egg whites
2 5-fl. oz. cartons of apricot yoghurt	Chocolate curls or coarsely grated chocolate

Drain the grapes. Turn the yoghurt into a bowl. Whisk the egg whites stiffly and fold into the yoghurt. Layer the yoghurt, grapes and more yoghurt in small glasses. Decorate with curls of chocolate. (Serves 6.)

Note. Gather together all the ingredients, but combine at the last minute – although the chocolate curls can be prepared in advance.

MENU 4

Hors d'Oeuvre
Gris Sticks

Beef and Chestnut Casserole
Château Potatoes   Vichy-style Carrots
Green Salad

Pears Felicie

The Wine

The flavourful main dish needs a sturdy red wine as partner – an Hermitage or Côte Rotie, perhaps.

Planning

The mainstay course for this meal is the rich beef casserole, and it's a really hot, spicy, winter-evening dish. You can prepare and cook it the day before, and then glaze the chestnuts and add just before serving. The sponge base for the dessert can also be made the previous day. For the hors d'oeuvre for 6 you will need a 3¾-oz. can of brisling, 3 oz. each of thinly sliced salami and of ham sausage, 1 can of artichoke hearts (1–2 hearts each), 3 hardboiled eggs (one half for each plate, stuffed with mayonnaise-creamed yolk). You could also add raw leek – one is enough for 6 servings – very finely chopped and marinaded in a sweetened French dressing. If you are having sherry before the meal, you could carry it through to drink with the hors d'oeuvre as well, and save the red wine for the casserole. This wine should be brought to room temperature by being kept in a warm part of the house for several hours – but never near artificial heat; uncork it about an hour before serving.

On the Day: Prepare and dice 2 lb. carrots. Complete the pear dessert. In the evening (while the casserole is reheating for an hour) blanch and drain the carrots. Return them to the pan with ¾ pint of water, a good knob of butter and very little salt, and bring to the boil. Reduce the heat and cook gently without a lid for 45 minutes, by which time the liquid should have evaporated. Add another knob of butter and a squeeze of lemon juice, and serve garnished with a dusting of freshly milled black pepper and chopped parsley. Canned new potatoes reduce the work. Toss the salad in its French dressing just before serving it.

Beef and Chestnut Casserole

(See colour picture facing p. 168)

3–3½ lb. chuck steak	¼ pint hot water
2 oz. seasoned flour	1 beef stock tablet
2 oz. lard	¼ pint dry red wine
1 medium-sized onion, sliced	A 3-oz. pkt. of sliced garlic sausage
A 15-oz. can of peeled tomatoes	Canned whole chestnuts
A 4-oz. can of pimientos, sliced	Butter Chopped parsley

Oven temperature: warm (325 °F, mark 3).

Trim the steak of any excess fat; cut into approximately 2-inch pieces and toss in seasoned flour. (Retain the surplus flour.) Melt the lard in a frying-pan and fry the meat until sealed, browning a few pieces at a time. Place the meat in a large casserole. Add the onion to the frying-pan and fry gently until beginning to brown; stir in any excess flour. Gradually add the tomatoes and pimientos. Blend the water and stock tablet and add with the wine to the frying-pan. Bring to the boil and check the seasoning. Cut the sausage into strips, add to the beef in the casserole and pour the pan contents over. Cover the casserole and cook in the oven for about 3 hours, then transfer to a clean casserole. (Serves 6.)

To re-heat on the Day: Place the casserole in the oven at moderate (350 °F, mark 4) for 1 hour. Sauté 12 drained chestnuts in a little melted butter until browned and add to the casserole. Serve garnished with parsley.

Château Potatoes

2 19-oz. cans of new potatoes	Salt and pepper Parsley or chives
3 oz. butter	

Drain the potatoes thoroughly. Heat the butter in a frying-pan and when hot add the potatoes, if possible in a single layer. Cook covered, shaking the pan frequently, until the potatoes are a golden-brown. Season lightly during the cooking. Serve garnished with snipped parsley or chives. (Serves 6.)

Pear Felicie

2 eggs	A 2.75-fl. oz. carton of double cream
2 oz. caster sugar	
2 oz. plain flour	½ oz. walnut halves, chopped
Sieved apricot jam	
Pistachio nuts, blanched and chopped	½ oz. glacé cherries, chopped
	½ oz. ratafias, crushed
A 1¾-lb. can of pear halves	1 piece of stem ginger, chopped
2 tbsps. sherry	

For the Glaze and Decoration

½ lime jelly tablet	Green colouring
¼ pint water	Crystallized rose petals
¼ pint double cream	Angelica

Oven temperature: hot (425 °F, mark 7).

Prepare a fatless sponge in the usual way, using the eggs, sugar and flour, and bake in a lined 7½-inch sandwich tin for 12–15 minutes. Cool. Brush the sponge edge with warm sieved apricot jam and coat with chopped pistachio nuts. Place on a serving dish. Sprinkle the top with a mixture of 4 tbsps. pear juice and 2 tbsps. sherry. Whip the cream and add the walnuts, cherries, ratafias and ginger. Chop all but 6 of the pear halves and add to the filling. Use to stuff the hollow of each pear half.

Dissolve the jelly tablet in the water, cool to the consistency of unbeaten egg whites, then fold in the unwhipped double cream and colour pale green. Use to double-coat the rounded side of each pear. When set, arrange the pears on the sponge. Decorate with crushed rose petals and angelica leaves. (Serves 6.)

MENU 5

Cream of Cucumber Soup   Melba Toast

Salmon Mayonnaise
Rolled Brown Bread and Butter

Veal Fricandeau
New Potatoes   French Beans   Broad Beans

Raspberry Napolitain

Coffee

The Wines

As apéritifs, chilled fino sherry (La Ina, perhaps) and Chambéry, that fragrant, subtle vermouth. A dry, refreshing young white wine, a Chablis Premier Crû 1964, to take with the first two courses. Next, for this very special dinner party, a superb, full-flavoured German wine such as a Johannisberger Vogelsang Riesling Spätlese, 1959. Then, with a leisurely pause to savour what has gone before, demitasse coffee, with a choice of Cognac or Port.

Planning

A very special, very elegant dinner, which entirely justifies invitation cards and dinner jackets, and which has just the right menu – not too rich, not too heavy – for the meal before a grand ball. It's fairly simple to cook, with the minimum of last-minute touches, so that you have leisure and energy to dress, welcome your guests and drink an apéritif with them before serving the first course.

The recipes below give you the amounts of ingredients needed for 6 people. You will also need a small tin loaf, bought two days earlier, for making the Melba toast. For the fish course, 1½–2 lb. tail-piece of fresh salmon; a small crisp lettuce (or more, so that you have enough heart to make cups for the salmon), a jar of good bought lemon mayonnaise (e.g. Salarad), if you don't normally make your own; 1 small brown loaf; paprika; and your favourite butter, which is to be served separately for the Melba toast, and used in making the rolled brown bread fingers. Also you'll need 3 lb. new potatoes, 3 lb. broad beans, 1 lb. French beans and some fresh savory.

The Day Before: Make some stock with veal bones for the Fricandeau and store when cool in the refrigerator. Make the puff-pastry discs for the Raspberry Napolitain and store in an airtight tin.

Morning of the Party: Prepare the soup up to, but not including, the stage of adding the egg yolks (see recipe). Loosely wrap the trimmed, well-seasoned salmon in liberally buttered foil, put on a baking sheet and pop in a cool oven (300 °F, mark 2) for about 1 hour; leave to cool. Wash and dry the lettuce, store in a plastic bag and crisp in the refrigerator. Roll the thinly sliced and buttered brown bread, and foil-wrap until required. Also cut from the tin loaf 12 to 16 slices, ⅛-inch thick, and remove the crusts. Get all the ingredients ready for the veal dish. Top and tail the French beans and pod the baby broad beans. (Both vegetables will take about 10–15 minutes to cook in boiling salted water, when the time comes: add a sprig of savory, if available, to the broad beans.)

Later in the Afternoon: Scrape the potatoes and leave under cold water (they will take about 20–25 minutes to cook in boiling salted water). Finish the Raspberry Napolitain.

During the Last 3 Hours before Guests Arrive: Start cooking the Veal Fricandeau. Once cooked, it will come to no harm if left in a cool oven (300 °F, marks 1–2) without attention.

Garnish just prior to serving. Lightly fold enough mayonnaise through the salmon to look creamy; just before the guests arrive, spoon it into lettuce leaf 'cups' on individual plates, and finish each with a sprinkling of paprika. Toast the Melba bread slowly until brown on both sides, then put into the bottom of the oven, until ready to serve in a napkin-lined basket with the soup. Arrange the rolled brown bread and butter on a separate plate to pass with the salmon. If you like asparagus, put some young, fresh tips into some of the bread fingers before you roll them.

Last-minute Jobs: Re-heat the soup and thicken with the egg yolks and cream. Best non-spill way to serve hot soup is from a jug or tureen, into soup cups or bowls which are already waiting on the hot tray (either electric, turned low, or the night-light type), with the cucumber and mint garnish ready alongside. Just before you serve the soup, put on the vegetables to start cooking over a gentle heat.

Cream of Cucumber Soup

1½ pints chicken stock	Green colouring
1 large cucumber	2 egg yolks
1 tsp. finely chopped, shallot or onion	4 tbsps. milk
1 oz. butter	Freshly grated cucumber and chopped mint for garnish
¾ oz. flour	
Salt and pepper	

If home-made chicken stock is not available, use 1½ pints water with 1 chicken stock cube. Peel the cucumber and cut into ½-inch slices. In a saucepan, bring to the boil the stock, cucumber and shallot. Reduce the heat and simmer for 15–20 minutes, until the cucumber is soft, Either rub the mixture through a fine sieve or put it in the electric blender. Melt the butter in the pan, stir in the flour and cook over a low heat for a few minutes. Slowly stir in the sieved cucumber and stock. Bring to the boil, check the seasoning and simmer for 5 minutes; cool. Use a mere drop of the colouring to make the mixture a delicate green. Blend the egg yolks and milk, add a little soup, stir well and pour back into the pan. Reheat but *do not boil;* garnish before serving. (Serves 6.)

Veal Fricandeau

2½ lb. lean boned veal	¼ lb. carrots, peeled
Butter	A bouquet garni
1 tbsp. corn oil	1 pint veal stock, made from the veal bones
A ¼-lb. slice of green back bacon	¼ pint dry white wine
¼ lb. small onions, skinned	¼ lb. mushrooms
	Chopped parsley

Oven temperature: warm (325 °F, mark 3).

Buy if possible noix of veal, cut from the leg and tied into a sausage shape. Less expensive cuts that suit this recipe are rolled best end or shoulder. In a frying-pan, melt 1 oz. butter and add the oil, then brown the veal evenly on all sides. Trim the bacon free of excess fat and cut into thick strips. Slice the onions and carrots thinly. Prepare a bouquet garni to include a sprig of parsley, a bay leaf, a sprig of thyme or tarragon, a few peppercorns, and a sliver each of orange and lemon peel. In a casserole place the bacon, onions and carrots; add the veal joint and bouquet garni. Pour the stock and wine over the meat, cover and cook in the oven for 2–3 hours, depending on the cut – the veal should be fork-tender. Lift the joint from the casserole. Remove the string and slice the joint with a sharp knife into 6–8 pieces. Keep warm on a serving dish while sautéing the mushrooms in butter. Strain the liquor into a small pan and reduce it. Check the seasoning, then spoon over the meat. Garnish with the sliced sautéd mushrooms and some chopped parsley. (Serves 6–8.)

Raspberry Napolitain

1 lb. puff pastry. frozen or chilled	3 egg whites
¼ lb. raspberry jam	1 oz. caster sugar
¾ pint double cream	1 lb. fresh raspberries
	Icing sugar

Oven temperature: hot (425 °F, mark 7).

Allow frozen pastry to thaw as directed on the packet. Roll out into 3 wafer-thin 10-inch rounds. Lift on to baking sheets, using a rolling-pin, prick well and leave to relax for 15 minutes in a cool place. Bake for about 10 minutes, until golden-brown: cool. Using scissors, trim each disc to the same size; crush and retain the trimmings. Spread sieved jam over one surface of 2 of the discs. Whisk together the cream, egg whites and sugar until the mixture holds its shape. Place a jam-spread disc, jam side uppermost, on a flat serving place and spread a film of cream over the surface. Halve the raspberries and place all but a spoonful from one portion in the centre of the disc. Use half the cream mixture to make a 'collar' level with the berries. Repeat with the second disc. Mount the top plain disc in position and press lightly. Level off the cream edges, if necessary, then dust with icing sugar. Spoon a band of pastry trimmings round the top edge and arrange a spoonful of berries in the centre. Press a few berries at intervals into the cream. Refrigerate for up to 1 hour before serving. (Serves 6–8.)

MENU 6

Midsummer Soup

Chaudfroid of Chicken
Sunflower Tomatoes   Sweet Pepper Rice

Cherry Cream Cones

The Wine

Beaujolais Blanc – a young, fragrant wine that should be served well chilled.

Planning

A formal dinner-party, ideal for a warm summer evening, but best eaten inside. Apéritifs, with nuts and olives, can be served out on the terrace or lawn; open windows all over the house will make the whole meal feel summery. If the meal finishes while the air is still warm, a trolley stacked with the coffee things could be stationed outside, but near the house, so that guests have a choice of being out or in. The menu has been carefully chosen, and preparations can be spread out over several days; the only hot course to worry about is the starter – Midsummer Soup.
A Few Days Ahead: Make the cones for the dessert and, when cold, store in an airtight container.

Order fresh food items, check the store-cupboard ones, including the niblets for apéritifs. Order wines and other drinks in advance. Decide on the table setting, checking on table linen and so on. This includes considering flowers for a centre-piece.
The Day Before: Make the soup, cover and keep in a cool place. Cook the chicken and leave covered in the stock, overnight in a cool place.

Make a sweet-pepper dressing, and put the mushrooms in it to marinade overnight.

Cook the rice and leave, covered, in a bowl.

Make the mayonnaise.

Wash the endive, dry and store in a plastic bag in the refrigerator.
On the Day: In the morning: remove and discard the skin and bones from the chicken.

Make the chaudfroid coating, coat the chicken, garnish and glaze with aspic and put in refrigerator.

Before guests arrive: lay the table and prepare the coffee tray.

Drain the mushrooms and arrange the Sunflower Tomatoes. Mix the sweet-pepper dressing with the rice and parsley and arrange on a serving dish with the chicken breasts.

Chill the white wine for 1 hour before serving. Prepare and assemble the dessert.

Midsummer Soup

1 lettuce	¼ lb. lean streaky bacon,
1 bunch of watercress	rinded and chopped
2 cartons of mustard	1 oz. flour
and cress	2½ pints chicken stock
½ lb. onions, skinned	Salt, pepper and 1 bay
and chopped	leaf
2 oz. butter	

Wash and shred the lettuce; prepare the watercress and mustard and cress. Place in a large saucepan with the onions, butter and bacon, and sauté gently for 10 minutes, stirring constantly. Add the flour and mix well, then slowly add the stock, stirring continuously. Bring to the boil, season to taste, then add the bay leaf. Cover and simmer for 20 minutes. Discard the bay leaf. Pour the soup a little at a time into an electric blender and blend until smooth. Return to a clean saucepan, bring to the boil and re-check the seasoning. (Serves 8.)

Note. Although the soup will not be quite as smooth, a sieve can be used to purée the ingredients, in which case increase the simmering time to 40 minutes.

Chaudfroid of Chicken

8 chicken breast portions	4 tbsps. lemon juice
2 large carrots, peeled and sliced	1 pint water
	2 bay leaves
2 large onions, skinned and sliced	Salt
	Freshly ground pepper

For the Coating

1½ level tbsps. aspic jelly crystals	¾ pint boiling water
	½ pint mayonnaise

For the Garnish

Black olives, stoned and halved	Radishes, sliced

Oven temperature: moderate (350 °F, mark 4).

Arrange the chicken breasts in one layer in a large, shallow oven-proof dish. Add the carrots, onions, lemon juice, water, bay leaves, salt and pepper. Cover with a lid or kitchen foil and cook in the oven for 1 hour, until tender. Leave until the chicken breasts are quite cold, and then carefully remove and discard the skin and bones.

Make up the aspic jelly as directed on the packet and leave until beginning to set. Fold ½ pint aspic jelly into the mayonnaise. When it is of a coating consistency, use to glaze the chicken. To do this, arrange the chicken breasts on a cooking rack placed over an oven sheet or board. Spoon mayonnaise over each breast – either coat thickly once, or thinly twice. Leave until set. To garnish, dip the halved olives and radish slices in the remaining aspic and arrange on the chicken. When set, finely glaze the chicken with the rest of the aspic jelly when it is of the consistency of egg white. (Serves 8.)

Sunflower Tomatoes

8 button mushrooms	8 large firm tomatoes
Sweet-pepper dressing (see recipe)	1 curly endive
	Salt and pepper

Remove the stalks from the mushrooms. Mari-

nade the mushroom caps in the sweet-pepper dressing overnight. To arrange the salad, cut each tomato into 6 segments, taking care not to slice right through to the base, and open out carefully like a flower. Place each tomato on a bed of endive and season with salt and pepper. Sit a mushroom in each tomato. (Serves 8.)

Sweet-pepper Dressing

½ pint oil	2 level sps. caster sugar
¼ pint wine vinegar	
1 level tsp. salt	7-oz. can of pimientos, drained and chopped
1 level tsp. dry mustard	

Place all ingredients together in a jar with a screw-top lid. Shake vigorously until well mixed; chill and use as required.
Note. Best made the day before required to allow the pimiento flavour to permeate the dressing.

Sweet-pepper Rice

1 lb. long-grain rice	Sweet-pepper dressing
2 pints water	Chopped parsley
2 level tsps. salt	

Put the rice, 2 pints water (or according to packet directions) and 2 level tsps. salt into a large pan. Bring to the boil and stir once with a fork. Reduce the heat so that water is simmering, cover tightly and cook for about 15 minutes without disturbing. Remove the lid. If some of the water has not been absorbed, replace the lid and cook for 1–2 minutes longer. Remove the rice from the heat and fluff with a fork. Leave to cool.

To serve, fold the sweet-pepper dressing through the rice, together with plenty of parsley. (Serves 8.)

Cherry Cream Cones

4 oz. butter	Vanilla essence
5 oz. icing sugar, sifted	4 oz. plain flour
	4 tbsps. water
3 egg whites	

For the Filling

½ pint double cream	Fresh ripe cherries
¼ pint single cream	

Oven temperature: fairly hot (400 °F, mark 6).

Grand Buffet for a Wedding: p. 52

Cream together the butter and sugar. Beat in the un-whipped egg whites and a few drops of vanilla essence, then the flour and water. Drop spoonfuls of the batter in heaps about 1½ inches across on a lightly greased baking sheet, keeping them well apart. Flatten them by banging the baking sheets on the table. Do not bake more than one sheet at a time. Bake until the edges turn golden-brown and the centres are lightly tinged – about 8 minutes. With a palette knife quickly remove and shape into cornets round cream-horn cases; cool on a wire rack, then carefully slip them off the cases.

To serve, fill the tip of each cone with a little whipped cream, add a couple of stoned cherries, then a final whirl of cream. Decorate the cones with whole stemmed cherries. (Makes 24.) *Note.* Whip the double cream and single cream together until the mixture just holds its shape. Fill the cones not more than 1 hour before they are required. The empty cases will keep in an airtight tin for several days.

Curry and Rice Party: p. 86

3
Lunch Parties

LUNCH MENU FOR EIGHT

Grapefruit and Avocado Salad

Cheese-crusted Chicken Pie
Buttered Green Beans   Carrot Rings

Oranges à la Turque

Coffee

The Drink

If you're not sure of your wines, this is not the time to start experiments. Serve one kind only, which will blend well with all the courses in the meal: this could be a white Burgundy or a Sancerre, either of them very lightly chilled.

Planning

This is a sophisticated menu, which is nevertheless homely enough for a family-and-friends Sunday lunch, and especially suitable for a young cook with perhaps in-laws, her own parents and another young couple to impress. But it's not really suitable for a meal which has the unavoidable accessory of young children – they'll wrinkle their noses at the strong flavours of the hot chicken pie and turn them right up at the idea of 'oranges for *pudding*?'

It's an easy meal to cope with single-handed, for the preparations will work themselves into three simple stages, but you do need to devote the whole morning to the cooking. The Oranges à la Turque can be made the night before, covered over and left in either the coldest part of the house, or right at the bottom of the fridge. On the Sunday morning, concentrate on the chicken pie, and especially on its timing, so that it completes its cooking as near as possible to the scheduled start of the lunch-party. Its peaceful 65 minutes in the oven will give you loads of time to prepare the salad and set the table. The setting, incidentally, should be unfussy, with wedding-present china and cutlery diplomatically in evidence; two small and simple bowls of fresh flowers will be all the extra decoration you'll need, plus napkins in one of the flower colours.

Grapefruit and Avocado Salad

8 oz. cream cheese	French dressing
3–4 grapefruit	Lettuce
2 avocado pears	

Shape the cream cheese into 16 small balls. Peel the grapefruit, removing the membranes as well as the skin. Remove the sections with a very sharp knife. Peel the avocados and cut in half lengthwise, through to the stone. Twist the halves in opposite directions, discard the stones and slice the avocados. Marinade the grapefruit and avocados in the French dressing. On individual plates arrange the lettuce, grapefruit, avocado and cream cheese balls.

Cheese-crusted Chicken Pie

For the Cream Cheese Pastry

3 oz. plain flour	1 oz. butter
¼ level tsp. salt	1 oz. white vegetable
A pinch of cayenne	fat
pepper	2 oz. firm cream cheese

For the Filling

12 oz. cooked	¼ lb. mushrooms,
chicken	sliced
3 oz. butter	2 level tbsps. flour
½ a red and ½ a	¼ pint chicken stock
green pepper	¼ pint single cream
seeded and	Salt and pepper
chopped	

74

Oven temperature: fairly hot (400 °F, mark 6).

Sift together the flour, salt and cayenne. Lightly rub in the fats, followed by the cream cheese; knead lightly and chill. Dice the chicken. Melt 2 oz. of the butter and sauté the peppers and mushrooms. Add to the chicken. Melt the remaining 1 oz. butter, stir in the flour and cook slowly for 2–3 minutes. Gradually add the stock, stirring continuously, and cook for a few minutes. Blend in the cream and pour over the chicken. Adjust the seasoning, turn the mixture into an 8½-inch pie plate and leave until cold. Roll out the pastry and use to cover the filling. Bake for 20 minutes. Reduce the heat to moderate (350° F, mark 4) and continue to cook for a further 45 minutes approximately. (Serves 4 – make 2 pies for 8 people.)

Oranges à la Turque

8 large juicy oranges   1 lb. caster sugar
Water   2 cloves

Thinly pare the rind from half the oranges and free them of white pith. Cut the rind into very thin julienne strips with a sharp knife or scissors. Put into a small pan, cover well with water, cover and cook until the peel is tender; strain. Cut away all the pith from the 4 peeled oranges and the rind and pith from the 4 remaining oranges – hold them over a bowl to catch the juice.

Dissolve the sugar in ½ pint water with the cloves. Bring to the boil and boil until caramel coloured. Remove from the heat, add 3 tbsps. water, return to a very low heat to dissolve the caramel, and add the orange juice. Arrange the oranges in a single layer in a serving dish and top with the julienne strips. Spoon the caramel syrup over the oranges and leave for several hours in a cold place, turning the oranges occasionally.

Note. Serve the oranges sliced and reassembled, or whole, with knife, fork and spoon to eat them.

HEN-PARTY LUNCH FOR 10

Melon Wedges

Chilli Con Carne
Tossed Green Salad   French Bread

Charlotte Russe

Coffee

Planning

Most hen-party lunches, understandably enough, revolve round something light and quick to make – a fluffy cheese and onion omelette, say, with frozen peas – which two or three gathered together can just squeeze into the middle of the day. But once in a while you could, if you planned your time carefully, try a more adventurous lunch-party for ten or a dozen of your favourite local friends. It could be a real life-saver, and perhaps become a weekly habit, with each friend taking it in turns to open her house and do the cooking.

It's a splendid opportunity to plan a show-off menu that is special, sophisticated and not at all the sort of thing which you – or they – would dish up for a week-end family meal. It's a challenge which can actually become cooking for pleasure, and well worth finding a spare day for. We've chosen as a sample menu one that is quite impressive, without needing over-much trouble or time to prepare. You could either make the Charlotte Russe the previous night, covering it and leaving it in a cool place to set, or start on it first thing on the day of the lunch, as soon as you've got the family out of the way. Either way, make it before you start on the main dish (which can be served straight off the top of the cooker), so that it has ample setting time. If you plan the lunch for 12.30 or 1.00 prompt, this should give you plenty of time for a really leisurely meal and coffee before the end-of-school dash at 3.30.

P.S. If you can persuade your harassed mums to drink wine with their lunch – just this once – it should be a thirst-quenching red or rosé.

Chilli Con Carne

2½ lb. lean chuck steak, minced	2 level tsps. salt
2 large onions, skinned	¼ level tsp. paprika pepper
1 level tbsp. American chilli powder	2 29-oz. cans of tomatoes
	2 16-oz. cans of red kidney beans

Brown the meat in a large saucepan, stirring frequently, for about 10 minutes. Finely slice the onions and add to the mince. Blend well together the chilli powder, salt and paprika pepper and sprinkle over the mince. Add the canned tomatoes, bring to the boil, cover and simmer for 1½–2 hours. Add the drained kidney beans and cook gently for a further 15–20 minutes.

Charlotte Russe

16 soft sponge fingers, approx.	4 level tsps. powdered gelatine
A 15-oz. can of apricot halves	2 tbsps. water
8 egg yolks	1 pint double cream
5 oz. sugar	2 tbsps. apricot liqueur
1 pint milk	Pistachio nuts and cream to decorate

Line the sides of a 7-inch straight-sided soufflé dish or a charlotte mould with sponge fingers; if necessary, trim the long edges of the fingers so that they fit snugly together. Drain the apricots, reserve 4 halves for decoration and cut the rest into small pieces. Beat the egg yolks and sugar together until pale in colour. Heat the milk and when almost boiling pour on to the egg and sugar mixture; return it to the pan and cook over a low heat until the mixture coats the back of the spoon. Dissolve the gelatine in water in the usual way – in a basin over hot water – and stir into the cooled custard. Lightly whip the cream until it will just hold its shape. When the custard mixture is beginning to thicken and hold its shape, fold in the cream, chopped fruit and liqueur. When the mixture is just on the point of setting, spoon it in to the lined soufflé dish. Leave until completely set.

When ready to serve, warm the base of the soufflé dish for a second in hot water, turn the charlotte out on to a plate and quickly reverse it on to a serving dish. Tie a ribbon round and decorate with the reserved apricot halves, pistachio nuts and piped cream. (Serves 8–10.)

Vary the decoration if you wish.

4
Informal Entertaining

PIE, PATTY AND PUNCHBOWL PARTY

There can't be many people who'd turn their noses up at the offer of a home-made pie, and if you enjoy this kind of cookery, a pie-and-patty-party is one of the easiest and most versatile to organize. It's applicable to any time of the year, and particularly suitable for Christmas Eve – see the colour picture facing page 49 and the one facing page 121. If you want to throw the house wide open for the whole evening to guests of all ages, you'll do best to provide individual pies, which won't spoil as batch after batch are kept warm in the oven. Frozen pastry cuts down the work and the pies can be made in advance. One of the well-filled pork and egg pies, say, and two of the sugar-sprinkled mince pies should make an adequate snack for each guest; but spin them out with scattered bowls of snippets in contrasting flavours – sticks of celery, Ritz biscuits, and the dated-but-still-delicious combination of cheese and pineapple side by side on cocktail sticks. Keep these bowls topped up during the party, and leave a couple of pots of ready-made mustard around for the savoury pies, plus a sugar shaker for the mince pies.

If you're planning a more select party, and want to pin your guests down a bit, invite them for a definite time, prop their hunger up with nuts, olives and a glass of sherry, and then, when they're all assembled, serve these pies piping hot and straight from the oven.

You'll be biting off more than you can chew if you try to offer all these pies for one party, but two or three varieties, big pies being combined with little individual ones, should placate the appetites of about a dozen hungry guests. We also give sausage rolls and an unusual fried pastry recipe. As accompaniment, what about an ample winter salad? And instead of the mince pies, you could offer slices of fresh pineapple.

Serving

Pare down eating arrangements to the absolute minimum – for your guests' sake as well as your own. If it's to be open house and individual pies, all you really need is an abundant supply of large paper napkins in the strongest, brightest colours you can find – then let people cope, hand-to-mouth, Wimpy-style. For the larger pies they'll need plates – paper again – and forks. And if you can mock up a large carton in flamboyant covering as a litter-bin and leave it prominently near the serving table, you might even find your guests posting their litter as they create it. *One word of warning:* don't get carried away and try to get out of using proper glasses for the wine – there's nothing more likely to kill drink stone-dead than the waxy tang of a paper cup; and besides, half the cheerful noise of a really good party comes from the clinking of bottle against glass.

The Drink

If the party's for Christmas Eve, or some other particularly festive occasion, a punch-bowl of warm mull makes good company for the pies. Try making it with Vila Real, a Portuguese red wine which is quite inexpensive. Or, as claret is the traditional base for a mull, you could use a non-vintage *Commune* wine like St. Émilion or St. Julien for just a little more. But if there's any straightforward red wine that you know and like, go ahead and use it. If the occasion doesn't really merit a punch-bowl – or if you simply can't be bothered – choose a wine to suit the pies you're serving. A full red seems the obvious choice for the beef-and-wine pies, but pink wines would blend with any of them. Keep a delicately flavoured Portuguese rosé for the fish one; the others will take the stronger rosés from Italy, Yugoslavia or Spain.

Beef-and-Wine Pies

(See colour picture facing p. 49)

2¼ lb. chuck steak	6 oz. mushrooms, sliced
½ lb. kidney	2 cloves of garlic,
3 oz. plain flour	skinned and crushed
Salt and pepper	1 pint stock
3½ oz. butter	½ pint dry red wine
3 tbsps. corn oil	A 13-oz. pkt. of bought
1 large onion,	puff pastry
chopped	Beaten egg

Oven temperature: warm (325 °F, mark 3).

Trim the meat and cut into 1-inch pieces. Remove and discard the core from the kidney, cut the kidney into pieces and toss with the meat in seasoned flour. Melt 2 oz. of the butter with 3 tbsps. oil in a large frying-pan. Quickly and evenly brown the meat and any excess flour, then transfer to a casserole. Melt the remaining 1½ oz. butter and fry the onions for a few minutes. Add the mushrooms and garlic and fry for a further few minutes. Pour the stock and wine into the pan, bring to the boil and pour over the meat. Cover and cook in the oven for 1½–2 hours until the meat is tender. Divide between 6 ½-pint individual ovenproof dishes and leave to cool. Cover with lids of thinly rolled puff pastry, making sure the edges are well sealed. Brush with beaten egg. Bake in a very hot oven (450 °F, mark 8) for about 15 minutes until the pastry is well risen and golden-brown. Serve hot, with a parsley garnish. (Makes 6.)

Fisherman's Potato-crusted Pie

(See colour picture facing p. 49)

3 lb. potatoes	1 medium-sized onion
Salt	3½ oz. plain flour
5 oz. butter	Freshly ground white
1½ pints milk	pepper
2 lb. fresh haddock	½ level tsp. dried fennel
fillet	A 3½-oz. can of shrimps

Oven temperature: fairly hot (400 °F, mark 6).

Boil the potatoes in salted water. Sieve, and cream with 1½ oz. of the butter and 5 tbsps. milk; keep warm. Poach the haddock with thin slices of onion in the rest of the milk until tender – about 15 minutes. Strain off the liquor

and if necessary make up to 1½ pints with more milk. Remove and discard any skin or bone and flake the haddock; discard the onion. Melt the remaining 3½ oz. butter in a saucepan and stir in the flour. Cook for 1–2 minutes over a low heat. Gradually add the milk, stirring; bring to the boil and simmer for 5 minutes. Season well with salt, pepper and fennel. Add the haddock and the shrimps, and transfer to a 4½-pint shallow pie dish. Pipe whirls of creamed potato over the fish filling, using a large star vegetable nozzle. Brown in the oven for about 40 minutes. (Serves 6–8.)

Chicken and Grape Pie

(See colour picture facing p. 49)

A 4½-lb. oven-ready	Milk
chicken	3 oz. butter
¾ pint water	3 oz. plain flour
3 carrots, peeled and	4–6 oz. white grapes,
sliced	skinned and pipped
1 large onion,	Salt and pepper
skinned and sliced	12 oz. shortcrust pastry
A few peppercorns	(12 oz. plain flour,
A bay leaf	etc.)
Thinly pared rind	Beaten egg to glaze
and juice of 1	Maldon salt, if
lemon	available

Oven temperature: fairly hot (400 °F, mark 6).

Remove the giblets from the chicken. In a saucepan large enough to take the chicken, put the water, carrots, onion, peppercorns, bay leaf and lemon rind. Place the chicken in the pan, bring to the boil, cover and simmer for about 1 hour. Strain the liquor and make up to 1½ pints with milk. Remove the flesh from the chicken and cut into strips. Melt the butter, add the flour, blend together and cook for 2–3 minutes. Gradually add the liquor a little at a time, stirring; bring to the boil and cook for a few minutes. Add the lemon juice, chicken flesh and grapes, and adjust the seasoning. Turn the mixture into a 3-pint ovenproof dish and cool it before covering with a lid of pastry. Trim, knock up and flute the edge, brush with beaten egg, decorate with pastry leaves and sprinkle with Maldon salt. Bake for about 40 minutes. Serve hot. (Serves 8.)

Double-crust Cheese and Tomato Patties

8 oz. shortcrust pastry (8 oz. flour, etc.)	3 oz. soft cream cheese
	Salt and pepper
4 oz. streaky bacon rashers, crisply fried	6 small tomatoes, skinned and sliced
	Worcestershire sauce
6 oz. Lancashire cheese	Beaten egg

Oven temperature : fairly hot (400 °F, mark 6).

Line 6 4½-inch shallow patty pans with pastry, reserving enough to make 6 lids. Mix the snipped bacon, crumbled Lancashire cheese, soft cheese and plenty of seasoning. Put 1 sliced tomato in each pastry-lined case, sprinkle with Worcestershire sauce and top with cheese mixture. Lid, glaze with egg and bake for about 25 minutes.

Pork and Egg Pies

1 oz. butter	2 level tsps. dried tarragon
1 medium-sized onion, chopped	
	Salt and freshly ground pepper
4 oz. streaky bacon, rinded and chopped	1½ lb. shortcrust pastry (1½ lb. flour ,etc.)
1 lb. lean pork, minced	17 small eggs

Oven temperature : hot (425 °F, mark 7).

Melt the butter in a frying-pan and sauté the onion and bacon for 5 minutes. Add the pork and continue cooking for a further 10 minutes. Add the tarragon and season well with salt and pepper; cool. Thinly roll about half the pastry and use to line 16 individual Yorkshire pudding tins. Divide the meat between these tins, hollow the centre and carefully break an egg into each. Roll out the remaining pastry and cut 16 4-inch plain rounds for lids. Damp the edges, press on to the pies, knock up and crimp the edges. Beat the remaining egg and brush over the pastry. Prick the lids and bake for 25–30 minutes, until golden-brown. Serve warm. (Makes 16.)

Cheese and Onion Pies

(See colour picture facing p. 121)

1½ lb. onions, skinned	A pinch of salt
	12 oz. mature Cheddar cheese, grated
3 oz. margarine	
3 oz. lard	Freshly ground pepper
12 oz. plain flour	Beaten egg to glaze

Oven temperature : fairly hot (400 °F, mark 6).

Halve or quarter the onions if large. Cook in boiling salted water until just tender but not mushy; drain well. Roughly chop the onions and leave to cool while making the pastry. In a bowl rub the fats into the flour and salt to resemble fine breadcrumbs, mix with cold water to give a firm but manageable dough. Form into one piece with the finger-tips and knead lightly on a floured board. Roll out and use to line 8 4½-inch shallow patty pans, leaving enough pastry to prepare lattice strips. Damp the edges of the pastry. Mix together the onions and cheese, season with pepper and divide between the patties. Cover with pastry strips, 6 on each, to form a lattice. Brush with beaten egg and bake in the centre of the oven for about 30 minutes. Serve warm. (Makes 8.)

Garlic Sausage Rolls

(See colour picture facing p. 121)

An 11-oz. pkt. of frozen puff pastry, de-frosted	½ lb. pork sausage-meat
	1 onion, skinned
	Beaten egg to glaze
½ lb. pork boiling ring	

Oven temperature : fairly hot (400 °F, mark 6).

Roll out the pastry into a rectangle about 19 inches by 12 inches. Cut in halves lengthwise. Remove the skin from the boiling ring and mince, together with the sausage-meat and onion. Blend well. Divide the meat mixture into two. Form each piece into a long sausage shape the length of the pastry (19 inches). Brush the egg on the long edge of each piece of pastry. Place a 'sausage' slightly to one side of the centre, fold the pastry over and press the edges together. Knock up the edges with a knife and brush with beaten egg. Cut the long sausage rolls at an angle into pieces about $1\frac{1}{2}$ inches long. Score the top of each roll twice. Place on baking sheets and bake for about 20 minutes, until golden. (Makes about 20.)

Brisling Fried Pastries

(See colour picture facing p. 121)

An 11-oz. pkt. of frozen puff pastry, defrosted	Mango chutney
	2 eggs, beaten
2 $3\frac{3}{4}$-oz. cans of smoked brisling	5 oz. flaked almonds
	Oil for frying

Roll the pastry out into a rectangle 19 inches by 12 inches. Cut it into halves lengthwise. Drain the brisling and lay in pairs side by side down the centre of each strip of pastry. Dot with a little chutney. Brush one long edge of each piece of pastry with egg, fold over and press the edges well together. Cut into pieces about $1\frac{1}{2}$ inches long. Brush each roll with beaten egg, then toss in flaked almonds. Heat oil to 375 °F and fry the rolls for about 3 minutes, until crisp and golden-brown. Drain on absorbent kitchen paper and serve at once. (Makes about 2 dozen.)

Note: These pastries are at their best served straight from the pan, but if this is not convenient, they can be kept warm in a hot oven.

Winter Salad

(See colour picture facing p. 49)

2 lb. white cabbage, finely shredded	1 celery heart, finely sliced
4 carrots, sliced wafer-thin	2 oz. flaked almonds
	$\frac{1}{4}$ pint soured cream
1 onion, skinned and finely chopped	$\frac{1}{4}$ pint mayonnaise
	1 tbsp. lemon juice
4 oz. seedless raisins	Salt and pepper

Combine all the salad ingredients; mix the cream, mayonnaise and lemon juice and season well, then toss the salad in this dressing.

Puff-Top Mince Pies

$\frac{1}{2}$ lb. shortcrust pastry (8 oz. flour, etc.)	$\frac{3}{4}$ lb. ready-made puff pastry
	1 egg, beaten
$\frac{3}{4}$ lb. mincemeat	Icing sugar

Oven temperature: very hot (450 °F, mark 8).

Roll out the shortcrust pastry thinly and stamp out 20 $3\frac{3}{4}$-inch plain rounds. Use to line deep patty tins. Put a good teaspoonful of mincemeat into each. Thinly roll the puff pastry and cut out 20 3-inch fluted rounds. Damp the shortcrust pastry edges and top each with a puff pastry lid. Press the edges firmly together and glaze with egg. Make a slit in each lid and bake the pies for 15–20 minutes, until well risen and golden-brown. Serve warm, dusted with icing sugar. (Makes 20.)

Note. These pies can be made a day ahead and re-heated in a warm oven (325 °F, mark 3) for 10 minutes.

Sugar-dusted Mince Pies

(See colour picture facing p. 121)

12 oz. shortcrust pastry	$\frac{3}{4}$ lb. mincemeat
	Icing sugar

Oven temperature: fairly hot (400 °F, mark 6).

Roll out the pastry to about $\frac{1}{8}$ inch thickness. Stamp out 20–22 3-inch fluted rounds and 20–22 $2\frac{1}{4}$-inch fluted rounds. Line $2\frac{1}{2}$-inch patty pans with the large rounds. Fill with mincemeat, but not right to the top. Damp the edges of the small rounds and place in position; snip the top with scissors. Bake in the oven, at the centre or above, for about 20 minutes, until pale brown. Serve warm, half-dusted with sifted icing sugar. To do this, lines the pies up in rows and cover half of each pie with a strip of paper. Dredge with icing sugar through a sieve. (Makes 20–22.)

Note: These pies can be made a day ahead and re-heated in a warm oven (325 °F, mark 3) for 10 minutes.

Meringue-topped Mince Pies

(See colour picture facing p. 121)

$\frac{1}{2}$ lb. shortcrust pastry	1 egg white
	2 oz. caster sugar
8–12 oz. mincemeat	

Oven temperature: hot (425 °F, mark 7).

Roll the pastry out to $\frac{1}{8}$ inch in thickness and cut into plain rounds large enough to line 12-

deep fluted brioche tins. Line the tins with pastry, prick the pastry well and place the tins on baking sheets. Bake 'blind' in the usual way for 20 minutes. Remove the pans from the oven, fill with mincemeat and top with whirls of meringue made in the ordinary way with the egg white and sugar. Return to the oven and bake for 15 minutes, until the meringue is lightly coloured. (Makes 12.)

Christmas Eve Mull

Thinly pared peel of 1 lemon, 1 orange	1 level tsp. grated nutmeg
4 level tbsps. Demerara sugar	¼ pint water
	2 bottles of red wine
½ level tsp. ground cinnamon	6 tbsps. rum or cherry brandy (optional)

Simmer the peel, sugar and spices in the water to extract the full flavour. Add the wine and spirit (if used) and heat gently until hot but not boiling, then strain into a heat-resistant punch bowl or pitcher. (This makes about 3 pints.)

For a fruit float to add to the mull, bake one or more oranges, each stuck with a dozen cloves, in a moderate oven (350 °F, mark 4) for about 30 minutes. Added to the punch bowl they not only look good but smell delicious.
Note. The rum or cherry brandy will 'spike' the mull and round out the flavour. If you like, whiskey, ordinary brandy, or indeed any full flavoured liqueur, can be used to add a little something to a mull.

DIP AND SPREAD PARTIES

This kind of party is ideal for warm summer evenings, when the food needs to be refreshing and varied, but *you* don't want to exhaust yourself with long, steamy cooking sessions. If you like playing different food flavours and textures off against each other, you can get a lot of pleasure out of the planning. The recipes below will keep a party of about 15 going for the evening. With larger parties, as well as multiplying up on quantities, you will have a splendid opportunity for a bit of daring experimental work; it doesn't matter if one or two of your mixtures don't quite come off.

As a basis for a good, varied table, you should serve one hot dip – like the lemon barbecue one – for hot cocktail sausages or meatballs. Then three or four of the cool, creamy dips, for dunking things like whole radishes, cauliflowers, carrot sticks, celery, spring onions – plus the plain tastes of pretzels, crisps and crackers. There's no reason why you shouldn't buy delicatessen-made leberwurst and truffle-pâtés, but have a rougher-textured home-made meat pâté as contrast, and to accompany these and the taramasalata, offer plenty of coarse brown loaves, pumpernickel, oatcakes, and assorted plain crispbreads.

If you want to serve a dessert, wait till later on, then bring in baked apples fresh from the oven – they'll look delectably good served with perhaps a topping of clotted cream or well-chilled whisky marmalade cream. For this whip double cream till firm, then fold in either bought whisky marmalade or your favourite thick marmalade plus 1 tbsp. whisky.

The Drink

There's little point in spoiling your guests with special wines at this informal party – they'll be more interested in quenching a thirst than in sipping and savouring. So make your choice from among the less expensive brands, like those from Peter Dominic, Waitrose or Nicolas.

Taramasalata

(*See colour picture facing p. 48*)

A thin slice of white bread	1 clove of garlic, skinned
An 8 oz. can of pressed cod's roe	Juice of ½ lemon
	1 tsp. cooking oil
1 small boiled potato	Salt and pepper
A few sprigs of parsley	Olives for garnish

Using an electric blender, make breadcrumbs from the slice of bread. Add the cod's roe to the breadcrumbs in the goblet, switch to 'high' and blend until smooth. Add the potato, parsley and garlic, blend for a few seconds. Add the lemon juice, oil and seasoning and blend until smooth. Turn into a shallow dish, spread evenly, fork into lines, chill and garnish.

Hunter's Pâté

1 lb. fat streaky rashers, rinded	½ lb. garlic sausage
1 lb. rabbit or hare flesh	4 oz. onions, skinned
1 lb. belly of pork, trimmed	3 tbsps. sherry
	2 tbsps. chopped parsley
½ lb. pigs' liver	2 level tbsps. dried sage
½ lb. pork sausage-meat	Salt and freshly ground pepper

Oven temperature : warm (325 °F, mark 3).

Grill or fry the bacon rashers until beginning to colour. Cut the rabbit or hare into small pieces. Put the pork, liver, sausage-meat, garlic sausage and onion through the mincer. Mix in the rabbit pieces, sherry, parsley and sage, and season well with salt and pepper. Take a loaf tin measuring (at top) about 9½ by 5½ inches by 3¼ inches deep, and line it with the bacon. Turn the pâté mixture into the prepared tin and fold the bacon edges over the mixture. Cover with kitchen foil, place in a second tin containing ½ inch water and cook for about 3 hours; cool in tin. Unmould and serve in thick slices.

Cool, Creamy Dips

SHRIMP AND YOGHURT: Drain a 3½-oz. can of shrimps and roughly chop them. Fold into the contents of a 5-fl. oz. carton of natural yoghurt. Season to taste with a little sherry and freshly milled black pepper.

MYCELLA: Gradually blend 8 oz. Mycella cheese with 8 tbsps. milk and beat to a creamy consistency. Season with freshly milled black pepper. Serve in a shallow glass dish, garnished with tomato wedges and a few sprigs of chives.

LEEK AND CHEESE: Blend together 8 oz. cottage cheese, the contents of a 5-oz. carton of soured cream and 1 pkt. of leek soup mix. Fold in 2 tbsps. chopped parsley and 2 tbsps. lemon juice. Turn into a serving dish and leave to chill for up to 1 hour.

WENSLEYDALE AND WALNUT: With a fork work 8 oz. Wensleydale cheese until creamy, adding a little at a time, about 12 tbsps. top-of-the-milk. Beat in a little grated onion, tomato paste and salt and pepper to taste. Finally, fold in 16 walnut halves, finely chopped.

Hot Lemon Barbecue Dip

4 oz. butter	Freshly ground pepper
1 clove of garlic, skinned and crushed	½ level tsp. dried thyme
	¼ tsp. Tabasco sauce
	Grated rind of 1 lemon
4 level tsps. flour	4–6 tbsps. lemon juice
2 level tbsps. sugar	¼ pint chicken stock
¼ level tsp. salt	

Heat the butter in a saucepan. Add the garlic, stir in the flour and cook for a few minutes. Stir in the remaining ingredients and simmer, covered, for 15 minutes. Serve hot as a dip for hot baby chipolatas.

SOUP AND SALAD PARTIES

Hot soup is amazingly filling and can make any snack seem like a meal. Follow it with a table full of really interesting salads – which means lots of contrasting tastes and some original thinking about dressings – and you've got the menu for a party of any age-group, at any time of the year. The recipes below add up to enough for a dozen people, and there's variety enough to appease their individual likes and dislikes.

We've chosen ingredients that will be available in any season, but of course you can and should include any summer or winter salad favourites of your own.

Appraise carefully, and make the most of any of the ready-prepared foods that your store-cupboard or local delicatessen can offer – this will leave you more time and energy for conjuring a super spread of cold dishes out of your imagination. The only vital extras you need are French bread, warm, fragrant and crisp from the oven, a large, fresh-as-you-can-get-it farmhouse loaf, and two kinds of butter – salted and unsalted and labelled accordingly – both of them cold and firm, but spreadable. And you'll be much appreciated if, later on, you appear with a board of varied cheeses and/ or bowls of fresh seasonal fruit – black and white grapes, apples, bananas, pears, oranges, and possibly some nuts into the bargain.

The Drink

For a buffet like this, where you're serving so many different, highly individual flavours, the drink selection must be proportionately wide. They don't all have to be alcoholic – you can run the whole range from fruit juices to dry bottled minerals, sparkling or still cider, beer or wine.

Cream of Mushroom Soup

12 oz. onions, finely chopped	3 pints chicken stock (made from 4 stock cubes)
6 oz. butter	Salt
1 lb. button mushrooms, chopped	Freshly milled black pepper
4 oz. plain flour	¼ level tsp. garlic salt
1 pint milk	Lemon juice

Sauté the onions in the butter for 10 minutes, till soft but not coloured. Add the mushrooms and continue cooking for 5 minutes. Stir in the flour and cook for 3 minutes, then slowly add the stock, stirring all the time. Bring to the boil and simmer for 20 minutes. Add the milk and seasonings, including lemon juice to taste, and simmer for a further 10 minutes. Serve piping hot. (Serves 10.)

Pineapple and Pepper Salad

(See colour picture facing p. 24)

A 28-oz. can of pineapple pieces	¼ of a cucumber, diced
1 green pepper, blanched, seeded and finely sliced	2 oz. sultanas
	1 lettuce, chopped
	4 tbsps. French dressing

Drain the pineapple, reserving the juice. **Mix** the pineapple pieces with the pepper, cucumber, sultanas and lettuce. Combine the French dressing and 2 tbsps. pineapple juice, pour over the salad and toss well.

Danish Sherry Herrings

(prepared 2 days ahead)

(See colour picture facing p. 24)

1½ lb. salted herrings	A few allspice, crushed
6 tbsps. sherry	2–3 small onions, skinned and thinly sliced
2 tbsps. water	
2–3 tbsps. wine vinegar	Fresh dill or dill seeds
2 oz. brown sugar	

Clean the herrings and soak in plenty of cold water for about 12 hours; skin, wash and drain the fillets. Mix together the sherry, water, vinegar, sugar and allspice, pour over the herrings and leave for 24 hours, turning them occasionally. Drain the fillets and cut diagonally into small pieces. Arrange in a dish, pour a little sherry liquor over and garnish with onions and dill.

Other Salads

(See colour picture facing p. 24)

BEETROOT AND SARDINE: Dice 1 lb. cooked beetroot and arrange on a flat platter. Blend together 2 5-fl. oz. cartons of natural yoghurt, some snipped chives and black pepper to taste. Spoon this over the beetroot. Drain the oil from 2 large cans of sardines. Arrange the sardines on top of the dish and garnish with watercress sprigs.

PRAWN AND RICE: Cook, drain and cool 8 oz. long-grain rice. Slice and lightly fry 4 oz. mushrooms. Mix together with 1 medium-sized onion, skinned and chopped, 1 green pepper, blanched, seeded and chopped, and 8 oz. frozen prawns, thawed. Toss in ½ pint French dressing. Serve garnished with parsley.

TOMATO AND ONION: Skin and finely slice 1 lb. tomatoes and chill. Put 8 oz. onions, skinned and finely sliced, into a bowl and cover with salt; leave covered for at least ½ hour and rinse with cold water, then drain. On a flat platter arrange the tomatoes, onion and (optionally) $\frac{1}{4}$ of a cucumber, finely sliced. Spoon a little French dressing over, and chill if desired.

SALAMI AND DILL PICKLE: Arrange thinly sliced salami in a serving dish and garnish with thick slices of dill pickle.

GARLIC EGGS: Hard-boil 6 eggs and cool. Blend $\frac{1}{4}$ pint mayonnaise with 1 large clove of garlic, skinned and crushed, and 4 tbsps. milk, until of a coating consistency. Halve the eggs, place cut side down on a platter and coat with the mayonnaise. Garnish with tomato quarters and sprinkle with chopped parsley.

PORK AND POTATO: Dice the contents of a 12-oz. can of pork luncheon meat and mix with 1 lb. potatoes, cooked and diced. Combine 4 tbsps. French dressing with the grated rind of 1 lemon, 12 sliced stuffed olives and chopped chives to taste. Mix well with the pork–potato mixture and serve on a flat platter.

TUNA AND BEAN: Flake the contents of 2 7-oz. cans of tuna into a bowl, with 1 large onion, skinned and sliced, and 2 8-oz. cans of red kidney beans, drained. Toss in $\frac{1}{4}$–$\frac{1}{2}$ pint French dressing until well coated. Leave for $\frac{1}{2}$ hour. Spoon on to bed of roughly chopped lettuce, and garnish with raw onion rings.

HAM AND ASPARAGUS ROLLS: Divide drained asparagus spears from a large can between 8 slices ($\frac{1}{2}$ lb.) of ham. Roll up and arrange side by side on serving dish. Coat with mayonnaise and garnish with watercress.

AFTER-THEATRE PARTY

The Menu

Burgundy Beef with Rice
Winter Salad
French Bread Sticks and Butter

Raspberry Coffee Vacherin
Black-currant Velvet
Refrigerator Cheese Cake

The Drink

This is a budget-watching party, so match the inexpensive menu with some of the best and cheapest of the *vins ordinaires*, like Peter Dominic's Carafinos of red, white or rosé wine in litre bottles, $\frac{1}{2}$-gallon or gallon jars. Cider is equally good with the strong-flavoured beef – so try Merrydown's Vintage Apple, dry or medium sweet (but remember its potency).

Planning

Assuming that it's been a good play and you've all enjoyed it, there's no better way to round off the evening than by inviting everyone back for supper. And even if the play was a failure, good hot food and a few glasses of wine or cider-cup can repair the damage of disappointment quicker than anything – certainly quicker than an expensive supper 'out', where you can't shout across the table to out-critic the man five seats away. But of course, unless you're happy about the supper situation at home, the last person likely to enjoy any play, good or bad, is *you*. So get ahead with the cooking – a day or two in advance, if need be.

For the main dish of beef, choose the cheaper – and tastier – cuts; trim off the fat and marinade the lean meat overnight in wine and herbs. And follow the directions carefully, for the winning points of this dish are in the subtle details – like the meat cut in generous chunks, and not swamped in too much liquid, and the rice cooked in stock till all the grains are separate, fluffy and full of flavour. For the salad, choose white cabbage, celery, tomato, raw onion rings, shredded raw carrot, eating apples, beetroot and chopped nuts. They are so crisp that they will improve if you toss them in French dressing before you leave for the theatre. All of the sweet dishes can be made the day before, covered and chilled until needed. (Incidentally, this menu assumes that a theatre party is more of a cold-month event; if your party takes place on a warm evening, use any of the cold buffet menus in this book.)

Burgundy Beef with Rice

(See colour picture facing p. 144)

7 lb. topside of beef or chuck steak	2 bay leaves
A 1-lb. piece of lean streaky bacon	2 cloves of garlic, skinned and crushed
4 oz. lard	Salt and freshly ground pepper
6 level tbsps. flour	24 shallots or small onions
1 pint Burgundy	
¾ pint beef stock, made with a cube	¾ lb. button mushrooms
1 level tsp. dried mixed herbs	1½ lb. uncooked long-grain rice

Oven temperature: warm (325 °F, mark 3).

Trim the beef and cut into 1½-inch squares. Dice the bacon. Melt 2 oz. of lard in a large frying-pan (or in a 6-pint ovenproof casserole, which can be used throughout). Brown the beef evenly, a little at a time, re-heating the fat each time. Keeping the browned meat on one side, drain off nearly all the fat. Add the bacon, sprinkle the flour over and brown gently, stirring occasionally. Transfer to the casserole with the beef. Stir the wine and stock into the drippings. When these are loosened, add the herbs, bay leaves, garlic and seasonings. Pour into the casserole, cover and cook in the oven for 1½–2 hours. Rather more than half-way through, lightly brown the shallots and mushrooms in 2 oz. lard; drain and add to the casserole. Continue to cook for a further ¾ hour. Meanwhile, cook the rice in boiling salted water. To serve, remove the bay leaves and border the meat with rice. (Serves 12.)

Note. To re-heat, put the Burgundy Beef in a large casserole, set the oven to moderate (350°F, mark 4) and allow 1¼ hours.

Raspberry Coffee Vacherin

(See colour picture facing p. 200)

3 large egg whites	1–2 tbsps. coffee liqueur (optional)
6 oz. caster sugar	
1 level tbsp. instant coffee	½ lb. raspberries
½ pint double cream	Curled or coarsely grated chocolate
¼ pint single cream	

Whisk the egg whites until really stiff. Add half

the caster sugar and whisk again, add the instant coffee and whisk until the mixture is really stiff and the coffee no longer gives a speckled effect. Fold in the rest of the sugar. Pipe this meringue into 24 shell shapes, using a large rose vegetable nozzle on non-stick (silicone-treated) paper.

Mark an 8-inch circle on a second piece of paper and spread the remainder of the meringue to make a disc. Dry these meringues in a cool oven – lowest setting – until crisp and firm (about 3 hours). Peel off the paper, cool the meringues and store in an airtight container. About ½–1 hour before serving, whip together the two creams and the liqueur, until the mixture is stiff enough to hold its shape. Use some of the cream to build a double row of meringue shells to form a basket. Spoon the remaining cream into the centre. Top with hulled raspberries and leave in a cold place. Just before serving, decorate with chocolate. (Serves 8–12.)

Black-currant Velvet

1 lb. black-currants	¼ pint coating custard
A large can of condensed milk	Whipped cream

Stalk the currants and cook until soft in the minimum of water, blend or sieve to obtain a purée, then cool. Fold in the condensed milk until evenly mixed. Fold in the custard. Divide between 4 individual glasses and chill. Decorate with a whirl of cream. Serve sponge fingers separately. (Serves 4.)

Refrigerator Cheese Cake

(See colour picture facing p. 200)

2 level tbsps. powdered gelatine	2 tbsps. lemon juice
6 oz. caster sugar	20 oz. plain cottage cheese, sieved
A pinch of salt	¼ pint double cream
2 eggs, separated	½ lb. strawberries, hulled
½ pint milk	
Grated rind of 1 lemon	
For the Crumb Topping	
4 oz. digestive biscuits	1 level tbsp. caster sugar
1½ oz. butter, melted	

In a saucepan blend together the gelatine, 5 oz. of the sugar and the salt. Beat together the egg yolks and milk and gradually stir into the saucepan. Bring just to the boil, stirring, and remove from the heat. Add the lemon rind and juice. Cool until beginning to set, then stir in the sieved cheese. Whisk the egg whites until stiff, add the remaining sugar and whisk again. Fold quickly into the cheese mixture. Lastly, fold in the whipped cream. Turn half the mixture into an 8½-inch base, spring-release cake tin, fitted with a fluted tubular base. Cover

with a layer of sliced strawberries and spoon over the remainder of the cheese-cake mixture. Crush the digestive biscuits and stir in the butter and sugar until evenly blended. Sprinkle the cheese-cake mixture with an even layer of crumb topping and chill until firm. Turn out carefully, crumb-side down, on to a serving plate. Decorate with berries. (Serves 10–12.) *Note.* Remove from the refrigerator for a short time before turning out. Carefully ease away the mould. If it is obstinate, warm the base by placing a hot cloth over the surface.

CURRY AND RICE PARTY

You have to be careful who you invite to this one – not everybody raves about curry; but if you have enough friends who do, then this is another fairly simple party to organize, and a great conversation-saver too, since you'll probably spend most of the meal swapping recipes. Cook the meat and poultry curries a day – or even two – in advance; covered over in the fridge, they'll have had a chance to mellow and mature by party time, and all you'll have to do is re-heat them. But you can't apply this method to curried prawns; they're quick and very little trouble to do, so cook them just before guests start arriving.

The three main dishes below plus cooked rice – allow 2 oz. long-grain rice per person – should more than fill 12 people. The sambals (side-dishes to the uninitiated) can be as many and varied as you like, and you'd be a spoil-sport not to include mango chutney – even though Indians never eat it – and poppadums as well. For dessert you'll need something light and refreshing, like a lemon, raspberry or pine-apple sorbet; you can buy these ready-made, but if you've time to make them yourself, they'll taste that much better. You could, of course, serve lychees.

The Drink

Practically anything long and cool – fruit juices, a light-strength lager, iced water, or amber-coloured iced tea with wafer-thin slices of lemon afloat in it.

Pakistan Chicken Curry

(*See colour picture facing p. 73*)

6 oz. desiccated coconut	3 level tsps. strong curry powder
1½ pints milk	3 level tsps. flour
2 3-lb. oven-ready chickens	3 level tsps. salt
Corn oil	4 level tbsps. ground almonds
2 oz. blended white vegetable fat	A 6½-oz. tube of concentrated tomato paste
1½ lb. onions, skinned and sliced	3 cartons of natural yoghurt
A little green ginger	

Oven temperature: warm (325 °F, mark 3).

Soak the coconut in the milk for ½ hour. Joint and skin the chickens. Heat just enough oil in a large saucepan to cover the base. (A flame-proof casserole can be used for preparing the curry from start to finish.) Fry the chicken until golden, and put aside. To the clean pan add the vegetable fat and sauté the onions until soft but not coloured. Stir in the chopped ginger, curry powder, flour, salt and almonds and simmer for 10 minutes. Add the tomato paste and mix well. Strain the liquid from the coconut into the pan and add the yoghurt; mix well. Add the chicken joints and turn the contents into a large casserole. Cover and cook in the oven for 2 hours. Lift the chicken from the sauce, and separate the meat from the bone; cut the meat into manageable pieces and return it to the sauce, stirring well. (Serves 8.)

West African Beef Curry

(See colour picture facing p. 73)

4 lb. chuck steak	2 level tbsps. desiccated
2 oz. flour	coconut
¼ level tsp. paprika	4 level tbsps. curry
pepper	powder
¼ level tsp. cayenne	2 level tbsps. curry paste
pepper	A clove of garlic,
¼ level tsp. chilli	skinned and crushed
powder	A few drops of Tabasco
Corn oil	sauce
1 lb. onions, chopped	2 pints stock

Trim the steak and cut into serving-size pieces. Toss in the flour seasoned with the paprika, cayenne and chilli powder – use just enough flour to coat the steak thoroughly. Heat 3 tbsps. oil in a large saucepan and fry the onions until evenly browned. Add the coconut, curry powder, curry paste, garlic, Tabasco and stock, and bring to the boil. In a large frying-pan, heat enough oil to just cover the base and fry the meat a little at a time, until sealed and brown. Add the drained meat to the curry sauce, cover and simmer until the meat is tender – about 2 hours. (Serves 8.)

Sambals

(See colour picture facing p. 73)

The curry accompaniments that add so much interest are items such as sliced hard-boiled egg; sliced cucumber in soured cream; shredded pineapple and sliced banana; thick lemon wedges; blanched red and green pepper rings; guavas, paw-paw, mango (all from cans); desiccated coconut; ground peanuts; raw onion rings marinaded in lemon juice, salt, sugar and pepper. Poppadums, the savoury, wafer-like biscuits, are simplest bought ready-made; fry in hot fat for 20–30 seconds, then drain and serve piled upon a large plate. They can be nibbled on the side or crumbled over the curry.

Curried Prawns

(See colour picture facing p. 73)

8 shallots or small	½ pint double cream
onions, skinned	1 tbsp. lemon juice
and finely chopped	Salt and pepper
4 oz. butter	1½ lb. frozen prawns,
2 level tbsps. curry	thawed
powder	Chopped parsley
½ pint chicken stock	

Fry the shallots in the butter until soft and beginning to colour, add the curry powder and cook for 5 minutes. Pour in the stock, bring to the boil and simmer for 15 minutes. Add the cream and lemon juice and adjust the seasoning. Bring to simmering point, 'bubble' for 5 minutes, add the prawns and heat through without boiling. Garnish with chopped parsley. (Serves 8.)

HOUSE-WARMING PARTY

Turning house into home takes more than just adding furniture, but there's nothing does it so quickly as the whiff of home-cooking, especially savoury casseroles, seeping out under the door of the kitchen. And there's no better way than this to greet the first group of friends over a new threshold. The three main dishes below make an ideal winter menu for such a party. Rice is as good a partner for them as anything – simple and quick to cook, too – with the added refresher of a crisp 'Ribbon' salad.

You can do nearly all the preparation of the main dishes on the day before the party, leaving just final touches and re-heating to the last minute. Allow 1½ lb. long-grain rice, cooked in plenty of boiling salted water, for each 12 servings. The hot-pots and salad together make an ample meal, but you could have a fruit flan to round it off.

The Drink

Each of the savoury dishes is rich and full in flavour, so you would do best to choose one of the no-nonsense red wines.

Spiced Beef and Coconut

3 lb. lean minced beef	Salt
½ lb. fresh white breadcrumbs	Freshly ground pepper
	2 eggs, beaten
½ lb. onions, chopped	2 oz. lard

For the Sauce and Garnish

4 oz. lard	4 oz. flour
2 lb. onions, sliced	4 pints stock, made from stock cubes
4 level tsps. curry powder	A 5-oz. can of pimientos drained and sliced
A dash of Tabasco sauce	1 oz. long-shred coconut, toasted
4 oz. ground almonds	

Oven temperature: moderate (350 °F, mark 4).

Mix together the beef, breadcrumbs, onions, salt, pepper and egg; form into 48 balls. Heat the lard in a frying-pan and fry the meat balls a few at a time, until golden-brown. Place in 2 shallow casseroles, if possible in a single layer. *To make the sauce:* Heat the lard in a saucepan and gently fry the onions until golden-brown. Stir in the curry powder, Tabasco sauce, ground almonds and flour. Slowly add the stock, stirring continuously to prevent lumping. Add the pimientos and bring to the boil. Simmer for a few minutes, then divide between the casseroles. Cover, and cook in the oven for 1½ hours. Garnish each casserole with a line of coconut. (Serves 12.)

Note. This dish can be made the day before the party; cool quickly and refrigerate. On the day, bring to the boil and simmer, covered, for at least 15 minutes.

Beef and Aubergine Moussaka

3 aubergines, sliced	1 lb. minced beef
4 tbsps. olive oil	Salt and pepper
4 medium-sized onions, chopped	¼ pint stock
	¼ pint puréed tomatoes
4 tomatoes, skinned and sliced	2 eggs, beaten
	¼ pint single cream

Oven temperature: moderate (350 °F, mark 4).

Fry the aubergines in some of the oil, and arrange in an ovenproof dish. Fry the onions in the rest of the oil until lightly browned. Fry the tomatoes in the same oil. Layer the meat and onion on top of the aubergine, season, and cover with the fried tomatoes. Pour in the stock and the puréed tomatoes; bake for about 30 minutes. Beat together the eggs and cream, season, and pour over the tomatoes. Return the moussaka to the oven for 15–20 minutes, until set. (Serves 4–6; for larger numbers, make 2 dishes.)

Chicken Marengo

3 2½-lb. oven-ready chickens	Salt
	1 lb. mushrooms, sliced
2 oz. lard	2 oz. butter

For the Sauce

3 oz. butter	2 fresh tomatoes, quartered
4 sticks of celery, chopped	A sprig of parsley
1 medium-sized carrot, chopped	A blade of mace
	A bay leaf
2 medium-sized onions, chopped	Salt, pepper
	3 oz. plain flour
2 oz. bacon, rinded and diced	A 5½-oz. can of concentrated tomato paste
1 oz. mushrooms, chopped	2 pints chicken stock
	2 tbsps. sherry

Oven temperature: fairly hot (375 °F, mark 5).

If the chickens are frozen, allow them to thaw thoroughly, then place in a deep roasting tin. Heat the lard and pour over the chickens. Season the skin with salt. Cook in the oven for 20 minutes per lb. Meanwhile make the sauce. Heat the butter in a saucepan. Add the celery, carrot, onions, bacon, mushrooms, tomatoes, parsley, mace, bay leaf, salt and pepper. Fry gently, stirring until dark golden-brown all over. Add the flour, stir well, then add the tomato paste. Slowly add the stock, stirring constantly to prevent lumps appearing. Add the sherry, bring to the boil, stirring, cover and simmer for 1 hour. When the chicken is cooked remove all the flesh and cut into 1-inch cubes; place in an 8-pint casserole. Sauté the mushrooms in the butter and add to the casserole. Strain the sauce into the casserole, discarding the vegetables. Cook in a moderate oven (350 °F, mark 4) for ½ hour. (Serves 12.)

Note. The chicken can be roasted and the sauce made the day before. Cook together for ¾ hour.

BOUNTIFUL BREAKFASTS OR BRUNCH

You may not be so dashing as to invite guests specially for breakfast, but if you have friends staying with you for a weekend or a longer spell, you might like to spoil them with a big, leisurely Sunday breakfast. In summer, there's a real holiday feel to eating out of doors.

Newly baked croissants or soft, floury rolls served just warm, with plenty of butter, add a continental touch, with honey, a variety of preserves and plenty of fresh coffee. If you choose chilled fruit juices for starters, look for the newer flavours. As alternative, what about lightly cooked apples, cinnamon flavoured; or honeydew melon rings with sugared raspberries or strawberries piled in the centre; or orange segments mixed with poached prunes and served in the orange shells?

When it's a more substantial English breakfast, eggs and fish are a classic choice. Scrambled eggs are splendid – served, perhaps with snippets of smoked salmon folded in, Succulent Arbroath smokies make a fine breakfast dish – so do plain grilled mackerel, especially when they're fresh from the sea. If you're planning to make croissants for the weekend, the dough is prepared a day or so in advance, but it wants an hour for final shaping and baking. So unless you're up with the dawn, reckon on a late breakfast or, even better, a brunch.

Here are three breakfast specials – plus our yeast-dough recipe for light, golden croissants.

Muesli with Yoghurt

6 tbsps. porridge oats	1 tbsp. condensed milk
3 tbsps. wheat germ (optional)	(or top of the milk or single cream)
2 tbsps. raisins, chopped	¼ pint milk
Prunes or chopped dried apricots	1 eating apple, washed but not peeled
Juice and grated rind of 1 lemon	Yoghurt or soured cream
	Demerara sugar

Mix together the oats, wheat germ, fruit, lemon juice and rind, condensed milk and fresh milk. Grate in the apple, mix well and leave to soak overnight. Serve in 4 individual dishes, garnished with yoghurt or soured cream and with Demerara sugar. In season, include thickly sliced strawberries. (Serves 4.)

Spicy Marmalade Bread

Cut a plump French loaf into 1–1½-inch diagonal slices. Spread with softened butter, then add a generous helping of marmalade. Sprinkle powdered cinnamon over the top. Place the slices, marmalade side up, on an ungreased baking sheet. Heat in a hot oven (400 °F, mark 6), for about 8 minutes.

Framed Eggs

With a plain round cutter, or the rim of a glass, remove the centre from a thick slice of bread from a large loaf. Brown the frame each side in hot fat. Turn it over, break an egg into the centre and fry till set. It's delicious. (Serves 1.)

Croissants

(See colour picture facing p. 120)

1 lb. strong plain bread flour	1 oz. fresh baker's yeast
	½ pint water less 4 tbsps.
2 level tsps. salt	1 egg, beaten
1 oz. lard	4–6 oz. margarine
For the Egg Glaze	
1 egg, beaten	½ level tsp. caster sugar
A little water	

In a bowl mix together the flour and salt and rub in the lard. In a small basin blend together the yeast and water. Stir into the flour together with the egg. Mix to a firm dough, turn on to a lightly floured surface and knead until the dough is smooth – 10–15 minutes. Roll the dough into a strip 20 inches by 6 inches. Divide the margarine into three. Place little flakes of margarine over the top two-thirds of dough, as for flaky pastry. Fold in three by bringing up the plain part, then folding the top part over. Turn the dough so that the fold is on the right. Seal the edges by pressing with the rolling pin.

Roll out again as above, keeping the corners square. Repeat with the other two portions of margarine as above.

Place the dough in an oiled plastic bag and allow to relax in the refrigerator for 30 minutes. Roll out as before, but without any fat. Repeat the folding and rolling three times. At this stage place the dough in an oiled plastic bag and leave overnight, or for up to 3 days.

Making-up and Baking

Oven temperature: hot (425 °F, mark 7).

Remove from the refrigerator and roll into a rectangle 21 inches by 12 inches. Cover with an oiled bag and leave for 10 minutes. Trim the edges and divide in halves lengthwise. Cut each strip into 6 triangles, 6 inches high with a 6-inch base. Mix the ingredients for the egg glaze and brush each triangle with it, then roll up loosely from the base towards the point and shape into crescents. Place on ungreased baking sheets, well apart. Brush again with egg. Place inside the oiled bag and leave at room temperature for about 30 minutes, until light and puffy. Brush again with egg and bake in the centre of the oven for about 20 minutes. Serve warm. (Makes 12.)

BRUNCH FOR EIGHT

A variation on the theme is the Brunch Party (see colour picture on back cover). This is for easy, informal people who rise late on Sundays, take the day as it comes. The food should be substantial enough to take one through to the evening meal – except perhaps for an afternoon cup of tea. Brunch starts about 11.30 a.m., and is often centred on the kitchen. If the kitchen itself is too tiny, then this is the perfect occasion to bring out the plug-in frying-pan, hot-plate and the like, and do the cooking where you want the food – in the breakfast room, living/dining-room, on the terrace or balcony.

The Food

For first course you might offer a choice of Muesli, flavoured yoghurts, tomato and other fruit juices, and perhaps a fruity dish like a prune and orange compote; the main course could be omelettes with a selection of sautéed mushrooms, shrimps, buttered whole tomatoes, bacon rashers and so on keeping warm on the hot-plate ready to add or include, and perhaps small bowls of grated cheese and chopped fresh mixed herbs, and some watercress. Floury rolls and butter, coffee (served in large cups) and cream are obvious necessities. Sheer greed inspires the addition of Danish pastries!

Catering and Preparation

Muesli: See the recipe overleaf and double up.

Other Starters: Buy in a selection and keep them in the fridge. The compote is made by combining the contents of a chilled can of prunes with 2–3 peeled, sliced and seeded oranges.

Omelettes and Flavourings, etc. Allow 1½ doz. fresh eggs, 2 lb. small firm tomatoes, 1 lb. streaky (back) bacon, 1 lb. mushrooms, 1 lb. cheese, 4 oz. prepared shrimps, herbs as available. If you wish to provide an alternative for those who don't like eggs, either have a little more bacon, or get some kipper fillets.

And buy 18 soft or crisp rolls to heat in the oven, 1–1½ lb. butter, coffee of your favourite blend, ½ pint cream (order Saturday for Sunday delivery), 1 doz. Danish pastries.

Sunday morning tasks: Skin tomatoes, wash, stalk and slice the mushrooms, grate the cheese and rind the bacon. Start to cook the mushrooms and tomatoes gently in butter in separate pans. Cook the bacon and keep it warm.

For each two-some omelette, whisk 4 whole eggs, with 2 tbsps. water and some seasoning. Melt 2 oz. butter in an 8-inch pan (have a couple on the go); when it is bubbly but not too brown, pour in the egg mixture and stir with a fork until nearly set. Then it is golden underneath, fill with grated cheese and shrimps or mushrooms, and fold in halves. For a *fines herbes* version, add snipped herbs to the mixture before cooking.

5
Wine and Pâté; Wine and Cheese

WINE AND PÂTÉ PARTY

This is one of the best and most versatile of informal parties, for the wine and pâté menu can cover a multitude of occasions, from pre-theatre or cocktail to casual lunch or evening buffet. And when it happens, it can be as much of a pleasant surprise to you as to your guests: for pâtés and terrines are actually *better* made a few days – or even a week – in advance. Once they're made, cover them over and leave them to mature in the fridge. Then, when *the* evening arrives, all you've got to do is set out the accompanying breads, butter, salads and wine, whisk the pâtés out of the fridge, and there's your party ready made.

The pâté recipes below will give a dozen or more guests some real variety of textures and flavours to get their tongues around. The chicken-liver pâté – creamy, soft and subtle – should be spooned out on to the individual plates, and so should the fish-fanciers' kipper pâté. The terrine of duck has a much coarser texture and is better served in slices from its dish; and you should also serve the stiff farm-house pâté in slices, but turn this one out of its mould first.

Pâtés don't really demand any special kinds of salad, so you've a free hand to choose whatever you like, or whatever is easiest to get hold of. But again, variety of flavours is the most important factor; chicory, celery, watercress, olives, radishes, lettuce hearts, tomatoes, carrot sticks and chopped raw white cabbage would all be good – and are best kept labour-saving and simple by being dished up individually. If you spend hours arranging them elaborately in huge bowls, your visitors will only have a harder time picking and choosing the morsels they like most.

An oven-full of warm French bread is still the most satisfying starchy base to put pâté on, but you may be harbouring dieters in your midst, so leave some crispbreads lying around, and, if possible, some carefully-crustless toast for the connoisseurs. Apart from these, the only other props you'll need are lots of fresh, firm butter, a pile of plates, a stack of knives, paper napkins, pepper and salt – in mills if possible – and dressings for the salads; and, as this is much too informal a party to bother about concocted sweets, add the most enormous bowl of fresh, ripe fruit. Leave all these casually and easily to hand on the buffet table.

The Drink

You'll be choosing your wines to match and mate with the pâtés you've made. A crisp, full-bodies white wine will suit the milder chicken-liver and fish pâtés best – like Beaujolais blanc or Mâcon blanc; or try one of the fruity and fragrant Traminer wines of Alsace. But you will also need a good solid red wine – especially with the farmhouse pâté; two possible choices are the fruity Château de Julienas 1964, or Lebègue's 1964 Fleurie.

Chicken Liver Pâté

4 oz. butter	A pinch of dried thyme
1 small onion, skinned and chopped	2 lb. chicken livers
	Salt
	Freshly ground pepper
4 bay leaves	

Melt the butter in a pan and add the onion, bay leaves and thyme. Cook gently for 2–3 minutes. Prepare the chicken livers, cut each into 2–3 pieces, add to the pan and simmer gently for 5–7 minutes, until the liver is cooked. Remove the bay leaves. Mince the liver twice (or put in an electric blender till smooth). Season well and place in one large serving dish or several small ones; fork up the top. Chill well before serving. (Serves 4–6.)

Terrine of Duck

1¾ lb. frozen duck breast portions, defrosted	1 clove of garlic, skinned and crushed
Salt	Freshly ground black pepper
1 lb. belly of pork	1 small orange, washed and sliced thinly
1 lb. pie veal	Aspic jelly to glaze
¼ lb. pork back fat	
¼ pint dry white wine	

Oven temperature: warm (325 °F, mark 3).

Place the duck portions in a roasting tin, sprinkle with 2 level tsps. salt and cook in the centre of the oven for 40 minutes. Meanwhile, trim the surplus fat from the belly of pork and trim the pie veal into neat pieces. Cut 4–6 thin strips from the pork fat and reserve for a garnish. Put the belly of pork, the veal and the rest of the pork fat through the mincer twice. Add the wine, garlic, salt and pepper and mix thoroughly. Take the duck from the oven, remove the skin, cut the flesh from the bones and dice it. Add 1 tbsp. of the cooking juice to the minced ingredients.

Put half this mixture in a 2- or 2½-pint terrine or casserole, add the duck meat and cover with the rest of the minced ingredients. Arrange the strips of pork fat in a lattice on top and cover the dish with a foil cap, pressed well down over the edges of the terrine. Stand the terrine in 1 inch of water in a roasting tin and cook in centre of oven for 1½–2 hours.

Remove the terrine from the oven, take off the foil and leave for 15 minutes. Then cover the meat with folded foil, place some weights on top and chill thoroughly. When chilled, arrange the orange slices in a pattern on top, glaze with nearly-set aspic and chill again before serving from the cooking dish. (Serves 6.)

Farmhouse Pâté

1 lb. belly pork	2 level tsps. salt
1 lb. lean veal	A pinch of powdered mace
½ lb. pig's liver	
8 oz. streaky rashers, rinded	4 tbsps. dry white wine
	2 tbsps. brandy
Freshly ground black pepper	1 clove of garlic, skinned and crushed

Oven temperature: warm (325 °F, mark 3).

Finely mince the pork, veal and liver two or three times. Cut 2 oz. of the bacon into small dice. To the minced meat add the diced bacon, pepper, salt, mace, wine, brandy and garlic. Blend together thoroughly and leave to stand for 2 hours. Stir again. Line a 2-lb. loaf tin with the remaining bacon. Turn the pâté into the tin, stand this in 1 inch of water in a roasting tin and cook (uncovered) in the centre of the oven for 1¼–1½ hours, until the contents show signs of shrinking. Some fat will have separated out, so work it back into the pâté with a fork. Leave to cool. When almost cold, cover with greaseproof paper, press with a weight and leave till completely cold. Store in the refrigerator until required. Turn out before serving. (Serves 8.)

This is a full-flavoured pâté, fairly rough-textured; for a smoother texture, put the mixture in an electric blender after cooking, then press as above.

Kipper Pâté

2 8-oz. pkts. of kipper fillets	1 onion, skinned and finely chopped
2 oz. butter	Black pepper

Boil the kippers in the bag as directed on the packet. Melt the butter and fry the onion gently until really soft but not brown. Flake the kipper flesh and mix it with the onion. Add freshly ground pepper to taste. Remove the mixture from the heat and mash until really smooth, then turn it into an earthenware dish suitable for the table. Cover well and keep in the fridge until you wish to serve it. (Serves 6.)

Watercress is a pleasant garnish and fresh accompaniment to this pâté.

WINE AND CHEESE FOR 50

The typical pub or 'farmhouse' lunch of crusty bread, cheese and onions will transform very easily into an informal but still highly sophisticated evening party. It's a particularly good party to throw if you've large numbers to feed, as most of the ingredients come straight from shop, can or greengrocer, and are then just strung together. But somehow food is appreciated that much more when it's obvious that some time and trouble have gone into it, so make the effort to blend some of the cheeses into dips, and to bake your own farmhouse loaves or the splendid Crown Loaf we give here. As well as these – or instead, if you really can't face baking – have a good selection of breads, crispbreads and biscuits. Allow about 6 biscuits or crispbreads and the equivalent of 3 hunks of French bread per person. Breads to choose from could be French, granary, rye, pumpernickel, Dorset knobs and Scotch baps; biscuits could be oatcakes, water biscuits, digestive, crackers and wheat-meal. In standard half-pound packs you get about 16 digestive biscuits, 32 crispbreads and 24 water biscuits. And from 1 lb. of butter you get about 40 pats. P.S. It would be very good diplomacy to label each cheese with its name, character and country of origin; it's a mystery why people should feel they're expected to be omniscient, but most of us are strangely embarrassed by not knowing what we're eating.
P.P.S. You don't *have* to invite 50 people to make this party work – but as it's an informal one, it won't really do for less than a dozen; it would also mean buying small and fiddly quantities of everything to get enough variety.

The Food

Allow about 4 oz. of cheese for each guest, excluding the dips, and give them at least eight varieties of cheese to choose from, including soft, semi-hard and veined types. The flavour of a lot of the cheeses will 'come alive' if you match them up with juicy fruits, vegetables, nuts or fishy things, like the examples mentioned in the list below. Radishes, gherkins or onions go well with tangy Double Gloucester,

and smoked Austrian or German Limburger cheese is surprisingly good with blackcurrant conserve. Some of the cheese can be pre-cut into cubes (you'll get about 3 dozen little pieces from a 1-lb. slab), set out with plenty of cocktail sticks alongside, but the Swiss cheeses-with-holes and also Danish Havarti and Samsoe, are better if cut in wafer-thin slices with a special cheese slice. You'll probably have to avoid the crumbly, loose-textured varieties of cheese, or use them in made-up form.

The dips should be creamy and light in consistency; if they're too stiff or too soft, dunking can become a complicated and sometimes embarrassing affair.

The Drink

For a small party it would be splendid – and quite possible – to find a regional wine to match each cheese, but for a larger party, like this one, the complications would be enormous. So content yourself with two kinds each of white and red wine. The white pair could be a Bordeaux, like Mouton Cadet Blanc, and Liebfraumilch–Kellergeist; the red could include Portuguese Sao Pedro Dao Tinto, Italian Valpolicella or Bardolino. Serve the white wines well chilled to go with the creamy cheeses, the reds for the English section and the continental 'blues' – but leave people free to make their own choice.

Mix-and-Match

Double Gloucester speared with pineapple and maraschino cherries; *Caerphilly* speared with melon and black grapes or with white grapes alone; *Port Salut* speared with anchovy fillet; *Samsoe* or *Havarti* with thick banana slices and halved walnuts; *Danish Blue* speared with strips of canned pimiento or grapes. *Gorgonzola* speared with black grapes; *Marc de Raisin* speared with apple; *Emmenthal* with William pears; *Edam* speared with melon slices; *Pipo Cream* with walnuts and celery; *Blue Cheese Dip* with carrot sticks.

93

Bacon Dip

1 carton (5 fl. oz.)
single cream
3 pkts of cream
Demi-sel cheese
½ level tsp. made
mustard

4 oz. rinded bacon, fried
crisply and crumbled
small
Freshly ground black
pepper

Slowly beat the cream into the cheese and mix
in the mustard, bacon and pepper to taste.

Blue Cheese Dip

3 pkts of
Philadelphia
cream cheese
4 oz. Danish Blue
cheese

1 carton (5 fl. oz.) of
soured cream
Garlic powder or
crushed garlic

Beat together the two types of cheese; when
smooth, slowly beat in the soured cream. Add
garlic to taste.

Chive Dip

4 oz. cream cheese
2 tbsps. chopped
chives

1 tbsp. cream or top of
the milk if necessary

Blend the ingredients to a soft cream.

Garlic Dip

4 oz. cream cheese
1 clove of garlic,
skinned and
crushed

1 tbsp. cream or top of
milk if necessary
Salt and pepper

Blend the ingredients to a soft cream and season
to taste. (Garlic salt can be used instead of the
crushed garlic.)

Crown Loaf

1 lb. 'strong' plain
flour
1 level tsp. sugar
½ oz. fresh yeast or
1 level tsp. dried
yeast

7–8 fl. oz. warm milk
1 level tsp. salt
2 oz. margarine
1 egg, beaten
Beaten egg to glaze
Poppy seeds

Oven temperature: fairly hot (375 °F, mark 5).

Grease a 9-inch sandwich tin. In a large bowl
stir together 5 oz. of the flour, the sugar, yeast
(crumble fresh yeast) and milk; mix well. Set
aside in a warm place until frothy – about 20
minutes. Sift the remaining flour with the salt
and rub in the margarine. Add the egg and the
sifted flour to the frothy yeast mixture and mix
well. Knead the dough thoroughly for about
10 minutes on a lightly floured surface – it will
be sticky at first, but will 'tighten' with kneading, and no extra flour should be necessary.
Place the dough in an oiled polythene bag, tie
it loosely and allow to rise until it springs back
when pressed; this will take 45–60 minutes in a
warm place, 2 hours at average room temperature and 12 hours in a cold room or larder (24
hours if the dough is refrigerated).

When you are ready to use the dough, shape
it into 12 equal-sized pieces and roll each into
a ball. Place them in a circle round the edge
of the sandwich tin, with 3 or 4 in the centre.
Brush with beaten egg and sprinkle with poppy
seeds. Put inside an oiled polythene bag and
leave to rise until doubled in size. Bake in the
centre of the oven for 45–60 minutes, until the
loaf is lightly browned and sounds hollow when
tapped. Cool on a wire rack. (Serves 12.)
Note. You may be able to buy 'strong' flour
from a baker, if you cannot find it at your usual
grocery store.

6
Instant Parties

SOMETHING OUT OF NOTHING

There's so much exotic food around, and so much unnecessary snobbery attached to cooking, that it's tempting to ignore the rather mundane cans and packets of store-cupboard foods when it comes to entertaining. In fact, these packets and tins, with a dash of ingenuity, some herbs, onions or whatever, can nearly always be turned into an exciting, even impressive 'something'. Easiest and most obvious 'somethings' are the small tit-bits – accessories for sherry-drinking, and a welcome change from nuts and olives; like Ritz biscuits topped with a mixture of John West tuna spread, chopped onion, chives or parsley and green pepper. Or it could be a Philly-and-almond-roll. (For this, you beat the contents of 2 packets of Philadelphia cream cheese spread until smooth, then add 1½ oz. of sharp blue cheese, 2 oz. of finely chopped ham, and 8–10 stuffed olives, also chopped. Form the cheese mixture into a roll and coat with chopped almonds; then chill the roll well, cut into ½-inch slices and serve these on buttered biscuits.)

However, you can also conjure really substantial and highly presentable party meals out of some basic store-cupboard foods. We've worked some of these dishes into three-course menus, with *planned* dinner or lunch parties in mind, but any of them, individually, could be the life-saver for a totally unplanned, unexpected and even unwanted party which would otherwise have caught you out.

MENU 1

Jellied Consommé

Beefeater Pie

Pears Marguerite

Jellied Consommé

Simply canned consomme, chilled and served with a slice of lemon and packet Melba toast.

Beefeater Pie

Pkt. of Lawry's beef stew seasoning mix	2 16-oz. cans of baked beans with tomato sauce
½ pint water	2 3½-oz. packets of instant mashed potato
2 level tbsps. dried sliced onions	2 oz. butter
1 level tbsp. dried marjoram	Salt and pepper
2 12-oz. cans of corned beef	Chopped chives

Mix together the seasoning mix and water in a saucepan until smooth. Add the onions and marjoram. Bring to the boil, then simmer. Cut the corned beef into 1-inch cubes and add to the sauce, with the baked beans. Mix well, cover and simmer gently. Meanwhile make up the potatoes with water as directed on the packet. Beat 2 oz. butter and some seasoning into the mashed potato. Turn the meat mixture into an oven-proof casserole, spoon the potato over the top, fork up and brown under a hot grill. Sprinkle with chopped chives. (Serves 6.)

Pears Marguerite

4 oz. seedless raisins	1 oz. angelica, chopped
3 tbsps. brandy	A 29-oz. can of pear halves, drained
¼ pint double cream	
1 oz. glacé cherries	Angelica for decoration

Put the raisins in a small pan with the brandy and bring to the boil; chill. Whisk the cream until it begins to thicken. Stir in the raisins and brandy, chopped cherries and angelica. Pile on the pear halves, placed hollow side up. Decorate with angelica. (Serves 6.)

MENU 2

Cream of Tomato Soup

Frankfurter Roka Salad

Peach and Brandy Fool

The Soup

Serve canned soup hot, with a dash of sherry or a dollop of cream, accompanied by gris sticks or crispbread.

Frankfurter Roka Salad

2 12-oz. cans of frankfurters	2 tsps. chopped parsley
2 12½-oz. cans of new potatoes, drained	A 4¾-fl. oz. jar of stuffed olives, drained and halved
An 8-fl. oz. bottle of Kraft Roka (blue cheese dressing)	1 lettuce, washed Paprika pepper

Cut the sausages into ½-inch pieces, halve the potatoes and mix well together in a bowl, with the dressing, parsley and olives. Arrange the lettuce on a serving dish, pile the frankfurter mixture in the centre, and sprinkle with paprika pepper. (Serves 8.)

Peach and Brandy Fool

2 29-oz. cans of peach halves, drained	1 tbsp. brandy 8 slightly rounded tbsps. of Marvel
8 tbsps. syrup from the canned fruit	Double cream for decoration
1 tbsp. lemon juice	

Cut the peach halves in halves again and put in a large blender goblet with 4 tbsps. of the syrup, ½ tbsp. lemon juice, ½ tbsp. brandy and 4 tbsps. Marvel. Replace the lid and blend until smooth – about 2–3 minutes. Pour into a serving dish or individual glasses. Repeat with the remainder of the ingredients. Pour over the first portion of fool and chill for 1 hour. Decorate with the lightly whipped double cream. (Serves 8.)

Note. If you haven't an electric blender, take a softer fruit like apricot, put it through a sieve, then whisk in the other ingredients.

MENU 3

Grapefruit

Tuna Catalina

Strawberry Ambrosia

The Grapefruit

Use chilled canned fruit; put it in individual glasses and top with a cherry or two.

Tuna Catalina

A 15-oz. can of cut green beans	2 level tbsps. Catalina dressing
A 15-oz. can of peeled tomatoes	1 lettuce heart 2 eggs, hard-boiled
2 7-oz. cans of tuna steak	A small can of anchovy fillets
A 4-oz. can of pimiento	Black olives

Drain the beans and the tomatoes. (The tomato juice can be reserved and used later as a starter or added to soups.) Drain the juice from the tuna and flake the fish. Drain the pimiento and roughly slice the caps. In a basin lightly toss together with 2 forks the beans, tomatoes, tuna, pimiento and dressing. Turn the mixture into a dish lined with lettuce heart, cut in eighths. Arrange quarters of hard-boiled egg on top and lattice with anchovy fillets and black olives. (Serves 8.)

Note. The dressing is garlic-based, but for a more pronounced flavour you can add a puff of 'Lazy Garlic'.

Strawberry Ambrosia

A 14-oz. can of Robertson's strawberry fruit filling	1 tbsp. lemon juice 2 egg whites 1 oz. caster sugar 1 tbsp. brandy (optional)
A small (6-fl. oz.) can of evaporated milk	Coarsely grated chocolate

Melon and Egg Salad;
Cheese-and-Grape Mousse;
Burgundy Beef Galantine;
Ham and Asparagus Mould:
pp. 131, 155, 161, 163

Turn the strawberry filling into a basin and stir in the milk and lemon juice until the mixture is thick and evenly blended. Whisk the egg whites until stiff, add the sugar and whisk again until stiff; fold into the strawberry mixture. Lastly, stir in the brandy. Spoon the ambrosia into small stemmed glasses and top with grated chocolate. Serve chilled, and hand shortbread or wafer biscuits separately. (Serves 6.)

VERY-NEARLY -IMPROMPTU

The great thing about this kind of party is that, although there's a bit more initial planning behind it than the guests should – or would want to – know about, once it's under way, everyone joins in and assumes equal responsibility for its success. But it's as good as ringing its death knoll to plan it and invite people too far in advance – nobody could look forward for a whole week to a bean-feast in the kitchen; so if it's not to be an anti-climax, invitations must be of the last-minute, come-as-you-are and-if-you-can't-come-somebody-else-will kind, leaving yourself just enough time to get the ingredients if the offer's taken up all round.

SAUSAGE AND MASH PARTY

Best suited to large appetites and a large kitchen. For any more than 6 people, the sausages are best baked. For every 4 guests, allow about 1 lb. of pork sausages; put them on baking trays and cook in a fairly hot oven (400° F, mark 6) for about half an hour. You'll want about 1 pint of apple sauce for every 4–6 helpings, and lots of fluffy creamed potatoes. Or you could break with tradition and serve the sausages with jacket potatoes, cole slaw (see page 59) and a sweet and sour or barbecue sauce. A pudding isn't really necessary if you have some fresh fruit around, but you could always spoil your guests with fruit salad, meringues and cream. And plenty of fresh, hot coffee.

HAWAIIAN PARTY

A winter-winner. For 12 people you want 2–4 yard-long French loaves and plenty of butter, and a mixed salad made with 2 large lettuces, 3 bunches of watercress, a green pepper and French dressing. You could start with a cream cheese dip, and finish with a Tropical Fruit Salad and cream (see page 60). A fruit punch might be offered – if you surround the party with some exotic pot plants, people won't perhaps notice that their punch is being served out of your largest mixing bowl. Otherwise, play safe and have an inexpensive red 'plonk'.

South Sea Island Pork

3 lb. shoulder of pork	Thinly pared rind of 2
1½ lb. collar bacon, rinded	oranges, cut in julienne strips
2 oz. seasoned flour	A 12-oz. pkt. of
2 oz. lard	frozen peas
3 tbsps. oil	¼ pint double cream
1½ pints stock (made with stock cubes)	3 oz. blanched almonds, shredded
Juice of 4 oranges (about ½ pint)	Chopped parsley

Oven temperature: moderate (350 °F, mark 4).

Cut the pork into 1-inch cubes, discarding any excess fat. Cut the bacon into cubes. Toss the meats together in seasoned flour. Heat the lard and oil together in a frying pan and fry the meat, a few pieces at a time, until sealed all over. Place in an 8-pint casserole, with the stock, orange juice and rind. Cover and cook in the centre of the oven for 1½ hours. Check the seasoning, add the peas and cook for a further ½ hour. Then add the cream and almonds and return the casserole to the oven for 5 minutes to heat through. Before serving, sprinkle with parsley. (Serves 12.)
Notes. 1. This dish can be cooked, up to the addition of the peas, on the day before the party; cool it quickly and refrigerate; the next day, add the peas and bring to the boil either on top of the stove or in the oven. Continue as in the main recipe. 2. If the bacon is on the salty side, soak for 2 hours before cooking it.

Christmas Eve Snacks: p. 98

7
Family Christmas

CHRISTMAS EVE SNACKS

On this busy day it's hospitality at its most in-formal, but warm and welcoming for all that. Offer help-yourself food mostly, on hot-plate or trolley. Make some soup in advance and heat it up when needed, to serve in hearty mugs. (We give one good recipe below.) Jacket potatoes look after themselves in a low oven, even when dressed up with their savoury fillings. Hot dogs – party piece in our colour picture – can be put together as the evening goes along; what makes these different is the wonderfully fresh rolls, specially ordered, and the variety of relishes. The fruit salad makes a pretty, palate-tempting contrast, and again, it may be made in advance. To drink: a golden cider mull, or lashings of coffee.

Cream of Celery and Tomato Soup

6 oz. onions, skinned and sliced	½ level tsp. sweet basil
3 oz. butter	Salt and freshly ground black pepper
1½ lb. celery, sliced	
1½ lb. tomatoes, skinned and sliced	2 oz. flour
	1 pint milk
2 pints chicken stock	Chopped parsley and croûtons (optional)

Fry the onions in 1 oz. butter in a large pan, for 5 minutes. Add the celery and cook for a further 5 minutes. Add the tomatoes, stock and basil, season well and bring to the boil. Reduce the heat, cover the pan and simmer for about ¾ hour. Put the soup through a sieve, or purée it in an electric blender. Melt the remaining 2 oz. butter in the clean pan and stir in the flour. Cook over a low heat for 2–3 minutes. Remove from the heat and add the milk slowly, stirring. Gradually add the vegetable

purée, bring to the boil, adjust the seasoning and simmer for a further 15 minutes. Serve with parsley and croûtons. (Makes 6 servings.)

Stuffed Jacket Potatoes

12 large potatoes	Oil

For the Curried Egg Filling

4 eggs, hard-boiled	4 oz. apple, peeled and diced
4 oz. onion, chopped	
1 oz. butter	Salt
1 level tsp. curry powder	Black pepper

For the Golden Bacon Filling

2 oz. onion, skinned and chopped	½ level tsp. marjoram
	1 tbsp. milk
1 oz. butter	Salt and black pepper
6 oz. bacon rashers, rinded and chopped	4 oz. Lancashire or Gloucestershire cheese, grated

Oven temperature: moderate (350 °F, mark 4).

Wash, scrub and dry the potatoes. Prick with a fork and brush with oil, then place on baking sheets and cook in the oven for about 1½ hours.

Meanwhile, for the first filling, sieve 2 of the eggs; fry the onion in the butter until soft but not coloured; add the curry powder and apple and fry for a further 5 minutes, then add the sieved egg. Cut a lid from 6 of the potatoes; scoop out the centres, leaving a wall. Mix the soft potato with the curried mixture and season well; replace inside the potato shells and garnish with the remaining 2 eggs, sliced. Serve with mango chutney.

For the second filling, fry the onion in the butter until soft but not coloured; put aside; add the bacon to the pan and fry until crisp.

Scoop out the remaining 6 potatoes as above. Cream the soft potato with the milk, add the onion and bacon and season well. Refill the potato cases. Top with grated cheese and keep warm in a low oven. Brown under a hot grill just before serving.

Hot Dogs

(See colour picture facing p. 97)

You have a choice of frankfurters and chipolatas. 'Franks' are usually sold in pairs, reckon on about 16 chipolatas to the lb. To cook frankfurters, either bring some water to the boil, turn off the heat and immerse the sausages for 5 minutes, or grill them under a moderately hot grill.

Hot Diggety Dogs: Slit frankfurters lengthwise, almost to the ends. Stuff with cottage cheese mashed with snipped chives. Wrap a bacon rasher spiral fashion round each sausage and fasten the ends with wooden picks, then grill. Or make slits at an angle, about 4 to each sausage, and slot in a slice of Cheddar cheese before grilling.

Chipolatas should be grilled or fried, either plain or pre-wrapped in a spiral of very thin streaky bacon.

Get your baker to make long, soft hot-dog rolls, or order long, crisp finger batons dusted with poppy seeds. Split the rolls, leaving a hinge, butter, insert a sausage in each and offer with these accompaniments:

Sweet corn relish.

Thick apple sauce.

Tomato relish.

Mustards – French, Dijon, German and Fines Herbes.

Crisp fried onion rings: dip onion rings in milk, drain, toss in flour and fry in deep fat until crisp. Drain on absorbent paper.

Winter Fruit Salad

Juice of 2 large lemons	A 1-lb. can of pineapple slices
1 lb. bananas, peeled and sliced	4 tangerines, peeled and segmented
½ lb. black grapes, pipped	½ pint water
½ lb. white grapes, pipped	4 oz. brown sugar
	1 tbsp. Kirsch
	1 tray of ice cubes

Pour the juice of the lemons into a bowl. Add the bananas, grapes, quartered pineapple and tangerines, and gently turn them over together. Make the water up to ¾ pint with the pineapple juice. In a saucepan heat the liquid with the sugar until dissolved, then reduce to ½ pint by boiling rapidly. Cool until there is no steam, then pour over the fruit. Chill, add the Kirsch, and just before serving, add the ice cubes. Serve with cream. (Makes 4 servings.)

Golden Cider Mull

(See colour picture facing p. 97)

¼ pint water	Thinly pared rind of 1 lemon and 1 orange
8 cloves	
1 cinnamon stick, broken up	1 oz. brown sugar
2 blades of mace	2 pints still cider
A little grated nutmeg	Clove-studded oranges to garnish

In a small saucepan heat all but the cider and garnish, bring to the boil and simmer gently for about 15 minutes. Bake the oranges in a moderate oven (350 °F, mark 4) for about 15 minutes. Add the cider to the saucepan and heat thoroughly before straining the liquid into the punch bowl. Add a float of the clove-studded oranges.

TRADITIONAL CHRISTMAS DINNER FOR 8

The Menu

Roast Turkey   Mushroom Stuffing

Bacon-wrapped Sausages

Bread Sauce   Cranberry Sauce   Gravy

Roast Potatoes   Sprouts with Almonds

Carrots with Parsley Sauce

Flamed Christmas Pudding   Brandy Sauce

Chilled Orange Soufflé

Dessert Bowl

The Schedule

At Christmas, and probably for at least 6 weeks beforehand, the whole of family life seems to revolve round the kitchen, culminating in that desperate last-minute sprint which lands the turkey on the dining-table just before 3 p.m. – if you're lucky. It seems an infinitely more civilized idea – if the family will let you do it – to resign yourself to the fact that Christmas Dinner is by nature a late affair, and actually *plan* to have it at about 5 or 6 o'clock. In this way, even the cook can have a fairly leisurely day. Ideally, it should start at about 9.30 or 10.00 a.m. with a long, lazy breakfast – in bed if possible. Make it a light meal – grapefruit, perhaps boiled eggs, toast or croissants and coffee – so that doling it out to the various relatives staying with you doesn't become just one more chore. The younger members of the family will have been up for hours, banging, blowing, munching and free-wheeling round the landing, so as well as giving them breakfast, you may have to fill in their appetites with another light snack mid-day. And both you and your guests will benefit from a cup of tea mid-afternoon. This done, you should all be able to enjoy the late dinner, and a long evening by the fire afterwards, especially if you can bear to save the presents round the tree till after the meal.

The Food

All the details for preparing the Christmas Dinner are given here – prop the book open at the appropriate page and work step by step. So far as the menu itself is concerned, although we suggest some 'starters' below, it's really more sensible to wade straight into the turkey, and so leave plenty of room for pudding. You can always serve appetizers like peanuts, olives and crisps with a couple of glasses of sherry about half an hour before the meal. If you feel you should have a first course, choose from Californian Cocktail (prawns and fresh grapefruit segments on lettuce, with cocktail sauce); Melon Wedges with Lemon; Egg and Anchovy Mayonnaise; Melon and Black Grape Cocktail (Melon with seeded grapes, garnished with frosted mint); Consommé (with an optional spoonful of sherry per cup).

It's considerate to have a second sweet ready, just in case someone doesn't like – or can't eat – Christmas pudding. The Cold Orange Soufflé – recipe below – makes a perfect contrast. And it *is* worth the effort of flambé-ing the pudding, whether you're serving individual ones or a family-sized effort. Do this at the table: allow 1 dessertspoonful for individual puddings, 3 tablespoonfuls for family-sized; warm the brandy slightly, spoon it on to the pudding and light it immediately with a taper. There's nothing to stop you flambé-ing the children's puddings as well – the alcohol evaporates away with the burning; there wouldn't be enough to let them get a taste for it, anyway, let alone do any harm. But if for any reason you don't want the flambé effect, rum butter makes a luscious alternative.

The Drink

Beforehand: Gin-and-tonic with lemon-zest is as good an apéritif as any, but give your guests a choice, and have one or two other alternatives to hand. Domecq's La Ina – served chilled – is a light, dry, fino sherry; or try Casal Garcia, served well-chilled; it's a young wine with a slight natural sparkle. And there's a new French sparkling wine called Kriter; it's refreshingly dry and should be served well chilled.

With: If you'd rather have a red wine with your turkey, there's a splendid reasonably priced Burgundy from the Côte de Nuits – La Ricardière 1961. Or, if you want to be really selective and are prepared to spend more, you could try French-bottled Chambolle–Musigny Tastevin 1959 from Pasquier des Vignes. One of the nicest white wines to serve with turkey is Kanzlerberg Gewürztraminer Réserve Spéciale. It's a fruity, full-bodied, inexpensive Alsatian wine, and best chilled for half an hour only before serving.

After: To pass round with bowls of fruit, nuts and sugared-almonds, Morgan's Top Honours Rare Old Tawny, or the pricier Morello Cherry Brandy; you can also get this in miniatures.

The Table

Make it fresh and simple, with a bowl of fruit

as the centre-piece, and fresh flowers, either in the middle or in tiny posies, next to each glass. And place a small individual gift at each side-plate, instead of crackers. Find stocky candles and paper table napkins in the same colour, either to match your colour scheme, or in brightest red, the ultimate Christmas colour.

Advance Tactics

CHOOSE the menu: calculate amounts; plan your programme.

MAKE detailed shopping list out; stock up in advance.

CHECK on supplies of kitchen foil (turkey size) and greaseproof paper.

PUT aside bread 2–3 days before for making breadcrumbs.

USE dried chestnuts for stuffing – canned for desserts.

ORDER flaked and nibbed almonds.

PREPARE fruit and nut bowls; dishes of muscatels and stuffed dates.

PLACE frozen or chilled puff pastry in the refrigerator 2 days in advance.

KEEP fresh parsley in a plastic bag in the refrigerator.

The Cookery Countdown

Make well in advance: Christmas pudding, mincemeat, cake, freezer items.

Two days ahead: Put frozen turkey to thaw.

Make breadcrumbs for stuffing and sauce.

Christmas Eve: Make stuffing; put in cool place.

Make stock from giblets.

(Thaw frozen prawns in normal part of refrigerator, and make cocktail sauce, if you are serving California cocktail as starter.)

Make cranberry sauce.

Make rum butter and chill.

Make orange soufflé; put to set.

Make mince pies.

Prepare potatoes and carrots, keep under water.

Trim sprouts and keep in refrigerator in plastic bag.

On the day: Serving the meal either at 1.30 p.m. or 7.30 p.m. and using a 12–14 lb. oven-ready turkey cooked by the quick method.

(See page 102 for other weights.)

4 hours before: Turn on oven. Stuff and truss bird. Rub over with butter. Wrap loosely in foil and put in roasting tin. Wrap sausages in thin streaky rashers. Leave in tin in cool place.

3½ hours before: Put bird in oven.

Put pudding to steam.

(Prepare California cocktail, if required, and put in cool place.)

2 hours before: Lay table and prepare wines.

Put plates and serving dishes to warm.

Set tray with coffee cups.

1¼ hours before: Parboil potatoes (5–7 minutes), drain.

Heat dripping; put potatoes in hot fat and roast on lower shelf.

Put bread sauce to infuse for 1 hour.

Put bacon-wrapped sausages into the oven alongside potatoes for about 1 hour.

Last hour: Cook carrots and sprouts.

Make gravy from giblet stock.

Make brandy sauce and parsley sauce. Cover.

When bird is cooked, remove trussing. Keep bird warm on serving dish, with bacon-wrapped sausages.

Simmer bread sauce for 5 minutes with lid off the pan and serve.

Brown flaked almonds in butter.

Drain potatoes and keep hot.

Coat carrots with parsley sauce, and add almonds to sprouts.

Re-heat mince pies.

Turn out pudding, keep warm with basin left in position.

Make coffee.

The Turkey

Stuffing and Trussing

Stuff turkey at the breast (or neck) end first, pulling flap of skin evenly and firmly to tuck underneath. Any remaining stuffing (or the second stuffing) is put into the tail end. Split the skin of the vent and put the parson's nose through this. Place pinions towards the backbone so that they hold the neck and skin in place. Press legs well into the sides to plump up the breast. Thread a trussing needle with fine string. Place turkey on back, with breast uppermost and legs on the right-hand side. Insert needle through top joint of one leg, through body and out through top joint of other leg. Catch in wing with needle and pass through the body to catch in the bottom of the leg on opposite side. Again insert the needle through the bottom end of the leg and pass through bottom part of the other leg. Pass needle diagonally through body to catch in the remaining wing, and tie the ends of string tightly together.

Working Out the Times

Oven-ready Weight	No. of servings (approx.)
6–8 lb.	6–10
8–12 lb.	10–20
14–16 lb.	30–40
20–24 lb.	40–50

Frozen turkey must have time to thaw completely before roasting. Allow 20–30 hours in a cool larder for a turkey weighing up to 12 lb. A bigger one can take up to 48 hours. If you do get landed with a frozen turkey at short notice, immerse it in warm water.

Approximate cooking times for quick oven method with foil, 450° F (mark 8).

6–8 lb.	$2\frac{1}{4}$–$2\frac{1}{2}$ hours
8–10 lb.	$2\frac{1}{2}$–$2\frac{3}{4}$ hours
10–12 lb.	$2\frac{3}{4}$–2 hours 50 mins
12–14 lb.	2 hours 50 mins–3 hours
14–16 lb.	3–$3\frac{1}{4}$ hours
16–18 lb.	$3\frac{1}{4}$–$3\frac{1}{2}$ hours

Approximate cooking times for slow oven method, 325° F (mark 3) without foil.

6–8 lb.	3–$3\frac{1}{2}$ hours
8–10 lb.	$3\frac{1}{2}$–$3\frac{3}{4}$ hours
10–12 lb.	$3\frac{3}{4}$–4 hours
12–14 lb.	4–$4\frac{1}{4}$ hours
14–16 lb.	$4\frac{1}{4}$–$4\frac{1}{2}$ hours
16–18 lb.	$4\frac{1}{2}$–4 hours 50 minutes

Cooking Tips

1. Foil is not necessary with the slow method, except to protect the legs and breast if the bird is large. You can wrap the whole bird in foil, but remove it 30 minutes before the end of the cooking time; baste and raise temperature to hot (425 °F, mark 7), to brown and crisp the skin.

2. With either method, turn the bird at half-time.

3. To know if it's done: pierce the deepest part of the thigh with a skewer. If the juices are colourless the bird is ready; if pink-tinged, cook a little longer.

4. Calculate your time to be ready 30 minutes before serving. If the bird is ready, lower the oven and keep the bird warm. If not, continue cooking.

Carving the Turkey

1. Remove the leg by pulling slightly away from the body and cutting through the ball and socket joint.

2. Holding end of drumstick in the left hand, cut slices from the leg in a downward slant away from you, turning the leg to get slices from all round the joint.

3. Carve long, thin slices from the breast. Start first below point of breastbone down towards the wing, including the stuffing.

4. Serve a portion of breast meat and leg meat with a scoop of stuffing from the tail end.

Stuffings

(For a 12–14 lb. bird, oven-ready weight. A different stuffing can be used at each end, or half of 2 recipes used to give a double stuffing at the breast or neck end.)

Forcemeat

8 oz. fresh white breadcrumbs	1 level tsp. mixed herbs
4 oz. shredded suet	Grated rind of 1 lemon
4 oz. lean bacon, rinded and minced	Salt and pepper
2 tbsps. chopped parsley	1 egg, beaten
	Milk or giblet stock to bind

Combine the ingredients, using just enough liquid to bind. The stuffing should not be too stiff.

Sausage Forcemeat: Omit bacon and include 1 lb. sausage-meat. Reduce amounts of breadcrumbs and suet by half.

Mushroom Stuffing

6 oz. mushrooms, chopped	2 oz. shredded suet
1 small onion, skinned and finely chopped	8 oz. fresh white breadcrumbs
1 oz. butter	1 level tsp. mixed herbs
4 oz. streaky bacon, rinded and chopped	1 tbsp. lemon juice
	1 egg, beaten
	Salt and pepper
	Milk

Fry the mushrooms and onion in the butter for 5 minutes; put in a bowl. Fry the bacon until crisp and add to the mushrooms, along with the rest of the ingredients, except the milk. Stir well and add just enough milk to bind.

Chestnut Stuffing

2 oz. bacon rashers, rinded	Grated rind of ½ a lemon
4 oz. fresh white breadcrumbs	16 oz. unsweetened chestnut purée
1 tsp. chopped parsley	Salt and pepper
1 oz. butter, melted	1 egg

Fry the bacon until crisp; drain and crumble. Add the breadcrumbs, parsley, butter, lemon rind and chestnut purée. Mix well, season and bind with egg. A little chopped fried onion may be added.

Bread Sauce

1 onion, skinned	4 oz. fresh breadcrumbs
2 cloves	Salt and pepper
1 pint milk	1 oz. butter

Stud the onion with the cloves. Place in a pan with the milk, breadcrumbs and seasoning. Leave to infuse in a warm place for about 1 hour. Just before the sauce is required, simmer for 5 minutes. Remove onion and add butter.

Cranberry Sauce

6 oz. sugar	½ lb. cranberries
¼ pint water	Sherry

Simmer the sugar with the water in a pan until the sugar dissolves. Add the cranberries and cook over a medium heat for about 10 minutes; cool. Add sherry to taste before serving.

Note. Use fresh or thawed frozen cranberries.

Christmas Pudding

6 oz. plain flour	8 oz. currants, cleaned
1 level tsp. mixed spice	8 oz. sultanas, cleaned
½ level tsp. grated nutmeg	4 oz. peeled, cored and chopped apple
3 oz. fresh white breadcrumbs	3 oz. Demerara sugar
4 oz. shredded suet	Grated rind of 1 lemon
4 oz. stoned raisins, chopped	Grated rind of 1 orange
	2 eggs, beaten
	⅓ pint brown ale

Grease a 2-pint pudding basin. Sift together the flour, mixed spice and nutmeg. Add the breadcrumbs, suet, dried fruit, apple, sugar, lemon and orange rind. Mix the ingredients well. Gradually stir in the beaten eggs and ale and stir thoroughly. If liked, leave overnight.

Turn the mixture into the prepared basin, then cover with greased greaseproof paper and kitchen foil or a pudding cloth. Either place in a pan with water half-way up the side and, after bringing to the boil, reduce heat and boil gently for 5–6 hours, or place in a steamer and cook for 8 hours. A piece of lemon in the water during the boiling prevents discoloration of pan. (Serves 6–8.)

Note. On the day, reboil for 3 hours.

Orange Soufflé

3 juicy oranges
1 lemon
4 large eggs, separated
4 oz. caster sugar
2 level tsp. gelatine
2 tbsps. water

2 tbsps. orange Curaçao
¼ pint double cream
2 tbsps. nibbed almonds, toasted
Whipped cream and slices of fresh orange for decoration

Prepare a 6-inch (1½-pint) soufflé dish with a band of non-stick paper in the usual way. Wipe the oranges and lemon. Grate the rind and squeeze the juice into a large deep bowl. Add the egg yolks and sugar. Whisk over a pan of hot (not boiling) water until thick; this will take a little time. Add the gelatine dissolved in the water and the liqueur. When the egg mixture has cooled and is nearly setting, fold in the lightly whipped cream. Lastly, fold in the stiffly beaten egg white quickly and evenly. Turn the mixture into the prepared dish and leave to set. To serve, ease the paper away with a knife, decorate the sides with nibbed almonds and top with whipped cream and twisted orange slices. (Serves 6.)

Brandy Sauce

1 pint sweet cornflour sauce (1½ oz. cornflour)
4 tbsps. brandy
A knob of butter

Make the sauce and just before serving, stir in the brandy and butter. When available, stir in also a couple of spoonfuls of cream.

Rum Butter

8 oz. butter (preferably unsalted)
4 oz. light soft brown sugar
2–3 tbsps. rum
Icing sugar to dredge

Cream the butter and beat in the sugar. When soft, slowly beat in the rum. Chill in the serving bowl. To serve, dust with icing sugar.

CHRISTMAS DINNER WITH A DIFFERENCE FOR 6

The Menu

Mushrooms à la Grecque
 or
Melon and Grape Cocktail

Roast Stuffed Goose
Gooseberry Sauce   Roast Potatoes
Buttered Carrot Sticks   Haricots Verts

Marron Pêche Mont Blanc
 or
Christmas Pudding and Rum Butter

Cheeseboard

Coffee

Planning

If you're really bored with all the traditional food trappings of Christmas, and particularly if you're to be an entirely adult party, you might like to try this menu as an alternative. It's an altogether more sophisticated meal, and not likely to lie so heavily on the poor beleaguered Christmas stomach. This form of Christmas dinner is better eaten at the normal lunch-time, but you needn't have too much of an agonized rush, as there's a lot that can be done in advance. Like the gooseberry sauce, which, if made a day or two before Christmas, can be covered and chilled in the fridge and will only need gentle re-heating. You can prepare the mushroom dish the day before, and, provided you've got ahead with the actual making of your meringues, the Marron Pêche Mont Blanc need only take about 10 minutes to complete – as near serving time as possible. Follow the sweet with a board of three or four well-varied types of cheese, accompanied by crackers, water-biscuits or preferably oatcakes, if you can get them. Round off with small doses of good, strong, fresh coffee and chocolate peppermint creams.

Mushrooms à la Grecque

1 onion, skinned and finely chopped
2 tbsps. olive oil
¼ pint dry white wine
A bouquet garni
A clove of garlic, skinned
Salt and freshly ground pepper
1 lb. button mushrooms, de-stalked
½ lb. tomatoes
Chopped parsley

Sauté the chopped onion in the oil until soft but not coloured. Add the wine, bouquet garni and garlic and season with salt and pepper. Wipe the mushrooms. Skin, halve and seed the tomatoes. Add to the onion mixture, and cook gently, uncovered, for about 10 minutes. Remove from the heat, and allow to cool. Remove the herbs and garlic and, if wished, add 2 more tbsps. olive oil. Serve chilled, sprinkled with chopped parsley.

Roast Stuffed Goose

8-lb. goose (oven-ready weight)
2 medium-sized onions, minced
1½ level tsps. dried sage
6 oz. fresh white breadcrumbs
Grated rind of 1 orange
1 oz. butter, melted
Salt and black pepper

Oven temperature: fairly hot (400 °F, mark 6).

Wipe the goose and put the giblets on one side. Combine the remaining ingredients in a bowl and use to stuff the tail end. Place the bird on a rack in a roasting tin. Sprinkle with salt and rub this well in. Cover the goose with 2 layers of greaseproof paper, but don't wrap completely. Protect the feet by wrapping them in foil. Cook for 15 minutes per lb. plus 15 minutes over. After the first hour, baste with the fat from the bird. Remove the greaseproof paper for the last 15 minutes, if not sufficiently brown.

Note. Allow ¾ lb. oven-ready weight per person. Serve with gooseberry sauce; use the giblet stock for the gravy.

Gooseberry Sauce

½ lb. gooseberries, topped and tailed
1 oz. butter
1–2 oz. sugar

Stew the fruit in as little water as possible, or until soft and pulped. Beat well, then sieve or put in a blender. Add the butter and a little sugar if the fruit is very sour.

Marrons Pêches Mont Blanc

3 egg whites
4 oz. caster sugar
½ pint double cream
4 trifle sponge cakes
Rum
A 2¾-oz. tube of sweetened marron purée
A 15-oz. can of white peaches

Use the 2 egg whites and caster sugar to make a meringue mixture. Using a star vegetable nozzle, pipe into 24 small rosettes and dry in the usual way. These may be stored in an airtight tin for 2–3 weeks. Arrange the meringues round a serving dish, fixing with a little of the whipped cream (see below). Break up the sponge cakes, put into the centre of the meringues and moisten well with rum. Top with the remainder of the cream. Pipe over it a good layer of marron purée, straight from the tube. Cover with drained peach halves and finally cover with a 'net' of piped marron purée. (Serves 6–8.)

Whipped Cream: Lightly whip the cream until light and fluffy and fold in the beaten egg white.

TWELFTH NIGHT PARTY FOR 12

The Eve of the Feast of the Epiphany, January 5th – otherwise Twelfth Night – is a splendid night for a party. It gives a lift to the heart when Christmas festivities are over and the New Year is already prosaic with the British weather and sheaves of bills.

The traditionally significant food item is the cake in which a bean (haricot) is buried. When the cake is cut, the guest who has the slice with the bean becomes the bean-king (or queen) and is rewarded with a good-luck gift. If you had a golden coin or small silver trinket, you could use that instead of a bean, and let it do double duty as the good-luck gift.

Twelfth Night is the ideal night for a teenage party, for bachelor flat-dwellers or for people with bigger houses. Imaginative choice in food and drinks can make it reasonably cheap and very simple to prepare. Christmas decorations are not usually taken down until the next day, so the friendly, decorative background for a party is still there in the Christmas cards, the holly and the ivy.

The Menu

Burgundy Beef with Rice
Winter Salad
French Bread Sticks
Butter

Twelfth Night Cake

Wine or Cider Cups

The Food

We've borrowed for this affair a couple of recipes from the After-Theatre Party.

Prepare and cook the main dish of Burgundy Beef a day or two in advance if need be.

The Beef recipe appears on p. 85, and directions for making the Winter Salad on p. 84.

The simple cake recipe lends itself to varying decorative finishes for many party occasions.

The Drink

As for the After-Theatre Party.

Twelfth Night Cake

(*See colour picture facing p. 144*)

10 oz. butter	Lucky 'bean' (see
10 oz. caster sugar	note in the in-
5 eggs	troduction)
10 oz. self-raising	Orange butter cream
flour	Orange glacé icing
Grated rind of 2	Silver balls
oranges	

Oven temperature : fairly hot (375 °F, mark 5)

Grease and line two 9½-inch straight-sided sandwich tins.

Make an orange flavoured Victoria sandwich cake-mix with the first 5 ingredients. Divide the mixture between the tins and put the lucky bean in one. Bake for about 30 minutes. When cool, sandwich together with orange butter cream. Decorate the cake-top with orange glacé icing, and on it outline a crown with silver balls before the icing has time to set. Pipe the sides with close-set stars of butter cream.

Orange Butter Cream: 6 oz. butter, 1 lb. sifted icing sugar, 3 tbsps. evaporated milk and orange colouring.

Glacé Icing: 8 oz. sifted icing sugar, 3 tbsps. fresh orange juice, orange colouring.

8
Children's Parties

CHILDREN'S PARTIES: THREE TO FIVES

It's the easiest thing in the world to over-complicate a party for this age-group. The secrets of its success are basically very simple: lots of colour around, tempting food – fairly mild in flavour, and in sizes and quantities they can manage – and a series of little gifts which they can clutch on to and enjoy. Don't make the party too long – a couple of hours is quite enough, as once one child starts to wail with fatigue, the fever very quickly spreads. Don't make it too large either. If you invite twelve children, you'll have large enough numbers for the various boisterous games, yet few enough to be able to give all the children sufficient attention and make sure no one is feeling lost or left-out.

You shouldn't have much difficulty interesting the children in the tea-table, but use any device you can think up which rivets their ever-wandering attention, and makes them feel at home with strange company in a strange place. Colour can be your most important aid. Quite a few firms produce party paperware in colours more delectable than most china. And a scene-stealing centre-piece is essential. Our tri-colour Maypole cake, layered in pink, chocolate and white, has been tried and tested on toddlers, who appreciated its edible decorations and, even though they'd already consumed a mountain of sandwiches, came back for second helpings. But if you haven't the time for making and baking, order an ice-cream novelty cake in advance – in ordinary cake shape, or practically any shape you care to name, including a teddy-bear.

So far as the food is concerned, the 'don'ts' are every bit as important as the 'do's'. Children of this age don't appreciate strong flavours, and won't like the fizzy mineral drinks which hold such charm for the age-groups just ahead of them. But even at this tender age, they'd probably feel supremely insulted if you gave them jam in their sandwiches. The mainstay of a party tea is still the savoury sandwich, with fairly bland fillings like lightly scrambled egg, cheese spread, tomato and paste; cut the sandwiches into manageable pieces – small fingers or triangles. Other savoury possibilities would be a couple of bowls of crisps, to go with the sandwiches, and cocktail sausages on sticks, served cold. If you can't get these small sausages, chippolatas can be twisted and cut to the same size.

When it comes to sweet things, your best bet is still jellies – little ones in individual paper dishes – in a variety of flavours like orange jelly with mandarins, lemon with slices of banana, and raspberry with canned raspberries (fresh if they're plentiful). And another diplomatic trick is to home-make biscuits in letter-shapes and place each child's initials on his own plate. These, along with chocolate and sponge fingers and the vast cake, should really see you through. The simplest, most acceptable, least trouble-causing drinks are orange juice and milk, with orange juice probably more in demand, as the better thirst-quencher.

After tea, plan to get in two or three more games before going-home time. 'Specially for Children' (p. 28) gives help, but just a final thought: As you shoosh each small guest into its coat and out the door with his or her collecting Mum, your parting gesture could be a cracker-wrapped tube of Smarties pressed into each sticky paw.

Maypole Cake

5 oz. plain flour	Thick white glacé icing
1 oz. cornflour	(made with 1 lb.
2 level tsps. baking	icing sugar)
powder	Ribbon or tape
½ level tsp. salt	A candy-striped
5 oz. caster sugar	drinking straw or
7 tbsps. corn oil	stick of rock or
7 tbsps. water	barley sugar for the
2 eggs, separated	maypole
Chocolate butter	12 tiny figures in wood,
cream (made with	plastic, etc., or 12
3 oz. icing sugar)	jelly baby sweets

Oven temperature : fairly hot (400 °F, mark 6).

Grease 2 8-inch straight-side sandwich tins and line the bases with greaseproof paper.

Sift the dry ingredients into a basin. Mix together the corn oil, water and egg yolks. Make a well in the centre of the dry ingredients and gradually stir in the liquid, beating well to form a smooth batter. Beat the egg whites till stiff and fold into the mixture. Turn the mixture into the prepared tins and bake for about 25 minutes, until pale golden and firm to the touch. Cool on a rack.

When the cakes are cold, sandwich them together with the butter cream. Make up the glacé icing. Cut 12 lengths of ribbon long enough to reach from the top of the maypole, when it is erected in the centre of the cake top, down to the outside edge of the cake, plus an extra couple of inches. Attach the ends of the ribbons to the top of the maypole, using a glass-headed pin in the case of a straw, or transparent sticky paper in the case of a stick of rock or barley sugar. Coat the cake with the glacé icing, leave to half-set, then place the maypole in the centre. Attach the free end of each ribbon to one of the figures or sweets and put the figures in place round the base of the cake. (A spot of stiff icing should hold them firmly.)

CHILDREN'S PARTIES: FIVES TO ELEVENS

The Menu

Egg Triangles   Ribbon Sandwiches
Cheese Pictures
Hot Sausages on Sticks
Crisps and Twiglets

Money Cake   Brandy Snaps
Meringue Whirls   Gingerbread Men
Jelly Galore

Citrus Fruit Cup

Planning

This is a rather wider-than-usual age-group to cater for, but it's exactly the kind of mixture that you frequently get at Christmas, when families come together, and it can be made to work very well. Many of the principles for the toddlers' party apply to this one – lots of colour, gifts, and one splendid big cake are essentials. But the food can be that much more sophisticated, so that it holds the interest of the youngest *and* the oldest at the party. Cocktail sausages are invaluable – they're really a universal party food for all ages; this time, serve them hot on their sticks. Keep the sandwiches small, but blend together some more interesting fillings. The selection of sweet things can be richer and more imaginative; brandy snaps and meringues filled with fresh-whipped double cream will be snaffled by the adults around if – remotest of possibilities – there are any left at the end of half an hour. The Gingerbread Men look their best if stuck into a crisp and shiny apple at each place. The Jelly Galore, made the day before and decorated on party day, is a much more exciting mixture than the tots' plain jellies, and can be served from its large bowl straight on to paper plates.

Children of these ages won't care about interesting drinks, only about quenching their considerable thirst; large jugs of the punch would hit exactly the right note, as it's simple to make – and innocent, although in appearance it parodies lethal grown-up party punches. It's made with orange squash, sharpened with fresh lemon juice and suitably diluted, then topped with apple and orange slices. The rim of each jug is hung with little bunches of grapes, and it's served in goblets, with a cherry at the bottom of each for colour.

The Food

Egg Triangles: Mash 4 lightly boiled eggs with a little softened butter and seasoning. Butter 12 slices of bread (cut from a 1¾-lb. loaf). Sandwich the buttered slices with egg filling, wrap, and store whole in a cool place. Trim the crusts and cut each sandwich into 4 triangles just before the party. (Makes 24.)

Ribbon Sandwiches: Spread a large slice of buttered white bread with potted meat or canned liver pâté. Cover with a similar-sized slice of brown bread topped with a spread of cream cheese and chopped chives. Add another slice of white bread and a potted meat layer, then top with a brown bread 'lid'. Wrap and store until required, then cut each decker sandwich into ½-inch fingers. (Makes 8–10.)

Cheese Pictures: Top 16 slices of buttered bread each with a slice of cold luncheon meat and trim the edges. Top the meat with cut-outs made from 8 slices of processed Cheshire or Cheddar cheese. This you do quite simply by using fancy biscuit-cutters, topping 8 of the open sandwiches with the centre cheese cut-outs, and using the remainder of the 8 cheese squares as 'frames' to the meat on the other sandwiches. (Makes 16 sandwiches.)

Sausages on Sticks: 1 lb. chipolatas (twisted in half and separated) or cocktail-size pork sausages can be baked in a fairly hot oven (400 °F, mark 6) for 25–30 minutes – turn them occasionally for even browning. Or simply heat through in bubbling-hot water the contents of a can of cocktail Frankfurters. Spear each sausage with a cocktail stick, then fix them all into a small Vienna loaf for the table. (Makes about 32, if chipolatas are used.)

Meringues (see picture facing p. 25): Can be made and stored a week before the party and filled with fresh cream on the day. You can get about 4 dozen small meringue halves from 2 egg whites and 4 oz. caster sugar, to pair up with ¼ pint whipped cream (see p. 201).

Brandy Snaps (see picture facing p. 25): Ready-to-serve brandy snaps are a useful and time-saving buy. Some called Tilly, nicely packed in drums of eight, are quite inexpensive. For a recipe for home-made brandy snaps, see p. 202.

Money Cake

(See colour picture facing p. 25)

8 oz. butter	White and chocolate
8 oz. caster sugar	butter cream (see
4 eggs	below)
6 oz. self-raising	Foil-covered chocolate
flour	coins to decorate
2 oz. cocoa	

Oven temperature: fairly hot (375 °F, mark 5).

Use the first 5 ingredients to make a chocolate Victoria sandwich cake (sifting the flour and cocoa together before mixing). Divide the mixture between 3 greased and lined straight-sided sandwich tins 8½ inches in diameter and bake for 20–25 minutes. When the cakes are cool, sandwich them together with white butter cream. Coat the top and sides with chocolate butter cream and decorate with the foil-wrapped coins.

Note. If you make and decorate the cake a day or two before the party and leave it in a cool place, it will be easier to slice.

Butter Cream for Cake

8 oz. butter	A few drops of
1 lb. icing sugar,	vanilla essence
sifted	2 oz. cocoa blended
4 tbsps. evaporated	with a little water
milk	

Cream the butter. Gradually beat in half the icing sugar, with the evaporated milk and a few drops of essence. Then beat in the rest of the sugar. Use some of this filling to layer the cake, and turn the rest into chocolate butter cream by adding the blended cocoa and mixing well.

Gingerbread Men

(See colour picture facing p. 25)

12 oz. plain flour	6 oz. soft brown sugar
1 level tsp.	4 tbsps. golden syrup
bicarbonate of	(3 oz.)
soda	1 egg, beaten
2 level tsps. ground	Currants for decoration
ginger	White royal or glacé
4 oz. butter	icing for decoration

109

Oven temperature : fairly hot (375 °F, mark 5).

Sift together the flour, bicarbonate of soda and ground ginger. Rub the butter (or margarine) into the sifted ingredients, add the sugar and mix well. Stir in the slightly warmed syrup and the egg, to give a pliable dough. Knead until smooth and roll out on a floured surface to ⅛ inch in thickness. Place a gingerbread man form (cut from greaseproof or non-stick paper) on the dough and cut round it with a sharp-pointed knife. Carefully lift the 'men' on to a greased baking sheet, keeping them well apart. On to each 'man' put 3 currants for buttons and 3 more to represent his eyes and mouth.

Bake for 10–15 minutes, until evenly coloured Cool on a wire rack. Store in an airtight tin for up to a week. To decorate, outline the neck and sleeve ends, etc., with piped white icing. (Makes 12.)

Note. The gingerbread men need a template from which the paste can be cut before baking. Artists in the family can no doubt draw one. The man is about 5½ inches high and 4½ inches broad.

THE PANTOMIME TEA

The Menu
Savoury Choux Buns
Decker Sandwiches
Fruit-jelly Castle
Chocolate Layer Cake
Tea   Milk Shakes   Fruit Cup, etc.

Plans and Variations
As a party, this high-tea-after-the-pantomime has to embrace guests of all ages, and while the menu is planned mainly to please the young-sters – after all, it's *their* day – no crusty aunt could with reason turn her nose up at it. It will fill out into an even higher tea if you add hot sausage on cocktail sticks, mince pies, cream-filled meringues and freshly-baked scones or date-bread. Placate the aunt with gallons of tea, but have milk shakes, fruit cups, coke and other minerals for the more broad-minded young.

This menu makes a very movable and vari-

Jelly Galore
(*see colour picture facing p. 25*)

3 lemon jelly tablets	2 15-oz. cans of red
Juice and grated	cherries, drained
rind of 3 oranges	and stoned
6 tbsps. rosehip syrup	A small can of
½ lb. white grapes,	evaporated milk
skinned and pipped	Double cream for

Dissolve the tablets of jelly separately in ¼ pint boiling water. To each jelly add the juice and rind of 1 orange, with 2 tbsps. rosehip syrup. Keep at the liquid stage. To the first jelly add ½ pint cold water, stir and pour into a 3- or 4-pint glass goblet or bowl; leave to set, then put half the cherries and grapes on top. To the second jelly add ½ pint cold water, stir and when nearly set, whisk until frothy. Spoon over the fruit and leave to set. To the third jelly add ½ pint cold water, and chill until of the consis-tency of unbeaten egg white. Whisk in the evaporated milk until mixture is light and fluffy and spoon on to the second jelly; leave to set. Before serving decorate with the remain-ing fruit and the cream. (Serves 10–12.)

able feast: it could easily be used for an evening party for young people, if you served with it a sparkling non-alcoholic grape-juice or some-thing similar.

Savoury Choux Buns

1½ oz. butter	2½ oz. plain flour
¼ pint water	2 eggs, lightly beaten

For the Filling

4 oz. cream cheese	Salt and freshly milled
2 oz. butter	black pepper
Lemon juice	Chopped parsley

Oven temperature : fairly hot (400 °F, mark 6).

Melt the 1½ oz. butter in the water and bring to the boil. Remove the pan from the heat and add the flour all at once. Beat until the paste is smooth and leaves the side of the pan, forming a ball. Cool slightly, then gradually beat in the eggs. Using a ½-inch plain nozzle, pipe the mixture into 25 walnut-sized balls on to greased baking sheets. Bake for 15–20 minutes, until the buns are golden-brown and cooked through. Make a small slit in the side of each to let the steam out. If necessary, put them back in the oven to dry out; cool. Beat the filling ingredients together and put some in each bun.

Fruit-jelly Castle

For the Base

A 1-pint cherry jelly tablet	A small can of evaporated milk

Middle Layer

A lime or lemon jelly tablet	A 30-oz. can of fruit cocktail

Top Layer

A raspberry jelly tablet	A small can of raspberries

Make up the cherry jelly to ½ pint with hot water and stir till the jelly has dissolved. When almost setting, add the evaporated milk and whisk until really frothy. Turn the mixture into a 7-inch round cake tin and leave to set. Make up the lime jelly to ¾ pint, using the juice from the fruit cocktail with some hot water. Stir till the jelly has dissolved; then add the fruit. When the mixture is beginning to set, turn it into a 6-inch round cake tin and leave to set. Make up the raspberry jelly to 1 pint with the contents of the can of raspberries and some hot water; stir till the jelly has dissolved. Pour into a 1-pint jelly mould, or a small straight-sided 4- or 5-inch cake tin; leave to set. Just before the sweet is required, turn out the cherry jelly on to a serving dish, then unmould and turn out the fruit jelly on to the cherry one, followed by the raspberry jelly.

TEENAGER'S HALLOWE'EN PARTY FOR 20

The Menu

Spiced Beef
Green Salad
French Bread or Poppy-seed Rolls

Dutch Apple Tart

Mulled Cider   Coffee

The Drink

A mull based on cider is ideal for this party. Although it's quite mild enough to keep parent's minds at rest, its alcoholic content will satisfy teenage egos, and it will team well in flavour with the Hallowe'en apples.

Planning

The menu for this party would be equally appropriate for teenagers on any winter evening – it's just dolled up for Hallowe'en with a few details of setting and serving. Unfortunately, our modern houses aren't the perfect setting for Witching-Eve parties; you need something the size and shape of a barn to hold them in, with the fire for the cauldron crackling in an enormous hearth.

However, you should, despite the drawback, be able to make it spooky enough if your main lighting is the unearthly glow from candles in hollowed-out pumpkins and turnips. Rough pottery on the buffet table could be set on hessian strewn with bracken, and black candles surrounded with apples, could sit next to anything that you absolutely must be able to see.

Nearly all the food is either hot or spicy or both. The quantities here are planned for about 20, and it's all highly casual and help-yourself. A heavy iron saucepan or giant skillet does the job of the cauldron and stays simmering on the kitchen stove. It can contain either the spicy beef dish, or the cassoulet of canned beans, sausage-meat (spiced up with herbs and seasonings, shaped into sausages and wrapped in streaky bacon), apple slices and onion rings.

The buffet table can boast a large, rough pottery bowl of green salad with a sharpish dressing, poppy-seed rolls and chunks of butter. If you have time and energy, the spiced Dutch apple tart would make a delicious sweet; otherwise all that's needed is a tray of fresh fruit, and possibly some accompanying bowls of hot curried nuts. (Make these by spreading any salted nuts in a shallow pan, pouring some melted butter over and sprinkling with curry powder, then putting them in a moderate oven for a few minutes, shaking them well several times.)

Spiced Beef for a Crowd

10 lb. chuck steak	6 lb. old potatoes
¼ pint water	A little butter
Salt and pepper	

For the Sauce

3 lb. tomatoes, skinned and chopped	½ lb. sugar
	2 level tbsps. salt
	1 level tsp. pepper
1 green pepper, seeded and chopped	2 level tsps. powdered cinnamon
1 onion, skinned and chopped	2 level tsps. powdered nutmeg
2 large cooking apples, peeled and chopped	2 level tsps. powdered allspice
	½ pint wine or cider vinegar

Oven temperature: moderate (350 °F, mark 4).

Trim the beef, cut into cubes and cook with the water and seasoning in a covered dish for 1½ hours, until tender. Meanwhile, make the sauce. Put the tomatoes, pepper, onion and apples in a saucepan, cover and cook slowly for 45 minutes; add the rest of the ingredients and boil, uncovered, for a further 15 minutes, or until thick. Parboil the potatoes for 7 minutes and cut into ¼-inch slices. Spread a layer of sliced potatoes on the bottom of a shallow, ovenproof casserole or meat tin, add a layer of cooked meat, pour on some sauce and continue, finishing with a layer of potatoes. Pour ½ pint of beef liquid down the side of the dish and brush the potatoes with a little melted butter. Raise the oven temperature to fairly hot (400 °F, mark 6) and cook the beef, covered for ½ hour; uncover and cook for a further ½ hour, until the potato is golden. (Serves 20.) *Note.* It may be more convenient to use 2 or 3

smaller dishes, in which case the cooking time may be slightly reduced.

Dutch Apple Tart

1½ lb. cooking apples	Sugar to taste
3 oz. sultanas or raisins	8 oz. rich shortcrust pastry
¼ level tsp. mixed spice	Icing sugar

Oven temperature: fairly hot (400 °F, mark 6).

Peel and core the apples and cut into eighths. Poach in a very little water until nearly soft. Lightly stir in the dried fruit and spice mixed with a little sugar; use more sugar to sweeten to taste. Leave to cool while making the pastry. Roll out two-thirds of the pastry, line a flan ring and place on a flat baking sheet. Fill the pastry case with apple mixture and cover with a pastry lid rolled from the rest of the pastry, damp the edges to seal and roll off any excess trimmings. Bake at about the centre of the oven until lightly browned – 40–45 minutes. Remove the flan ring and carefully lift the tart with a flat spatula on to a serving plate. Serve warm or cold, dredged with icing sugar. (Serves 6, make 3 tarts for a party of 20.)

Mulled Cider

6 inches of cinnamon stick	8 oz. Demerara sugar
2 level tsps. whole allspice	1 orange, sliced
8 pint cider	1 lemon, sliced
	Whole cloves

Put the cinnamon stick and allspice in a muslin bag. Heat the cider, sugar and spices in a saucepan and bring to near boiling point. Remove the spices. Stud the centre of each fruit slice with a clove, float the slices on top of the mull and simmer gently for a few minutes. Ladle into ⅓-pint tumblers or mugs – a spoon in the glass to stop cracking. (24 servings.)

9
Barbecues

INFORMAL SUMMER NIGHT BARBECUE FOR 12

The Menu

Foil-roasted Corn Cobs
Spare-rib Chops   Piquant Barbecue Sauce
Tandoori Chicken
Jacket Potatoes   Picnic Cole Slaw
Hot Bread Rolls

Fresh Peaches, Apples, Bananas

Cookies and Coffee

Verandah Punch   Chilled Lager
Aveleda Wine Cup

The best summer barbecues take the shape of a long, leisurely eating session which lasts from dusk till around midnight. You don't have to worry too much about whom you invite; youngsters too young to stay up that late will be kept at home by their parents, older people will know whether or not they want to stand about chewing in the chilly evening air.

The menu here simplifies the cooking by cutting down on the number of grills which are actually barbecued. We've suggested quantities for a dozen and erred on the generous side. It's corny but true that food tastes ten times better in the open air, and in these conditions, guests' appetites can expand alarmingly. You can, of course, adapt the menu to feed larger or smaller numbers, and vary it to include other grills, like beefsteak or lamb chops. Smaller things like sausages, bacon, hamburgers and mushrooms can be cooked in a frying-pan or on a griddle. And if you want to be mediaeval, roast whole eggs beside the embers, turning them in case – as Touchstone says in *As You Like It* – they get 'ill roasted, all on one side'. But that goes for plenty of other barbecued foods, too! It's best to make the

barbecue sauce back-stage and keep it hot at the side of the barbecue, when you can also warm the foil-wrapped bread rolls.

Don't burden yourself by creating mountains of washing-up. Eating equipment can be narrowed down to throwaway paper plates and really large, tough, absorbent paper napkins – you'll need forks for the cole slaw, but it wouldn't cost much to make these plastic, and therefore equally disposable. The cooks in the party will need foil, long-handled tongs and forks for turning the grilling meats, pastry brushes for basting, a slice for turning griddle scones, and, above all, thick gloves.

Amounts

1 dozen corn cobs, 18 spare-rib chops, 12 chicken legs or joints, 1 dozen jacket potatoes; amounts for barbecue sauce and cole slaw are given in each recipe; 1 dozen each fresh peaches, apples, pears, 18 soft rolls, butter.

Foil-roasted Corn Cobs

Remove the husks and silk from the cobs. Mix 3 oz. butter and plenty of salt and fresh-milled black pepper. Spread some on each cob and put each in a 12-inch square of foil. Fold over the sides for a double seal in the centre, and make double folds at each end to seal completely. Cook at the side of the grid for 25 minutes, turning them occasionally.

Jacket Potatoes

Scrub and dry the potatoes and brush with melted butter, or bacon fat. Wrap each loosely in foil and cook, turning once or twice, at the side of the grid.

Barbecued Meat and Poultry

Trim off excess fat from any meats. For the spare-rib chops, marinade them for an hour or so in twice as much oil as lemon juice and seasoning. Use the marinade for basting.

Cooking times (turning the meat or poultry half-way). For spare-rib chops: 20 minutes; for chicken joints or less: 25–35 minutes; for 1-inch thick lamb chops and steaks: 12–18 minutes.

Piquant Barbecue Sauce

2 tbsps. malt or cider vinegar	¼ level tsp. cayenne
¼ pint water	1 thick slice of lemon
2 level tbsps. sugar	1 onion, skinned and thinly sliced
1 level tbsp. prepared mustard	2 oz. butter
½ level tsp. pepper	¼ pint tomato ketchup
1½ level tsps. salt	2 tbsps. Worcestershire sauce

In a saucepan, mix together the vinegar, water, sugar, mustard, pepper, salt, cayenne, lemon, onion and butter. Bring to the boil, reduce the heat and boil gently, uncovered, for 20 minutes. Add remaining ingredients and bring back to the boil. (Makes ¾ pint approx.)

Tandoori Chicken

12 chicken joints	A good pinch of ground coriander
Salt and pepper	
2 cartons of plain yoghurt	2 cloves of garlic, skinned and crushed
2 level tsps. chilli powder	Juice of 2 lemons, strained
A good pinch of ground ginger	4 tbsps. melted butter

Remove any protruding bones from the chicken joints, wipe, and season with salt and pepper. Combine the yoghurt with the chilli powder, ginger, coriander, garlic, lemon juice, 1 level tsp. freshly ground black pepper and 2 level tsps. salt. Mix well and add the chicken pieces. Allow to stand for 3–4 hours, turning several times. Remove the chicken from the marinade, shaking off as much of the liquid as possible, then pour a little melted butter over each chicken joint. Place the pieces on the barbecue grid and brown them quickly on all sides. Remove the chicken and place each piece on a 15-inch square of foil. Fold over the sides of the foil, making a double join in the centre, and make a double fold in each end of the foil to seal completely. Place each packet on the grid and cook for a further 20 minutes turning once during the cooking time. Heat the spicy marinade and serve separately. (Serves 12.)

Picnic Cole Slaw

2 lb. nutty-flavoured cabbage	2 level tbsps. caster sugar
½ lb. carrots, peeled	1 tbsp. lemon juice
2 eating apples, grated	1 tbsp. mayonnaise
A 5-fl. oz. carton of soured cream	Salt and freshly ground pepper

Remove the cabbage stem and shred the leaves very finely. Grate the carrots and apples coarsely. Blend together the soured cream, sugar, lemon juice and mayonnaise. Season well. Toss together all the ingredients in a bowl. (Serves 12.)

Verandah Punch

2 large, juicy oranges	3 'splits' of ginger ale, well chilled
3 thin-skinned lemons	3 'splits' of soda water
¼ pint sugar syrup (see below)	Ice cubes and slices of orange to decorate
½ pint freshly made tea	

Squeeze out the fruit juices and mix with the sugar syrup and tea. Cool, then strain into a bowl. Just before serving, mix in the ginger ale and soda water. Add the ice cubes and sliced orange. (Makes 10 servings.)

Aveleda Wine Cup

¼ bottle (⅓ pint) dry sherry	1 tbsp. Curaçao
1 bottle of Portuguese Vila Real	1 'split' of soda water Borage, cucumber and unpeeled sliced apple to decorate

Mix the liquids well, chill in a jug, and garnish before serving. (Makes 6 servings.)

10
Picnics

FAMILY PICNIC FOR EIGHT

The Menu
Crumbed Lamb Cutlets   Picnic Eggs
Bacon and Pineapple en Croûte
Glazed Beetroot   Fresh Salads

Variety Breads, Rolls and Butter
Pear Trifles   Bran Tea-bread

French and cream bottled dressings
Mustard and condiments

Planning
The soup, hard-boiled eggs and bread-and-butter kind of picnic is easy enough to organize – it's usually an impromptu affair, and somehow the paper-bags, petty discomforts and tantrums over mislaid can-openers are all an essential part of it. But if you're making the picnic an 'occasion' and inviting another section of the family, it must be well organized and include as many home comforts as can reasonably be expected. This rather elaborate menu anticipates eight people, made fairly hungry by the open air, and will cover a mid-day meal and an afternoon snack. It needs a day or so's forethought, and will if necessary happily adapt to the dining-room table.

Vital props for the picnic include: unbreakable crocks, kitchen cutlery, a hold-all for the paper napkins and milk, plastic bags for all the food-stuffs, and a large basket for the screwtop containers and jars. You won't really be able to get away with vacuum-flask tea at a picnic of this scale, but a kettle and spirit burner, plus tea-bags (and/or instant coffee) are relatively simple extras to take; don't bother with fresh milk – some people *can* tell Marvel Instant from real, but not many.

Make a list and tick off everything as you pack it; among the mundane things (Chapter 4, p. 22 lists many more) which easily get forgotten are mustard, salt and pepper, sugar and the bottle opener. One or two toilet things are also fairly essential, like damp cloths for sticky fingers and tissues; take also a large junk bag. *P.S.* This picnic-plan does assume that you have the one most essential prop of all – a car which can whisk you and the food to an idyllic country meadow; but – although you'd need to economize on space in your packing and probably leave out such luxuries as the kettle and picnic stove – train, feet or bicycle could carry you and the goodies to green fields.

Amounts
Apart from basic store-cupboard items and ingredients for the recipes detailed below, you will need: 8 eggs, 8 lamb cutlets, a selection of salad stuffs – lettuce, cucumber, tomatoes, spring onions, 1 green pepper, watercress, 1 lb. box of lump sugar, $\frac{1}{2}$ lb. butter, 2 pints milk. Work out the quantities of your chosen breads and drinks according to ages and appetites.

Preparation
The Night before the Picnic: Brush the lamb cutlets with beaten egg and dip into a mixture of equal quantities of breadcrumbs and grated cheese. Press the crumbs well in to coat thoroughly. Melt 2 oz. dripping in a baking tin and turn the chops in dripping. Bake in a fairly hot oven (400° F, mark 6) for 45–50 minutes. Cool, wrap and refrigerate overnight. *On the Picnic Morning:* Hard-boil the eggs. Put under cold running water and shell when cold. Cut in half lengthwise, scoop out the yolks and press these through a sieve; blend with 2 level

tsps. mustard, 1½ tsps. Worcestershire sauce, 2 tsps. lemon juice, 1 level tsp. grated lemon rind, season to taste and spoon back into the hollows in the eggs. Sandwich the egg halves together in pairs, wrap each in a twist of plastic film and pack into original egg boxes, filling up any empty spaces with tomatoes.

Glazed Beetroot

2 lb. cooked beetroot	¼ pint water
3 oz. sugar	3 tbsps. vinegar
½ oz. arrowroot	1 level tsp. salt

Dice the beetroot. Blend the sugar and arrowroot together with a little of the water to a smooth paste. Add the rest of the water, bring to the boil and cook until thick and clear. Add the beetroot, stir and heat through. Stir in the vinegar and season with salt. (Serves 8.)

Bacon and Pineapple en Croûte

A 3-lb. joint of lean shortback bacon	1 lb. bought chilled puff pastry
A small can of pine-apple rings	1 egg, beaten

Oven temperature: very hot (450 °F, mark 8).

If you can, buy the delicious Wiltshire sweet-cure bacon. Other joints may need soaking before cooking, so ask about this when you buy.

Place the joint, skin side down, in cold water, bring to the boil, remove the scum, then reduce the heat, cover the pot and simmer the meat for 25 minutes per lb. plus 20 minutes over. Let the joint cool in the cooking liquid. When it is cool, remove the rind and trim off surplus fat. Arrange drained pineapple rings over the fat.

Roll out the pastry to a size large enough to enclose the joint completely. Lift the pastry on the rolling-pin and lay it over the joint. Press it down lightly on the pineapple, then carefully turn the joint upside-down, wrap the pastry round it and seal, using beaten egg. Turn it over again and place, joined side underneath, on a baking sheet. Brush the surface lightly with beaten egg. Use the pastry trimmings to make some leaves, place in position on the pastry case and brush with egg. Make a small hole or slit in the pastry top. Bake the croûte above the centre of the oven for about 20 minutes. Reduce the heat to moderate (350° F, mark 4), cover the pastry with greaseproof paper and cook for a further 30 minutes. Cool on a wire rack. (Serves 8.)

Pear Trifles

1 jam Swiss roll	Sugar
A 29-oz. can of pears	Grated rind of 1 lemon
6 level tbsps. custard powder	2 oz. chocolate dots
	8 glacé cherries
2 pints milk	

Cut the Swiss roll into 8 even slices and place 1 slice in the base of each of 8 individual lidded picnic containers. Drain the canned pears and pour 1 tbsp. of juice over each piece of roll. Retain 8 pear halves, chop any extras and divide between the containers. In a bowl blend the custard powder with a little of the milk. Put the rest of the milk in a saucepan, bring to the boil and pour on the blended powder. Stir and return to the pan, bring to the boil, stirring, and sweeten to taste. Add the lemon rind and boil for 1–2 minutes. Cool the custard, stirring occasionally. Spoon over the Swiss roll, dividing equally between the containers and adding a few chocolate dots, half-way through. Place a pear half, hollow side up, on top of each. Place a glacé cherry in the centre. Leave in a cool place until required. (Serves 8.)

Bran Tea-bread

3 oz. All-bran	½ pint milk
8 oz. sultanas	6 oz. self-raising flour
8 oz. soft brown sugar	1 level tsp. baking powder

Oven temperature: fairly hot (375 °F, mark 5).

Grease and line a loaf or other oblong tin with base measurements of about 8½ by 4½ inches. Overnight, soak together the bran, sultanas, sugar and milk. The next day, add the flour and baking powder sifted together, stir well and turn the mixture into the lined tin. Bake for about 1–1¼ hours. Turn out, remove the paper and cool on a wire rack. Slice and butter.

PART THREE

1
Soups and Starters

Scotch Broth

Backbone of winter lunch in Scotland

6 pints water	1 lb. carrots, grated or
1 lb. flank of mutton	diced
1 cupful of pearl	½ lb. turnips, grated or
barley	diced
2 onions, chopped	Salt and pepper
3 leeks, chopped	

Put the water and mutton into a pot, bring to the boil and skim off the scum; add the barley and vegetables, a scant dessertspoonful of salt and a little pepper. Simmer for 3½ hours. (Serves 4.)

You can add a little of any vegetable available, and of course some chopped parsley.

Potage Breton

Peasant-style

2 rashers of lean	1 pint stock (made with
streaky bacon	a chicken stock cube)
1 oz. butter	Salt and pepper
1 onion, chopped	2 large carrots, grated
1½ lb. potatoes, sliced	Chopped parsley

Rind the bacon and cut into snippets with kitchen scissors or a sharp knife, then fry slowly in a saucepan to extract the fat. Add the butter and, when this has melted, add the onion and potatoes. Continue to fry slowly for a further 5 minutes, but do not allow to colour. Add the stock, bring to the boil, cover, reduce the heat and simmer for ½ hour, or until the potatoes are tender and begin to break up. Put through a sieve or Mouli, then return to the saucepan and check the seasoning. Add the grated carrots and continue to cook for a further 10 minutes. Serve garnished with chopped parsley or snipped fresh chives. (Serves 4.)

French Onion Soup

(See picture below)
Increasingly popular 'hearty' soup

½ lb. onions	Salt and pepper
1½ oz. butter	A bay leaf
½ oz. plain flour	Slices of French bread
1½ pints boiling stock	Grated cheese

Slice the onions finely, then fry in the melted butter until well and evenly browned – take care not to let the pieces become too dark. Add the flour, mixing well. Pour in the boiling stock, season, add the bay leaf and simmer for 30 minutes. Put the slices of bread into individual bowls or into a soup tureen, pour on the soup and top with cheese. Alternatively, put the soup in a fireproof casserole, float the slices of bread on it and cover with grated cheese; then heat the soup in a hot oven for a few minutes. (Serves 4.)

Cream of Chicken Soup

Traditional favourite

1 oz. butter	8 oz. cooked chicken
2 level tbsps. plain	pieces
flour	½ pint milk
Salt and pepper	Chopped parsley
1 pint chicken stock	

Melt the butter in a saucepan, add the flour and ½ level tsp. salt; blend and cook for 1–2 minutes. Add the chicken stock and chicken pieces and simmer gently for 10–15 minutes. Add the milk and heat thoroughly, but do not boil. Season to taste with salt and freshly ground pepper and serve immediately, sprinkled with chopped parsley and accompanied by a herb loaf – see below. (Serves 4.)

Herb Loaf

Appetizing accompaniment

4 oz. butter	A pinch of salt
2 level tsps. mixed	A French loaf
herbs	

Oven temperature: hot (425 °F, mark 7)

Melt the butter, and add the herbs and salt. Slice the loaf to within ½ inch of the bottom crust and brush the slices with the melted butter. Wrap in foil, then crisp in the oven for 20–30 minutes. (Serves 4.)

Watercress Soup

Delicately-flavoured and attractive

1 lb. potatoes	A bunch of watercress
(weighed after	1 oz. butter
peeling)	Freshly ground pepper
1½ pints milk	Lemon slices for
1 level tsp. salt	garnish

Cook the potatoes until soft in boiling salted water (about 15 minutes); drain, and mash well or sieve. Heat the milk to boiling point and gradually add to the potatoes; add the salt. Pick off the watercress leaves and chop, discarding the stems, then stir into the soup and simmer for 5–6 minutes. Just before serving, stir in the butter, cut into small pieces. Check the seasoning, adding a little to taste. Garnish with a thin slice of lemon – or a sprig of watercress. (Serves 4.)

Bortsch

Chilled soup from Eastern Europe

1 onion, finely	½ a bay leaf
chopped	2 pints well-flavoured
1 large carrot, sliced	beef or chicken stock
1 lb. raw beetroot,	Salt and pepper
skinned and grated	Juice of ½ a lemon
2–3 sprigs of parsley	Soured cream

Put the prepared onion, carrot and beetroot into a saucepan with the parsley, bay leaf, stock and seasoning. Bring to the boil, reduce the heat, cover and simmer for about 45 minutes. Strain, and add lemon juice to taste. Chill, and serve each portion with a good spoonful of soured cream. (Serves 6.)

Chilled Cream of Celery Soup

(See colour picture facing p. 217)
Celery is now available almost the year round

1 oz. butter	1 tsp. lemon juice
1 head of celery,	Salt
prepared and	Freshly ground pepper
chopped	2 oz. carrots, finely
1 oz. plain flour	diced
1 pint chicken stock	½ pint milk
A blade of mace	

Melt the butter in a saucepan, add the celery and sauté for 5 minutes. Stir in the flour, cook for a few minutes, then gradually add the stock, stirring. Add the mace and lemon juice, season with salt and pepper; bring to the boil, cover and simmer for 20 minutes. Discard the mace. Blend or sieve the soup, return it to the pan, add the diced carrot and simmer until the garnish is tender – about 15 minutes. Remove from the heat, cool slightly, add the milk and check the seasoning. Turn the soup into a bowl and chill. (Serves 4.)

Chilled Cream of Spinach Soup

(See colour picture facing p. 217)
Green soup for sunny days

1 lb. spinach	Freshly ground pepper
2 oz. butter	2 tsps. lemon juice
1 small onion,	A bay leaf
chopped	½ oz. plain flour
1½ pints chicken stock	4 tbsps. single cream
¼ level tsp. salt	Cheese croûtons

Wash and drain the spinach, discard the stalks. Melt 1 oz. butter in a large pan and sauté the onion until soft but not coloured. Add the spinach and sauté for a further 5 minutes, stirring frequently, then add the stock, salt, pepper, lemon juice and bay leaf. Bring to the boil, cover and simmer for about 20 minutes. Discard the bay leaf and blend or sieve the soup. In the clean pan make a roux with the flour and the rest of the butter. Slowly add the soup, stirring, bring to the boil and simmer for 5 minutes. Check the seasoning. Turn it into a bowl and chill. Just before serving, stir in the cream. Hand round cheese-topped croûtons separately. (Serves 4–6.)

Chilled Curry Soup

New twist for curry addicts

¾ lb. onions, chopped	1 oz. plain flour
2 oz. butter	1 pint beef stock made
3 level tsps. curry	with a cube
powder	1 tsp. lemon juice
¼ level tsp. paprika	½ pint milk
¼ tsp. Tabasco sauce	4 tbsps. single cream
Salt and pepper	Crisp-fried onion rings

Sauté the onions in butter for 5 minutes, stir in the curry powder, paprika, Tabasco, salt, pepper and flour. Cook over a low heat for a further 5 minutes, stirring. Slowly stir in the stock and lemon juice, bring to the boil, cover and simmer for 20 minutes. Blend or sieve the soup, turn it into a bowl, add the milk and chill. Just before serving stir in the cream and garnish with onion rings. (Serves 4.)

Gazpacho

Spanish delight

1 lb. tomatoes	1 tbsp. olive oil
1 small onion	1–2 tbsps. lemon juice
1 small green pepper	Salt and pepper
1 clove of garlic	¼ of a cucumber
1 tbsp. wine vinegar	Toast croûtons

Wash the tomatoes, dry and slice roughly. Prepare the onion and green pepper and cut into slices. Crush the garlic. Place the tomatoes, onion, pepper, garlic, vinegar and olive oil in a liquidizer and combine well together. Turn into a basin, and add lemon juice and season-ing to taste. Chill thoroughly in a refrigerator. Serve with diced cucumber and croûtons of toast. (Serves 4.)

Fish Stock

Essential for many fish soups

1 cod's head (or	Peppercorns, mace
equivalent in fish	1–2 sticks of celery
bones and skin	2 onions

Boil all the ingredients together in 2 pints water for 40 minutes, then strain before using.

Fish Chowder

Meal in itself

1 lb. cod or haddock	1 green pepper, sliced
fillet	and seeded
1 onion, roughly	1½ pints fish stock (see
chopped	below)
1 oz. butter	½ pint milk
2 tbsps. chopped	A 16-oz. can of whole
fried bacon	corn kernels
¾ lb. potato, diced	

Skin and dice the fish fillet. Sauté the onion in the melted butter and add the bacon, fish, potato and green pepper. Add the fish stock and simmer gently for 30 minutes, then add the milk and drained corn kernels. Heat thoroughly and season to taste. Serve with crisp toast fingers. (Serves 4–5.)

Crab-and-Sweetcorn Soup

(See colour picture facing p. 241)

Chinese delicacy

1½ tbsps. corn oil	A 12-oz. can of whole
4 oz. cooked crab	sweetcorn kernels
meat	2 pints chicken stock
Salt	2 level tbsps. cornflour
1 tsp. rice wine (Shao	2 eggs, lightly beaten
Hsing) or dry sherry	

Heat the oil in a saucepan, add the crab meat and season with salt and wine or sherry. Add the drained corn and stock and bring to the boil. Reduce the heat and simmer for 5 minutes. Add the cornflour, blended to a paste with a little water, and cook for a few minutes. Lastly add the eggs and cook for a further minute. (Serves 6.)

Globe Artichokes

(See picture above and colour picture facing p. 209)
Still slightly exotic

Globe artichokes are served with a herb-flavoured vinaigrette dressing. The leaves should be pulled out with the fingers, dipped in the dressing and the soft end sucked. When the centre is reached the choke, or soft flowery part – if not already taken out – is removed, and the 'bottom', which is a special delicacy, is eaten with a knife and fork.

Choose young, fresh artichokes, allowing one per person. Cut off the stem close to the base of the leaves. Take off the outside layer of leaves and also any others which may be dry or discoloured. Remove the choke from the centre. Wash very thoroughly and, if liked, tie the tops of the leaves neatly together. Cook in boiling, salted water until tender (that is, until the leaves pull out easily) for anything from 20 to 40 minutes. Drain upside-down.

The artichokes may also be served hot with Hollandaise sauce or with melted butter and lemon.

Canned artichoke hearts are a delicious hors d'oeuvre ingredient; add a piquant French dressing.

Filled Avocado Pears

Three interesting variations: See also p. 63

Cut open the avocado pears: using a stainless knife, make a deep cut through the flesh, up to the stone and entirely encircling the fruit. Separate the halves by gently revolving them in opposite directions. Discard the stones. If the pears are not to be served at once, sprinkle the flesh with lemon juice or cover closely with waxed paper to prevent it from discolouring. Just before serving, fill or finish as desired. Allow one-half per person.

Fill the hollow with shelled shrimps, prawns, flaked crab or lobster meat, moistened with mayonnaise or soured cream, or with flaked tunny fish bound with mayonnaise and flavoured with a little chutney.

Dice a small piece of sharp-flavoured cheese such as Danish Blue or Roquefort and mix with some cottage cheese. Carefully take out all the flesh, dice it and combine with the cheese mixture, then return all to the 'shells'.

Dice the avocado pear flesh as above and combine with a little chopped celery heart, a squeeze of lemon juice and some mayonnaise. Return the mixture to the 'shells'.

Melon Cocktail

Melon in party dress

3–3½ lb. honeydew melon	Cointreau
	Orange peel
Caster sugar	

Cut the melon in halves and remove the seeds. Scoop out 18–24 balls from the melon flesh, using a 'parisienne' potato cutter, and cut the remainder into cubes. Divide the cubes between 6 glasses, cover with melon balls and drain any juice over the top. Dredge with a little sugar and add a few drops of Cointreau. Garnish with very finely cut strips of orange peel. (Serves 6.)

Insalata di Peperoni

Italian-style starter

A 6½-oz. can of pimientos (peperoni)	1 tbsp. chopped chives
	Lemon juice
1 oz. long-grain rice, cooked	Freshly ground pepper
	Salt
1 tbsp. double cream	Lettuce leaves
1 tbsp. capers, chopped	

Drain the pimientos and carefully pull into shape ready to hold the stuffing. Mix together the rice, cream, capers, chives and sufficient lemon juice to sharpen. Season with pepper and salt. Fill 4 pimiento caps with stuffing and serve on small, crisp lettuce leaves. Serve a little French dressing separately. (Serves 4.)

Note. 'Peperoni' is the Italian name for fresh sweet peppers – which can be red, yellow or green. 'Pimiento' is the name you will find on cans of red peppers. The green variety is only available fresh from the greengrocers. Fresh red and yellow ones are seasonally in the shops.

120

Mixed Hors d'Oeuvre

(See picture above)
Often the best choice if you don't know your guests'
individual tastes

Choose 4 or 5 items from the following, either
arranging them on individual plates or leaving
the guests to make their own selection. (The
latter is more wasteful, as you are bound to
have some left over.) Do not forget to add
salad greenery; on occasions add thinly sliced
or diced cheeses and meats. Flaky, twisted
cheese straws grouped in bowls make handy
munchers.

The picture illustrates the first six items:

Glazed onions – particularly good with sliced
liver sausage or cold rare-roast beef. Melt some
butter in a pan over a low heat, add 1 level
tbsp. sugar and some prepared pickling onions,
cook slowly until tender and caramelised and
allow to cool.

Swedish cucumber – thinly slice some cucumber, sprinkle with salt and leave to stand. Drain
thoroughly. Cover with French dressing and
freshly chopped parsley or dill.

Shredded celery and salted peanuts, in a dressing
made by combining 1 tbsp. oil, 1 tbsp. lemon
juice and lots of black pepper.

Bermuda salad – thinly sliced orange and raw
onion.

Peaches and cottage cheese – drain peach halves
and fill the centre of each with a good teaspoonful of cottage cheese.

Rice and ginger salad – fold together 4 oz. long-
grain rice (cooked); ½ oz. stem ginger, chopped; 1 small green pepper, chopped; 2–3
spring onions, chopped; 1 eating apple, diced;
3–4 tbsps. lemon mayonnaise seasoned with
¼ level tsp. curry powder.

French beans and sour cream – cut the cooked
beans in 1-inch pieces and dress with soured
cream seasoned with lemon juice and ground
pepper.

Chicory Salad

Pleasantly crisp and crunchy

1 crisp eating apple	1 firm tomato, skinned
1 small head of	seeded
chicory	2 tbsps. French dressing
3 or 4 inner leaves of	Melba toast and
lettuce	butter

Core the apple and cut the flesh into tiny
cubes; finely slice the chicory; break the lettuce
leaves into small pieces; roughly chop the
tomato. Toss all together with French dressing
and chill for ½ hour. Serve in small bowls, with
slices of buttered Melba toast. (Serves 3–4.)

Guacamole

A Mexican dish that's good to start a meal

1 small firm tomato,	2 tbsps. lemon juice
skinned and	2 level tbsps.
finely chopped	mayonnaise
1 tiny onion, minced	1 tsp. salad oil
or chopped	4 drops of Tabasco
6 avocados	sauce
2 level tsps. salt	Shredded lettuce

Just before serving, place the tomato and onion
in a bowl. Halve the avocados and remove the
stones. Scoop out the flesh, cut it into small
pieces and add to the tomato. Add all the other
ingredients except the lettuce, toss lightly until
blended, and arrange on a bed of shredded
lettuce. (Serves 8.)

Stuffed Eggs

Ways of using one of the most popular hors d'oeuvre
items

There are many delicious fillings for eggs: here
are a few *Good Housekeeping* favourites (for each,
use 4 hard-boiled eggs).

Scandinavian Eggs: Cut a thin slice off the white
at the blunt end of each egg so that they stand
upright on the dish. From the pointed end cut
a slice to reveal the yolk; scoop out and sieve
the yolks. Beat to a smooth consistency with a

121

Christmas Pie and Patty
Party: pp. 79–80

knob of butter and a little mayonnaise. Press a little into the egg-white cups, and top with Danish-style caviare.

Creamy Eggs: Cut the eggs in halves, lengthwise. Remove the yolks and sieve them. Beat in enough soured cream to give a smooth consistency, and season to taste with salt and pepper. Pipe back into the whites, or pile with a spoon. Garnish with sprigs of cress, and serve each with a curled lettuce leaf.

Eggs Pâté Style: Sieve the egg yolks and beat thoroughly with 4 oz. of leberwurst. If necessary, add a little top of the milk to give a creamy consistency. Return the mixture to the egg whites, and garnish with sliced olive.

Danish Blue Mousse

Fresh-tasting and light

4 oz. Samsoe cheese	$\frac{1}{2}$ oz. gelatine
4 oz. Danish Blue cheese	Water
	2 egg whites
$\frac{1}{2}$ pint double cream	Salt and pepper
1 oz. almonds, chopped and toasted	Mustard

Grate both cheeses into a large bowl. Half-whip the cream and fold with the toasted almonds into the cheeses. Fold in the gelatine, dissolved in 2 tbsps. water in a small bowl over a pan of hot water, then fold in the stiffly whipped egg whites. Season to taste, and set in a 1-pint dish. Serve with lettuce hearts, Melba toast and butter. (Serves 6–8.)

Crab Gratiné

Hot and piquant

1 medium-sized cooked crab (8 oz. crab meat)	$\frac{1}{2}$ level tsp. salt
	$\frac{1}{4}$ level tsp. pepper
	A few drops of Worcestershire sauce
2 oz. breadcrumbs	
4 oz. cheese, grated	About 3 tbsps. cream or top of the milk
$\frac{1}{4}$ level tsp. dry mustard	
	Watercress
$\frac{1}{2}$ level tsp. cayenne pepper	2 bananas
	$\frac{1}{2}$ oz. butter

Oven temperature: hot (400 °F, mark 6)

Prepare the crab: lay it on its back and, holding the shell firmly with one hand and the body (to which the claws are attached) with the other, pull apart. Using a spoon, remove and discard the stomach bag (which lies just below the head), and the greyish-white frond-like pieces ('dead man's fingers') from the shell. Carefully scrape all the meat from the shell into a basin and reserve. Wash and if necessary scrub the shell, then dry and polish. Knock away the edge as far as the dark line.

Remove the flesh from the claws, except the tiny ones. Mix the flaked white and dark meat with the breadcrumbs, cheese and seasonings, and add sufficient cream or milk to bind to a fairly soft consistency. Replace the crab mixture in the shell and bake for 20 minutes. Place the shell and claws on a bed of watercress and serve garnished with the sliced bananas fried in butter until lightly browned.

Crab Viroma

An unusual starter

1 lb. crab meat	Celery salt
3 oz. butter	Tabasco sauce
1 small onion, finely chopped	Worcestershire sauce
	4 oz. Cheddar cheese, grated
4 oz. button mushrooms, sliced	2 tbsps. double cream
3 tbsps. dry sherry	Salt and pepper

Flake the crab meat. Melt the butter and sauté the onion until soft but not coloured, add the mushrooms and cook for a further 3 minutes. Stir in the crab meat, add the sherry and a dash each of celery salt, Tabasco and Worcestershire sauces. Simmer gently for 7–10 minutes, then add the grated cheese and stir until melted. Remove the pan from the heat and add the cream, re-season if necessary. Put back into the crab shell, or make individual portions by putting into natural scallop shells.

For a somewhat more substantial dish, serve with boiled rice.

Caviare

For a very special occasion

This is served ice-cold, with freshly made toast and butter. Lemon juice may be sprinkled over it if you wish. Alternatively, spread the caviare on croûtes of fried bread or toast, and sprinkle with a few grains of cayenne pepper.

Moules Marinière

Classic and good

4 doz. mussels (about 6 pints)	Chopped parsley to flavour and garnish
Butter	2 sprigs of thyme, if available
4 shallots or 1 medium-sized onion, finely chopped	1 bay leaf
½ bottle of dry white wine	Freshly ground black pepper
	2 level tsps. plain flour

Place the mussels in a large bowl under running water, and scrape off the mud, barnacles, seaweed and 'beards' with a small sharp knife. Discard any that are open or even just loose (unless a tap on the shell makes them close) or are cracked. Rinse again until there is no trace of sand in the bowl.

Melt a large knob of butter and sauté the shallots until soft but not coloured. Add the wine, a small handful of chopped parsley and the thyme, bay leaf and several turns from the pepper mill. Simmer, covered, for 10 minutes. Add the drained mussels a handful at a time; cover and 'steam' for about 5 minutes, shaking often until the shells open. Remove the top shells over a saucepan to catch the juices, and place the mussels in wide soup plates; keep warm. Strain the liquor and reduce it by half; thicken a little by adding a small knob of soft butter creamed with 2 level tsps. flour (whisked in piece by piece). Adjust the seasoning. When cooked, pour over the mussels. Sprinkle with freshly chopped parsley and serve at once with plenty of crusty bread. Use forks for the mussels, soup spoons for the juices.

Oysters

Another special-occasion delight

Medium-sized oysters are best; they should be tightly shut when purchased. Wash them before opening, and open only just before use. (Always open on the deep shell, so as to conserve as much as possible of the natural liquid.) Arrange 5–7 on each plate, if possible embedded in crushed ice. Garnish with lemon slices, and hand thinly cut brown bread and butter separately, together with salt and freshly ground black pepper.

A sharp cocktail, such as a blending of chilli sauce, ketchup, horseradish and Worcestershire sauce, may be placed in a small container in the centre of the oysters; alternatively, use a little very finely chopped shallot.

Prawn Pyramid

(See colour picture facing p. 240)

Spectacular presentation

Choose 3 glass bowls in varying sizes that fit into each other to form a pyramid shape. Arrange freshly cooked unpeeled prawns over the rims, snugly fitting together to prevent them falling off, the heads of the second layer locking with the tails of the bottom layer. Fill the small top bowl with shredded lettuce. Hand round *sauce verte* separately.

Sauce Verte: Remove the stalks from a bunch of washed watercress, and very finely chop the leaves; add to the basic mayonnaise, with a crushed garlic clove. Alternatively, add a little spinach purée just before serving.

Baked Scallops

(See picture below)

The scallops' own flavour remains unmasked

8 scallops	Shavings of butter
1 egg, beaten and seasoned	Lemon slices and watercress to garnish
Breadcrumbs	

Oven temperature: fairly hot (375 °F, mark 5)

Wash the scallops and discard the beard and black parts; if they are large, divide in two. Well grease 8 scallop shells. Dip the scallops in beaten egg, then toss in breadcrumbs; place in the shells, dot with pieces of butter and bake for 20–30 minutes. Garnish and serve.

Scallops in Cream

French cuisine provides an exquisite first course

6–8 scallops, prepared	1 shallot, skinned and
2 tbsps. olive oil	finely chopped
Lemon juice	2–3 tbsps. white wine
Seasoned flour	¼ pint single cream
2 oz. butter	Salt and cayenne
2 oz. button	pepper
mushrooms,	2 level tbsps. Parmesan
sliced	cheese, grated

Cut up the scallops. Mix the oil with 1 tsp. lemon juice, and marinade the scallops for 1 hour; drain well, then toss in flour and fry gently in the butter. Place the scallops in 4 shells, then fry the mushrooms and shallot lightly in the butter. Add the wine and reduce well, then stir in the cream. Heat gently, season and add a few drops of lemon juice. Pour over the scallops, sprinkle with cheese and brown under the grill.

Sea-Food Cocktail

Consult your fishmonger about his 'best buy' for this starter

4 level tbsps.	A dash of Worcester-
mayonnaise	shire sauce
2 tbsps. double cream	8 oz. shelled prawns,
1 level tbsp. tomato	shrimps, crab or
ketchup	lobster
1 tsp. lemon juice	Shredded lettuce

Mix together the mayonnaise, cream, ketchup, lemon juice and Worcestershire sauce; fold the sea-food through the mixture. Half-fill 4 glasses with shredded lettuce and pile the sea-food mixture on top. Garnish as desired with lemon wedges, whole prawns, etc., as available. Serve with thinly sliced brown bread and butter. (Serves 4.)

Smoked Trout

Fish for the connoisseur

Remove the skin from the body of the fish, but leave the head and tail intact. Serve with lemon wedges and horseradish sauce.

Alternatively, skin the fish, remove the fillets from the bone and serve on lettuce leaves, with lemon and brown bread.

Smoked Salmon

Expensive, but worth it

Just serve it with lemon juice, capers and freshly ground pepper to accentuate the flavour. Cut very thinly, allowing 1½–2 oz. per serving. Hand thinly cut brown bread and butter.

Note. Norwegian or Pacific salmon is a good alternative if the Scottish type proves to be too expensive.

Fried Whitebait

(See picture below)
Old-world delicacy that's still in favour

Wash the fish and dry in a cloth. Put 2–3 level tbsps. flour in a dry cloth and toss the whitebait in it a few at a time. Place them in a frying basket. Heat some deep fat until it will brown a 1-inch cube of bread in 1 minute. Fry the whitebait for 2–3 minutes, until lightly browned, then drain them on crumpled kitchen paper. Serve at once, sprinkled with salt and garnished with lemon and little sprigs of parsley. Serve slices of brown bread and butter separately.

Snails à la Bourguignonne

For the returned Continental traveller

1 can of snails	2 cloves of garlic,
½ pint dry white wine	skinned and crushed
1 onion stuck with	A bouquet garni
cloves	Salt and butter
¼ pint brandy	

For the Snail Butter

4 oz. softened butter	1–2 tbsps. chopped
½ a shallot, skinned	parsley
and finely chopped	A good pinch of mixed
1 clove of garlic,	herbs
crushed	Salt and pepper

Remove the snails from the can and place in a pan, with the rest of the ingredients. Simmer gently for 1 hour, remove from the heat and allow to cool in the liquor. Meanwhile, mix the ingredients for the snail butter, blending well. Put a snail into each shell, fill up with snail butter and put the shells in an ovenproof dish. Bake them for 10 minutes in a very hot oven (450 °F, mark 8) and serve hot.

Note. If shells are not provided with the can of snails, simmer the snails as before, put them into an ovenproof dish, place the butter over and round them and bake as above.

Home-made Pâté de Foie

Well-balanced blend of flavours

1 lb. calves' or	A little water
chickens' liver	2 oz. cooked tongue
4 oz. pork fat	A little truffle, if
A small clove of	available
garlic	Aspic jelly
A pinch of mixed	Truffle or green leek
herbs	for garnish
Salt and freshly	
ground pepper	

Mince the liver and pork fat with garlic and mixed herbs; season lightly. Heat a thick frying-pan; when hot, add the minced liver and stir well. When the liver has changed colour add a very little water and allow to simmer for 5 minutes. Press through a fine sieve, or put in a liquidizer. Add the tongue chopped in diamonds, and the truffle, finely chopped. Re-check the seasoning. Line the bases of 4 tiny soufflé dishes, ramekins or their equivalent, with a layer of aspic and some decoration. A simple decoration is most effective, cut from thin slices of truffle and leek; the latter should be blanched to set and brighten the colour. When the decoration has set, fill each mould with pâté, spread evenly, and chill until firm. When required, turn out in the usual way on to individual plates.

Note. Powdered garlic is now available in a convenient pack, and is a reasonable substitute, used carefully, when fresh garlic is not to hand.

Steak Tartare

Something of an acquired taste

6 oz. raw fillet beef	2 tsps. parsley
2 small onions,	2 tsps. lemon juice
skinned	Worcestershire sauce
1 oz. gherkins	Salt and pepper
2 tsps. capers	2 unbroken egg yolks

Scrape the meat on to a board; shape into 2 rounds about 1 inch deep, make a hollow in each round, then put on to a dish or on a slice of brown bread and butter. Chop the onions, gherkins, capers and parsley separately and put in piles round the meat. Sprinkle the meat with lemon juice and sauce, season and place an egg yolk in the centre of each round. (Serves 2.)

The ingredients of this appetizer are mixed as you eat. Once you have acquired the taste for this 'starter' (which is very popular on the Continent, especially in Scandinavia) you will find it a delightful dish.

2
Meat, Poultry and Game

Roast Lamb

Everyday and party versions

All cuts of lamb are suitable for roasting. Allow per person: 12–16 oz. for loin, saddle or shoulder; other cuts, with bone, 8–12 oz.; without bone, 4–6 oz.

Roasting temperature: Moderate (350 °F, mark 4) for all cuts.

Roasting Time: For leg, shoulder and saddle, 25–30 minutes per pound. Stuffed joints, 40–45 minutes per pound.

Method: Wipe the joint, rub seasoned flour well into the surface. Dot with lard or dripping, put direct into the roasting tin.

Variations:

1. Rub the surface with a cut clove of garlic.
2. Brush over with oil and dredge with flour.
3. Spoon over 4 tbsps. orange or pineapple juice half-way through the cooking time.
4. Baste at 10-minute intervals and, just before the joint is cooked, sprinkle with 3 level tbsps. Demerara sugar.
5. Make insertions in the fat with the point of a sharp knife. Insert a little rosemary and a sliver of orange rind. Place the joint in a roasting tin, with about ½ inch water, and roast uncovered.

Gravy: First remove the excess fat, then thicken the dripping in the pan with flour, adding stock to extend it.

Stuffing: Boned shoulder and breast taste good with mushroom forcemeat.

Accompaniments: Mint, caper or cranberry sauce, red-currant jelly.

Roast Crown of Lamb

(*See colour picture facing p. 145*)

Party piece

Oven temperature: moderate (350 °F, mark 4)

Buy 2 pieces of the best end of neck, each with 6–7 cutlets (and taken if possible from the opposite sides of the animal, though this is not essential). They should be chopped – not chined – and sliced between the bones to about half-way down, the ends of the bones being scraped clean. Trim neatly and bend the two best ends round backwards, fat side innermost, to form the crown, securing them with skewers and string. Stuff the centre with sausage-meat or sage and onion stuffing and twist some pieces of buttered paper or foil round each of the exposed bones to prevent their burning. Roast in the centre of the oven, allowing 30 minutes per pound, plus 30 minutes. Serve with the bones capped with cutlet frills, if available, or spear potato balls on the ends of the bones to form 'jewels'.

Alternatively, the centre of the joint can be left unstuffed and filled just before serving with vegetables such as diced carrots and peas or small boiled potatoes garnished with parsley butter.

Garnish the joint with piped creamed potato, etc., to look like a crown, and serve separately some gravy and also red-currant or some other sharp-flavoured jelly.

Cutlets en Croûte

Surprise presentation – tender meat in crisp pastry

½ lb. bought puff pastry	Salt
1 oz. butter	Freshly ground black pepper
1 clove of garlic, skinned and crushed, or ½ level tsp. minced dried garlic	4 lamb cutlets, trimmed 2 medium-sized tomatoes, skinned and sliced
	Beaten egg

Oven temperature: hot (450 °F, mark 8)

Roll out the puff pastry into a long strip 15 by 4 inches; leave to rest while preparing the cutlets.

Cream the butter, beat in the garlic and season to taste. Spread the garlic butter over one side of each cutlet, and top with sliced tomato.

Cut the pastry lengthwise into 4 narrow strips and brush with beaten egg. Use one strip to wrap round each cutlet; overlap each turn fractionally, and keep the egg-glaze side uppermost. Place the pastry-wrapped cutlets on a baking sheet and bake for 10 minutes. Reduce the temperature to moderate (350 °F, mark 4) and cook for a further 20 minutes. Serve really hot. (Serves 4.)

Cumberland Cutlets

Good for January, when New Zealand lamb is at its excellent best

8 lamb cutlets	Juice of 1 lemon
Seasoned flour	3 tbsps. red-currant
1 oz. butter	jelly with port
Juice and finely	preserve
grated rind of	1½ level tsps. arrowroot
1 orange	Sugar

Oven temperature: moderate (350 °F, mark 4)

Dip the cutlets in the seasoned flour. Fry several at a time in the hot butter for 7–10 minutes, until golden; turn them once. Remove the cutlets and keep warm. Drain off the dripping and add to the pan the orange juice and rind, the lemon juice and the red-currant jelly. Simmer, stirring occasionally, until the residue is scraped from the pan and the jelly has melted. Add the arrowroot, blended to a cream with a little water; stir, and adjust the sharpness by adding a little sugar. Return the cutlets to the pan, turning them in the glaze, and re-heat. Serve piping hot. (Serves 4.)

Roast Beef

So simple, so good

Suitable Cuts: Sirloin on or off the bone; rib on or off the bone; topside; rump. Allow per person: 8–12 oz. with bone; 4–6 oz. without bone.
Roasting Temperatures: Prime cuts, hot (425 °F, mark 7) lesser cuts, fairly hot (375 °F, mark 5).
Roasting Times: For rare meat, of prime cuts, 15 minutes per pound and 15 minutes over; for medium to well done, 20 minutes per pound and 20 minutes over. Cheaper joints, topside, thick flank, 25 minutes per pound. Boned and rolled, 30 minutes per pound for 'medium rare'.
Method: Put on a rack in the baking tin. Do *not* salt before cooking. Baste every 30 minutes, adding extra fat only if the joint is very lean.
Variations: 1. Red wine and beef are perfect partners. Add some wine to the pan after the first half-hour, and then baste well. 2. As a marinade, use red wine, seasoning, herbs and garlic.
Gravy: Serve a thin gravy made from the pan juices. Add a little stock or red wine (if not already included).
Accompaniments: Nothing to beat horseradish – 2 oz. of it, freshly grated, ¼ pint double cream, lightly whipped, salt, pepper, 2 tsps. lemon juice, all folded together and chilled.

Boeuf en Daube

Gorgeous French way with beef

2½ lb. top rump of beef	¼ pint beef stock
1 oz. butter	1 level tsp. dried basil
2 tbsps. cooking oil	½ level tsp. dried
½ lb. onions, finely	rosemary
sliced	1 bay leaf
1 lb. carrots, finely	½ level tsp. powdered
sliced	mixed spice
½ lb. salt pork, rinded	Salt and pepper
and cubed	6 black olives
½ pint dry white wine	

Oven temperature: warm (325 °F, mark 3)

Secure the beef firmly with string. Fry quickly in butter and oil to seal the meat; drain on absorbent paper and place in a casserole. Fry the onions, carrots and salt pork until golden-brown; drain and place around the beef. Pour the wine and stock over, and stir in the basil, rosemary, bay leaf and mixed spice; season well. Bring to the boil in a flameproof casserole, replace the lid and cook for 2½–3 hours until fork-tender. Half an hour before the end of the cooking time, add the stoned olives. When the meat is cooked, remove the string and slice the beef. Skim the fat from the juices. Serve from the casserole, accompanied by plain boiled potatoes and Brussels sprouts. (Serves 6.)

127

Filet de Boeuf en Croûte

(See picture on right)
Impressive, delicious

2 lb. fillet of beef	An 11-oz. pkt. of frozen
Salt and pepper	puff pastry
2 oz. butter	(defrosted)
1 tbsp. oil	1 egg, beaten
8 oz. liver pâté	

Oven temperature: fairly hot (400 °F, mark 6)

Place the meat on a board, and, using a sharp knife, trim and discard all the excess fat and sinewy parts. Sprinkle all over with salt and pepper. Tie some fine string round the meat at intervals to form it into a neat shape, carry the string round the end and across to the other side as for a parcel, and tie firmly.

Heat 1 oz. butter with the oil in a frying-pan and fry the meat until browned all over, turning frequently. Put the meat in a roasting tin, and dot with the remaining butter. Cook at the top of the oven for 10 minutes. Remove and leave in a cool place until cold; untie the string.

Mix the pâté in a small basin until smooth; season to taste. Using a small palette knife, spread pâté over the top and sides of the meat. Roll out the pastry about ⅛ inch thick, to a rectangle large enough to well-cover the meat; place the beef, pâté side down, in the centre of the pastry, then spread pâté over the rest of the surface. Brush one long side of the pastry with beaten egg, fold the unbrushed side over the meat, fold over the second side and press together. Cut the top piece of pastry at an angle, then cut straight across. Reserve this piece for decoration. Brush the inner edge of the remaining pastry with egg and fold up on to the join. Raise the oven temperature to hot (425 °F, mark 7.) Place the meat join-side down in a roasting tin. Roll out the pastry trimmings and cut into leaves. Brush the pastry surface with beaten egg, arrange the leaves in the centre and brush them with egg. Bake in the centre of the oven for 40 minutes, until the pastry is golden.

Arrange on a flat platter, with a garnish of watercress and tomato. Serve at once, accompanied by buttered asparagus and creamed potatoes. (Serves 6.)

Fondue Bourguignonne

Excellent main course for a small party – 6–8 at most

You need a fondue set consisting of an iron or copper pot over a spirit lamp and a set of long-handled forks. Alternatively, use a thermostatically controlled electric table cooker or frying pan.

Allow 6 oz. best grilling steak per person, cut into 1-inch cubes. Fill the pot two-thirds full with oil (corn oil is suitable) and heat on a cooker to 375 °F. Transfer to the stand or to a table cooker which will keep the oil at just the correct temperature. (If you are using an electric frying-pan, half-fill it with oil, set the dial to 375 °F and heat up.) If possible, have a second pot of oil heated up, so that the first bowl can be replaced when the temperature of the oil begins to drop. Place a plate of steak and a long-handled fork in front of each diner; it is a good idea to give each a second fork, so that the cooked steak can be transferred to it for eating.

Each person impales a piece of steak on the long-handled fork and dips it into the oil until it is sufficiently cooked. It is then transferred to the cold fork and dipped into one of the sauces or garnishes on the table.

Have 3–4 of the following sauces and 1–2 side dishes on the table and serve crusty French bread and butter and a green salad.

Accompaniments

Hollandaise sauce

Tartare sauce

Tomato mayonnaise (mayonnaise flavoured with tomato paste)

Curry mayonnaise (mayonnaise flavoured with curry powder)

Horseradish sauce (mix whipped double cream with enough horseradish relish to flavour)

Side Dishes

Chopped banana	Chopped parsley
Sliced gherkins	Chopped chives
Sliced olives	

Boeuf Bourguignonne

Full of flavour, a rich classic dish

2 lb. topside of beef	$\frac{1}{4}$ pint stock, made with
1$\frac{1}{2}$ oz. lard	a stock cube
4-oz. piece streaky	A pinch of thyme
bacon, diced	$\frac{1}{2}$ a bay leaf
1 level tbsp. flour	1 clove of garlic,
3 tbsps. brandy	crushed
$\frac{1}{4}$ pint red wine	Salt and pepper
(Burgundy)	6–8 shallots, left whole

Oven temperature: warm (325 °F, mark 3)

Cut the meat into 2-inch squares. Melt 1 oz. lard in a saucepan and brown the meat on both sides, a few pieces at a time. Drain off nearly all the fat, add the bacon, sprinkle with flour and allow to brown, stirring occasionally. Transfer to a 3$\frac{1}{2}$-pint ovenproof casserole. Warm the brandy, ignite and pour while still flaming over the meat. Add the wine and stock, stirring all the time, then stir in the thyme, bay leaf, garlic and seasoning. Cook for 2 hours.

Melt the remaining lard in a small pan and brown the shallots. Drain them thoroughly and add to the meat. Reduce the temperature of the oven to cool (300 °F, mark 2) and cook for a further $\frac{1}{2}$ hour, or until the meat is tender. Remove the bay leaf. Serve with creamy mashed potato. (Serves 4–5.)

Carbonnade of Beef

Beef and beer – it should be British, but hails from the Continent!

2 lb. lean stewing	A 2$\frac{1}{4}$-oz. can of con-
steak	centrated tomato
1 oz. butter	purée
2 tbsps. cooking oil	1 clove of garlic,
$\frac{3}{4}$ lb. onions, sliced	skinned and crushed
1 pint pale ale	$\frac{1}{4}$ pint beef stock
A little grated nutmeg	Salt and pepper

Oven temperature: cool (300 °F, mark 2)

Discard the excess fat from the meat; cut the meat in 1$\frac{1}{2}$ to 2-inch squares and heat the butter and oil in a large frying-pan. Fry quickly to seal the meat – do not over-brown. Drain the meat and place it in a casserole, or put aside if a flameproof casserole is being used. Add the onions to the frying-pan and cook until transparent, then drain and add to the casserole.

In a clean saucepan, reduce the ale by half by boiling rapidly. Add the tomato purée, nutmeg, garlic and stock, and adjust the seasoning. Pour over the meat in the casserole and stir well. Cover tightly and cook in the oven for about 3$\frac{1}{2}$ hours, until the meat is fork-tender. (Serves 4–5.)

Boeuf Stroganoff

Top-of-the-stove special

1$\frac{1}{2}$ lb. fillet of beef	Salt
$\frac{1}{2}$ lb. onions	Freshly ground black
$\frac{1}{2}$ lb. button	pepper
mushrooms	$\frac{1}{4}$ pint soured cream
2 oz. butter	

Trim the beef free of any fat; cut in thin strips about 2 inches long and $\frac{1}{4}$ inch wide. Slice the onions finely. If necessary, wipe the mushrooms, but do not wash; slice finely. Melt 1 oz. butter in a frying-pan, add the onions and fry very slowly, until evenly browned. Add the mushrooms and fry for a few minutes longer, adding a little more butter if required. Remove the onions and mushrooms from the pan and keep warm. Add the rest of the butter to the pan and heat. Put in the prepared steak and fry rapidly to seal – about 4 minutes — turning it occasionally. Return the onions and mushrooms to the pan, season well with salt and freshly ground pepper and shake the pan over the heat. Add the soured cream, stir once and cook for a minute over a high heat. Serve at once, with rice or puréed potatoes and a French-dressed green salad. (Serves 4.)

Note. For more sauce, increase the soured cream to ½ pint.

Grilled Steaks Garnis

(See picture on right)

The ever-popular steak in various guises

Brush the meat with melted butter or oil and place under a preheated grill. Cook under a really high heat for 1 minute on either side, then reduce to moderate heat and cook, turning from time to time until brown outside yet tender and juicy inside.

Total Cooking Times

Thickness	Rare (mins.)	Medium (mins.)	Well done (mins.)
¾ inch	5	9–10	14–15
1 inch	6–7	10–12	15
1½ inches	10	12–14	18–20

Steaks may also be fried in shallow fat (preferably butter) – quickly at first on both sides to seal the outside, then gently until they are cooked.

Serve with chipped, creamed or sautéed potatoes, and garnish with fresh sprigs of watercress.

Grilled tomatoes and grilled or sautéed mushrooms are often served as well. Onion rings dipped in milk or egg white and then in seasoned flour and fried until crisp are popular (see picture).

Steak au Poivre

The famous classic 'pepper' steak

1 oz. white peppercorns	2 tbsps. brandy
1½ lb. rump steak	¼ pint dry white wine
1 oz. butter	2 tbsps. double cream
	Salt and pepper

Crush the peppercorns roughly and coat both sides of the steak with them. Heat the butter. Add the steak and cook in the usual way. Place on a serving dish and keep hot.

Pour off the fat, leaving the peppercorns in the pan. Pour in the brandy and wine, add the cream and warm through. Taste and season: pour over the steak and serve at once.

Steak Diane

Good flavour, enhanced by skilful seasoning

4 pieces of fillet steak, ¼ inch thick	2 tbsps. Worcestershire sauce
1 oz. butter	1 tbsp. grated onion
2 tbsps. oil	2 tsps. chopped parsley
1 tbsp. lemon juice	

Fry the steaks in the butter and oil for 1–2 minutes on each side. Remove them (keeping them hot) and add the lemon juice and Worcestershire sauce to the juices in the pan, stir well and warm through; add the onion and parsley and cook gently for 1 minute. Serve the sauce spooned over the steaks.

Fried Beef with Green Peppers

(See colour picture facing p. 241)

A Chinese speciality

½ lb. fat-free rump steak	1 spring onion stalk, chopped
Corn oil	1 tsp. Chinese wine –
½ a clove of garlic, skinned and crushed	Shao Hsing if available – otherwise
4 thin slices of green ginger root	substitute sherry

Seasoning for Beef

¼ level tsp. bicarbonate of soda	1½ tbsps. peanut oil
½ level tsp. salt	¼ tsp. vinegar
2 tsps. dark soy sauce	Freshly ground pepper
1 level tbsp. cornflour	6 tbsps. water

For the Green Peppers

2 medium-sized green peppers	4 tbsps. good chicken stock
1 tbsp. corn oil	A pinch of salt

For the Gravy

1 tbsp. oyster sauce	A few drops of sesame oil
1 tsp. dark soy sauce	
1 tbsp. good chicken stock	A pinch each of salt, pepper and sugar
1 level tsp. cornflour	

Using a sharp cook's knife, slice the beef against the grain into very thin slices. Wipe and halve the green peppers, discard the seeds and slice the 'shells' very thinly. Put the beef into a dish; add all the beef seasonings listed, giving a good turn of the pepper mill, and then gradually add the water, mixing well.

Heat the oil for the green peppers in a large, deep frying pan. Add the peppers, stock and a pinch of salt and boil for 15 seconds, then drain.

Heat 1 pint corn oil for the beef in a frying pan over a medium heat. Add the meat and cook for 15 seconds. Strain off the oil. Put in 2 tbsps. fresh corn oil, add the garlic, ginger, spring onion, beef and green pepper, and quick-fry over full heat for 15 seconds. Sprinkle the rice wine or sherry over, then add the ingredients for the gravy. Mix well and re-heat. Turn the mixture into a hot serving dish and serve at once.

Burgundy Beef Galantine

(See colour picture facing p. 96)

Excellent cold dish

A 3-lb. piece of chuck steak	1 large carrot, sliced
	1 bay leaf
¾ lb. back bacon rashers, rinded	1 level tsp. dried herbs
	½ pint red wine
Salt and pepper	(Burgundy-style)
2 oz. butter	½ lb. button
1 tbsp. oil	mushrooms, sliced
1 large onion, sliced	½ oz. gelatine

Oven temperature: moderate (350 °F, mark 4)

Trim all excess fat from the meat and discard. Lay the bacon rashers over the meat and tie into a long roll with string. Season with salt and pepper. Heat 1 oz. butter and the oil in a large flameproof casserole. Add the meat and fry, turning until sealed all over. Add the onion, carrot, herbs, wine and ½ pint water. Bring to the boil, cover and cook in oven for 3 hours.

Remove the meat from the stock and leave until quite cold. Place the stock in the refrigerator; when it is cold, skim off and discard the fat. Make the stock up to 1 pint with water if necessary. Sauté the mushrooms in the remaining 1 oz. butter, then leave until quite cold. Cut the meat into thin slices; arrange half of these in a 3 to 4-pint loaf tin, cover with the mushrooms, then the remaining meat. Dissolve the gelatine in 2 tbsps. water in a basin in a pan of hot water, add to the stock and mix well. When beginning to set, pour over the meat. Leave until quite set, then unmould and serve sliced. (Serves 6–8.)

Steak, Oyster and Mushroom Pudding

Victorian favourite

For the crust

8 oz. self-raising flour	4 oz. shredded suet
½ level tsp. salt	Water to mix

For the filling

1 lb. best stewing steak, trimmed	Oil
	4 oz. mushrooms
4 oz. ox kidney	A 7-oz. can of oysters
2 level tbsps. seasoned flour	Salt and pepper
	½ pint stock

Sift together the flour and salt, add the suet and mix well. Add enough water to make a soft but not sticky dough. Leave to stand.

Cut the steak into $\frac{3}{4}$-inch pieces. Toss the steak and kidney in seasoned flour and fry in a little oil until browned. Allow to cool. Wipe the mushrooms and slice them; drain the oysters.

Roll out three-quarters of the pastry into a round about $\frac{1}{4}$ inch thick. Grease a $1\frac{1}{2}$-pint basin, lower the pastry in and gently press it in to line the basin to the rim. Fill with alternate layers of steak, kidney, juice from the pan, mushrooms, oysters, seasoning and stock. Roll out the rest of the pastry into a round to fit the top; damp the edges with water and fit on the lid, pressing the edges together. Cover with greased greaseproof paper and a foil cap. Boil the pudding for $3\frac{1}{2}$–4 hours in a pan with water half-way up the basin. Top up occasionally with hot water to maintain the level.

Roast Veal

Veal requires a little more 'dressing up' than beef or lamb

Suitable Cuts: Loin, leg, shoulder and breast (boned and rolled). Allow per person: 8–12 oz. on the bone; 4–6 oz. boned.

Roasting Temperatures: Moderate (350 °F, mark 4) or hot (425 °F, mark 7) in foil.

Roasting Time: 40 minutes per pound for boned and stuffed joints (at 350 °F). In foil, on the bone, 25 minutes per pound plus 25 minutes over (at 425 °F).

Method: Put the joint direct in the roasting tin. Ideally, cover it with overlapping rashers of streaky bacon, or lard it with bacon strips. If roasting it plain, rub it with salt and pepper, add a bay leaf to the pan for subtle flavour, and baste every 30 minutes.

Good Housekeeping's Special Stuffing: Suitable for a 3-lb. piece of boned loin or breast. Mix together 3 oz. breadcrumbs, $\frac{1}{2}$ lb. minced pork, 4 oz. minced beef, 1 tbsp. chopped parsley, 4 oz. Emmenthal or Gruyère cheese (cubed), 1 level tsp. salt, $\frac{1}{2}$ level tsp. pepper. Blend the dry ingredients, then add 1 beaten egg.

Gravy: With a stuffed joint, reduce the liquor from the roasting pan and thicken. Or use this as the basis of a tomato sauce, Italian style.

Accompaniments: Bacon rolls, forcemeat balls, sautéed prunes and apple wedges.

Veal à la Crème

Rich and creamy

4 escalopes (total weight about 12 oz.)	3 tbsps. brandy
	$\frac{1}{4}$ pint double cream
Salt and pepper	A dash of sherry and of
Lemon juice	Worcestershire
$1\frac{1}{2}$ oz. butter	sauce
4 oz. mushrooms, sliced	Chopped parsley

Flatten the escalopes and season with salt, pepper and a little lemon juice. Melt 1 oz. butter and fry the escalopes until just brown on both sides; remove from the pan and keep warm on a serving dish. Add the remaining butter and sauté the mushrooms until tender. Add the brandy and set it alight. Loosen any residue in the pan and add the cream, sherry and Worcestershire sauce; check the seasoning. Re-heat gently but do not boil. Pour over the escalopes, and serve garnished with chopped parsley.

Note. A quickie speciality – forget about vegetables and serve a crisp green salad, with shoestring potatoes, oven-warm rolls or crispbread, and fresh fruit for dessert.

Veal with Oranges

Sophisticated flavouring

$1\frac{1}{2}$ lb. shoulder of veal, boned	2 carrots, thinly sliced
	2 oranges, peeled and thinly sliced
1 oz. butter	
$\frac{1}{2}$ level tsp. salt	$\frac{1}{4}$ pint white stock
$\frac{1}{8}$–$\frac{1}{4}$ level tsp. pepper	3 tbsps. sherry
Caster sugar	

Oven temperature: warm (325 °F, mark 3)

Cut the veal into strips about 1 inch wide and 3 inches long; fry the strips in the butter for 3 minutes on each side. Remove from the pan, drain well and place in a 3-pint ovenproof casserole. Mix together the salt, pepper and sugar and sprinkle over the meat. Place the carrots and oranges on top, pour the stock over, cover and cook for 1½ hours. Stir in the sherry and cook, uncovered, for a further 15 minutes. Spoon over some fluffy boiled rice and serve with green salad on side plates. (Serves 4.)

Hungarian Goulash

Paprika-flavoured Continental casserole

2 lb. boned shoulder or leg of veal	Garlic salt
2 oz. dripping or lard	Black pepper
¾ lb. onions, thinly sliced	¾ pint stock
1 level tbsp. flour	½ level tsp. carraway seeds
1 level tbsp. paprika	1½ lb. potatoes
1 level tbsp. concentrated tomato purée	A 5-oz. carton of soured cream
	Chopped parsley

Oven temperature: warm (325 °F, mark 3)

Cut the meat into large serving pieces and fry quickly in the fat until sealed and brown. Drain the meat from the fat and place in a casserole. Fry the onions until soft and golden-brown. Add the flour, paprika, tomato purée, garlic salt, pepper and stock, bring to the boil and pass through a sieve or liquidize in an electric blender. Pour the sieved ingredients over the meat, stir in the carraway seeds and cover tightly. Cook in the oven for about 1½ hours; add the potatoes, roughly cut into ½-inch cubes, and return the goulash to the oven for a further hour to finish cooking.

Put the soured cream in a small pan and bring gently to the boil. Pour over the casserole, top with chopped parsley. (Serves 4–5.)

Vitello Tonnato

An Italian cold dish to include in a buffet spread

1½ lb. boned leg of veal	A 3-oz. can of tuna fish
1 small carrot, sliced	4 anchovy fillets
1 onion, quartered	¼ pint olive oil
1 stick of celery, chopped	2 egg yolks
4 peppercorns	Pepper
1 level tsp. salt	1 tbsp. lemon juice
	Capers and lemon slices for garnish

Tie the meat into a neat roll, put into a saucepan with the meat bone, carrot, onion, celery, peppercorns, salt and some water; bring to the boil, cover and simmer till tender – about 1 hour. Remove the meat and cool.

Meanwhile, mix together the tuna fish, anchovy fillets and 1 tbsp. olive oil. 'Break down' the fish with a wooden spoon, then stir in the egg yolks and pepper. Press all through a sieve into a small basin and add the lemon juice. Stir in the remaining oil a little at a time, beating thoroughly after each addition; continue until the sauce resembles thin cream.

Cut the meat into slices, arrange in a shallow dish and coat completely with the sauce; cover and leave overnight. Serve cold, with a garnish of capers and lemon slices. (Serves 6.)

Roast Pork

What could be more appetising on a cold day?

Suitable Cuts: Loin, spare ribs, blade, hind leg, hand and spring. Allow per person: 8–12 oz. with bone; 4–6 oz. without bone.

Roasting Temperature: 425 °F (mark 7).

Roasting Time: Allow 25 minutes per pound plus 25 minutes.

Method: Pork rind should be smooth and pliable when raw, if it is to give a good crisp crackling. Ask the butcher to score the rind deeply at ¼-inch intervals. Rub it well with oil and salt before cooking, on a rack.

Variations: For a herb glaze, mix 2–3 tbsps. powdered thyme and a crumbled bay leaf with made mustard, rub into the rind and sprinkle generously with salt and black pepper a few hours before cooking. Alternatively, the crackling can be brushed with honey during the last 15 minutes of cooking time.

Gravy: Leave 2 tbsps. fat in the roasting tin, dredge in 2 level tbsps. flour, blend well and cook gently until beginning to brown. Stir continuously, then mix in ½ pint stock and boil for 2–3 minutes. Finally, add 1 tbsp. dry cider or white wine. Season well and strain.

Stuffing: For boned, rolled loin, use a prune and apple mixture.

Accompaniments: Peaches in brandy or spiced with cloves for high days; Lyonnaise potato.

Pork Roast with Prunes

Warming main dish for winter-time

A 4-lb. blade-bone of pork, boned, rolled and scored	A little grated lemon rind
12 plump Californian prunes, stoned	Cooking oil Savoury or plain salt

Oven temperature: fairly hot (375 °F, mark 5)

Make a 'pocket' in the joint and insert the prunes and grated lemon rind. Rub the rind generously with cooking oil and sprinkle with salt – celery, onion, garlic or plain. Stand the joint on a rack in a roasting tin and cook, allowing 30 minutes per pound plus 30 minutes over. Serve with rich gravy, braised celery and roast potatoes. The remainder can of course be served cold, with salad and hot jacket potatoes. (Serves 6–8.)

Pork Stroganoff

Similar to the better-known beef dish

1 lb. pork fillet or tenderloin	$\frac{1}{2}$ lb. mushrooms, thickly sliced
Seasoned flour	$\frac{1}{2}$ lb. tomatoes, skinned, quartered and seeded
1 oz. butter	
1 tbsp. corn oil	2 5-fl. oz. cartons of soured cream
4 oz. lean streaky bacon rashers, rinded	

Cut the pork into strips about 2 inches by $\frac{1}{2}$ inch, and coat well in seasoned flour. Heat the butter and oil in a 9-inch frying-pan. Add the meat and fry until lightly browned all over, turning frequently. Put the meat on one side and keep warm.

Scissor-snip the bacon into strips, add to the pan and fry until browned; put aside with the meat. Cook the mushrooms in the same pan until tender and then add the tomatoes. Return the pork and bacon to the pan, stir well and add the soured cream. Loosen the residue from the pan base, bring to the boil and check the seasoning; reduce the heat and simmer for about 20 minutes, stirring occasionally.

Serve with diced potatoes, golden-fried in shallow fat, and leaf spinach.

Note. For a less rich sauce, replace 1 carton of soured cream by $\frac{1}{4}$ pint stock. (Serves 4.)

Sweet–Sour Pork

Chinese-type dish

1 small carrot, very thinly sliced	2 tsps. soy sauce
2 medium-sized onions, very thinly sliced	3 oz. dark, soft brown sugar Cornflour
2 tbsps. corn oil	2 tbsps. water
An 8-oz. can of pineapple tid-bits	Salt and pepper
$\frac{1}{4}$ pint pineapple juice	1–2 lb. belly or shoulder pork
$\frac{1}{4}$ pint malt vinegar	2 eggs
Juice and grated rind of 1 small lemon	2 level tsps. flour Oil for frying

Gently fry the carrot and onions in the oil for 10 minutes. To the saucepan add the pineapple and $\frac{1}{4}$ pint juice, vinegar, lemon juice, rind, soy sauce and sugar. Cover and simmer for 15 minutes. Blend 2 level tsps. cornflour to a cream with the water; stir into the ingredients in the saucepan and simmer, stirring, for 5 minutes. Check the seasoning and keep hot.

Cut the pork into 1-inch cubes. Beat the eggs with 2 level tsps. cornflour and the flour. Dip the pork cubes in the mixture and fry in deep oil until golden-brown – about 10 minutes. Drain well on kitchen paper.

Pour most of the sauce into a hot dish, pile in the pork, add the remaining sauce and serve at once. (Serves 4.)

Pork Chops with Plums

The superb plums of southern Germany led to this dish

4 pork chops	4 cloves
$\frac{1}{2}$ lb. fresh plums	1 glass dry red wine
1 oz. sugar	Salt and pepper
Powdered cinnamon	

Oven temperature: moderate (350 °F, mark 4)

Trim the chops free of excess fat and heat the trimmings to extract some fat; use this to fry the chops until lightly but evenly browned. Stew the plums with sugar and just enough water to prevent the fruit from burning; pass the mixture through a sieve. Put the chops in a shallow heatproof dish in a single layer. Add a pinch of cinnamon and the cloves to the plum purée, and pour over the chops. Add the wine, season with salt and pepper, cover and bake for 1 hour, adding a little water if necessary during the cooking. (Serves 4.)

Roast Gammon

(See picture below)

Hard to beat as a cut-and-come-again joint

A 4-lb. gammon joint	Cloves
2 oz. Demerara sugar	2 tbsps. honey
	2 tbsps. orange juice

Oven temperature: moderate (350 °F, mark 4)

Soak the bacon for several hours in cold water, then drain. Place the joint in a pan, skin side down, cover with water and add the sugar. Bring slowly to the boil and remove the scum.

Reduce the heat and simmer, covered, for half the calculated cooking time, allowing 20–25 minutes per pound and 20 minutes over. Top up the pan with extra boiling water when necessary.

Drain the joint, carefully strip off the rind and score the fat into squares, then stud with cloves. Blend the sugar, honey and orange juice and spread over the joint. Place it in a roasting tin and roast in a moderate oven for the rest of the cooking time, basting two or three times. About 20 minutes before the end of the cooking time, raise the oven temperature to hot (425 °F, mark 7).

Serve hot, garnished if desired with apricot halves and glacé cherries impaled on cocktail sticks. (Serves 10.)

Gammon and Onion Pizza

(See colour picture facing p. 208)
Unusual version of the famous Italian dish

For the Dough

½ lb. plain bread flour	¼ oz. fresh baker's yeast
1 level tsp. salt	¼ pint water
¼ oz. lard	Oil

For the Topping

1 lb. gammon, cut in ½-inch slices and rinded	2 level tsps. dried marjoram
3 tbsps. oil	Salt and pepper
1 lb. onions, sliced	4 oz. Bel Paese cheese, grated

Oven temperature: very hot (450 °F, mark 8)

Grease a shallow rectangular tin measuring about 12¼ by 8½ inches by ¾ inch deep.

Roll out the dough to fit the base of the tin. Trim the gammon slices and cut into ¼-inch cubes. Fry in oil until sealed all over. Remove the gammon from pan, add the onions and sauté until soft but not coloured. Mix with the gammon. Spread the gammon mixture over the dough and sprinkle with marjoram, salt and pepper, then cover with grated cheese. Bake in the centre of the oven for 20 minutes, cover loosely with kitchen foil and continue to cook for 20 minutes. Serve hot. (Serves 6.)

Mixed Grill

Traditional fare, but it lends itself to variation

4 best end of neck lamb chops	4 rashers of bacon, rinded
2 lamb's kidneys	4 tomatoes, halved
4 mushrooms	Salt and pepper
½ lb. chipolatas	Melted butter or oil

Trim the chops; skin, halve and core the kidneys; trim the ends of the mushroom stalks. Sprinkle all the meats and vegetables with salt and pepper and brush with melted fat. Heat the grill, and if it has an open grid place the tomatoes (cut side up) and the mushrooms (stalks up) in the pan, where they will be basted by the juices from the other food and will cook without further attention. Replace the grid and put on the chops, sausages and kidneys. Cook them under a medium heat, allowing 14–16 minutes altogether and turning the food frequently to ensure even cooking. The kidneys will probably be cooked first, so remove these and keep them warm. Replace them by the bacon rashers and cook for a further 3–5 minutes. (If necessary, keep the cooked meats hot in a low oven.)

Serve the food on a large plate, with a simple garnish of watercress. Traditional accompaniments are chipped or matchstick potatoes, and for formal occasions maître d'hôtel butter.

Note. Small pieces of fillet or rump steak are often substituted for the lamb chop; calf's or lamb's liver is sometimes included in a grill.

Kebabs

This Eastern dish has become very popular in recent years

A thick slice of lamb taken from the leg (approx. 1 lb.)	8 rashers of streaky bacon, rolled up
3 tbsps. olive oil	8 button mushrooms
1 tbsp. lemon juice	A few bay leaves (optional)
Salt and pepper	2 small onions, quartered (optional)
A clove of garlic, skinned and crushed	Melted butter
4 small tomatoes	Boiled long-grain rice

Remove any fat and gristle from the meat and cut the meat into 1-inch cubes. Marinade for 2 hours (or preferably overnight) in the olive oil, lemon juice, seasoning and crushed garlic. Thread 8 skewers alternately with meat cubes, halved tomatoes, bacon rolls and whole mushrooms. If liked, a bay leaf or an onion quarter may be placed on each side of the meat pieces, to give more flavour. Brush with melted butter and cook under a low grill for 10–15 minutes, turning the kebabs about 3 times, until the meat is tender. Serve on plain boiled rice. If wished the skewer may be carefully removed from each kebab, so that pieces of food rest in a line as it was cooked. However, if small, decorative skewers are used, the kebabs may be served on them.

Lamb's kidneys may also be used; allow ¼ kidney per person, removing the core. Thread the pieces on to the skewers with the other ingredients and cook as above.

Kebab Cookery with a Rôtisserie Unit

Special kebab attachments are now supplied with some rôtisserie units. They consist of a number of skewers which are revolved by means of the rôtisserie motor. The exact manner of assembling the attachment varies with the particular model, but details will be supplied with your cooker.

General hints for using a kebab attachment:

1. Choose a mixture of fatty and drier foods and cut them into even-sized pieces.

2. Grease the skewers before use. (Allow as a rule one skewerful per person.)

3. Skewer the food and use the discs provided to hold the pieces firmly in position.

4. Brush the foods over with oil or melted fat.

5. Turn on the heat and let the grill or oven become very hot.

6. Put the kebab attachment in place and turn on the motor. Cook for 10–20 minutes, basting if necessary, until all the foods are done.

Rich Raised Pie

(See picture on right)
An unusual mixed meat filling

Veal bones	½ lb. lean pork
A 2½-lb. oven-ready chicken, boned	½ lb. shoulder veal
	2 tbsps. chopped
Salt and pepper	parsley
½ lb. lean streaky bacon, rinded	1 lb. pork sausage-meat

For the Hot-water Crust

1 lb. plain flour	¼ pint milk or water
2 level tsps. salt	approx.
4 oz. lard	

Oven temperature: fairly hot (400 °F, mark 6)

Chop the veal bones and use them, together with the chicken bones, skin and giblets, to make a well-seasoned, concentrated jellied stock; leave to cool in the refrigerator.

Separate the chicken breasts and cut into pieces; mince the remainder of the flesh, together with the pork and half the bacon rashers. Dice the veal.

Blend the parsley into the sausage-meat. Cut the remaining bacon rashers in half, stretch each piece on a flat surface with a knife; spread a thin layer of sausage-meat over the bacon and roll up.

Sift the flour and the salt together into a basin. Heat the lard and liquid until boiling and add to the flour, stirring. The consistency should be soft but manageable; knead until smooth. Roll out about two-thirds of the pastry and use to line an 8-inch oval fancy pie mould, placed on a baking sheet. Press the pastry well into the base and the pattern. Use three-quarters of the remaining sausage to make a lining over the pastry. Fill the centre alternately with bacon rolls, minced pork mixture, veal and chicken breast, piled well up. Season well, and cover with the remaining sausage-meat. Damp the edges of the pastry and roll out the remaining piece for a lid. Trim the edges and seal. Decorate with pastry trimmings, and make a hole in the centre of the pie. Brush well with beaten egg. Bake in a hot oven for 30 minutes, reduce the heat to moderate (350 °F, mark 4) and cook for about a further 2 hours. Cover with foil once the pastry is a good golden-brown.

When the pie is quite cold, fill up with cool but not cold liquid stock. (Serves 6–8.)

Orange Sweet–Sour Tongue

This meat combines well with orange

3 lb. fresh ox tongue	1½ oz. flour
1 medium-sized onion, sliced	⅛ level tsp. pepper
1 carrot, sliced	1 level tsp. soft brown sugar
2 stalks of celery, sliced	¼ pint fresh orange juice
2 sprigs of parsley	1 level tbsp. grated orange peel
2 level tsps. salt	
Boiling water	1 orange, segmented
2 oz. butter	

Wash the tongue and place it in a large saucepan. Add the onion, carrot, celery, parsley and salt and pour on enough boiling water to just cover the meat. Cover the pan and simmer for 2½–3 hours, or until the meat is tender. Remove the tongue from the liquor and trim off the bone and gristle at the thick end; skin the tongue, slice lengthways and keep warm. Strain off the vegetables and 1 pint of the cooking liquor. Purée the vegetables. Melt the butter in a pan, stir in the flour and cook gently for 1 minute. Stir in the liquor, with the puréed vegetables, and simmer till thickened. Flavour with the pepper, sugar, orange juice and peel; if necessary, add a little more salt. Stir in the orange segments and heat through. Pour the sauce over the warm tongue just before serving. (Serves 6.)

Rice goes well with this dish.

Liver and Bacon Provençale

Party version of a popular partnership

1 lb. lambs' liver	1 level tsp. dried marjoram
2 oz. flour	
2 tbsps. olive oil	1 bay leaf
½ lb. bacon, rinded and chopped	1 tbsp. Worcestershire sauce
1 lb. onions, chopped	¾ pint stock
14-oz. can tomatoes	Seasoning

Oven temperature: warm (300 °F, mark 2)

Slice the liver into long thick strips, coat with flour and fry in oil until golden-brown. Place in a casserole.

Add the bacon and onions to the frying-pan, cook until golden. Stir in excess flour, in which the liver was coated. Add the tomatoes, marjoram, bay leaf and Worcestershire sauce. Stir in the stock, season well, place in a casserole. Cover with a tight-fitting lid and cook for about 1½ hours. Serve with noodles tossed in butter and a side salad – perhaps a crisp cole slaw. (Serves 4.)

Liver with Marsala

A popular Italian dish, served with fluffy rice and an individual green salad

1 lb. calf's or lamb's liver	3 tbsps. Marsala
	¼ pint stock, made with a stock cube
Lemon juice	
Seasoned flour	Mushrooms to garnish
2 oz. butter	

Cut the liver into 12 thick slices; sprinkle with lemon juice and coat with seasoned flour. Melt the butter in a frying-pan and fry the liver on both sides until just brown. Stir in the Marsala and stock and simmer gently until the liver is just cooked and the sauce syrupy. Arrange on a serving dish and garnish with the lightly sautéed mushrooms. (Serves 4.)

Kidney Royale

A good flambé dish

8 lambs' kidneys	Salt
1½ oz. butter	Black pepper
1 medium-sized onion, chopped	2 tbsps. Irish whiskey
	4 tbsps. soured cream
2 canned red pimiento caps	8 oz. long-grain rice
	diced chopped parsley

Halve the kidneys, remove and discard the skin and cores, then cut into pieces. Melt the butter in a frying-pan and sauté the onion gently for about 5 minutes, till transparent but not coloured. Add the kidneys and sauté for about 10 minutes. Stir in the pimiento, season with salt and pepper and simmer for a further 5 minutes. Pour the whiskey over and flambé. Remove the pan from the heat, stir in the cream and re-heat gently.

Arrange freshly boiled rice around the edge of a serving dish, and pile the kidneys in the centre. Garnish generously with the chopped parsley. (Serves 4.)

Sweetbreads in Onion Sauce

The Continental-type sauce makes this dish

1 lb. calves' sweetbreads	1 clove of garlic, crushed
Juice of 1 lemon	1 bay leaf
Salt	¼ pint dry white wine
Pepper	¼ pint stock (made with a cube)
2 oz. butter	
1 onion, sliced	¼ level tsp. dried thyme
1 carrot, sliced	

For the Sauce

1 oz. butter	½ pint sweetbread stock (see below)
1 large onion, grated	
1 oz. flour	4 tbsps. double cream

Put the sweetbreads in a bowl, cover with water, add the lemon juice and leave for 1 hour. Drain and place in a pan with fresh water to cover. Season, bring to the boil, then cover and simmer for 15 minutes. Drain off the liquor and discard. Trim the sweetbreads and cut into manageable pieces. Melt the butter in a saucepan, add the sweetbreads and fry until golden. Place the onion, carrot, garlic and bay leaf under the sweetbreads, add the wine, stock and thyme, bring to the boil, cover and simmer for 30 minutes. Strain the stock and make up to ½ pint with water.

Heat 1 oz. butter for the sauce in a pan. Add the onion and sauté for 5 minutes. Add the flour, cook for a few minutes, then add the stock, stirring. Bring to the boil, simmer for a few minutes, and add the cream and sweetbreads. Re-heat without boiling. Serve with plain boiled rice.

Sausage and Egg Roll

Quick and easy, as well as cheap

12 oz. shortcrust pastry	Salt
	Pepper
1 lb. pork sausage-meat	2 level tsps. dried mixed herbs
1 clove of garlic, skinned and crushed (optional)	4 eggs
	Milk to mix

Oven temperature: fairly hot (400 °F, mark 6)

Roll out the pastry into a 12-inch square and place on a baking sheet. Work together the sausage-meat, garlic, seasoning and herbs.

Press out to a thick oblong 10 by 3 inches and place in the centre of the pastry. Make 4 'pockets' and break in the eggs. Damp the edges of the pastry with milk, shape the pastry up over the eggs, and press and twist the edges together. Brush with milk. Bake for about 1 hour, until the pastry is golden. Serve hot. (Serves 4.)

Roast Chicken

Standard recipe for an ever-popular dish

Oven temperature: fairly hot (400 °F, mark 6)

If the bird is frozen, allow it to thaw out completely, then remove the bag of giblets. Wash the inside of the bird and stuff it at the neck end with herb stuffing, sausage-meat or another stuffing as you wish. Don't stuff too tightly, as the bread or rice in the forcemeat mixture tends to swell and might cause the skin of the bird to split. To add extra flavour you can put an onion, a thick lemon wedge or a knob of butter in the body of the bird. Brush the chicken with melted butter or oil and sprinkle with salt and pepper. Put it in a shallow roasting tin, and if you like put a few strips of streaky bacon over the breast to prevent the flesh from becoming too dry during the cooking.

Cook in the centre of the oven, basting from time to time and allowing 20 minutes per lb. plus 20 minutes. Put a piece of greaseproof paper over the breast if the flesh shows signs of becoming too brown. Alternatively, wrap the chicken in foil before roasting, making the join along the top; allow the same cooking time, but open the foil for the final 15–20 minutes, to allow the bird to brown.

Serve with roast potatoes and a green vegetable or – for a change – a tossed green salad. Bacon rolls, forcemeat balls, small chipolata sausages, bread sauce and thin gravy are the most usual accompaniments for roast chicken.

Note. An older bird can be roasted if you first steam or boil it for about 2 hours, to make it tender; it is best to do this the previous day, so that the chicken has time to get cold before it is stuffed. Roast for 30–45 minutes to make it crisp, brown and really hot.

Roast Chicken with Pecan Stuffing

American influence is seen here

A 4-lb. roasting chicken (oven-ready weight)	Melted butter or oil

For the Stuffing

Heart and liver from the chicken	A pinch of ground mace
2 oz. fresh white breadcrumbs	A pinch of dried thyme
	1 tbsp. chopped parsley
2 oz. shelled pecans, chopped	A pinch of celery salt
	2 oz. mushrooms, chopped
1 hard-boiled egg, chopped	1½ oz. butter
	1 small onion, chopped
A pinch of ground nutmeg	2 tbsps. sherry
	Freshly ground pepper

Oven temperature: fairly hot (375 °F, mark 5)

Place the chicken heart and liver in a small saucepan and cover with water; simmer for 10 minutes, drain, finely chop or mince, then cool. Add the mixture to the crumbs, pecans, egg, spices, herbs and celery salt in a bowl. Sauté the mushrooms in half the butter for 3–4 minutes and add to the bowl. Fry the onion in the remaining butter and add to the bowl, then mix all the ingredients with sherry and season with pepper.

Wipe the chicken, stuff and truss. Brush with melted butter or oil, season and roast (allowing 20 minutes per pound plus 20 minutes over) until the bird is tender. (Serves 6.)

Chicken Beaujolais

Pre-cut chicken is practical for casseroling

4 rashers of back bacon, rinded and cut up	¾ oz. plain flour
	¼ pint Beaujolais
	¼ pint water
Corn oil	1 chicken stock cube
4 chicken portions, skinned	Salt and pepper
	4 tomatoes, skinned and quartered
2 oz. onion, finely sliced	Chopped parsley

Oven temperature: warm (325 °F, mark 3)

In a shallow flameproof casserole (large enough to take the chicken in a single layer), gently fry the bacon snippets until beginning to brown; drain from the fat. Add just enough oil to the casserole to cover the base. Brown the chicken evenly and lightly, remove from the casserole and strain off all but 1 tbsps. fat. Add bacon and onion; when beginning to colour stir in flour and cook for a minute or two. With the casserole still over the heat, slowly stir in the wine, water and crumbled stock cube. Loosen the residue from the pan base and bring to the boil, stirring. Adjust the seasoning, replace the chicken, flesh side down, and tuck the tomato quarters into the corners. Cover and cook for about 1¼ hours. Serve the chicken with the sauce spooned over and garnish with parsley.

To re-heat from cold give it 30 minutes in a moderate oven (350 °F, mark 4).

Coq au Vin

One of the glories of the French kitchen

A 3-lb. oven-ready roasting chicken	4 tbsps. brandy
	3 level tbsps. flour
3 oz. bacon, rinded and chopped	½ bottle red wine
	¼ pint stock
6 oz. mushrooms, sliced	1 level tbsp. sugar
	A bouquet garni
15 button onions	A pinch of ground nutmeg
½ oz. butter	
1 tbsp. oil	Salt and pepper

Oven temperature: moderate (350 °F, mark 4)

Prepare the chicken and joint into 8 portions. Fry the bacon, mushrooms and onions in the butter and oil for about 3–4 minutes, until lightly browned; remove from the pan. Re-heat the fat and fry the chicken for 8–10 minutes, until golden-brown. Pour the brandy over the chicken, remove the pan from the heat and 'flame' it by igniting the liquid in the saucepan with a match. Remove the chicken from the pan when the flames have died down and place it in a casserole. Stir the flour into the fat remaining in the pan and cook for 2–3 minutes. Stir in the wine and stock gradually, bring to the boil and continue to stir until the mixture thickens; add the sugar, herbs and seasonings. Add the cooked vegetables to the casserole and pour the sauce over the chicken. Cover and cook in the centre of the oven for 1–1¼ hours, until tender. Before serving, remove the bouquet garni. (Serves 4.)

Poulet en Cocotte

Superb casseroled chicken

A 3–3½-lb. chicken oven-ready weight	8 oz. lean back bacon, in one slice
Salt	1 lb. potatoes
Freshly ground pepper	6 oz. shallots
2½ oz. butter	1 lb. small new carrots Chopped parsley to garnish

For the Stuffing

4 oz. sausage-meat	1 chicken liver, chopped
2 level tbsps. fresh white breadcrumbs	2 level tbsps. chopped parsley

Oven temperature: moderate (350 °F, mark 4)

Mix together all the stuffing ingredients in a bowl until well blended. Stuff the chicken at the neck end, plump up and secure with a skewer. Truss the bird as for roasting and season well.

Melt the butter in a large frying-pan, add the chicken and fry, turning until browned all over. Place the chicken and butter in a large ovenproof casserole. Rind the bacon and cut into ¾-inch cubes; add to the casserole, cover and cook for 15 minutes. Meanwhile cut the potatoes into 1-inch dice. Remove the casserole from the oven and baste the chicken. Surround with the potatoes, shallots and carrots, turning them in the fat. Season, return to the oven and cook for a further 1½ hours. Garnish with chopped parsley. Have a hot plate to hand for carving the bird, but serve the vegetables and juices straight from the casserole. (Serves 4.)

Almond Chicken

(See colour picture facing p. 241)

Typically Chinese

12 oz. raw chicken breasts	3 whole blanched mushrooms, quartered
6 oz. whole almonds	1 spring onion stalk, cut lengthwise in thin strips
Salt	
Corn oil	
2 thin slices of green ginger root	½ tsp. Chinese rice wine – Shoa Hsing (if available) or sherry
½ a clove of garlic, skinned and crushed	

Seasoning for Chicken

½ an egg white	1 tsp. dark soy sauce
1 level tsp. cornflour	½ tsp. Chinese rice wine or sherry
A pinch of salt	
A pinch of pepper	

For the Gravy

1 tdsp. stock or water	1 tbsp. oyster sauce
A few drops of sesame oil	A pinch each of salt pepper and sugar
	½ level tsp. cornflour

Dice the chicken flesh. Blanch and halve the almonds, boil them in slightly salted water for 10 minutes; drain. Put 1 pint corn oil into a large, deep frying-pan and heat to 248 °F. Deep-fry the nuts until lightly coloured, then drain. Mix the chicken seasoning ingredients, add the chicken and blend well.

Re-heat the pan of oil to 248 °F, put in the chicken and fry for 15 seconds only, until the chicken becomes white. Strain the oil. Re-heat the pan with 1 tbsp. corn oil, put in the ginger, garlic, mushrooms, spring onion, chicken and gravy ingredients. Stir well. Sprinkle with the rice wine or sherry, add a further 1 tbsp. corn oil, mix well, add nuts and serve hot.

Chicken Maryland

An American recipe that's becoming a British classic

A 3-lb. oven-ready chicken	½ oz. flour
2 level tbsps. seasoned flour	½ pint chicken stock
Beaten egg	A 5-oz. carton of soured cream
4 oz. fresh white breadcrumbs	Salt and pepper
3 oz. butter	Corn fritters (see below)
1 tbsp. oil	Fried bananas (see below)

Divide the chicken into 8 portions. Remove and discard the skin and dip each piece of chicken in seasoned flour. Coat with egg and then with breadcrumbs, patting the crumbs firmly on to the chicken.

Melt the butter in a large frying-pan, and add the oil. When the fat is hot add the chicken, reduce the heat and cook slowly, allowing 35–45 minutes, until evenly browned and well cooked. Drain and keep warm.

Pour off all but 2 tbsps. of the fat. Add the flour and cook, stirring, for 2–3 minutes. Stir in the stock and soured cream, bring to the boil and check the seasoning. Serve the chicken surrounded by corn fritters and fried bananas, with the gravy in a sauceboat. (Serves 4.)

Corn Fritters

Sift 2 oz. flour with some salt and pepper into a basin, make a well in the centre and add 1 beaten egg and 4 tbsps. milk. Beat till smooth. Add more milk to give a coating consistency, then add an 8-oz. can of corn kernels, drained. Fry the batter in spoonfuls in hot fat for about 5 minutes, turning once.

Fried Bananas

Peel 1 banana per person and cut into 3 or 4 pieces. Just before you make the gravy, fry the banana in the chicken fat until lightly browned.

Chicken Paprika

Central European in flavouring

4 large chicken joints	1 clove of garlic, skinned
Salt	and crushed
Black pepper	A 14-oz. can of round
2 oz. flour	skinned tomatoes
2 oz. dripping	½ pint chicken stock
1 lb. onion, sliced	1 bay leaf
1 green pepper,	A 5-oz. carton of
seeded and sliced	soured cream
1 level tbsp. paprika	Chopped parsley

Oven temperature: warm (325 °F, mark 3)

Season the chicken joints with salt and black pepper and toss in flour. Fry quickly, skin side down, in the dripping until golden-brown. Remove from the frying-pan and place in a casserole large enough to take the chicken in a single layer. Add the onion and green pepper to the pan and cook without colouring. Stir in the remaining flour used for coating the chicken joints, with the paprika and garlic. Cook gently for a few minutes. Add the tomatoes, with the juice, stock and bay leaf, to the frying-pan, season and pour over the chicken. Cover tightly with the lid and cook for about 1½ hours. Discard the bay leaf.

Before serving, gently heat the soured cream in a small saucepan and add to the chicken; stir well. Serve on a bed of buttered noodles, sprinkled with parsley. (Serves 4.)

Chicken à la Kiev

For the small dinner party with important guests

4 oz. softened butter	1 egg, beaten
1 tbsp. chopped	4 oz. fresh breadcrumbs
parsley	Fat for deep frying
4 chicken breasts, boned	

Beat the softened butter and chopped parsley together, form into a roll and chill. Beat the boned chicken with a rolling pin until very thin. Divide the butter into 4, place a piece on each of the chicken breasts, wrap the chicken round the butter like a parcel and tie with cotton. Dip each parcel in beaten egg and coat with breadcrumbs. Heat the fat or oil until a 1-inch cube of bread will brown in 60–70 seconds, then fry the chicken for 5 minutes. Remove from the fat, drain on crumpled kitchen paper and remove the cottons before serving.

Arroz Con Pollo

Mexican and flavourful

3-lb. oven-ready	2 chicken bouillon
chicken	cubes
2 level tbsps.	8 stuffed olives
seasoned flour	6 oz. long-grain rice
4 tbsps. oil	Salt and pepper
1 medium-sized	½ lb. pork chipolata
onion, chopped	sausages
A 14-oz. can of	A small pkt. of
skinned tomatoes	frozen peas, thawed
Mole (if available) –	Small whole tomatoes
see note below)	and watercress for
A 6-oz. can of	garnish
pimientos	

Cut the chicken into 8 pieces and toss in seasoned flour till well coated. Heat the oil in a large saucepan, brown the chicken well, drain and set aside. Add the onion to the pan and brown. Drain the tomatoes and make up the juice to ¾ pint with water. To the saucepan add the tomato juice, *mole*, pimientos, crumbled bouillon cubes, olives, rice, seasoning and sausages (cut into ½-inch slices). Mix well. Arrange the chicken joints on top; cover and simmer for 30 minutes, occasionally lifting the rice with a fork to prevent sticking. Add the peas and simmer for a further 15 minutes, or until the chicken is tender. Serve garnished with small whole baked or grilled tomatoes and watercress. (Serves 4.)

Note. Mole, the Mexican chilli sauce which is the traditional ingredient for this dish, is available from some high-class grocery counters.

Risotto with Variations

(See picture above)
Comparatively cheap, but excellent for an informal get-together

1 onion	1½ pints stock
2 oz. flat mushrooms	Salt and pepper
2 oz. butter	1 oz. Parmesan or
8 oz. long-grain rice	Cheddar cheese

This is the basic risotto, which can be varied in many different ways – see below. Risotto is ideal for a party, as it can be kept hot well.

Skin the onion; wash the mushrooms in a sieve and drain them well. Chop the onion finely and slice the mushrooms. Melt the butter in a saucepan, add the onion and mushrooms and fry for about 5 minutes, or until golden-brown. Meanwhile, place the rice in the sieve, rinse in cold water and drain. Add the rice to the vegetable mixture in the saucepan and heat

gently, stirring till the butter is absorbed. Pour the stock over and stir thoroughly; season well. Cover pan with a tight-fitting lid and simmer gently for about 20 minutes, or until all the water has been absorbed. Meanwhile, grate the cheese on a plate, using the fine holes on the grater. When the risotto is ready, stir in the cheese. Transfer to a dish, garnish and serve at once. Alternatively, keep the mixture hot by leaving it in a pan with a close-fitting lid over a low heat or – a safer way – in a casserole covered with a lid or foil in a cool oven (300 °F, marks 1–2). Add some extra stock before serving, if it is rather dry.

Variations

1. Rind 2 oz. streaky bacon and chop the rashers in ½-inch strips; fry with the onion.

2. Stir in ½ lb. skinned and quartered tomatoes or 2 level tbsps. tomato paste when adding the stock.

3. After about 10 minutes' simmering, add 1 small pkt. of frozen peas or prawns.

4. Pour a can of mushroom or tomato soup over the rice instead of stock.

5. Hard-boil 4 eggs, slice and chop them and add to the risotto just before serving.

6. For the chicken risotto pictured, fry some sliced green peppers with the onion and mushrooms. About half-way through the cooking time, stir in a few sultanas or seedless raisins, some cooked peas and some pieces of cooked chicken flesh. Do not add cheese. Serve garnished with wedges of raw tomato.

Paella

(See picture overleaf)
Fish and chicken meet in this gorgeous blend

6–8 mussels, fresh or bottled	1 clove of garlic, skinned
2–4 oz. Dublin Bay prawns (or frozen scampi)	4 tomatoes, skinned and chopped
1 small cooked lobster	8–12 oz. long grain rice
1 small chicken	2–3 pints chicken stock (made from a cube)
4 tbsps. olive oil	Salt and pepper
1 onion, chopped	A little powdered
1 green pepper, seeded and chopped	saffron
	A small pkt. of frozen peas

This famous Spanish dish takes its name from the pan in which it is cooked – a shallow oval metal dish with handles at each side. There are few hard-and-fast rules about making a paella, although the following ingredients are traditionally included – chicken, lobster, shellfish of various kinds, onion, green or red peppers and rice. Paella is rather elaborate and somewhat expensive to prepare in this country, but it makes an attractive party dish.

Prepare the mussels and prawns in the usual way, if fresh. Remove the lobster meat from the shell and dice it, retaining the claws for decorating. Cut the meat from the chicken into small pieces. Put the oil into a large paella or frying-pan and fry the onion, green pepper and crushed garlic for 5 minutes, until soft but not browned. Add the tomatoes and chicken pieces and fry until the chicken is lightly browned. Stir in the rice and add half the stock, the seasoning and saffron (blended with a little of the stock). Bring to the boil, then reduce the heat and simmer for about 20–25 minutes, until the chicken is tender and the rice just cooked. Stir in the mussels, prawns, lobster meat and peas and simmer for a final 5–10 minutes, until heated through. Serve garnished with a few extra strips of green pepper or pimiento and the lobster claws. Mussels in their shells can also be used as a garnish. (Serves 6–8.)

Chicken Vol-au-Vent

Effective, delicious, and surprisingly simple

8 oz. ready-made puff pastry 3 oz. cooked ham
6 oz. cooked chicken ½ pint thick white sauce
Salt and pepper

Oven temperature: very hot (450 °F, mark 8)

Roll the pastry out ½ inch thick and cut into an oval, using a cutter or a knife; mark a lid also, brush the top with egg, and bake in the centre of the oven for about 25 minutes. Remove the lid, take out any damp pastry that is inside and put the case back in the oven for a minute or two to dry.

To make the filling, cut the chicken and ham into pieces and mix with the sauce and seasoning; heat in a saucepan, and when you are ready to serve the vol-au-vent, pour the mixture into the case and put on the lid.

Note. Many other savoury mixtures may be served in this way. The case may also be allowed to cool and can then be filled with a sweet mixture, such as soft fruit or peaches combined with whipped cream.

Cold Roast Duckling

Oranges, the traditional accompaniment for duck, used in a different way

A 4-lb. frozen duckling, thawed
Orange jelly marmalade
Orange slices, sweet pickled cucumber and olives for garnish

Oven temperature: moderate (350 °F, mark 4)

Prick the duckling all over with a fine skewer, then place on a rack in a roasting tin, breast side down. Calculate the cooking time as 20 minutes per pound, plus 20 minutes over. Put it in the oven and after ½ hour turn it so that the breast is uppermost for the rest of the time. Allow to cool. To finish, with a sharp knife mark the carving lines for easy cutting at the table. The wings are removed first with a small portion of breast, the breast then being carved in slanting slices. Lastly the legs are removed. Glaze the ducklings with orange jelly marmalade which has previously been warmed and garnish. Serve with celery

Twelfth Night Party: p. 105

and orange salad and watercress and chicory salad, and with these stuffing balls:

Stuffing Balls

2 oz. liver sausage	1 tbsp. chopped parsley
4 oz. bacon rashers, rinded	1 cooked duckling liver, chopped
2 oz. fresh breadcrumbs	1 egg, beaten
Grated rind of 1 orange	1 tbsp. stock
	Salt and pepper

Remove the fat from the sausage; cut the sausage in small dice. Mince the bacon. Mix all the ingredients together, seasoning the stuffing to taste. Shape into balls; roll these in melted lard and bake in a fairly hot oven (400 °F, mark 6) for about 20 minutes, or fry in a frying-pan.

Duck in Red Wine

A splendid, fairly rich casserole

A duckling (about 5–6 lb.)	2 oz. mushrooms, sliced
½ a clove of garlic, skinned and crushed	A bay leaf
	Sprigs of parsley
	½ level tsp. dried thyme
2 oz. flour	1 level tsp. salt
¾ pint red wine	1 lb. small onions
	1 lb. small carrots

Oven temperature: moderate (350 °F, mark 4)

Remove the skin and fat from the duck and put them with the giblets into a pan; cover with water and simmer for 1 hour. Skim off the fat from the surface and let the stock cool. Cut the duck into joints. Heat 2 tbsps. of the duck fat in a pan, then brown the duck joints on all sides. Remove them from the fat and put in a casserole. Add the crushed garlic to the fat, fry for 1 minute and stir in the flour. Add the wine, mushrooms, herbs and salt. Bring to the boil, stirring constantly until the sauce thickens. Put the prepared onions and carrots into the casserole, pour the sauce over, cover and cook in the centre of the oven for ¾–1 hour, until tender. (Serves 5–6.)

Note. If preferred, use 4 frozen duckling joints (about 12 oz. each). Thaw, remove any excess fat, and fry in 1 oz. dripping until well-browned. Drain, put in a casserole and proceed as described above.

Turkey Sauté Annette

A full-flavoured, rich brown sauce using the turkey carcass stock, enhances the left-overs

2 oz. turkey dripping	2 level tsps. powdered tarragon
2 oz. flour	
1 pint turkey stock	3 tbsps. chopped parsley
Salt and pepper	
3 oz. butter	3 tbsps. dry red wine
12 oz. cooked turkey, cubed	Lemon juice
	Lemon slices or twists to garnish
1 medium onion, chopped	

Melt the turkey dripping, stir in the flour and cook slowly over a low heat until brown, stirring occasionally. Gradually add the turkey stock, stirring. Bring to the boil, simmer for about 3 minutes and season. Melt the butter, add the turkey and sauté until it is heated through. Lift the turkey from the fat and place on a serving dish. Keep warm.

Fry the onion in the pan, add to the turkey sauce and bring to the boil. Add the tarragon, parsley and wine. Check the seasoning and sharpen with a little lemon juice to taste. Coat the turkey with the sauce and garnish with lemon slices or twists. (Serves 4.)

Note. Potato croquettes and frozen peas mixed with sweet corn kernels are good accompaniments.

Turkey Cranberry Salad

Ruby-capped moulded salad with good texture contrast

Powdered gelatine	2 tsps. finely chopped onion
¼ pint water	
2 tbsps. lemon juice	2–3 sticks of celery, chopped
A 7-oz. can of whole berry cranberry sauce	
	1 small green pepper, diced
½ pint turkey stock	1 red-skinned eating apple, diced
¼ tsp. Tabasco sauce	
2 tbsps. lemon juice	12 oz. cooked turkey, diced
5 level tbsps. lemon mayonnaise	

Sprinkle 3 level tsps. gelatine over the water in a bowl and stand this in a pan of hot water until dissolved. Add the lemon juice and cranberry sauce, stir thoroughly, pour into a

145

Roast Crown of Lamb: p. 126

mould and leave to set. Place the turkey stock in a saucepan, sprinkle 1 level tbsp. gelatine over the surface and dissolve over a low heat, but do not boil. Add the Tabasco sauce and lemon juice, pour into a bowl and leave until cool. Gradually whisk in the mayonnaise. When beginning to set, fold in the onion, celery, pepper, apple and turkey. Check the seasoning. Spoon the mixture on to the cranberry layer and leave to set. Unmould to serve. (Serves 4.)

Cole slaw and lots of crisp French bread make ideal accompaniments.

Canned Pheasant en Casserole

Start with a good 'convenience food', treat it well, and you end with a real party special

4 oz. fried bacon, chopped	1 level tbsp. red-currant jelly
A 3-oz. pkt. of thyme and parsley stuffing	Lemon juice to taste
2 oz. lard	A 1-lb. can of small whole onions, drained
A 3-lb. can of whole roast pheasant in Burgundy jelly	1 oz. butter
3 level tbsps. cornflour	Chopped parsley to garnish

Oven temperature: hot (425 °F, mark 7)

Mix the bacon with the stuffing and add just enough water to give a fairly stiff consistency; leave to stand for 5 minutes. Shape into 20 balls, place in a small baking dish with the melted lard and put in the top of the oven. Drain and joint the pheasant, arrange in a large ovenproof casserole, cover and put in the centre of the oven for 15–20 minutes. Blend the cornflour with a little of the stock from the can, add to the remaining stock and bring to the boil. Add the red-currant jelly and lemon juice. Simmer gently while frying the onions in the

butter for 3–4 minutes, till coloured. When the bird is heated through, add the onions, pour the sauce over and top with the stuffing balls. Sprinkle with parsley.

Casserole of Game

Excellent if you're not convinced the birds would roast well

2 partridges or pheasants	1 clove of garlic, skinned and crushed
Butter	Salt and pepper
2 tbsps. oil	1 bay leaf
1 small onion, chopped	4 tbsps. stock
	$\frac{1}{4}$ pint single cream
4 oz. minced veal	2 tbsps. brandy
4 oz. minced lean ham	Lemon juice (optional)
1 small cooking apple, peeled and sliced	4 oz. button mushrooms

Oven temperature: warm (325 °F, mark 3)

Prepare the game. Fry evenly in 1 oz. butter and the oil until well sealed and browned, then set aside.

To the pan add the onion, veal, ham, apple and garlic, and cook gently for 5 minutes. Turn the mixture into a casserole just large enough to take the birds, season and add the bay leaf. Place the birds on top of the veal mixture, breast side down, and pour the stock over. Cook in the oven for 1 hour. Remove from the oven, discard the bay leaf, turn the birds over and pour in the single cream. Ignite the brandy, add to the casserole, cover tightly, and return to the oven for $\frac{3}{4}$ hour.

To serve, carve the birds and keep hot. Adjust the seasoning in the gravy and sharpen if wished with lemon juice. Add the mushrooms sautéed in a little butter; re-heat but do not boil. Spoon over the birds, and serve accompanied by watercress, game chips and braised celery. (Serves 4.)

3
Fish, Eggs, Cheese and Pasta

Haddock with Lobster Sauce

Everyday fish enlivened by a special sauce

2 lb. haddock fillet
Juice of ½ a lemon
2 oz. butter, melted
A good pinch of
  marjoram
½ level tsp. salt

¼ level tsp. pepper
A small can of lobster
  bisque
3 tbsps. soured cream
A pkt. of frozen mixed
  vegetables (optional)

Oven temperature: moderate (350 °F, mark 4)

Wash the fish and cut into 4 portions. Place in a shallow fireproof casserole, sprinkle with the lemon juice and allow to soak for 5 minutes, then discard the juice. Pour the melted butter over the fish and sprinkle with the marjoram and seasonings. Grill for about 10 minutes, basting once. Mix the bisque and the cream together, pour over the fish and cook for 30 minutes in the centre of the oven. Serve garnished with the vegetables. (Serves 6.)

Haddock with Butter and Wine

Subtle main-dish recipe that is suited to most white fish

4 haddock cutlets
Salt
Freshly ground
  pepper
A squeeze of lemon
  juice

2 oz. butter
A pinch of marjoram
4 tbsps. white wine
1 tomato, quartered
Chopped parsley

Oven temperature: fairly hot (375 °F, mark 5)

Trim the cutlets and skewer the ends with cocktail sticks. Butter an ovenproof serving dish large enough to take the cutlets in a single layer and arrange them in the base. Season the fish with salt, pepper and lemon juice, then pour the melted butter over and round the

fish. Add a pinch of marjoram to the wine and pour round the fish. Cook in the oven for 30 minutes until tender, basting 3 times. After 20 minutes, insert a tomato quarter in the opening of each cutlet, baste, and continue cooking. Garnish with parsley and serve from the dish. (Serves 4.)

Herring Fillets Normandy Style

The slight tartness of the apples counteracts the richness of the fish

4 herrings (1 lb.)
Seasoned flour
2 tbsps. oil
2 oz. butter
2 eating apples

Juice of ½ a lemon
Pepper
Chopped parsley to
  garnish

Bone the herrings and cut in halves down the centre. Dip them in the seasoned flour and fry in the oil and 1 oz. butter until crisp and golden on each side; keep warm.

Peel and core the apples and cut into eighths, then add the rest of the butter to the pan and sauté the apple till tender but still whole. Add the lemon juice and a dusting of freshly ground pepper (with a little more butter if needed). Arrange the herring fillets on a dish, overlapping each other, spoon the apple mixture over and serve really hot, with a good sprinkling of fresh chopped parsley. (Serves 3–4.)

Plaice with Orange Butter

Appealing to eye and taste buds

2 whole plaice
  (about ¾ lb. each)
Rind and juice of
  1 orange

2 oz. butter
Salt
Freshly ground black
  pepper

Remove the head and fins from the cleaned fish and trim the tails. Cut shallow slits at an angle on each side of the fish. Coarsely grate the orange rind and beat into the butter, with the orange juice. Season with salt and pepper. Grease the grill rack (or the base of the pan without a rack), and lay the plaice in the centre, dark side down. Spread over them half the butter and cook under a medium grill for 10–15 minutes; baste from time to time. Turn them over carefully, using a large palette knife or fish slice. Spread on the rest of the butter and cook for a further 10 minutes. Serve at once, garnished with bacon-stuffed mushrooms. (Serves 2.)

Stuffed Mushrooms

Choose 4 large open mushrooms. Grill 4 rinded streaky bacon rashers until transparent, and snip into small pieces with scissors. Divide between the caps, place under the grill and continue to cook until the mushrooms are soft – about 6 minutes.

Plaice Veronique

From the French cook's repertoire; grapes 'make' the dish

4 large plaice fillets	4 tbsps. water
½ oz. butter	4 oz. large white grapes
1 tbsp. lemon juice	Milk
½ small onions, sliced	1 oz. butter
6 peppercorns	1 oz. flour
1 bay leaf	Salt and pepper
4 tbsps. dry white wine	Chopped parsley

Oven temperature: fairly hot (375 °F, mark 5)

Skin the fillets, fold each into three and arrange in a buttered 1-pint ovenproof *gratin* dish. Sprinkle the fish with lemon juice, add the onion slices, peppercorns, bay leaf, wine and water. Cover the fish with a cap of foil or greaseproof paper, put into the oven and cook for about 20 minutes.

Skin and pip the grapes, keeping them whole. Lift the cooked fish from the dish and strain the fish liquor into a pan. Return the fillets to a clean dish and keep warm. Reduce the fish liquor to 3 tbsps. by fast boiling. Melt the 1 oz. butter in the pan, remove from heat,

add 1 oz. flour and stir until the roux is smooth. Return to the heat, cook gently until bubbly, then gradually add the milk and fish liquor and stir well; simmer for a few minutes. Check the seasoning.

Coat the fillets with the sauce, and garnish with the grapes, piled at one end, and a line of chopped parsley. (Serves 2.)

Salmon for a Party

And what better fish for a special occasion?

1. *A 2–2½ lb. Piece of Salmon*

Foil Method: Pre-heat the oven to cool (300 °F, mark 1–2). Wipe the fish, removing the fins, etc. Butter well a large piece of foil. Place the fish in the centre and season lightly with salt and pepper. Package the foil loosely and place on a baking sheet. Bake for about 1 hour, depending on the thickness of the fish. Cool in the foil, unwrap and remove the skin. Carefully lift the flesh from the bones.

Slow-cooking Method: Prepare the fish. Fill a fish kettle or large saucepan with sufficient water to almost cover the salmon. Add ¼ pint white wine, a bay leaf, a sprig of parsley, salt and 2–3 peppercorns. Bring this to the boil and simmer for 10 minutes. Lower in the salmon, and boil gently for 3 minutes. Remove the fish kettle from the heat, remove the lid and leave on one side until cold. Lift out the fish, remove the skin and, if wished, lift the flesh from the bones.

2. *Salmon Steaks/Slices/Cutlets*

These should be cut about ¾ inch thick. If very large, serve one between two people rather than ask for the steaks to be cut thinly. Wipe, and remove any blood from the backbone area. Close the flaps, and to keep the pieces a good shape secure with a cocktail stick. If individual portions of cold salmon are required for coating with mayonnaise, etc. – and especially for small numbers – it is sometimes easier to cook cutlets. After cooking, carefully ease away the bones, remove the skin and portion the fish as desired.

To Poach: Place in a deep frying-pan (preferably not a saucepan, as a shallow utensil makes removal of the fish much easier) with a simple court-bouillon: for this, simmer 12 pepper-corns, a blade of mace, bouquet garni and 2 bay leaves with 6 pints water, ½ pint white wine, ¼ pint tarragon vinegar, 2 onions and 2 carrots (sliced) for ¼ hour. Cover the pan with a lid and simmer gently for 5–10 minutes. Serve hot or cold.

To Bake: Line a baking sheet with a larger piece of foil, and butter the surface. Place the prepared salmon on the foil. Dot each steak with butter and season with salt, pepper and lemon juice. Package loosely and cook in the centre of a warm oven (325 °F, mark 3) for 20–40 minutes, depending on its thickness. Serve hot with maître d'hôtel butter or Hollandaise sauce. To serve cold, leave to cool wrapped.

To Grill: Season the prepared fish with salt and pepper and brush well with melted butter. Cook on a greased grill grid under a medium heat. When the top side is cooked and tinged light brown, turn, brush with more butter and continue to cook for about 10–20 minutes altogether. Serve hot. Traditional accompaniments are poached diced cucumber, new potatoes and asparagus or peas.

Salmon Trout with Sauce Verte

(See colour picture facing p. 240)
The fish which spells the beginning of summer

A whole salmon trout	Butter
	Salt and pepper

For the Sauce Verte

Watercress leaves	Thick mayonnaise
A sprig or two of fresh tarragon or chervil	1 tbsp. lightly whipped cream
A few parsley sprigs	

Prepare a court-bouillon (see top of page). Lower in the cleaned fish and reduce the heat, so that the liquor just 'shivers' without boiling. Allow 10 minutes per lb. Leave the fish in the liquor until cold, then skin it, glaze with aspic and garnish.

Grilse: Allow 10 minutes per lb. for the first 6 lbs., then 8 minutes per lb.

Sauce Verte: Very finely chop the watercress leaves, tarragon and parsley sprigs. Just before serving add the mayonnaise, with the cream.

Fillets of Sole Dugléré

The characteristic sauce can be used with most white fish

2 sole, filleted	1 oz. butter
1–2 shallots, chopped	3 level tbsps. flour
½ a bay leaf	3 tbsps. single cream
A few sprigs of parsley	2 tomatoes, skinned and diced, with seeds removed
¼ pint white wine	
¼ pint water	
Salt and pepper	2 tsps. chopped parsley

Oven temperature: moderate (350 °F, mark 4)

Wash and wipe the fish and put in an oven-proof dish with the shallots, herbs, wine, water, salt and pepper. Cover with foil or a lid and bake in the centre of the oven for about 15 minutes, or until tender. Strain off the cooking liquid and keep the fish warm. Melt the butter, stir in the flour and cook for 2–3 minutes. Remove the pan from the heat and gradually stir in the cooking liquid from the fish. Bring to the boil and continue to stir until the sauce thickens. Remove from the heat and stir in the cream, tomatoes and parsley. Adjust the seasoning and pour over the fish. (Serves 4.)

Sole à la Meunière

French frying – simple, quick, delicious – makes a certain winner

Skin fillets of sole, season with salt and pepper and dust with flour. Add just sufficient butter to cover the base of a pan. Fry the fillets for 5 minutes, turn once. Place on a hot serving dish and coat with the following sauce.

In a saucepan put ¼ pint water, a bay leaf, 2–3 peppercorns, parsley stalk, thin slice of onion, piece of carrot and fish skin. Bring to the boil, cover, infuse for ½ hour. Strain. Make up to ½ pint with milk and 2 tbsps. dry white wine. Prepare a sauce in the usual way with 1 oz. butter and 1 oz. flour. Check the seasoning.

Variations

Véronique: White wine sauce with skinned and pipped white grapes.

Princesse: White wine sauce with lightly sautéed asparagus.

Hongroise: White wine sauce with sautéed onion and tomato, seasoned with paprika.

Héloïse: White wine sauce with sautéed mushroom and chopped parsley.

Suchet: White wine sauce with poached, thickly sliced leek, carrot and cucumber.

Bonne Femme: White wine sauce with sautéed shallots and button mushrooms.

Trout en Papillote

Delicate-flavoured river trout and red mullet taste sublime cooked in 'parcels'

For each person

1 river trout or red mullet	Slivers of lemon peel
Shallot slices	Butter
A sprig of fragrant fresh herbs	Salt
	Freshly ground pepper

Oven temperature: warm (300 °F, mark 1–2)

Butter well a rectangle of foil large enough to envelop the chosen fish completely. Lay the prepared fish on it, add some shallot, fresh herbs, lemon peel, dots of butter and seasoning. Close the 'parcels' and cook on a baking sheet for about 30 minutes. Bring the food to the table still wrapped.

Baked Turbot with Shrimp Sauce

(See top picture opposite)

Turbot, king of the flatfish, is worthy of a delicious sauce

4 6-oz. turbot steaks	Freshly ground pepper
¼ pint milk	Butter
Salt	

For the Sauce

Milk	2 oz. shelled shrimps
1 oz. butter	Parsley sprigs to garnish
1 oz. flour	

Oven temperature: moderate (350 °F, mark 4)

Butter an ovenproof dish and arrange the prepared turbot steaks in a single layer. Pour the ¼ pint milk over the fish, season, and dot with butter. Bake, uncovered, for 20–25 minutes, until cooked; baste twice. Drain off the liquor and make up to ½ pint with more milk. Keep the fish hot. Melt the butter in a saucepan, stir in the flour and cook over a low heat for 2 minutes. Remove from the heat and gradu-

ally stir in the liquor; return the pan to the heat and bring to the boil, stirring. Add the shrimps, check the seasoning and simmer for 3–4 minutes. Pour over the turbot and garnish with parsley. For the effect seen in the picture, pipe the edge of the dish with creamed potato and brown lightly before putting fish and sauce in centre. Garnish as shown. (Serves 4).

Tuna and Spaghetti Crisp

(See lower picture opposite)

Inexpensive and good for an informal supper

4 oz. short-cut spaghetti	3 oz. grated cheese
A 7-oz. can of tuna	Salt and pepper
½ pint white sauce	A small pkt. of potato crisps

Oven temperature: moderate (350 °F, mark 4)

Cook the spaghetti in boiling salted water until tender – 8–12 minutes. Drain well and place in a bowl. Add the drained and flaked fish, the white sauce, cheese and seasoning, mix well and transfer to a greased 2-pint casserole. Slightly crush the crisps and arrange on top. Bake for 20–30 minutes and garnish as desired – for example, with mushrooms.

Note. Use plain white sauce or, if you wish, flavour it with mushroom stalks. Alternatively, use a canned condensed mushroom soup, or a packet soup made up with slightly less water than stated on the packet and with a little top of the milk added.

Fish Curry

Bream and haddock are equally good curried, and other fairly firm fish can also be used

1 lb. bream or haddock fillets, skinned	1 sweet apple, peeled, cored and diced
1 oz. seasoned flour	1 clove of garlic, skinned and crushed
½ lb. onions, skinned and finely chopped	¼ lb. tomatoes, skinned and quartered
2 oz. butter	¾ pint water
2 tbsps. oil	1 level tbsp. mango chutney
1 level tbsp. curry powder	Toasted coconut to garnish
2 level tbsps. flour	Boiled rice
1 carrot, finely sliced	
2 celery stalks, diced	

Cube the fish and toss it in the seasoned flour. Sauté the onions in half the butter and oil until they are golden. Stir in the curry powder and flour and blend thoroughly. Add the carrot, celery, apple, garlic and tomatoes. Stir in the water and chutney, bring to the boil, cover and simmer for 40 minutes. Quickly brown the fish in the remaining oil, add to the sauce and simmer for 10 minutes. Dish up on the rice, garnished with the coconut. (Serves 3–4.)

Sweet–Sour Fish

(See colour picture facing p. 241)
A Chinese dish that's worth a little trouble

1 lb. fish fillet, e.g., haddock, cut up	1 pint corn oil
Light soy sauce	2 tbsps. white vinegar
Sherry	3–4 level tbsps. sugar
Salt and pepper	2 tbsps. tomato ketchup
Flour, cornflour	½ a garlic clove, crushed
1 level tsp. baking powder	6 tbsps. pineapple juice
A pinch of Accent	An 8-oz. can of fruit cocktail
2 tbsps. lard, melted	

Dip the fish into a mixture of 1 tsp. soy sauce, 1 tbsp. sherry, salt and pepper; dust with 1 tbsp. flour and leave for ½ hour. Sift together 4 level tbsps. flour, 2 level tbsps. cornflour and 1 level tsp. baking powder, add the Accent, lard and 1–2 tbsps. water, then beat until smooth. Heat the oil. Dip the fish into the batter and fry for about 3–5 minutes, until it is done and the batter is crisp, turning it once. Drain and keep warm.

Reheat 1 tbsp. of the oil in a saucepan and stir in the vinegar, sugar, ketchup, 1 tsp. soy sauce, garlic and pineapple juice; bring to the boil. Blend 2 level tbsps. cornflour with a little fruit cocktail juice and the drained fruit, add to the pan, bring to the boil, check seasoning and pour over fish. (Serves 4.)

Crab à la Dewey

Looks nice in individual soufflé dishes

4 button mushrooms, sliced	4 tbsps. double cream
1 small green pepper, chopped	2 tbsps. dry white wine
1 oz. butter	8 oz. crab meat
¾ oz. plain flour	Salt and pepper
	Chopped parsley for garnish

Sauté the mushrooms and pepper in the butter until they become soft. Stir in the flour and cook for a further 3 minutes. Gradually add the cream over a low heat, stirring. Add the wine and crab meat and re-heat slowly without boiling. Check the seasoning. Garnish with chopped parsley and serve with Melba toast. (Serves 3–4.)

Lobster Newburg

(See picture above)
Very rich, very delicious

2 lb. cooked lobster (approx. ¾ lb. meat)	Freshly ground black pepper
1 oz. butter	Paprika
6 tbsps. Madeira	Cayenne
2 tbsps. lemon juice	¼ pint single or double cream
2 egg yolks	

Split the lobster in half and remove the bag, intestine and thin grey or black line running through the tail meat. (These are the only inedible parts.) Remove the meat from the shell, keeping it as whole as possible. Melt the butter in a flameproof dish or frying-pan and add the pieces of lobster; heat gently for 5 minutes without browning. Place the lobster on one side and keep warm. Spoon the Madeira and lemon juice into the pan and boil to reduce the liquor by half. Beat the egg yolks with the seasonings, add the cream, stir into the juices in the pan and heat through, but do not boil. Add the lobster and re-heat; serve in the lobster shells, with hot buttered toast fingers. (This amount of Lobster Newburg makes a quick lunch for three with a tossed, green salad, or a luxury starter for four.)

Note. Lobster Newburg may also be served in hot pastry shells; for more sauce, step up the cream to ½ pint. Canned or frozen lobster may be used.

Prawns with Bean Sprouts

This delicate Chinese dish makes a main course if it is served with rice and a side-salad

6 oz. shelled prawns	6 oz. bean sprouts
2½ tbsps. sherry	1½ tbsps. light soy
3 tbsps. oil	sauce
½ level tsp. salt	½ tsp. sugar

Soak the prawns in the sherry for 1½ hours. Heat the oil and fry the drained prawns for 2 minutes with the salt. Add the bean sprouts and fry for 1 minute, then add the soy sauce and sugar. Mix, and serve with plain boiled or fried rice and salad. (Serves 2.)

Curried Eggs

Specially good served with Easter-type accompaniments

6 oz. long-grain rice	2 level tbsps. plain flour
1 oz. lard	¾ pint stock or water
2 medium-sized onions, chopped	1 medium-sized cooking apple, peeled and
1 level tbsp. curry powder	chopped
1 level tsp. curry paste	2 tbsps. mango chutney
1 level tsp. concentrated tomato paste	6 eggs
	Paprika to garnish

Cook the rice in the normal way; drain and keep hot. Melt the lard and sauté the onions for 5 minutes. Stir in the curry powder and

paste and cook slowly for 5 minutes. Stir in the tomato paste and flour. Gradually add the stock, stirring. Bring to the boil, check the seasoning and add the apple and chutney. Simmer for 10 minutes. Meanwhile boil the eggs for 8 minutes only. To serve, pile the rice in a ring round a serving dish. Cut the hot shelled eggs in halves lengthwise and arrange in the centre of the rice. Pour the curry sauce over and garnish with paprika. (Serves 6.)

Suitable accompaniments are tomato and onion salad, sliced banana tossed in lemon juice, and poppadoms.

Eggs à la Florentine

Florentine often means with spinach, as here

1 lb. spinach	4 eggs
Salt and pepper	2–3 tbsps. single cream
½ oz. butter	A sprig of parsley
2 oz. Parmesan cheese, grated	to garnish

Oven temperature: moderate (350 °F, mark 4)

Wash the spinach well, put it into a pan with a little salt and just the water that clings to the leaves, and cook for 10–15 minutes, until tender. Drain well, chop roughly and mix with the butter and seasoning. Put into an oven-proof dish and cover with most of the grated cheese. Break the eggs into a saucer and slide side by side into the cheese; bake in the centre of the oven for 10 minutes. Remove from the oven, spoon the cream over and sprinkle with the remaining cheese. Return the dish to the oven and bake for 10–15 minutes, until the eggs are firm. Garnish with parsley. (Serves 4.)

Alternatively, line small individual casseroles with the spinach purée, add cheese and an egg to each and finish as above.

Stuffed Eggs Mornay

A light, creamy main dish

6 eggs	2 level tsps. concentrated tomato paste
1 oz. butter	
2 tsps. oil	2 tbsps. chopped parsley
2 tbsps. chopped onion	Salt and pepper
4 oz. mushrooms, chopped	¾ pint cheese sauce
	Grated cheese for topping

Hard-boil the eggs just before they are required – they should be hot. Heat the butter and oil, and fry the chopped onion until soft but not coloured; add the chopped mushrooms and cook until soft. Mix in the tomato paste, chopped parsley and seasoning to taste. Cut the freshly boiled eggs in half lengthwise. Remove the yolks and pound them into the mushroom mixture; refill the whites and arrange in a dish. Coat with cheese sauce and dust with grated cheese. Brown under a hot grill. (Serves 4–6.)

Seafood Quiches

(*See picture above and colour picture facing p. 208*)
A skilful way of making fairly small amounts of expensive ingredients go further

6 oz. shortcrust pastry   Parsley to garnish
  (6 oz. flour, etc.)   (optional)

For the Filling
2 oz. shelled prawns   4 egg yolks
2 oz. smoked salmon   Salt and pepper
$\frac{1}{2}$ pint single cream   1 tbsp. chopped parsley

Oven temperature: fairly hot (400 °F, mark 6)

Use the pastry to line 6 4$\frac{1}{4}$-inch fluted patty pans (or one larger tin). Roughly chop the prawns and cut the salmon into narrow strips; divide the fish equally between the uncooked

pastry cases. Beat together the cream and egg yolks and season to taste. (Remember that the salmon is on the salt side.) Add the chopped parsley. Spoon the mixture into the pastry cases, which should be placed on a baking sheet. Bake in the centre of the oven for 10 minutes. Reduce the heat to moderate (350 °F, mark 4) and cook for a further 20–25 minutes, until the pastry is beginning to colour and the filling is lightly set. Garnish and serve warm. (Makes 6.)

Cheese and Spinach Quiche

(*See colour picture facing p. 208*)
Subtly flavoured, unusual

8 oz. shortcrust pastry   A knob of butter
$\frac{1}{2}$ lb. prepared $\frac{1}{2}$ pint single cream
  spinach   4 egg yolks
Salt and pepper   4 oz. cream chesee

Oven temperature: fairly hot (400 °F, mark 6)

Put 6 4-inch flan rings on baking sheets and line with pastry. Cook the spinach in a little water with salt, pepper and butter; drain thoroughly and cool. Divide it between the uncooked cases. Beat together the cream, egg yolks and cheese, season and spoon evenly over the spinach. Bake in centre of oven for 10 minutes, reduce to moderate (350 °F, mark 4) and cook for a further 20-25 minutes, until pastry begins to colour and filling is lightly set. Serve warm. (Makes 6.)

Quiche Lorraine

One of those dishes with many 'correct' versions

6 oz. shortcrust pastry (6 oz. plain flour, etc.)

For the Filling
8 oz. green back   2 oz. Gruyère cheese
  bacon rashers   (optional)
1 small onion, finely $\frac{1}{2}$ pint single cream
  chopped (optional)   4 egg yolks
Butter   Salt and pepper

Oven temperature: fairly hot (400 °F, mark 6)

Use the pastry to line an 8$\frac{1}{2}$-inch fluted French flan tin with a loose base. Rind the bacon rashers, removing about half the fat, cut the bacon into $\frac{1}{2}$-inch strips and fry gently to extract the fat; cook until tender but not too browned, then remove from the pan. Add the onion to the pan juices, with a knob of butter, and sauté until soft but not coloured; drain off the excess fat. Put the bacon, onion and very finely sliced or diced cheese in the flan case.

Beat together the cream and egg yolks and season to taste. (Remember that the bacon is salty.) Pour into the flan case. Bake in the centre of the oven for 15 minutes, reduce the heat to moderate (350 °F, mark 4) and cook for about 20 minutes longer, until the pastry is beginning to colour and the filling is lightly set. Serve warm. (Serves 6.)

Cheese-and-Grape Mousse

(See colour picture facing p. 96)

Splendidly different buffet party savoury

4 oz. cheese pastry (4 oz. plain flour, etc.)	1¼ lb. cottage cheese
2 eggs, separated	¼ lb. Danish Blue cheese
½ pint milk	Salt, pepper and made mustard
2 level tbsps. gelatine	Cream cheese and
6–8 spring onions, roughly cut up	black and white grapes for garnish

Oven temperature: fairly hot (375 °F, mark 5)

Roll out the pastry to line the base of a 7½-inch-square tin, letting the pastry come a little way up the sides to allow for shrinkage. Prick the base. Bake just above the oven centre for about 25 minutes, until lightly coloured and crisp. Carefully turn out and cool; wash the tin. Beat the egg yolks, gradually blend in the milk and pour into a saucepan. Sprinkle the gelatine over and heat gently but do not boil, until the gelatine has dissolved; cool slightly. In an electric blender, blend a third each of the onions, the egg mixture, the cottage cheese and the Danish Blue; turn into a bowl. Repeat with the remainder, and season to taste. Fold in the stiffly beaten egg whites. Return the pastry base to the clean tin, pour the cheese mixture over and leave to set in the refrigerator.

Loosen the edges with a knife and turn out. With the pastry base down, pipe the surface with lines of softened cream cheese in a lattice; fill in with halved and pipped grapes. Cut into fingers to serve. (Serves 10–12.)

Note. Cheese mousse can be made one day ahead, turned out and garnished on the day.

Swiss Fondue

Traditionally, fondue is served at the table in the dish in which it is cooked, kept warm over a small spirit lamp or dish-warmer. Special fondue sets are available at the larger stores and specialized shops

1 clove of garlic, crushed	2 level tsps. cornflour
	A little pepper
¼ pint dry white wine and a squeeze of lemon juice	A little finely grated nutmeg
	1 liqueur glass of Kirsch
8 oz. cheese, cut in thin strips (half Gruyère and half Emmenthal)	French bread, cut into chunks

Rub the inside of a flameproof dish with the garlic, place the dish over a gentle heat and warm the wine and lemon juice in it. Add the cheese and continue to heat gently, stirring well, until the cheese has melted and begun to cook. Add the cornflour and seasonings, blended to a smooth cream with the Kirsch, and continue cooking for a further 2–3 minutes; when the mixture is of a thick creamy consistency, it is ready to serve.

To eat it, provide cubes of crusty bread which are speared on a fork and dipped in the fondue.

An anglicized version of fondue can be made using a strong-flavoured Cheddar cheese, cider instead of white wine and brandy instead of Kirsch.

Red House Soufflé

(See picture overleaf)

New world style

2 oz. butter	8 oz. tomatoes, skinned and thickly sliced
8 oz. onions, thinly sliced	2 tbsps. chopped parsley
1 small pkt. of frozen sweet corn	

For the Sauce

4 oz. butter	Salt
4 oz. plain flour	6 oz. strong Cheddar cheese, grated
1 pint milk	
Freshly ground black pepper	6 large eggs, separated

Oven temperature: moderate (350 °F, mark 4)

155

Heat 2 oz. butter in a frying-pan, add the onion and sauté until soft but not coloured. Add the corn and continue cooking for 5 minutes. Remove from the heat and add the tomatoes and parsley.

For the sauce, melt 4 oz. butter in a saucepan, stir in the flour and cook for a few minutes. Gradually add the milk, stirring all the time, bring to the boil and simmer for a few minutes. Add half the sauce to the vegetables and check the seasoning.

Turn the mixture into a 3½-pint greased soufflé or casserole dish. Add the cheese to the remaining sauce in the pan, beat in the egg yolks and check the seasoning again. Fold in the stiffly beaten egg whites. Spoon the mixture over the corn and bake for about 1 hour, until well risen and golden-brown. Serve at once. (Serves 6.)

Note: Drained canned corn may also be used.

Spaghetti alla Bolognese

Becoming almost hackneyed, but excellent for hungry teenagers

1 clove of garlic, skinned and chopped	¼ pint dry Italian white wine
1 onion, chopped	8 tomatoes, skinned and and quartered
1 stick of celery, chopped	2 level tbsps. tomato paste
1 carrot, chopped	Salt and pepper
2 tbsps. olive oil	8 oz. spaghetti
1 oz. margarine	Grated Parmesan cheese
1 bay leaf	
8 oz. lean minced beef	

Put the garlic and vegetables in a pan with the oil, margarine and bay leaf; fry gently for 5 minutes. Add the beef, wine, tomatoes and tomato paste and season well. Cook gently with the lid on for about ¾ hour.

Meanwhile, cook the spaghetti in plenty of boiling salted water for 20 minutes. Drain, put in a hot dish, top with sauce (don't forget to remove the bay leaf) and serve with grated Parmesan cheese. (Serves 4.)

Note. Stock may be used to replace the white wine, and an 8-oz. can of tomatoes substituted for the fresh tomatoes.

Lasagne al Forno

Sizzling, savoury baked Lasagne

2 medium-sized cans of Italian tomatoes	8 oz. cooked veal or ham, diced
A small (3-oz.) can of tomato paste	4 oz. lasagne
½–1 level tsp. dried marjoram	6 oz. Ricotta or cream cheese
Salt and pepper	2 oz. Parmesan cheese, grated
1 level tsp. sugar	8 oz. Mozarella cheese

Oven temperature: fairly hot (375 °F, mark 5)

Combine the canned tomatoes, tomato paste, marjoram, seasonings and sugar, simmer gently for about 30 minutes and add the veal or ham. Cook the lasagne in boiling salted water in the usual way for about 10–15 minutes (or as stated on the packet) and drain well. Cover the base of a fairly deep ovenproof dish with a layer of the tomato and meat sauce. Add half the lasagne, put in another layer of the sauce, then cover with the cheeses, using half of each kind. Repeat these layers with the remaining ingredients, finishing with a layer of cheese. Bake towards the top of the oven for 30 minutes, until golden and bubbling on top. Serve at once. (Serves 6.)

Note. The tomato and meat sauce can be replaced by a Bolognese sauce (see the recipe for Spaghetti alla Bolognese).

4
Vegetables and Salads

Asparagus

(See colour picture facing p. 209)
One of summer's highlights

Allow 8–10 stems per person. Choose spears that don't appear to have woody stems. Cut off a good portion but not all of the white part, and scrape the remaining white part to remove the coarse outer coat. Tie in easily handled bundles and place upright (stems down) in a large saucepan of boiling salted water, with the heads *above* the water. Boil for 10 minutes, then lay the bundles down to immerse the heads also and cook more gently until tender – about 10 minutes, according to age and size. Since the tips cook quite quickly, the whole cooking needs careful attention. Drain well, untie the bundles and serve.

With hot asparagus, serve melted butter or Hollandaise sauce separately; if it is cold, serve vinaigrette dressing or chiffon mayonnaise.

Young, very tender asparagus is entirely succulent, but with older spears the last piece of stem is usually discarded.

Dressed Aubergines

Redolent of the Mediterranean

Choose small aubergines and allow ¼ lb. per person. Do not peel, but cut in half lengthwise, sprinkle with salt and leave for 2 hours. Drain and wipe dry. Fry in a little oil until lightly coloured; remove from the pan, place in a bowl and almost cover with a mixture of 2 parts oil to 1 part dry white wine. Leave for 24 hours, turning occasionally. Drain, slice, and serve with chopped parsley and freshly ground pepper.

Note. Coarse wholemeal or granary bread and farmhouse butter are just the right accompaniment for these vegetables.

Broad Beans

Country-dwellers are most likely to enjoy this vegetable at its best

Young garden beans can be cooked whole in salted water until tender (about 20 minutes) then served with melted butter. When they get larger, remove the pods – about 4 lb. will shell out to 1 lb. Cook the beans in salted water until tender and serve in a thin white sauce to which is added a little cream, plenty of chopped parsley, a dash of lemon juice and a pinch of grated nutmeg. Top with crisp, crumbled streaky bacon rashers.

Glazed Carrots

A lively way to cook older carrots

In a saucepan, cook 2 level tbsps. chopped onion and 1 tbsp. chopped parsley in 1 oz. butter for about 5 minutes. Add medium-sized carrots, cut in ½-inch slices, a can of condensed consommé and a dash of grated nutmeg. Cook uncovered for about 30 minutes, until glazed.

Courgettes

(See picture overleaf and colour picture facing p. 209)
Two ways with this delicately flavoured vegetable

Choose small, even-sized firm courgettes, and allow ¼ lb. per person. Trim the stem end. Cook whole in boiling salted water for 6–8 minutes and drain. Serve hot with melted butter in which a little chopped onion has been sautéed until soft but not coloured; sharpen with lemon juice and garnish with chopped parsley or chervil.

Alternatively, slice the courgettes and while still warm toss in a vinaigrette dressing, then chill, to serve as a cold course.

French Beans

Hot or cold?

Choose young beans that snap crisply, and allow about ¼ lb. per person. Top and tail the beans with scissors, and cook whole in boiling salted water until tender but not soft – about 10–15 minutes. Drain well. Serve hot, with butter and freshly milled black pepper.

Alternatively, toss them, while still warm, in a French dressing with plenty of freshly chopped parsley and a squeeze of garlic juice. Then serve them cold, garnished with skinned, seeded and chopped tomato (see colour picture facing p. 209). Another version is given on p. 161.

Buttered Leeks

Worth a little extra trouble

Allow ¾–1 lb. leeks per person. Trim, leaving about 1 inch of green, and slice fairly thinly. Wash well to remove any grit; drain and plunge them into boiling salted water, off the heat. Leave for 2 minutes. Melt some butter in a saucepan (about ½ oz. for each 1 lb. of leeks). Lightly toss the leeks until shiny and add a good turn from the pepper mill. Cover the pan and cook gently, shaking occasionally, until tender but not mushy – up to 5 minutes.

Potato Parade

New and old ways of presenting our old friends

Pommes de Terre Château are delicious with roast beef. For this, scrape or scrub 1½ lb. new potatoes of even size. Heat 1½ oz. butter in a frying-pan and add the potatoes in a single layer. Cover with a lid or plate – preferably of ovenproof glass. Leave over a low heat for about 15 minutes, shaking occasionally. Turn the potatoes carefully and cook for a further 5–10 minutes, until tender and golden. Lightly salt before serving. (Serves 4.)

Potatoes in Cream are wonderful with roast veal. Boil 1½ lb. potatoes and when just tender, drain and allow to cool. Dice them and put into a large pan. Pour over them a mixture of 1 oz. melted butter, ¼ level tsp. salt, a pinch of pepper and the contents of a small carton of single cream. Cook slowly until the cream has thickened and the potato is thoroughly warmed through. Garnish with chopped parsley. (Serves 4.)

Rösti; a Swiss way, giving crisp and tasty result. First scrub ¾ lb. small potatoes and parboil in salted water for 7 minutes. Remove the skins and grate the potatoes on a coarse grater straight into a frying-pan in which 1½ oz. butter is bubbling. Using a palette knife, shape the potato edges to form a neat round. Fry gently for 5–7 minutes, until golden-brown. Carefully turn, and brown the second side. Serve piping hot with a parsley garnish. (Serves 2.)

Sauté left-over boiled potatoes which are firm, not broken; new potatoes are particularly good. Cut them into ¼-inch slices, heat some butter in a pan and fry the slices on both sides until they are really crisp and brown. Lift from the pan and drain on kitchen paper. Serve garnished with chopped parsley or chives, and sprinkle with salt.

Roast Potatoes. This method gives a crisp and golden finish, with a floury inside. Peel the required number of even-sized potatoes, parboil for 5–7 minutes and drain. Put in a baking tin with 4 oz. hot dripping or lard for each 1½ lb. potatoes. Spoon the fat over and cook in a hot oven (425 °F, mark 7) for about 1 hour. Turn them half-way through the cooking time.

Scalloped Potatoes are good with lamb, and can be cooked in foil for flavour and convenience. Peel 1½ lb. potatoes and slice thinly. Butter 2 12-inch squares of foil, and layer the potatoes in the centre of each piece, with 3 oz. butter divided between the two. Season well and add 1 tbsp. milk to each pile of potatoes. Shape the foil into parcels. Bake on a baking sheet in a fairly hot oven (400 °F, mark 6) for 50–60 minutes. Turn the potatoes into a hot serving dish and sprinkle with chopped parsley. (Serves 4.)

They can also be cooked in a closed casserole or foil-covered oven-dish.

Galette Lyonnaise. Boil 1 lb. potatoes and cream them with butter and milk until quite fluffy. Peel, chop, then sauté 1 lb. onions in 2 oz. butter until tender, without browning. Stir the onions into the creamed potatoes and add a little grated nutmeg. Check the seasoning. Turn the mixture into a shallow ovenproof dish, smoothing over the top; dot with 1 oz. butter and brown in a fairly hot oven (375 °F, mark 5) for about 20 minutes. Serve cut in wedges. A good partner for pork. (Serves 4.)

Mousseline Potatoes: A rich dish that's splendid with cold beef and green salad. Boil 2 lb. potatoes, drain, then sieve into another pan. Add ¼ pint hot milk or single cream, 2 oz. grated cheese, 1–2 oz. soft butter, 1 tbsp. chopped parsley and ½ level tsp. salt. Beat until really fluffy. Quickly beat 4 egg yolks until pale and creamy and fold into the really hot potato purée; next, fold in the stiffly beaten egg whites. Pile into a greased 2-pint ovenproof dish, and bake in a fairly hot oven (400 °F, mark 6) for about 30 minutes, until risen and gold-topped. Serve quickly straight from the dish. (Serves 4–6.)

Duchesse Potatoes: Mash or sieve 1 lb. freshly cooked boiled potatoes; melt 2 oz. butter in a saucepan, add the potatoes and, when warm, add half a beaten egg and 1 tbsp. of cream or milk. Season well and blend thoroughly. Put the mixture into a forcing bag with a large star nozzle and pipe on to a greased baking sheet in rosette or other shapes. Glaze with the remaining beaten egg and brown in a hot oven (425 °F, mark 7) for about 10–15 minutes. (Serves 4.)

Jade Spinach

(See colour picture facing p. 241)
Nothing pappy about this!

1 lb. leaf spinach	¼ pint chicken stock
6 tbsps. corn oil	Salt

Remove the coarse stems from the spinach. Wash the leaves thoroughly and drain well. Heat the oil and add the spinach, stock and seasoning. Cook over a high heat for 20 seconds, then strain off the stock. The spinach is now crispy and green. Serve hot. (Serves 2–4.)

Hot Stuffed Tomatoes

Treated this way, they make a substantial second vegetable

4 even-sized tomatoes	2 tbsps. fresh
1 oz. ham, chopped	breadcrumbs
1 tsp. chopped onion	Salt and pepper
½ oz. butter	2 level tbsps. grated
½ tsp. chopped parsley	cheese (optional)

Oven temperature: fairly hot (400 °F, mark 6)

Cut a small round from each tomato at the end opposite to the stalk and scoop out the centres. Lightly fry the ham and onion in the fat for 3 minutes. Add the parsley, crumbs, seasoning, cheese (if used) and the pulp removed from the tomatoes. Fill the tomatoes with this mixture, pile it neatly on top, put on the lids and bake for about 15 minutes. (Serves 4.)

Cauliflower Salad

This can be served as a side-salad to almost any fish dish, or as a starter

1 medium-sized cauliflower	1 tsp. finely chopped onion
7 anchovy fillets	Freshly ground pepper
Milk	1 tbsp. olive or salad
3 tsps. bottled capers	oil
10 green olives, stoned and sliced	1½ tsps. wine vinegar

Divide the cauliflower into small florets. Wash, cook in boiling salted water for 5 minutes, drain and chill. Meanwhile, soak the anchovy fillets in just sufficient milk to cover them. Drain and cut into small pieces. Toss together the cauliflower, anchovy fillets, capers, olives and onion. Sprinkle with freshly ground pepper and add the oil and vinegar blended together. Turn the salad in the dressing and leave to marinade for about 30 minutes, then arrange on small dishes. (Serves 4.)

Cheese and Grape Salad

Eat as a luncheon with wholemeal bread

¼ lb. green grapes
3 medium-sized heads of chicory
4 tomatoes
8 oz. Cheshire cheese, diced

Cut the washed grapes lengthwise and remove the pips. Wash and thinly slice the chicory. Skin and thinly slice the tomatoes. On individual plates arrange an outer circle of chicory and an inner circle of overlapping tomato. Pile the cheese in the centre, and garnish with the halved grapes. (Serves 4.)

Chicken and Banana Salad

Refreshing for hot days

6 oz. cooked chicken
6 oz. cooked ham
6 oz. cooked long-grain rice
2 bananas, sliced
1 small onion, finely chopped
3 tomatoes, skinned seeded and chopped
2 tbsps. mayonnaise
2 tbsps. soured or double cream
Salt and pepper
1 lettuce

Dice the chicken and ham and place in a large bowl. Add the rice, bananas, onion and tomatoes. Blend together the mayonnaise and cream and adjust the seasoning. Serve on lettuce. (Serves 4.)

Chicken and Peach Salad

As good to look at as it is to eat

8 oz. long-grain rice
A pinch of saffron
Salt
3–4 tbsps. French dressing
A 2½-lb. cooked whole chicken
A 15½-oz. can of peach halves
3 oz. cream cheese
1 oz. walnuts, coarsely chopped
A bunch of watercress
1 egg, hard-boiled and and sliced lengthwise
Freshly milled black pepper

Boil the rice with the saffron and salt in the usual way. Leave until cold and toss with French dressing. Remove the breast meat from the chicken in large pieces and cut into strips. Carve off the dark meat and chop; add this to the rice. Drain the peaches, retaining 4 halves; dice the remainder and add to the rice. Beat the cream cheese and stir in the walnuts. Divide between the peach halves, filling the hollows. Check the rice mixture for seasoning. Arrange as a base on a flat-rimmed platter. Top with peaches, watercress, chicken breast and egg. Garnish the egg with freshly milled black pepper. (Serves 4.)

Chicken, Rice and Corn Salad

(See picture below)
Serve this main-dish salad with cracker biscuits and butter

A 2–2½ lb. chicken, cooked
3 tbsps. French dressing
¼ pint lemon mayonnaise
1 tbsp. lemon juice
1 tbsp. single cream
Salt and pepper
6 oz. cooked long-grain rice
An 11-oz. can of sweet corn kernels
1 medium-sized green pepper, finely diced
Cos lettuce

Cut the chicken flesh into 1-inch pieces and toss in the French dressing. Put the mayonnaise, lemon juice, cream and seasoning in a bowl. Gently fold in the chicken, rice, drained corn and green pepper. Arrange in a salad bowl lined with torn leaves of lettuce (or hand a green salad separately). Garnish if desired with rings of peppers. (Serves 4.)

Chicory and Orange Salad

Ideal accompaniment to pork or bacon

2 heads of chicory (avoid those with green tips)   French dressing
2 thin-skinned oranges

Wipe the chicory and slice finely; marinade for ½ hour in just enough well-seasoned French dressing, turning it occasionally. Peel the orange and dice the segments of pith and membrane. Add to the chicory and toss very lightly together. (Serves 4.)

Curried Cheese Salad

Exotic talking point

1 lb. cottage cheese
1 level tsp. curry paste
Salt and pepper
2 oz. sultanas, roughly chopped

2 oz. peanuts, roughly chopped
4 bananas, sliced
Lettuce
Black olives to garnish

Season the cheese with the curry paste and add salt and pepper to taste. Combine the mixture with the sultanas, peanuts and bananas. Pile on a bed of crisp lettuce and garnish with black olives. (Serves 4.)

Egg Mayonnaise

One of many versions of this old favourite

4 eggs, hard-boiled
A small jar of shrimp or salmon spread
Salt and pepper
Mayonnaise
Chopped parsley
Lettuce

French dressing
½ lb. tomatoes, skinned, seeded and roughly chopped
Snipped chives
Black pepper

Cut the cold eggs in halves lengthwise. Scoop out the yolks and cream with the fish spread; adjust the seasoning. Use to re-fill the egg-white shells; place the rounded side uppermost and coat with mayonnaise. Garnish each half with a line of chopped parsley and arrange in a row on a bed of French-dressed lettuce. On either side pile some tomato, then garnish with snipped chives and freshly milled black pepper. Serve with crusty rolls and butter. (Serves 4.)

French Bean Salad

Good simple hors d'oeuvre with Melba toast or crusty fresh bread

1 lb. French beans
2 tbsps. salad oil
1 tbsp. vinegar
Salt

Freshly ground black pepper
Freshly chopped chives and chervil

Cook the beans in boiling salted water until tender. Whisk together the oil, vinegar and seasoning until well blended. Pour over the hot drained beans. When cold, arrange on small plates and garnish with chives and chervil. (Serves 4.)

Note. This is a particularly good way of using up left-over cooked beans.

Ham and Asparagus Mould

(See colour picture facing p. 96)
Cool for summer days, yet quite satisfying

½ pint aspic jelly
16 asparagus stalks (1 for each flute of mould), cooked
3 oz. sugar
1 level tbsp. dry mustard
½ level tsp. salt

3 eggs, lightly beaten
6 tbsps. vinegar
½ oz. gelatine, dissolved in 2 tbsps. water
½ pint single cream
¾ lb. ham, sliced ⅛ inch thick and cut in thin strips

Line a 1½-pint mould with the syrupy aspic and put asparagus round edge. Mix the sugar, mustard, salt and eggs. Bring the vinegar to the boil and slowly add to mixture, stirring; cook over a low heat, stirring, until thick – don't boil. Remove from the heat, add the gelatine and cool till beginning to set, then stir in the cream and ham. Pour into mould, set and turn out. (Serves 6.)

Ham Cornets with Orange Beetroot

(See picture overleaf)
Another eye-catching salad

½ lb. cooked beetroot
3 large oranges
1 oz. flaked almonds
Salt and pepper
1½ level tsps. gelatine
1 tbsp. wine or cider vinegar

8 thin slices of cooked ham
1 lettuce, washed
4 tbsps. French dressing
A carton of mustard and cress

Peel and finely dice the beetroot and place in a bowl. Add the grated rind of 1 orange. Remove the peel and pith from the orange and cut the flesh into pieces. Add to the beetroot, with the almonds and seasoning. From one of the other oranges cut 4 slices to keep for a garnish. Squeeze the juice from these oranges and make up to ½ pint with water. Dissolve the gelatine in a little of the juice in a bowl over hot water. Add the rest of the juice and the vinegar, and leave until beginning to set. Fold through the orange and beetroot, and leave to set. Roll the ham slices into cones and chill.

Just before serving, roughly tear the lettuce and toss with the dressing. Arrange as a bed on a large round plate. Spoon jellied beetroot into the cornets and arrange on the lettuce. Any extra jelly can be piled in the centre. Place a small bunch of cress with a twisted orange slice between every two cornets. (Serves 4.)

Herring and Tomato Salad

Inexpensive, hearty salad dish

A 14-oz. can of herrings in tomato	2 oz. onion, very finely sliced
8 oz. long-grain rice	Salt and pepper
8 oz. firm tomatoes, skinned and sliced	Watercress or mustard and cress to garnish

For the Creamy Mustard Dressing

The herring liquor	1 level tsp. made mustard
1 tbsp. top of milk	
1 tbsp. vinegar	Salt and pepper to taste

Carefully drain off (and keep) the liquor from the can of herrings. Remove the centre bones from the fish. Boil the rice in the usual way and allow to cool. Toss the rice in the mustard dressing and arrange on a flat serving dish. Top with overlapping slices of tomato and onion, and season with salt and pepper. Lay the herring fillets on top of the tomato slices and garnish with watercress or mustard and cress. (Serves 4.)

Creamy Mustard Dressing: Whisk all the ingredients together.

Hot Potato Salad

Serve with either hot or cold frankfurters, smoked country sausage or other cold cuts

2 rashers of streaky bacon, rinded	2 fl. oz. vinegar (malt, wine or herb)
1 small onion, diced	4 fl. oz. water
½ level tbsp. flour	1 egg, hard-boiled and chopped
½ level tbsp. sugar	
½ level tsp. salt	2 large potatoes, boiled and cubed
¼ level tsp. paprika	

Cut the bacon into 1-inch pieces. Sauté the onion with the bacon until golden-brown. Add the flour, sugar, salt, paprika, vinegar and water and cook for about 2 minutes, stirring. Add the egg and potatoes. Continue cooking slowly for about 10 minutes, until the potatoes are hot and the flavours blended. Stir occasionally, and serve hot, sprinkled with chopped parsley. (Serves 3–4.)

Marinated Kipper Salad

Try this unusual combination

¾ lb. boiled potatoes	10 oz. boil-in-the-bag kipper fillets
2 sticks of celery	
1 eating apple, cored and peeled	A 7-oz. can of sweet corn, drained
4 tbsps. mayonnaise	French dressing
Paprika	Lemon wedges

Cut the potatoes into ½-inch cubes. Dice the celery and the eating apple. Blend together with the mayonnaise, pile in the centre of a flat serving dish and dust with paprika. Using scissors, snip the kipper fillets into narrow strips. Mix with the sweet corn and the French dressing and arrange on the dish around the potato salad. Garnish with lemon wedges. (Serves 4.)

Melon and Egg Salad

(See colour picture facing p. 96)
Imaginative combination

2 lettuces	6 hard-boiled eggs
2 cartons of mustard and cress	The flesh of a small melon
1–2 bunches of radishes	Mint-flavoured mayonnaise

Prepare the salad vegetables in the usual way, slice the radishes thinly, chop the eggs and cut the melon flesh into small cubes. Arrange prettily in a bowl. Serve the mayonnaise separately. (Serves 8.)

Note. Accompanied by a slice of veal-and-ham or pork pie, this could make a meal in itself.

Minted Tomato Salad

A fragrant side salad – to be eaten with roast lamb and new buttered potatoes

A slice of onion	$\frac{1}{2}$ a cucumber, finely diced
6 tomatoes	French dressing
2 tbsps. chopped mint	Crisp lettuce

Rub the onion round a salad bowl. Skin and slice the tomatoes and put in the bowl. Add the mint and cucumber to the dressing, spoon over the tomatoes and garnish with small lettuce leaves. (Serves 4.)

Orange-dressed Beetroot

Adds zest to cold meats or roast poultry

10 small globe beetroots, cooked	Orange dressing (see below)

For the Dressing

1 spring onion, finely chopped	2 level tsps. sugar
Freshly ground pepper	1 level tsp. continental mustard
A pinch of salt	3–4 tbsps. corn oil
2 tbsps. tarragon vinegar	2 tbsps. orange juice
	Grated rind of $\frac{1}{2}$ an orange

Remove the beetroot skins. Leave the beetroot whole, or cut in halves, and place in a dish.

Pour the orange dressing over and leave for several hours, or overnight in a cool place. When possible, turn the salad occasionally in the dressing. (Serves 10.)

Dressing: Shake together all the ingredients in a screw-topped jar. Check the seasoning.

Pear and Grape Salad

American-style

2 fresh pears, peeled and halved (or 4 canned halves)	1 tsp. chopped chives
	Milk if required
	$\frac{1}{4}$ lb. black grapes, halved and pipped
2 tbsps. cream cheese	1 lettuce
$\frac{1}{4}$ oz. butter	2 tbsps. French dressing
Salt and pepper	

Core the pears if necessary. Blend the cream cheese, butter, seasoning and chives, adding a very little milk if necessary to soften the mixture. Put this mixture between the grape halves. Arrange each pear half on a crisp lettuce leaf, fill the hollow centres with the stuffed grapes, chill well and sprinkle with French dressing.

Peruvian Potato Salad

It's the dressing that makes this salad different! It's very good with cold meats

1 lb. medium-sized new potatoes	Salt and pepper
	2 tbsps. olive oil
2 hard-boiled eggs	1 tsp. finely chopped onion
8 oz. cottage cheese	
A few drops of Tabasco sauce	3 tbsps. chopped parsley
1 tbsp. cream or top of the milk	Lettuce
	Paprika

Wash the potatoes and cook in boiling, salted water for about 30 minutes until tender. Drain, peel and cut into $\frac{1}{4}$-inch slices; leave to cool. Cut the eggs in half lengthways and remove the yolks. Chop the egg whites and set aside. Put the egg yolks, cottage cheese, Tabasco sauce, cream, salt and pepper in a small bowl and beat until smooth. Gradually add the oil, beating all the time. Stir in the onion and parsley. Arrange the lettuce leaves around the edge of a large flat plate; overlap the sliced potatoes in the centre. Spread the cheese mixture on top of the potatoes. Garnish with chopped egg whites and paprika. (Serves 4.)

Salad Tongue Wrap-Around

Light main course for a summer lunch

4 hard-boiled eggs, chopped	A few drops of Worcestershire sauce
½ a cucumber, diced	8 thin slices of tongue
4 oz. seedless raisins	8 cocktail onions
¼ pint soured cream	Lettuce
Salt and pepper	

Mix the hard-boiled eggs, cucumber, raisins, cream, salt and pepper and Worcestershire sauce in a bowl. Divide the filling between the slices of tongue, arranging it down the centre; fold one side over the other. Pierce with cocktail sticks decorated with cocktail onions, and arrange on a bed of finely shredded lettuce. (Serves 4.)

Salade Julienne

This recipe does wonders for canned meats

A 12-oz. can of Danish pork with tongue	A pinch of salt
	1 level tsp. sugar
2–3 young carrots	1 level tsp. continental mustard
1 dessert apple	
2 sticks of celery	A good pinch of curry powder
2 level tsps. finely chopped onions	
	2 tbsps. cider vinegar
A little freshly ground pepper	4 tbsps. salad oil
	Shredded lettuce
	Celery seed

Slice the meat thinly and then cut into Julienne strips. Peel the carrots and cut into fine Julienne strips. Peel and core the apple, slice thickly and cut similarly. Prepare the celery in the same way. Place all together in a large bowl. In a closed jar shake together the next eight ingredients. Use to dress the salad, tossing until all the ingredients glisten. Pile on to a bed of shredded lettuce, then sprinkle judiciously with some celery seed. (Serves 4.)

Tomato Salad

Heavenly starter salad

Firm but really ripe and rich-coloured tomatoes make a refreshing cold course. Allow about 1 lb. tomatoes for 4 servings, skin and slice them and arrange, overlapping, on individual plates. Coat with lemon dressing and garnish

with finely grated lemon rind or mint and perhaps a sprig of watercress. To make enough dressing for four shake (or beat) together 2 tbsps. lemon juice, 1 tsp. olive oil, a pinch of salt and 1 level tsp. sugar. (Serves 4.)

Salade Niçoise

(*See picture above*)
From the South of France

½ lb. tomatoes, skinned	4 oz. cooked French beans
½ a small cucumber, thinly sliced	2 oz. black olives, stoned and chopped
Salt and freshly ground black pepper	½ a clove of garlic, skinned and finely crushed
1 tsp. chopped fresh basil	French dressing
1 tsp. chopped fresh parsley	8 anchovy fillets, halved
	Brown bread and butter
Grated rind of 1 lemon	Quarters of lemon

Slice the tomatoes, put in layers with the cucumber on a shallow dish, season well and sprinkle with the herbs and lemon rind. Pile the French beans in the centre of the dish, scatter the chopped olives over and season again. Add the garlic to the dressing and pour over the salad. Arrange the anchovy fillets in a lattice pattern over the salad and allow to stand for about ½ hour before serving, so that the flavours blend. Serve with the bread and butter and the lemon quarters.

Tomato Jelly Ring

(See picture on right)
Imposing and delicious

1 lb. firm ripe tomatoes	A pinch each of celery salt and grated nutmeg
2 small onions	
1 small clove of garlic	1 level tbsp. powdered gelatine
1 bay leaf	
1 tsp. peppercorns	1 tbsp. tarragon vinegar
1 level tsp. sugar	
½ level tsp. salt	3 tbsps. lemon juice

Skin the tomatoes and cut in quarters, removing the centres if tough. Chop the onions and crush the garlic. Add bay leaf and peppercorns tied in muslin. Cook with the tomatoes, onion, garlic, sugar, salts and nutmeg over a low heat until the onion is tender. Remove the muslin bag. Dissolve the gelatine in a little water, and add to the tomato mixture which has been liquidized and put through a sieve and turned into a measure. Add the vinegar and lemon juice and if necessary make up to 1 pint with water. When beginning to set, pour into a wetted ring mould and leave to set. Unmould, turn out and garnish. (Serves 4–5.)

Tuna Salad

Top with crushed potato crisps for a change

2 eating apples	A 7-oz. can of tuna
Juice of ½ a lemon	3 tbsps. French dressing
½ a cucumber	Lettuce

Core and dice the apples, and put in a bowl with the lemon juice. Dice the cucumber; flake the tuna and wash the lettuce. Toss together the apples with the lemon juice, cucumber, tuna and French dressing. Arrange crisp lettuce in a salad bowl and pile the tuna salad in the centre. (Serves 4.)

Watercress and Orange Salad

Adds piquancy to shellfish and egg dishes

A bunch of watercress	2 thin-skinned oranges
2 heads of chicory	French dressing

Sprig and wash the watercress. Thinly slice the chicory. Peel and slice the oranges. Arrange on a plate and sprinkle with dressing. (Serves 4.)

Walnut, Date and Apple Salad

Satisfying, sweet, crunchy

4 firm, juicy eating apples	Mild mayonnaise
2 oz. walnut halves	A few drops of lemon juice
4 oz. stoned dates	

Core the apples and dice the flesh. Roughly chop the walnuts, chop the dates and toss all together with mayonnaise and lemon juice.

White Cabbage Salad

Makes a meal with cold ham or bacon

1½ lb. finely shredded crisp white cabbage	2 level tbsps. caster sugar
2 carrots, grated	1 tbsp. lemon juice
1 eating apple, cored and cubed	¼ pint soured cream
1 small green pepper, very finely chopped	3 level tbsps. mayonnaise
1 level tbsp. chopped onion	Salt and pepper
	Celery seed

Toss together the cabbage, carrot, apple, pepper and onion. Blend together the sugar, lemon juice, soured cream and mayonnaise. Check the seasoning. Add the salad ingredients and lightly toss together; sprinkle with celery seed. On occasions add tiny cream-cheese balls tossed with chopped salted peanuts. (Serves 8.)

Whole Potato Salad

Secret of this salad made with baby new potatoes is that the dressing should be poured over while the potatoes are hot

Use a sharp, well-seasoned French or vinaigrette dressing, using wine vinegar, and don't forget a little onion and mustard. Just before serving, when the dressed potatoes are cold, either pour over a little thin mayonnaise or add some cream to more French dressing. Garnish with chopped parsley or chopped salted nuts.

5
Savoury Sauces and Stuffings

Simple White Sauce – Roux Method

I – Pouring Consistency

¾ oz. butter
¾ oz. (approx. 2 level tbsps.) plain flour

½ pint milk or milk and stock
Salt and pepper

Melt the butter, without allowing it to brown, add the flour and stir with a wooden spoon until smooth. Cook over a gentle heat for 2–3 minutes, stirring until the mixture (called a roux) begins to bubble. Remove from the heat and add the liquid gradually, stirring after each addition to prevent lumps forming. Bring the sauce to the boil, stirring continuously, and when it has thickened, cook for a further 1–2 minutes. Add seasoning to taste.

II – Coating Consistency

1 oz. butter
1 oz. (3 level tbsps.) plain flour

½ pint milk or milk and stock
Salt and pepper

Make the sauce as above.

For a thick coating sauce increase the quantities to 1½ oz. each of butter and flour.

III – Binding Consistency (Panada)

2 oz. butter
2 oz. (6 level tbsps.) plain flour

½ pint milk or milk and stock
Salt and pepper

Melt the butter, add the flour and stir well. Cook gently for 2–3 minutes, stirring, until the roux begins to bubble and leave the sides of the pan. Add the liquid gradually, bring to the boil, stirring all the time, and cook for 1–2 minutes after it has thickened; add salt and pepper to taste.

This very thick sauce is used for binding mixtures such as croquettes.

Simple White Sauce – Blending Method

I – Pouring Consistency

½ oz. (1½ level tbsps.) cornflour
½ pint milk

A knob of butter
Salt and pepper

Put the cornflour in a basin and blend with 1–2 tbsps. of the milk to a smooth cream. Heat the remaining milk with the butter until boiling; pour on to the blended mixture, stirring all the time to prevent lumps forming. Return the mixture to the pan and bring to the boil, stirring continuously with a wooden spoon. Cook for 1–2 minutes after the mixture has thickened, to make a white, glossy sauce. Season to taste before serving.

II – Coating Consistency

Increase the quantity of cornflour to 2 level tbsps.

Brown (Espagnole) Sauce

1 oz. streaky bacon, chopped
1 oz. butter
1 shallot, chopped (or a small piece of onion, chopped)
1 oz. mushroom stalks, chopped

1 small carrot, chopped
¾–1 oz. (2–3 level tbsps.) plain flour
½ pint beef stock
A bouquet garni
2 level tbsps. tomato paste
Salt and pepper

This classic brown sauce forms the basis of many other savoury sauces.

Fry the bacon in the butter for 2–3 minutes, add the vegetables and fry for a further 3–5 minutes, or until lightly browned. Stir in the flour, mix well and continue frying until it turns brown. Remove from the heat and gradually add the stock (which if necessary can be made from a stock cube), stirring after each addition. Return the pan to the heat and stir until the sauce thickens; add the bouquet garni, tomato paste, salt and pepper. Reduce the heat and allow to simmer very gently for 1 hour, stirring from time to time to prevent it sticking; alternatively, cook in the centre of a warm oven (325 ° F, mark 3) for $1\frac{1}{2}$–2 hours. Strain the sauce, re-heat and skim off any fat, using a metal spoon. Re-season if necessary.

Note. 1 tbsp. sherry may be added just before the sauce is served.

Béarnaise Sauce

4 tbsps. wine or tarragon vinegar	1 shallot, chopped
	2 egg yolks
A few sprigs of tarragon chopped	3 oz. butter
	Salt and pepper

Place the vinegar, tarragon and shallot in a small saucepan over a gentle heat and reduce to about 1 tbsp. Stir into the egg yolks in a basin and cook over a pan of simmering water until slightly thickened. Whisk in the butter a little at a time, then season to taste. The sauce should be slightly thicker than Hollandaise and with a more piquant flavour.

Serve with steaks or grills.

Note. 1 tbsp. vinegar can be replaced by 1 tbsp. water – this gives a slightly less piquant sauce, which is preferred by some people.

Béchamel Sauce

$\frac{1}{2}$ pint milk	$\frac{1}{2}$ a bay leaf
1 shallot, sliced (or a small piece of onion)	3 peppercorns
	1 oz. butter
A small piece of carrot, cut up	1 oz. plain flour
	Salt
$\frac{1}{2}$ a stick of celery, cut up	Pepper

Put the milk, vegetables and flavourings in a saucepan and bring slowly to the boil. Remove from the heat, cover and leave to infuse for about 15 minutes. Strain the liquid and use this with the butter and flour to make a roux sauce (see opposite). Season to taste before serving.

This classic sauce is excellent with fish, and is the basis of many variations.

Chaudfroid Sauce – Brown

$\frac{1}{2}$ an envelope of aspic jelly powder	$\frac{1}{4}$ pint Espagnole sauce
	Madeira, sherry or port to taste
$\frac{1}{4}$ pint hot water	
$\frac{1}{4}$ oz. gelatine	Salt and pepper

Put the aspic jelly powder in a small basin, dissolve in the hot water and stand the basin in a pan of hot water. Sprinkle in the gelatine and stir over a gentle heat until it dissolves. Warm the Espagnole sauce and beat in the aspic and gelatine mixture. Add wine to taste, and extra salt and pepper if necessary. Strain the sauce and allow to cool, beating it from time to time.

When it reaches the consistency of thick cream, use to coat game, duck or cutlets.

Chaudfroid Sauce – White

$\frac{1}{2}$ an envelope of aspic jelly powder	$\frac{1}{2}$ pint Béchamel sauce
	$\frac{1}{8}$–$\frac{1}{4}$ pint single cream
$\frac{1}{4}$ pint hot water	Salt and pepper
$\frac{1}{4}$ oz. gelatine	

Put the aspic jelly powder in a small basin and dissolve it in the hot water. Stand the basin in a pan of hot water, sprinkle in the gelatine and stir until it has dissolved, taking care not to overheat the mixture. Stir into the warm Béchamel sauce, beat well and add the cream, and extra salt and pepper if necessary. Strain the sauce and leave to cool, stirring frequently.

Use when at the consistency of thick cream, for coating chicken, fish or eggs.

Chestnut Sauce

$\frac{1}{2}$ lb. chestnuts, peeled	$1\frac{1}{2}$ oz. butter
$\frac{1}{2}$ pint stock	1 oz. plain flour
A small piece of onion	Salt and pepper
A small piece of carrot	2–3 tbsps. single cream

Put the peeled nuts into a pan with the stock and vegetables, cover, simmer until soft and mash or sieve. Melt the butter and stir in the flour to form a roux, then add the chestnut purée and bring to the boil, stirring – the sauce should be thick, but it may be necessary at this point to add a little milk or extra stock. Season well, remove from the heat and stir in the cream. Re-heat without boiling.

Use with turkey or other poultry.

Hollandaise Sauce

(See picture above)

4 tbsps. wine vinegar   4–8 oz. butter
2 tbsps. water   Salt and pepper
8 peppercorns,   A squeeze of lemon
   crushed   juice
4 egg yolks

Place the vinegar, water and peppercorns in a saucepan. Bring to the boil and reduce by half. Strain the mixture into a basin placed over a pan of hot water and gradually beat in the egg yolks. Cook until the mixture thickens, stirring constantly. Allow the butter to soften slightly, then gradually beat into the egg yolk mixture until a thin coating consistency is obtained. Add the seasoning and lemon juice. Serve as soon as possible. If the sauce is too thick, thin with a little hot water.

Serve with salmon and other fish dishes, asparagus, broccoli, etc.

Horseradish Cream

2 tbsps. grated   A pinch of dry mustard
   horseradish   (optional)
2 tsps. lemon juice   ¼ pint double cream
2 level tsps. sugar

Mix the horseradish, lemon juice, sugar and mustard. Whip the cream until it just leaves a trail, then fold in the horseradish mixture.

Serve with beef.

168

Maître d'Hôtel Butter

1 oz. butter   1 tsp. lemon juice
1 tsp. parsley, very   Salt and pepper
   finely chopped

Work the ingredients together with a fork until well combined; shape into little pats and leave in a cold place until required.

Serve with grilled meat, grilled fish, etc.

Mayonnaise

2 egg yolks   ½ pint oil
½ level tsp. dry   2 tbsps. lemon juice, or
   mustard   1 tbsp. lemon juice
¼ level tsp. salt   and 1 tbsp. wine or
¼ level tsp. sugar   tarragon vinegar
Freshly ground pepper

Put the egg yolks in a deep bowl with the mustard, salt, sugar and pepper; mix thoroughly. Add the oil drop by drop, holding the basin firmly and beating with a wooden spoon or, ideally, use a hand-held mixer, working it round the bowl. When half the oil is added, beat in 1 tbsp. lemon juice; beat well. Add the remaining oil drop by drop, then the remaining 1 tbsp. lemon juice or the vinegar.

Serve with salads.

Tartare Sauce

¼ pint mayonnaise or   2 tsps. chopped
   salad cream   gherkins
1 tsp. chopped   2 tsps. chopped parsley
   tarragon or chives   1 tbsp. lemon juice or
2 tsps. chopped capers   tarragon vinegar

Mix all the ingredients well, then leave the sauce to stand for at least 1 hour before serving, to allow the flavours to blend.

Serve with fish.

Apple and Prune Stuffing

4 oz. prunes, stewed   2 oz. almonds, blanched
   and stoned   and shredded
8 oz. cooking apples,   Salt and pepper
   peeled and cored   Juice and grated rind
4 oz. rice, cooked   of ½ a lemon
2 oz. shredded suet   1 egg, beaten

Beef and Chestnut Casserole: p. 68

Cut the prunes into quarters and roughly chop the apples. Mix the fruit, rice, suet and nuts, season to taste, add the lemon rind and juice and bind with beaten egg.

Use for stuffing pork and breast or shoulder of lamb.

Apricot Stuffing

(See top picture on right)

3 oz. dried apricots	¼ level tsp. salt
3 oz. fresh white breadcrumbs	¼ level tsp. pepper
	1 tbsp. lemon juice
¼ level tsp. mixed spice	1 oz. butter, melted
	1 small egg, beaten
1 tbsp. chopped parsley	

Soak the apricots overnight in cold water. Drain off the liquid and chop the fruit. Stir in the crumbs, spice, parsley, salt, pepper, lemon juice and butter. Bind with the egg.

For pork, turkey, chicken, etc.

Celery Stuffing

4 sticks of celery, finely sliced	Juice and grated rind of 1 orange
1 onion, finely chopped	Salt and pepper
2 tbsps. cooking oil	4 oz. white breadcrumbs

Place the celery in a pan, cover with boiling water and simmer for 15–20 minutes, until tender; drain. Sauté onion in oil until golden. Put the celery in a basin, mix with the onion, orange juice, and rind, season very well and add the crumbs. Mix carefully with a fork.

Use for stuffing any meat; especially good with pork or lamb.

Sage and Onion Stuffing

2 large onions, skinned and chopped	4 oz. fresh white breadcrumbs
½ oz. butter	2 level tsps. dried sage
	Salt and pepper

Put the onions in a pan of cold water, bring to the boil and cook until tender – about 10 minutes. Drain well, add the other ingredients and mix well.

Use for stuffing pork joints.

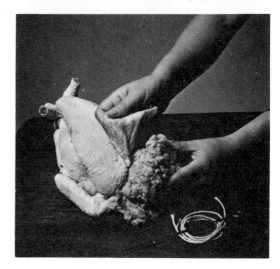

Sausage Stuffing

(See lower picture)

1 large onion, chopped	2 level tsps. chopped parsley
1 lb. pork sausage-meat	1 oz. fresh breadcrumbs (optional)
1 oz. lard	Salt and pepper
1 level tsp. mixed herbs	

Mix the onion with the sausage-meat. Melt the lard and fry them lightly for 2–3 minutes, add the rest of the ingredients and mix well.

Use with chicken; for turkey, double the quantities.

Roast Loin of Pork with Fantail Potatoes: p. 67

Bacon or Ham Stuffing

¼ of an onion, chopped   Salt and pepper
½ oz. dripping   A little dry mustard
2 mushrooms,   A few drops of
   chopped   Worcestershire sauce
2–3 oz. cooked bacon   Beaten egg or milk to
   or ham, chopped   bind
1 oz. fresh breadcrumbs

Lightly fry the onion in the dripping for 1–2 minutes; add the mushrooms and bacon or ham, and fry until the onion is soft but not coloured. Remove from the heat, add the crumbs, seasonings and sauce and bind with beaten egg or milk.

Use as a stuffing for vegetables, tomatoes, small marrows, peppers, etc.

Veal Forcemeat (also called Herb or Parsley Stuffing)

1–2 oz. cooked ham   2 level tsps. mixed
   or bacon   herbs
1 oz. suet (optional)   Grated rind of ½ a
4 oz. white   lemon
   breadcrumbs   Salt and pepper
1 tbsp. chopped   Beaten egg to mix
   parsley   Milk or stock to bind

Finely chop the ham or bacon and the suet (if necessary), then mix with the breadcrumbs. Add the parsley, herbs and lemon rind, season well and add the beaten egg, with milk or stock, if required, to bind.

Suitable for veal, shoulder of lamb, lamb's hearts, liver, chicken, etc.

6
Hot Puddings and Pies

Apfel Strudel

Popular Austrian sweet

8 oz. plain flour	½ level tsp. powdered
½ level tsp. salt	cinnamon
1 egg, slightly beaten	2½ lb. cooking apples,
2 tbsps. oil	peeled, cored, and
4 tbsps. lukewarm	grated
water	1½ oz. butter, melted
1½ oz. seedless raisins	4 oz. ground almonds
1½ oz. currants	Icing sugar and cream
3 oz. caster sugar	to serve

Oven temperature: fairly hot (375 °F, mark 5)

Put the flour and salt in a large bowl, make a well in the centre and pour in the egg and oil. Add the water gradually, stirring with a fork to make a soft, sticky dough. Work the dough in the bowl until it leaves the sides, turn it out on to a lightly floured surface and knead for 15 minutes. Form into a ball, place on a cloth and cover with a warmed bowl. Leave to 'rest' in a warm place for an hour.

Add the raisins, currants, sugar, and cinnamon to the apples and mix thoroughly.

Warm the rolling pin. Spread a clean old cotton tablecloth on the table and sprinkle lightly with 1–2 tbsps. flour. Place the dough on the cloth and roll out into a rectangle about ⅛ inch thick, lifting and turning it to prevent its sticking to the cloth. Gently stretch the dough, working from the centre to the outside and using the backs of the hands, until it is paper-thin. Trim edges to give an oblong about 27 by 24 inches. Arrange the dough with one long side towards you, brush it with melted butter and sprinkle with ground almonds. Spread the apple mixture over the dough, leaving a 2-inch border uncovered all round the edge. Fold these pastry edges over the apple mixture, towards the centre. Lift the corners of the cloth nearest to you up and over the pastry, causing the strudel to roll up, but stop after each turn, to pat it into shape and to keep the roll even. Form the roll into a horseshoe shape, brush it with the remaining melted butter and slide it on to a lightly buttered baking sheet. Bake in the centre of the oven for about 40 minutes, or until golden-brown. Dust with icing sugar and serve hot or cold, with cream. (4–6 servings.)

Note. Strudel paste is occasionally available at delicatessen shops.

Apple Brûlée

(*See picture above*)
'Apples again!' Yes, but what apples!

1 pint thick apple	¼ pint single cream
purée (see note)	Grated rind of 1 orange
¼ pint double cream	Soft light brown sugar

Turn the cold purée into ovenproof cocottes to give about 1-inch depth. Whisk the creams together until light and fluffy, but not over-firm. Fold in the orange rind, and spread the cream over the apple. Chill until just before required. Cover with a thick layer of sugar – about $\frac{1}{4}$–$\frac{1}{2}$ inch – and before serving place under a hot grill to melt the sugar quickly. Serve while still bubbling. (Serves 4–6.)

Note. To prepare 1 pint thick apple purée, peel, core and slice 2 lb. cooking apples. Cook with just enough water to cover the bottom of the pan. When soft, reduce to a thick purée by boiling. Add 3–4 oz. sugar and boil gently, stirring, for 5 minutes.

Apricot Soufflé Omelette

(*See picture on right top*)
Light, fluffy, with a luscious filling

A 15-oz. can of apricot halves	4 eggs, separated 2 oz. caster sugar
1 oz. cornflour	1 oz. butter

Drain the juice from the apricots and blend it with the cornflour. Heat in a small saucepan and bring to the boil, stirring. Add the apricots and simmer. Beat the egg yolks with the sugar until thick and pale; beat the egg white stiffly and fold into the creamed yolks. Melt the butter in an 8-inch frying- or omelette-pan, until tiny ripples can be seen. Pour the egg mixture into the pan and cook over a low heat until the underside is set and golden. Place the pan under a hot grill until the omelette mixture is risen and lightly browned.

Dust a piece of greaseproof paper with a little caster sugar. Slide the omelette out on to the paper and mark it across the middle with a knife. Spoon the apricot filling over one half. Lifting the other half by means of the paper, fold the omelette over on to a warm plate. Serve at once. (Serves 3.)

Baked Alaska

(*See picture on right bottom*)
This looks much more difficult than it actually proves to be

A 7-inch round sponge cake	A 'family' block of ice-cream
An 11-oz. can of fruit (e.g., raspberries)	3–4 egg whites 4–6 oz. caster sugar

Oven temperature: very hot (450 °F, mark 8)

Pre-heat the oven. Place the sponge cake on a flat heatproof dish and spoon over it just enough canned fruit juice to moisten the cake. Put the ice-cream in the centre of the cake and pile the fruit on top. Whisk the egg whites stiffly, whisk in half the sugar, then fold in the remaining sugar. Pile this meringue mixture over the cake, covering the cake, ice-cream and fruit completely and taking the meringue down to the dish. Place in the oven immediately, towards the top, and cook for 2–3 minutes, or until the outside of the meringue just begins to brown. Serve at once.

Variations
1. Use fresh crushed fruit, e.g., strawberries.
2. Sprinkle 1–2 tbsps. sherry or rum over the cake before the ice-cream is added.

Crêpes Suzettes

Practise once or twice so that you're slick and efficient in front of guests

4 oz. plain flour	2 eggs
½ level tsp. salt	½ pint milk
2 oz. caster sugar	Butter

For the sauce

2 oz. caster sugar	Grated rind of 1 lemon
2 oz. butter	3 tbsps. Cointreau
Juice of 2 oranges	2 tbsps. brandy

The pancakes may be made the previous day. Mix the flour, salt and sugar in a bowl. Make a well in the centre and add the eggs and a little milk. Gradually stir the flour into the liquid and when it is of the consistency of thin cream, beat until smooth. Stir in 1 oz. melted butter (which should be warm but not hot) and the remaining milk. Melt a very little butter in a small frying-pan. When the pan is hot, pour in 3 tbsps. batter and quickly turn the pan in all directions to spread it evenly and thinly over the base. When the underside is browned (after 1–2 minutes), turn the pancake and brown the second side. Put on a plate. This mixture makes 12 thin pancakes; stack them on the plate, cover and keep in a cool place until required.

Before serving the first course, fold the pancakes into four and arrange them in a shallow ovenproof dish. Next make the sauce. Put the sugar in a pan and heat gently until it melts and then browns. Add the butter, orange juice and lemon rind and stir well. Heat gently, stirring until all the caramel is dissolved, add the Cointreau and pour over the pancakes. Cover the dish, put in a cool oven (300 °F, mark 2) and leave while the first course is eaten. Uncover the dish and take it to the table. Warm the brandy gently, pour it over the pancakes and ignite. Serve at once. (Serves 4.)

Fruit Almond Puff

(*See picture below*)
Unusual mixed fruit filling

1 lb. bought (chilled) puff pastry	1 egg, beaten, to glaze

For the Filling

2 oz. butter	2 oz. Maraschino
2 oz. caster sugar	cherries, halved
½ tsp. almond essence	An 8-oz. can each of
1 egg, beaten	prunes, sliced peaches
½ oz. flour	apricot caps
2 oz. ground almonds	1 small apple, peeled and chopped

Oven temperature: very hot (450 °F, mark 8)

Cream the butter and sugar and beat in the essence, egg, flour, and almonds. Lightly fold in the cherries, well-drained canned fruits, and apple. Thinly roll out a quarter of the pastry and trim to an 8-inch round. Place on a baking sheet and prick with a fork. Brush a 1-inch rim with beaten egg. Divide the remaining pastry into 2 portions; roll out one piece and trim into a 9-inch round for the lid. Roll out the remainder in a strip 1 inch wide and about 14 inches long; divide in halves. Lay the strips over the egg-glazed rim to form a 'wall'. Leave the pastry to relax for 30 minutes.

Pile the fruit mixture within the 'wall', brush rim with beaten egg and place the pastry lid on top; press the edges together lightly. Roll out the trimmings thinly and cut into thin, narrow strips. Glaze the pastry with beaten egg and arrange the strips like spokes of a wheel.

Bake for 15 minutes, then reduce to moderate (350 °F, mark 4). Cover the puff with dampened greaseproof paper and cook for a further 45 minutes. Serve warm, cut in wedges and accompanied by whipped cream. (Serves 6.)

Lemon Bomb Pudding

There's a country air to this hearty sweet

8 oz. self-raising flour	Water
4 oz. suet	6 oz. soft brown sugar
½ level tsp. salt	1 large thin-skinned lemon

In a bowl mix together the flour, suet, and salt. Add just sufficient water to make a suet-crust dough. Roll out two-thirds of the dough and line a 1½-pint pudding basin. Half-fill the lined basin with some of the brown sugar, then put in the whole lemon (washed and dried and with the skin slightly scored). Fill up with the rest of the sugar. Damp the edges and cover with the remaining piece of dough, rolled to fit. Cover, place in a pan with water half-way up and boil gently for 4 hours. (Serves 4.)

Lemon Meringue Pie

One of the well-established old favourites, suitable for many occasions

4 oz. shortcrust pastry	1 oz. cornflour
$\frac{1}{2}$ pint water	2 eggs, separated
1 large lemon	$\frac{1}{2}$ oz. butter
2 oz. sugar	4 oz. caster sugar

Oven temperature: hot (425° F, mark 7)

Line an $8\frac{1}{2}$-inch pie plate with thinly rolled pastry. Knock up and crimp the edges and bake blind towards the top of the oven for about 25 minutes. Put the water, grated lemon rind and 2 oz. sugar on to boil. Blend the cornflour with the lemon juice (using about 3 tbsps.). Pour on the lemon juice mixture, stirring; return the mixture to the pan, bring to the boil and boil for 3 minutes. Remove the saucepan from the heat and beat in the egg yolks and the butter. Pour the mixture into the cooked pastry case. Whisk the egg whites until stiff, add 2 oz. of the caster sugar and whisk again, until stiff. Fold in almost all the remaining 2 oz. sugar. Pile the meringue on to the lemon filling, making sure that it covers the pastry edge, and swirl it decoratively. Dredge with the rest of the sugar and bake in the centre of a cool oven (300 °F, mark 2) for about 30 minutes, until the meringue is crisp and lightly coloured. Serve warm or cold, plain or with cream.

Marmalade–Apple Pie

Apple pie with a plus

8 oz. shortcrust pastry	A few sultanas (optional)
Coarse-cut orange marmalade	Milk to glaze
A 15-oz. can of apple pie filling	Granulated sugar for top of pie

Oven temperature: fairly hot (400 °F, mark 6)

Roll out the pastry and use a little less than half to line a 9-inch pie plate. Cover the base with a layer of marmalade. Add the pie filling (which should not be too juicy), with the sultanas, if used. Cover with the remainder of the pastry, rolled out to make a lid, and seal the edges. Brush the top with milk and lightly dredge with sugar. Make a slit in the centre top, put on a heated baking sheet and bake about 30 minutes. Serve hot or cold. (Serves 6.)

Orange Caramel Bananas

For banana addicts

4 oz. granulated or caster sugar	4 large bananas, peeled and halved length-
Grated rind and juice of 1 orange	wise
	Single cream

In a 6- or 7-inch frying pan, heat the sugar until it turns golden-brown. Shake the pan from time to time to move the sugar so that the caramel colours evenly. Remove from the heat, add the orange rind and juice, and return the pan to a low heat to dissolve the caramel; bring to the boil. Arrange the bananas in the the sauce and spoon the sauce over to coat. Simmer for 2–3 minutes, then serve hot, with single cream. (Serves 4.)

Peaches with Butterscotch Sauce

Easy and delectable

Drain the syrup from a 15-oz. can of peach halves. Melt 1 oz. butter in a small frying-pan, add the peaches, cut side up, and fill each centre with soft brown sugar. Simmer gently until the sugar melts into the butter to form a sauce. Serve hot, with cream. (Serves 4.)

Note. You can chill the peach syrup and mix it with fresh orange juice as an appetizer for another meal.

Rhubarb Meringue

A refreshing way of serving forced rhubarb

$1-1\frac{1}{2}$ lb. rhubarb, prepared	Grated rind and juice of 1 large orange
4 individual sponge cakes, sliced	2-egg meringue mixture (see p. 201)
2–3 oz. sugar	

Oven temperature: fairly hot (375 °F, mark 5)

Cut the rhubarb in ½-inch slices. In a 2-pint ovenproof dish put alternate layers of rhubarb and sliced sponge cakes, sugar, orange juice, and rind. Press down, cover and bake until the rhubarb is soft – about 30 minutes. Spoon or pipe the meringue mixture over top, and return the dish to the oven to tinge the meringue – about 10 minutes. Serve warm. (Serves 4.)

Swiss Apple Pudding

Gentle cheating makes this a very easy sweet

A 1-lb. can of apple	1 oz. butter
purée	4 oz. packeted Swiss
1 oz. brown sugar	Muesli

Oven temperature: moderate (350 °F, mark 4)

Empty the apple purée into a greased ovenproof dish and stir in the sugar. Melt the butter in a saucepan, remove from the heat and stir in the Muesli until the butter is absorbed. Sprinkle this mixture over the apple and bake in the centre of the oven for 20 minutes.

Vanilla Soufflé

A basic baked soufflé

2 oz. caster sugar	½ pint milk
5 large eggs	½ tsp. vanilla essence
1½ oz. plain flour	

Oven temperature: moderate (350 °F, mark 4)

Grease a 7-inch (2-pint) soufflé dish. Cream the sugar with 1 whole egg and 1 yolk until pale cream in colour. Stir in the flour, pour the milk over and mix until smooth. Bring to boiling point, simmer for 2 minutes, then leave to cool slightly. Beat in the remaining egg yolks and the vanilla essence. Fold in the stiffly beaten egg whites, pour the mixture into the prepared soufflé dish and bake in the centre of the oven for 45 minutes, or until well risen, firm to the touch and pale golden. Serve at once. (Serves 4–5.)

Note. If you wish, after 30 minutes' baking, quickly dust the soufflé with icing sugar, then continue to bake.

Coffee Soufflé: Instead of the milk use a mixture of half milk and half strong black coffee.

Chocolate Soufflé

Deliciously fluffy, and popular with children

3–4 oz. chocolate dots	½ oz. butter
2 tbsps. water	3 egg yolks
¾ pint milk	4 egg whites
2 oz. caster sugar	Icing sugar
1½ oz. plain flour	

Oven temperature: moderate (350 °F, mark 4)

Grease a 7-inch (2-pint) soufflé dish. Put the chocolate in a basin with the water and melt over a pan of boiling water. Heat the milk (reserving a little) with the sugar and pour on to the melted chocolate. Blend the flour to a smooth paste with the remaining milk, then stir in the chocolate mixture. Return the mixture to the pan, bring to boiling point and cook for 2 minutes. Add the butter, in small pieces. Leave until lukewarm. Beat in the egg yolks, then fold in the stiffly whisked whites. Turn the mixture into the soufflé dish and bake for 45 minutes, until well risen and firm to touch. Dust with icing sugar before serving. (Serves 4–5.)

Apricot Soufflé

One of the best fruit soufflés

A 15-oz. can of	¼ pint milk
apricots, drained	3 oz. caster sugar
1½ oz. butter	4 large eggs, separated
1½ oz. plain flour	1 tbsp. apricot brandy

Oven temperature: moderate (350 °F, mark 4)

Grease a 7-inch (2-pint) soufflé dish. Sieve the apricots. Melt the butter in a saucepan, stir in the flour, then the milk, and stir until smooth. Add the apricot purée, bring to boiling point and simmer for 2 minutes, or until the mixture begins to leave the sides of the pan. Remove from the heat. Stir in the sugar, egg yolks and brandy; fold in the stiffly whisked egg whites. Turn the mixture into the soufflé dish and bake in the centre of the oven for 45 minutes, or until well risen, golden-brown and just firm to the touch. Serve immediately. (Serves 4–5.)

Apple Soufflé: Replace the apricots by a purée made by stewing 1 lb. cooking apples (cored and sliced) with 1 oz. butter and 2 tbsps. water to a pulp and then sieving. Replace the apricot brandy by a pinch of powdered cinnamon. Serve the soufflé dusted with a mixture of powdered cinnamon and caster sugar and accompany by thin cream.

Liqueur Soufflé

Light and rich

2 trifle sponge cakes	1 oz. plain flour
5 tbsps. Kirsch	¼ pint milk
2½ oz. mixed glacé fruits	2 oz. caster sugar
	3 eggs, separated
2 oz. butter	Icing sugar

Oven temperature: moderate (350 °F, mark 4)

Cut the sponge cakes into fingers and soak them in 1 tbsp. Kirsch. Rinse the fruit in very hot water to remove excess sugar, cut up small and soak in 1 tbsp. Kirsch. Grease a 7-inch soufflé dish.

Melt the butter, and then stir in the flour. Remove from the heat and gradually beat in the milk; return the mixture to the heat and cook for 5 minutes. Cool slightly and beat in the sugar, egg yolks and 3 tbsps. Kirsch, then fold in the stiffly beaten egg whites. Pour half the mixture into the soufflé dish, place over it a layer of cake and fruit, then cover with the remaining mixture. Cook in the centre of the oven for 45 minutes, until well risen, just firm to the touch and light golden-brown. Serve at once, dusted with icing sugar.

Butterscotch Nut Sauce

1 heaped tbsp. golden syrup	2 level tsps. custard powder
1 level tbsp. brown sugar	¼ pint water
	Lemon essence
½ oz. butter	2 tbsps. nuts, chopped

Put the syrup, sugar and butter in a pan and heat gently until melted. Remove from the heat and mix in the previously blended custard powder and water. Bring the mixture to the boil, stirring, and mix in the essence and nuts. Serve hot or cold, with steamed or baked puddings.

Fruit Sauce

A 15-oz. can of fruit (e.g., apricots), drained	A squeeze of lemon juice or 1 tbsp. rum, sherry or fruit liqueur (optional)
2 level tsps. arrowroot or cornflour	

Sieve the drained fruit, make up to ½ pint with juice and heat until boiling. Blend the arrowroot with a little more juice until it is a smooth cream, then stir in the puréed fruit. Return the mixture to the pan and heat gently, continuing to stir, until the sauce thickens and clears. A squeeze of lemon juice or 1 tbsp. of rum, sherry or a fruit liqueur may be added just before the sauce is served. Good with meringue sweets, cold soufflés, ice-creams, hot baked puddings, and steamed puddings.

Lemon or Orange Sauce

Grated rind and juice of 1 large lemon or orange	1 level tbsp. cornflour
	2 level tbsps. sugar
	1 egg yolk (optional)

Make up the fruit rind and juice with water to ¼ pint. Blend the cornflour and sugar with a little of the liquid to a smooth cream. Boil the remaining liquid and stir into the mixture. Return it to the pan and bring to the boil, stirring until the sauce thickens and clears. Cool, add the beaten egg yolk (if used) and re-heat, stirring, without boiling. Serve hot or cold, as for Fruit Sauce.

To make a Spice Lemon Sauce, include a pinch of ground cinnamon.

7
Cold Sweets and Desserts

Apple and Orange Bristol

Festive-looking and fresh-tasting

4½ oz. caster sugar	2 oranges, washed
⅜ pint water	Cream as accompani-
4 dessert or cooking	ment (optional)
apples (or pears)	

First make the caramel topping: put 2 oz. of the caster sugar into a thick pan and heat gently until it becomes a light brown colour, taking care not to let it burn. Pour on to a greased tray, spreading it as thinly as possible, and leave to set. Put the water and the remaining 2½ oz. sugar into a thick frying-pan, dissolve and bring to the boil. Peel, core and quarter the apples and put into the boiling syrup; poach gently with a lid on until just tender, then leave them to stand in the syrup until they become transparent. Pare 3–4 very fine strips of peel from one of the oranges, cut into small 'matchsticks' and put them into cold water. Bring to the boil and cook for 5–10 minutes, until tender, then drain them and dip into cold water. Peel the oranges and divide in sections free of membrane. Arrange the apple and orange in a dish and pour a little of the syrup over them. Just before serving, sprinkle with the orange peel 'matchsticks' and the broken caramel. Serve with cream, or alone, as you prefer.

Apricot and Almond Flans

(See left-hand picture overleaf)
Very pleasant individual sweets

1 pkt. of sponge flan mix	A little Kirsch (optional)
A 1 lb. 12-oz. can of apricot halves	A few flaked almonds, toasted
¼ pint apricot syrup	A 2·75-fl.-oz. carton of
2 level tsps. arrowroot	double cream, whipped

Make up 8 small flans as directed on the packet, and leave to cool. Meanwhile, drain the apricot halves; select 24 and put on one side, roughly chop the rest. Measure ¼ pint syrup and blend this with the arrowroot in a small saucepan. Bring to the boil, stirring, and cook until clear. When almost cold, add Kirsch to taste; spoon a little into each flan, and top with chopped apricot. Arrange the whole caps in groups of three on each flan; brush with more glaze and scatter some nuts on each one. Just before serving, whip the cream sufficiently to hold its shape. Decorate with cream. (Serves 8.)

Note. This sweet can be prepared early in the day. Keep in a cool place but *not* in the refrigerator.

Brioche with Apricots

(See right-hand picture overleaf)
Unusual yeast sweet with fruit filling

8 oz. strong plain flour	1½ tbsps. warm water
A pinch of salt	2 eggs, beaten
½ oz. caster sugar	2 oz. melted butter
½ oz. fresh yeast	Egg to glaze

For the Filling

A 16-oz. can of apricot halves	1 level tbsp. icing sugar
3 tbsps. Kirsch	Icing sugar for dusting
½ pint whipping cream	

Oven temperature: very hot (450 °F, mark 8)

Brush a 2-pint fluted mould with oil. Sift together the flour, salt and sugar. Blend the yeast with the water and stir into the flour, with the eggs and butter. Work to a soft dough and knead for about 5 minutes. Put the dough in an oiled plastic bag and leave to rise at room temperature for 1–1½ hours, until doubled in size.

On a lightly-floured surface knead the dough

well. Shape three-quarters of the dough into a ball and place in the bottom of the mould. Press a hole in the centre and put the remaining piece of dough shaped as a 'knob' in the middle; press down lightly. Place the mould in the oiled plastic bag and leave at room temperature until the dough is light, puffy and nearly reaches the top – about 1 hour. Brush lightly with egg glaze and bake for 15–20 minutes, until brown and hollow-sounding when tapped. Turn out and cool on a wire rack. Cut away the 'knob' area for the lid, scoop out the centre of the brioche and discard. Drain the apricots, reserving a few for decoration and chopping the rest. Mix 3 tbsps. of the juice with the Kirsch, spoon over the inside of the brioche and leave for 5 minutes. Whip the cream until it holds its shape and add the sugar; fold in the chopped apricot and pile into the brioche. Decorate with apricot halves, replace the lid and dredge with sugar.

Black Forest Sundae

Really sophisticated ice-cream sweet

A 15-oz. can of red or black cherries, or ½ lb. fresh ripe cherries
¼ lb. strawberries
2 tbsps. Kirsch

5 oz. plain covering chocolate
1 tbsp. golden syrup
¼ pint double cream
A medium-size pkt. of Cornish ice-cream

Drain the canned cherries and stone them (or remove the stones from fresh cherries). Reserve 4 strawberries for decoration; thickly slice the remainder. Marinade the cherries and sliced strawberries in the Kirsch for ½ hour.

Coarsely grate 3 oz. of the covering chocolate; melt the remainder with the syrup in a small bowl placed over a pan of warm water.

To assemble, divide the grated chocolate between 4 tall chilled glasses. Cover with half the marinaded cherries and strawberries (include the marinade). Cover with nearly all the whipped cream; top with the remainder of the fruit and fill up with ice-cream. Quickly spoon the chocolate sauce over, and finish with a whirl of cream and the whole strawberries. Serve fan wafers separately. (Serves 4.)

Cherries Jubilee

So simple for such an exotic effect

A can of cherry pie filling
Grated rind of 1 orange or lemon

A little brandy
4 portions of vanilla ice-cream

Heat the pie filling in a saucepan, adding the grated orange or lemon rind. Just before serving, add a little brandy; ignite it and spoon the flaming cherries over the portions of ice-cream in their individual dishes.

Choc Rum Mousse

Although this recipe is suitable for setting in a domestic refrigerator, it deep-freezes well

5 tbsps. water	2 eggs, separated
2 oz. chocolate dots	1½ oz. sugar
(cooking chocolate)	¼ pint double cream
1½ level tsps.	Grated chocolate and
powdered gelatine	whipped cream to
1 tbsp. rum	decorate

Place 3 tbsps. water and the chocolate in a small bowl; sprinkle the gelatine over. Dissolve the gelatine and melt the chocolate by standing the bowl in a pan of hot water. Remove from the heat and add the rum. Meanwhile, beat the egg yolks and sugar with the remaining water in a bowl over hot water until thick, stir in the gelatine mixture. When the egg mixture is almost cold and beginning to set, quickly fold through the whipped cream and lastly the whisked egg whites. When the mixture is evenly blended, turn into a 1½-pint serving dish. (Glass is quite suitable, but obviously not your best glass, if it's going into the deep-freeze.) If you have no deep-freeze, chill until set; decorate just before serving. (Serves 4.)

To freeze: Omit the decoration. Place the unwrapped dish in the deep-freeze for 3 hours, until it is firm. Remove from the freezer and wrap in a polythene bag, seal in the usual way, and replace in the freezer. Store for not more than 2–3 months, at 0 °F, or below.

To thaw: Unwrap, place in a refrigerator, *not* in the ice-tray compartment, for 3—4 hours. Decorate with whipped cream and chocolate.

Crème Brûlée

A French classic sweet

4 egg yolks	½ pint double cream
1 level tbsp. caster	A vanilla pod
sugar	Caster sugar
½ pint milk	

Cream the egg yolks and sugar together until pale in colour. Warm the milk and cream with the vanilla pod in a double saucepan or basin over hot water. Strain on to the egg yolks, stir, and return the mixture to the pan. Continue to cook, stirring constantly, until the custard has thickened and coats the back of the spoon.

Strain into an ovenproof dish, until the mixture almost reaches the top. Leave in a cool place for 2–3 hours. Sprinkle enough caster sugar over the surface to form a thick layer; this should entirely cover the surface.

Place under a hot grill until the sugar turns to caramel, and cool before serving, to set the caramel. (Serves 4–5.)

Note. When serving, tap with the bowl of a spoon to crack the caramel. Banana wedges and frosted grapes make attractive partners.

Crème Marron

Really rich

2 egg whites	1 tbsp. Tia Maria
½ pint double cream	1½ oz. marrons glacés
4 tbsps. marron	Ratafia biscuits
purée	

Whisk the egg whites very stiffly. Whisk the cream and reserve 2 heaped tbsps. of it for decoration. Mix the marron purée with the Tia Maria. Chop 1 oz. marrons glacés finely and add with the purée mixture to the cream. Fold in the egg whites, pile into individual glasses, top with the remaining cream and decorate with a small piece of marron glacé. Serve with ratafia biscuits or wafers. (Serves 4–6.)

Dressed Pineapple

(See colour picture facing p. 200)
Centrepiece idea

First mark a whole fresh pineapple into 8 sections with a sharp knife. Remove the outer skin from alternate sections, then cut through the flesh of these sections almost to the base, so that they fall away. Fill the cavity with sugared strawberries.

Gooseberry Chartreuse

(See colour picture facing p. 200)
Unexpected way of using gooseberries

6 oz. sugar	Juice and rind of
¾ pint water	1 orange
2 lb. gooseberries,	Green colouring
topped and tailed	1 level tbsp. cornflour
4 level tsps.	½ pint milk
powdered gelatine	2 eggs, separated

Dissolve the sugar in the water, add the prepared fruit and poach gently until just tender. Lift the fruit out carefully and sieve about half, to give $\frac{1}{2}$ pint purée. Measure $\frac{1}{2}$ pint of the juice. Dissolve 2 level tsps. gelatine in the orange juice in the usual way, stir into the gooseberry juice and colour pale green. Pour a little into the base of a $2\frac{1}{2}$-pint fancy jelly mould and leave to set in the refrigerator. Spoon the whole fruit over the jelly, cover with the remaining cool jelly and leave to set.

Make up a cornflour sauce with the milk and beat in the egg yolks and grated orange rind. Dissolve a further 2 level tsps. gelatine in 1 tbsp. water and add to the cornflour mixture. Stir in the gooseberry purée and fold in the stiffly whisked egg whites. Check for sweetness, then pour over the jelly layer. Chill in the refrigerator until set. Unmould (Serves 6–8.)

Gooseberry Velvet

Sharp gooseberry jelly, fruit-cream topping

2 lb. gooseberries,	$\frac{1}{2}$ oz. gelatine
topped and tailed	Green colouring
Water	$\frac{1}{4}$ pint custard
7 oz. sugar	$\frac{1}{4}$ pint double cream

Cook 1 lb. of the prepared gooseberries with $\frac{1}{2}$ pint water and 3 oz. sugar until the fruit is soft; retain a few whole berries for decoration, and pass the rest through a sieve. To clear the liquid, pour it through muslin or a fine sieve. If necessary, add water to make up to 1 pint. Sprinkle the gelatine over the warm liquid and stir until dissolved. Tint to a delicate green with colouring. Cool, then spoon into 6 ($\frac{1}{4}$-pint) sundae glasses and set in the refrigerator.

Meanwhile, cook the remaining 1 lb. gooseberries with 2 tbsps. water and 4 oz. sugar until the fruit is soft and reduced. Sieve and leave to cool. Make custard with $\frac{1}{4}$ pint milk, 3 level tsps. custard powder and 3 level tsps. sugar; stir occasionally while cooling. Lightly whip the cream. Fold the custard into the gooseberry purée, and add colouring to complement the jelly layer. Fold in the whipped cream, and divide between the 6 glasses. Chill until required. Decorate with tiny ginger biscuits or chocolate buttons and the remaining poached whole berries. (Serves 6.)

Grape Flan

Meltingly tender and sweet

A rich shortcrust	1 large egg
flan case, baked in	1 tsp. grated orange
an $8\frac{1}{2}$-inch fluted tin	rind
$\frac{1}{2}$ pint milk	2 tsps. orange liqueur
2 oz. caster sugar	$\frac{3}{4}$ lb. grapes
1 oz. flour	Juice of 1 orange,
2 level tsps. cornflour	strained
	A little arrowroot

Cool the flan case. Heat the milk, blend the sugar, flour, cornflour and egg. Stir in a little hot milk to give a smooth paste, return the mixture to the pan and stir until it thickens and just comes to the boil. Add the grated orange rind and the liqueur, cool and spoon into the pastry case. Cover the surface with buttered paper and leave until cold. Halve and pip the grapes and arrange over filling. Glaze with the orange juice thickened with arrowroot. (Serves 6.)

Iced Charlotte Russe

Worth the time and patience needed

For the Vanilla and Raspberry Ice-Cream Layers

$\frac{1}{2}$ pint milk	1 pint water
15 oz. sugar	1 lb. raspberries
A vanilla pod	8 tbsps. lemon juice
2 eggs, beaten	2 6-oz. cartons of hazel-
$\frac{1}{2}$ pint double cream	nut yoghurt

For the Case

3 level tbsps. sugar	28 boudoir biscuits or
4 tbsps. water	sponge fingers
4 tbsps. sherry	(2 packets)

First prepare the ice-cream. Heat the milk with 3 oz. of the sugar and the vanilla pod, and pour on to the beaten eggs, stirring. Return the mixture to the saucepan and cook over a low heat, stirring, until the custard thickens. Strain, remove the vanilla pod and allow the custard to cool. Half-whip the cream and fold into the cold custard. Pour into the ice tray and freeze until mushy. Turn into a chilled bowl, whisk thoroughly, freeze again until mushy.

To prepare the raspberry ice-cream, dissolve 12 oz. sugar in the water; bring to the boil, reduce to 1 pint and cool. Sieve the berries to remove the pips and make a purée. Add the lemon juice, yoghurt and sugar syrup to the purée, put into the ice tray, freeze to a mush.

Screw up some kitchen foil and fashion it into a collar to fit inside the base of an 8½-inch round cake tin, leaving a small gap between the tin side and the foil to support the biscuits. Dissolve the 3 level tbsps. sugar in the water in a small pan and simmer for 5 minutes. Blend with the sherry in a flat dish. Soak the sponge fingers briefly in this sherry syrup, removing them before they soften. Place side by side in the gap made by the foil, and chill the tin.

Layer the vanilla and raspberry ices. Start with half the vanilla. Lift the foil ring as the vanilla layer is spooned in, but leave the foil in position above the vanilla layer to give support to the biscuits. Freeze the vanilla layer, then remove the foil. Add half the raspberry ice, and when frozen, repeat as above. Leave in the freezer until required, but remember to allow a little time for the ice-cream to start to soften. Turn out and cut with a knife dipped in warm water. (Serves 12–14.)

Mille-Feuilles Slices

Who can resist these melt-in-the-mouth creamy pastries?

8 oz. puff pastry ready-made weight	½ pint crème pâtissière 6 oz. glacé icing
¼ lb. raspberry jam	Cochineal

Oven temperature: very hot (450 °F, mark 8)

Roll out the pastry into a rectangle 10 by 9 inches and prick well. Place on a dampened baking sheet and bake in the centre of the oven for 25 minutes, until well risen and golden-brown. Cool on a rack. When cold, cut in half lengthwise and spread the top of one piece with raspberry jam; then cover with the crème pâtissière. Spread raspberry jam on to the base of the second piece of pastry and place on top of the crème pâtissière. Make the glacé icing and mix 1 tbsp. of it with a few drops of cochineal to make a deep pink colour. Pour this into a greaseproof paper piping bag and cut the tip off the bag just before it is required. Spread the white icing over the top of the pastry. With the pink icing, pipe lines across the mille-feuilles ½ inch apart. Draw a skewer down the length of the mille-feuilles at ½-inch

intervals to make the feathering. Leave to set, then cut into pieces. (Makes 6 slices.)

Orange Liqueur Trifles

Quick and easy, and with a bitter-sweet flavour that's most refreshing

4 individual trifle sponge cakes	A 1-pint orange jelly tablet
Some fine-shred orange marmalade	½ pint hot water Double cream and
1 orange	finely grated orange
2 tbsps. Cointreau or Curaçao	rind for decoration

Split the sponge cakes in half lengthwise and sandwich together in pairs with orange marmalade. Cut into cubes and divide equally between 4 sundae glasses. Grate a little orange rind and put this on one side for decorating the trifles.

Squeeze the juice from the orange; blend together 2 tbsps. orange juice and the liqueur. Soak the sponge cake with 1 tbsp. juice to each glass. Make up half the jelly tablet with the hot water. When the jelly has dissolved, add ¼ pint cold water. Spoon evenly over the soaked sponge cake and leave to set. Meanwhile, put the rest of the jelly tablet in a measure and add any left-over orange juice (unless you have other uses for it); make up to ½ pint with hot water. Stir to dissolve the jelly and leave until beginning to set. Whisk until light and fluffy and spoon on top of the jellied sponge. Very lightly whip 4 tbsps. double cream and trickle over the jelly. Dust with grated orange rind. (Serves 4.)

Peach Savarin

If you've eaten a Savarin in France you'll long to make one yourself

½ level tsp. caster sugar	½ level tsp. salt 2½ oz. butter, softened
4 tbsps. milk, slightly warmed	2 eggs, beaten A 1-lb. 12-oz. can of
1½ level tsps. dried yeast	sliced peaches Rum or Kirsch to taste
4 oz. plain bread flour	¼ pint double cream

Oven temperature: hot (425 °F, mark 7)

Dissolve the sugar in the milk. Sprinkle the yeast on top and leave in a warm place for

181

10 minutes, until frothy. Grease a 1½-pint fancy metal ring mould. Sift together the flour and salt and rub in the softened butter. Beat in the eggs and yeast until well blended – about 5 minutes. Pour the batter into the mould and cover with a plastic bag. Leave for the dough to rise in a warm place until doubled in size. Bake for about 30 minutes, until well risen and golden-brown.

Meanwhile, drain the sliced peaches and chop about half the fruit. Add rum or Kirsch to the juice to taste. Turn the Savarin out on to a shallow dish and prick with a fine skewer, then baste with the syrup until all has been absorbed. To serve, place the Savarin on a flat serving plate, fill the centre with chopped fruit and decorate with the lightly whipped cream and with the remainder of the sliced peaches. (Serves 8.)

Pineapple Fluff

Simple and refreshing

A 15-oz. can of pineapple pieces	A large can of evaporated milk
2 1-pint pineapple jelly tablets	¼ pint double cream
	Chocolate vermicelli

Drain the pineapple, reserve 8 pieces for decoration and chop the remaining pieces. Place the jelly tablets in a 2-pint measure, add the pineapple juice and make up to 1½ pints with boiling water; stir until the jelly has dissolved. Leave the jelly to cool, until it is the consistency of unbeaten egg white. Whisk until frothy, add the evaporated milk and whisk again until frothy. When beginning to set, fold in the chopped pineapple. Turn into a serving dish or divide between 8 individual glasses. When set, decorate with 8 whirls of whipped cream topped with the reserved pineapple and some chocolate vermicelli. (Serves 8.)

Note. Make first thing in the morning for lunch or the evening meal. Decorate it just before serving.

Variations on the pineapple flavour are: mandarin oranges and orange jelly, or canned apricots and lemon jelly. Crisp accompaniments are shortbread fingers, little macaroons or boudoir biscuits, any of which would look appetizing piled up in little glass bowls.

Raspberry Cream

Fruity, creamy, fluffy – and pretty!

2 level tsps. gelatine	1 tbsp. sherry
3 tbsps. water	1 level tbsp. ground almonds
2 egg whites	
3 level tbsps. caster sugar	½ lb. raspberries, hulled
¼ pint single cream	A chocolate milk flake bar
¼ pint double cream	

Dissolve the gelatine in the water in the usual way. Whisk the egg whites until stiff, add the caster sugar and whisk again until stiff. Whip the creams together until thick. Quickly fold in the cool – but not setting – gelatine, the sherry, ground almonds and, lastly, the egg whites and raspberries. Divide between 6 trifle cases. Decorate with a chopped milk flake bar, and chill. (Serves 6.)

Raspberry Jewels

The glistening red of the jelly and the matt crimson of the fruit make a delightful picture

2 1-pint raspberry jelly tablets	Double cream
1 pint boiling water	Toasted flaked almonds to decorate
¾ lb. fresh raspberries	

Dissolve the jelly tablets in the water. Leave in a cold place until of the consistency of unbeaten egg white. Beat with a rotary whisk or electric beater until really frothy. Pour into a 1½-pint refrigerator ice-cube tray; replace the divisions and leave to set in the refrigerator – not in the ice-cube compartment.

Unmould the jelly cubes and arrange in stemmed goblets, alternately with the hulled raspberries. Lightly whip the cream – it should still be of a pouring consistency – and drizzle it over the jelly cubes and raspberries. Top with flaked almonds. (Serves 6.)

Red-currant Chiffon

Enjoy the tartly delicious flavour of fresh red-currants in this party sweet

1 lb. red-currants	2 level tsps. gelatine
2 large eggs, separated	1 tbsp. water
3 oz. caster sugar	

Stew the red-currants in the minimum of water until soft; blend or sieve. Whisk the egg yolks and caster sugar, add the fruit purée, place the bowl over a pan of hot water and whisk until thick. Dissolve the gelatine in the water in the usual way and whisk into the purée. Continue whisking until the mixture is on the point of setting. Fold in the stiffly whisked egg whites, pile into individual glasses and chill. (Serves 4.)

Red-Currant Compote

Easy to make, lovely to eat

1 lb. red-currants   ⅛ pint water
6–8 oz. caster sugar

Stalk the red-currants and wash them quickly in cold water, not letting them soak at all. Put them in a pan and add the sugar and water. Shake the currants until the sugar is dissolved, then put them into a glass dish. Leave them for about 2 hours, by which time the juice should have formed a red jelly, making a delicious summer sweet.

Rhubarb Velvet

So quick, so delicious!

¾ pint custard   Whipped cream and
A 14-oz. can of   chocolate dots to
   rhubarb pie filling   decorate
Grated rind of 1 orange

Make the custard in the usual way with ¾ pint milk (or use cold left-over custard). Stir in the pie filling and orange rind. Spoon the mixture into 4 individual stem glasses and chill. Before serving, top with whipped cream and chocolate dots. (Serves 4.)

Rolla Torte

Meringue layers sandwiched together with a rich filling

⅛ level tsp. cream of   5½ oz. caster sugar
   tartar   1 oz. ground almonds
A pinch of salt   1 oz. cornflour
3 egg whites

For the Filling and Decoration

Chocolate crème au   2 oz. flaked almonds,
   beurre (see   lightly toasted
   recipe below)   Icing sugar

Oven temperature: warm (325 °F, mark 3)

Draw 3 7-inch circles on non-stick parchment paper and place on baking sheets.

Add the cream of tartar and salt to the egg whites and whisk until very stiff. Beat in two-thirds of the sugar, 1 tbsp. at a time. Mix together the remaining sugar, the almonds and cornflour and fold into the meringue mixture. Using a forcing bag and a ¼-inch plain vegetable nozzle, pipe the mixture on to the circles (start from the centre and work outwards in a coil, taking care to see that each ring of meringue touches the previous one). Alternatively, spread the meringue with a palette knife in smooth layers. Bake just below the centre of the oven for 30 minutes, until just coloured and dry. Peel off the paper and cool on a wire rack.

Meanwhile, prepare the crème au beurre and sandwich it between the meringue layers. Coat the sides with crème au beurre and decorate with flaked almonds. Dredge the top with icing sugar.

Leave the torte in a cool place for 24 hours to mature before cutting; the meringue layers should soften a little.

Chocolate Crème au Beurre

3 oz. caster sugar   4–6 oz. butter
4 tbsps. water   (preferably unsalted)
2 egg yolks, lightly   2 oz. chocolate dots
   beaten

Place the sugar in a fairly large heavy-based saucepan; add the water and leave over a very low heat to dissolve the sugar, without boiling. When completely dissolved, bring to boiling point and boil steadily for 2–3 minutes, or until a little of the syrup will form a thread when pulled between wetted finger and thumb (225 °F). Pour it in a thin stream on the egg yolks, whisking all the time. Continue to mix until the mixture is thick and cold. Gradually add to the creamed butter.

Put the chocolate polka dots (cooking chocolate) in a small bowl with 1 tbsp. water. Leave to stand over hot water until the mixture is smooth and the chocolate melted. Cool it slightly before beating it into the basic crème au beurre mixture.

183

Strawberry Galette

Tastes gorgeous – fit for a dinner party

9 oz. plain flour	1–1½ lb. strawberries
6 oz. butter	Red-currant jelly
3 oz. caster sugar	Red-currant glaze

Oven temperature: moderate (350 °F, mark 4)

Stand a 9-inch plain flan ring on a baking sheet. Sift the flour, rub in the butter and add the sugar. Continue lightly kneading the mixture until it forms a dough. Roll or press out to fit ring, drawing sides up to make a wall. Crimp edge and prick base. Bake for about 30 minutes, until lightly browned. Cool for 15 minutes on the tray, then remove the ring and, with a palette knife, lift on to a wire rack.

Cut the strawberries in halves lengthwise. Brush the base of the galette with red-currant jelly. Arrange the strawberries cut side uppermost over the jelly, coat with red-currant glaze and set. Serve with lightly whipped cream.

Red-currant Glaze: Heat 4 oz. red-currant jelly with ¼ pint water, bring to the boil and sieve. Blend with 2 level tsps. arrowroot, return the mixture to the pan and cook until clear.

Strawberry Nut Meringues

(*See picture above*)

Meringues with a couple of plusses

7 oz. icing sugar, sifted	Almond essence
3 egg whites	Double cream and
4½ oz. almonds, blanched and finely chopped	18 large whole strawberries to decorate the meringue

Oven temperature: cool (300 °F, mark 1–2)

Line 2 baking sheets with non-stick parchment paper. Put the icing sugar in a bowl with the egg whites and place over a saucepan of hot water. Whisk steadily with a rotary whisk or electric beater until the mixture forms stiff peaks. Remove the bowl from the heat and stir in the nuts and a few drops of essence. Place small discs of the mixture about 2 inches across on the baking sheet. Bake for about 30 minutes, until the meringue is crisp on the outside and creamy in colour. Cool on a wire rack. Store in an airtight tin. (Makes 18.)

To serve: Pipe a border of cream round each, and place a large strawberry in the centre.

Strawberry Shortcakes

Individual version of a popular sweet

8 oz. plain flour	Milk to mix
2 level tsps. baking powder	¾ lb. strawberries, prepared
2 oz. butter	Caster sugar for fruit
1 oz. caster sugar	¼ pint double cream
1 egg, beaten	whipped till fluffy

Oven temperature: very hot (450 °F, mark 8)

Lightly grease a baking sheet. Sift together the flour and baking powder. Rub in the butter and add the sugar. Mix to a stiff dough with the egg and a little milk. Roll out ½–¾ inch thick and cut out 12 rounds, using a 3-inch plain cutter. Place on the baking sheet and bake towards the top of the oven for 7–10 minutes, until well risen and golden-brown.

Crush the strawberries very lightly and add a little caster sugar to sweeten. While the shortcakes are still warm, split in halves and spread the base of each with crushed strawberries. Put on the top and decorate with more cream and strawberries.

Strawberry Wafer Dessert

A no-cook refrigerated dessert

A 5½-oz. pkt. of chocolate wafer biscuits	2 oz. butter
	1 egg
4 oz. icing sugar, sifted	An 11-oz. can of strawberry pie filling
	¼ pint double cream

Crush the biscuits to crumbs and sprinkle half these crumbs over the base of a buttered 9-inch sandwich tin. Cream the icing sugar and butter until very light and fluffy; beat in the egg. Spread this mixture over the crumbs in the tin. Spread the strawberry filling over the butter cream, and finish with a layer of whipped cream and the remaining crumbs. Use the back of a spoon to press mixture down. Chill for 12 hours, cut into fingers. (Serves 6–8.)

Stuffed Pears

An easy gala sweet

2 oz. macaroons, crushed	A little syrup
8 Maraschino cherries	8 pear halves
1 tbsp. apricot jam	Whipped cream

Mix the macaroons and 6 chopped cherries with sufficient jam and syrup to bind together. Divide the mixture between the pear halves, sandwich together in pairs. Arrange on a dish, top with whipped cream and decorate with the remaining cherries. (Serves 4.)

Syllabub

(See picture above)
The lightest of traditional sweets, which can be made well in advance. Here are two variants

Syllabub (solid): Pile high into glasses or custard cups. Keep for up to two days in a cool place but not the refrigerator. Serve sponge fingers or boudoir biscuits separately.

Thinly pared rind of 1 lemon	2 tbsps. brandy
	2–3 oz. caster sugar
4 tbsps. lemon juice	½ pint double cream
6 tbsps. white wine or sherry	Grated nutmeg or chopped nuts

Place the lemon rind, juice, wine and brandy in a bowl and leave for several hours, or overnight. Strain into a large bowl, add the sugar and stir until dissolved. Add the cream slowly, stirring all the time. Whisk until the mixture forms soft peaks. Spoon into ¼-pint glasses and sprinkle with nutmeg or nuts. (Serves 4–6.)

Syllabub (separated): Make in the morning for the evening meal; choose tall slim glasses rather than tubby ones. Gorgeous to eat – you dip a spoon through the frothy honeycomb layer into the wine–lemon whey beneath.

185

2 egg whites
4 oz. caster sugar
Juice of ½ a lemon

¼ pint sweet white wine
½ pint double cream,
lightly whipped

Whisk the egg whites until they form stiff peaks. Fold in the caster sugar, lemon juice, and wine. Finally fold in the lightly whipped cream. Spoon into ¼ or ½-pint glasses. Leave to separate. Decorate with a twist of lemon peel and serve home-made macaroons separately. (Serves 4–6.)

Black-Currant Trifle

A quickie worth trying

12 boudoir biscuits
2 tbsps. orange bitters
1 tbsp. water
¼ pint double cream

An 11-oz. can of black-
currant pie filling
Toasted flaked almonds
to decorate

Place 6 biscuits in the base of a rectangular dish and soak with the mixed orange bitters and water (or 4 tbsps. orange juice). Whip the cream till it can hold its shape and spread half over the biscuits. Cover with half the pie filling, then layer another 6 biscuits and the remaining pie filling and cream. Sprinkle with toasted almonds and chill before serving. (Serves 4–6.)

Chestnut Soufflé

Frankly rich and extravagant

3 eggs, separated
3 oz. caster sugar
¾ pint milk
4 oz. unsweetened
chestnut purée
3 level tsps. powdered
gelatine

1 tbsp. water
2 tbsps. rum
¼ pint double or
whipping cream
Whole chestnuts in
syrup and whipped
cream to decorate

Prepare a soufflé dish 5 inches in diameter and 2½ inches deep, adding a band of non-stick paper secured with paper clips, or use an ordinary glass serving dish. Cream the egg yolks with the sugar until pale and thick. Bring the milk just to the boil and pour on to the egg mixture. Place the bowl over a pan of hot water and stir until the mixture thickens (this takes about 20 minutes). Stir in the chestnut purée; cool. Dissolve the gelatine in the water and rum, and add to the custard. Chill to setting point, then quickly fold in the whipped cream, followed by the stiffly-whipped egg whites. Turn the mix-

ture into the soufflé dish and chill until set. Remove paper. Decorate with whipped cream and pieces of whole chestnut. Serve with sponge fingers. (Serves 4.)

Milanese Soufflé

First choice for many – light and refreshing to follow a roast

Finely grated rind of
2 lemons and juice
of 3 lemons
4 large eggs, separated
4–6 oz. caster sugar
2 tbsps. water

½ oz. gelatine
¼ pint double cream
3 level tsps. chopped
toasted almonds
Whipped cream for
decoration

Prepare a 6-inch (1½-pint) soufflé dish. Put the lemon rind, juice, egg yolks and sugar in a basin over a pan of hot water. Whisk the mixture until beginning to thicken. Place the water in a small basin or cup, sprinkle the gelatine over and dissolve by standing the bowl in a pan of hot water; stir into the lemon mixture. Leave to cool until just beginning to set, then whisk again. Fold in the lightly whipped cream, then quickly and evenly fold through the stiffly beaten egg white. Turn the mixture immediately into the prepared dish and leave to set. Remove the paper collar, then decorate the sides with almonds and the top with whirls of cream. (Serves 6.)

Raspberry Soufflé

A useful basic recipe; thick, sweetened, cooked gooseberry purée is a particularly good alternative flavouring

4 eggs, separated
4 oz. caster sugar
½ pint raspberry
purée
½ oz. powdered
gelatine
2 tbsps. water

1 tbsp. Curaçao
(optional)
¼ pint double cream
¼ pint single cream
Whole raspberries and
cream for decoration

Prepare a 7-inch (2-pint) soufflé dish. Put the egg yolks and sugar in a large bowl over a pan of hot water; whisk until thick and pale in colour. Add the raspberry purée and continue to whisk until beginning to thicken. Remove from the heat and stir in the gelatine dissolved in the water, and the liqueur. Allow the mixture to cool until just beginning to set, whisking occasionally. Meanwhile, whisk the two creams together until thick, and lightly fold through the raspberry mixture, followed by the whisked egg whites. Turn the mixture into the soufflé dish and leave to set. Remove the paper collar, and decorate the soufflé with whipped cream and whole berries. (Serves 6–8.)

Note. For the purée, put 1 lb. fresh or thawed frozen raspberries through a fine sieve.

Vanilla Ice-Cream

A good basic recipe

¼ pint milk
1½ oz. sugar
1 egg, beaten
¼–½ tsp. vanilla essence
¼ pint double cream

Heat the milk and sugar and pour on to the egg, stirring. Return the mixture to the saucepan and cook it over a gentle heat, stirring all the time until the custard thickens. Strain, and add the vanilla essence. Allow to cool, fold in the half-whipped cream, pour into a 1-pint ice tray and half-freeze (about ½ hour). Remove and turn into a cool bowl, whisk thoroughly with a rotary whisk, then replace in the frozen food compartment and leave until the ice-cream is firm. (Serves 4.)

Choc-de-Menthe

Embodies the favourite mixture of mint and chocolate flavours

Make up the basic vanilla ice-cream recipe, replacing the vanilla essence by 2 tsps. crème de menthe and a few drops of green colouring. When half-frozen, turn into a chilled bowl and whisk with a rotary whisk; fold in a small crumbled bar of flake chocolate. Return the mixture to the tray and continue as above.

Coffee Ice-Cream

For those who prefer a stronger flavour

6 oz. caster sugar
¼ pint water
5 egg yolks
½ pint double cream
1½ level tbsps. instant coffee
2 tsps. water

Dissolve the sugar in the water in a small saucepan; bring to the boil and boil to 217 °F

(about 5 minutes). Cool slightly, then pour into the beaten egg yolks in a thin stream, beating all the time. Place the bowl over a pan of hot water and continue to beat until thick. When cold, fold in the whipped cream and the coffee blended with the water. Put into 2 1-pint ice trays and freeze. (Serves 6–8.)

Honey Ice-Cream

Pleasantly exotic

1 lb. raspberries
¼ pint double cream
A 5-oz. carton of plain yoghurt
3 egg whites
2 tbsps. lemon juice
10 level tbsps. clear honey
A pinch of salt

Sieve the raspberries to give ½ pint purée. In a bowl, blend together the raspberry purée, cream, yoghurt, lemon juice, honey and salt. Turn the mixture into the ice trays and freeze until firm. Put into a bowl and beat until smooth. Fold in the stiffly whisked egg whites. Return the mixture to the ice trays and freeze until firm. (Serves 8.)

Lemon Ice-Cream

Refreshing, like every lemon sweet

½ pint double cream
2 eggs
Grated rind and juice of 2 lemons
10 oz. caster sugar, sifted
½ pint milk

Beat together the cream and eggs with a rotary whisk, until smooth. Add the lemon rind, the juice, sugar and milk and mix thoroughly. Pour into the freezing tray and freeze in the refrigerator frozen food compartment set at 'lowest', for about 2 hours. Do not stir while in the freezing tray. (Serves 6.)

Pineapple Ice-Cream

Slightly 'chewy' texture

Make up the basic vanilla ice-cream recipe, replacing the vanilla essence with 1 tsp. lemon juice and 1 tsp. Maraschino. When half-frozen, turn into a bowl and whisk with a rotary whisk until smooth; fold in the drained contents of a 15-oz. can of pineapple, finely chopped. Return the mixture to the trays, and freeze as usual. (Serves 4–6.)

Strawberry Liqueur Ice-Cream

Very hard to resist

½ pint double cream, Vanilla essence
  half-whipped 2 tbsps. rum or
1 lb. fresh straw- Maraschino
  berries, sieved 4 oz. caster sugar

Mix together all the ingredients, pour into a
1-pint ice tray and freeze for ¾–1 hour. Turn
out the whisk until smooth, then return the
mixture to the ice tray and freeze until firm.
(Serves 4–6.)

Neapolitan Bombe

Splendid party piece

Use a 1½–2 pint mould filled with basic vanilla,
choc de menthe, and strawberry liqueur ice-
cream. Use vanilla to line the chilled mould,
and freeze each layer before adding the next.

Sauces for Ice-Creams

*These sauces will add your personal touch to bought
ice-creams, and marry well with plain vanilla or
dairy blocks*

Apricot Sauce

Mix some apricot jam with a little lemon juice
and 2 tsps. sherry; pour over ice-cream, and
sprinkle with desiccated coconut or other
decoration.

Butterscotch Sauce

4 oz. sugar ½ pint milk
6 tbsps. boiling water ½ oz. butter
4 level tsps. cornflour

Put the sugar in a small, heavy-based saucepan
and heat gently till it dissolves and turns a pale
golden-brown; do not stir. Remove from the
heat, cool slightly and add the boiling water a
little at a time. Return the pan to the heat and
simmer gently until the caramel has dissolved,
then set aside. Blend the cornflour with half the
milk. Heat the remainder and pour on to the
blended cornflour. Add the caramel syrup. Return the mixture to the pan, bring to the boil,
add the butter and cook for 2 minutes. Serve
hot or cold. Chopped nuts may be added.

Cherry Sauce

½ lb. black or dark 2 level tsps. arrowroot
  red cherries Almond essence
Water 2 tsps. Cherry Heering
2 oz. sugar (optional)

Stone the cherries and cook in a little water
with the sugar until fairly tender. Drain the
fruit, make the juice up to ½ pint with water if
necessary. Blend the arrowroot with a little
juice, return with the rest of the measured
juice to the pan, and cook until transparent.
Pour over the cherries, add a little almond
essence and the Cherry Heering, if desired.

Chocolate Sauce

2 oz. plain chocolate 1 tbsp. milk
½ oz. butter 1 tsp. vanilla essence

Melt the chocolate and butter in a basin standing in a pan of hot water. Stir in the milk and
vanilla essence and serve straight away over the
ice-cream.

Chocolate Rum Sauce

Make a sauce from a chocolate blancmange
mixture and flavour with rum. This is very
good served over a mixture of ice-cream and
chopped banana.

Coffee Sauce

4 oz. Demerara or ½ pint strong black
  granulated sugar coffee
2 tbsps. water

Put the sugar and water in a heavy-based pan
and dissolve over a gentle heat, without stirring. Bring to the boil and boil rapidly until the
syrup becomes golden in colour. Add the coffee
and stir until the caramel has dissolved. Boil
for a few minutes, until syrupy. Allow to cool
before using.

Flambé Sauce

An 8-oz. can of 3 oz. sugar
  fruit cocktail 1½ oz. butter
Grated rind of 3 level tsps. cornflour
  ½ lemon 2 tbsps. brandy

Gently heat the fruit cocktail with the grated
lemon rind, sugar, butter, and cornflour, stir-

ring until it thickens. Add the brandy but do not stir. Ignite the brandy and spoon the sauce over and into the flame until it dies down. Pour the sauce at once over vanilla ice-cream.

Marshmallow Sauce

4 oz. sugar	1 egg white
3 tbsps. water	½ tsp. vanilla essence
8 marshmallows, cut up small	Red colouring (optional)

Dissolve the sugar in the water and boil it for 5 minutes. Add the marshmallows and stir the mixture until they have melted. Whip the egg white stiffly and gradually fold in the marshmallow mixture. Flavour with vanilla and tint pink. Serve at once over portions of coffee or chocolate ice-cream.

Melba Sauce

4 level tbsps. red-currant jelly	3 oz. sugar
¼ pint raspberry purée (from ½ lb. fresh fruit or a 15-oz. can)	2 level tsps. arrowroot or cornflour
	1 tbsp. cold water to blend

Mix the jelly, raspberry purée and sugar and bring to the boil. Blend the arrowroot with the cold water to a smooth cream, stir in a little of the raspberry mixture and return the sauce to the pan. Bring it to the boil, stirring with a wooden spoon until it thickens and clears. Strain and cool before using.

Pecan Rum Sauce

6 oz. soft brown sugar	1 oz. butter
2 level tsps. instant coffee	1 level tbsp. golden syrup
6 tbsps. single cream or evaporated milk	1 tbsp. rum
	2 oz. shelled pecans or walnuts

Combine together in a saucepan the sugar, coffee, cream or evaporated milk, butter, and golden syrup. Cook over a low heat to dissolve the sugar. Bring to the boil and boil gently, stirring, for 2–3 minutes, or until thickened. Stir in the rum and shelled pecans or walnuts. Bottle and store in a cool place. Serve either cold or warm, with dairy ice-cream.

Raspberry Sauce

An 8-oz. can of raspberries	2–3 level tsps. arrowroot

Blend the arrowroot with ½ pint of the liquid from the raspberries (made up if necessary with water) and boil until thickened. Stir in the fruit (whole or crushed) and chill the sauce before serving.

Other fruit sauces may be made in a similar way.

Black-Currant Sorbet

Good way of enjoying the rich flavour of this fruit

½ pint water	1 tsp. lemon juice
4 oz. sugar	2 egg whites
½ lb. black-currants	

Place the water in a saucepan with the sugar, bring to the boil and boil gently for 10 minutes. Cool.

Meanwhile, stew the stalked black-currants in a minimum of water for 10 minutes, then sieve and make the pulp up to ½ pint with water, if necessary; cool. Mix together the sugar syrup, lemon juice and fruit pulp, pour into an ice tray and freeze until nearly firm – about 1 hour. Whisk the egg whites till stiff but not dry. Turn the half-frozen fruit mixture into a chilled bowl, break down, and fold in the egg whites. Return to the ice tray and freeze until firm, but still of a slightly soft texture. Spoon into serving dishes. (Serves 4–6.)

Note. Follow the same method to make Strawberry and Raspberry Sorbets; simply sieve the raw fruit; do not cook, but make up to ½ pint with water.

Lemon Sorbet

Palate-refresher

6 oz. sugar	2 egg whites
1 pint water	Mint sprigs to decorate
Grated rind and juice of 4 lemons	

Put the sugar and water in a saucepan; dissolve the sugar, bring to the boil and boil for 10 minutes. Remove from the heat and add the lemon rind and juice (¼ pint). Cool in a bowl.

189

Pour when cold into a freezing tray and place in the refrigerator frozen food compartment set at 'lowest'. When half-frozen and slushy, turn into a bowl and fold in the stiffly beaten egg whites. Return to the tray and continue to freeze until firm. Serve spoonfuls of the sorbet in goblets and top each with a sprig of mint. (Serves 4.)

Orange Sorbet Cups

Prettily presented, attractively flavoured

4 large oranges	2 tbsps. lemon juice
4 oz. sugar	2 egg whites
½ pint water	

Cut the tops off the oranges and scoop out the flesh and membrane; discard the membrane. Wash the empty shells and put them, with their lids, into the frozen food compartment. Make a syrup with the sugar and water and leave to cool, as for sorbet. Blend or sieve the orange pulp, and make up to ½ pint with juice from an extra orange, if necessary. Combine with the syrup and lemon juice and continue as for Black-currant Sorbet. To serve, pack small spoonfuls of sorbet into the chilled orange shells and pile up well. Replace the lids and chill for up to 1 hour. (Serves 4.)

Pear Sorbet Meringue

Sorbet goes to town

A 15½ oz. can of pears	3 egg whites
12 oz. caster sugar	1 fresh pear, sliced and
½ pint water	cored
3 tbsps. lemon juice	Melted chocolate

Drain the pears, place in a measure and make up to ½ pint with some of the juice. Purée in an electric blender or put through a sieve. Dissolve half the sugar in the water, bring to the boil and reduce to ½ pint syrup. Pour on to the pear purée, add the lemon juice and stir well. Freeze this sorbet until firm.

Meanwhile, on a piece of non-stick parchment paper, draw a 9-inch circle; divide into 6 segments. Whisk the egg whites until stiff. Add 3 oz. sugar and whisk again until stiff. Fold in the remaining 3 oz. of the sugar. Spoon the meringue into a forcing bag fitted with a large star vegetable nozzle; using the pencilled lines as a guide, pipe a scalloped edge round the circle, indenting each section. Fill in the base with more meringue, then build up the scalloped edge and outline each segment. Dry in the oven set at lowest for 3–4 hours until crisp and firm. Cool, remove the paper.

To serve: Spoon the sorbet into the meringue 'nests'. Arrange slices of fresh pear dipped in lemon juice between them and drizzle with melted chocolate. Serve at once. (Serves 6.)

Pineapple Sorbet

Pineapple and the citrus fruits seem to have an affinity, well exploited here

2¾-lb. pineapple	11 oz. granulated sugar
6 tbsps. lemon juice	Whipped cream
4 tbsps. orange juice	(optional)
¼ pint water	

Peel the pineapple, remove the core, pulp the flesh in an electric blender, then put through a sieve to give ¾ pint purée. Mix the pineapple purée with the lemon and orange juice, water and sugar, stirring until the sugar has completely dissolved. Pour into freezing trays and freeze in the frozen food compartment of the refrigerator set at 'coldest' for 3½–4 hours, without stirring, until crystals have formed but a spoon still goes in. Serve accompanied by whipped cream, either in sundae glasses or returned to the empty pineapple shell, if this was kept in two halves. (Serves 6.)

8
Baked at Home

CAKES, PASTRIES, BUNS, COOKIES

Basic Victoria Sandwich

'Mother of thousands' you might call this mixture, so adaptable it is

8 oz. butter or margarine	8 oz. self-raising flour
8 oz. caster sugar	Vanilla essence
4 large eggs	

Oven temperature: moderate (350 °F, mark 4)

Grease and line a shallow tin measuring 14 by 9 inches (top measurement)

For a Plain Slab: Cream together the butter and sugar until light and fluffy. Beat in the eggs one at a time. Lightly fold the flour into the creamed mixture and then add a few drops of vanilla essence. Turn the mixture into the tin. Level the mixture and bake just above the centre of the oven for 35–40 minutes, until well risen and spongy to the touch. Turn out and cool on a wire rack.

For a Chocolate Slab: Make up the basic recipe above, adding to the creamed mixture 1 oz. cocoa, blended with a little water to a smooth paste.

For a Pink Slab: Make up the same basic recipe as above, and add a few drops of cochineal.

Storing: Wrapped in kitchen foil, these slabs will keep moist for several days, ready for finishing.

Basic Genoese Sponge

Foundation for a host of party gâteaux and small cakes

2½ oz. plain flour	4 oz. caster sugar
½ oz. cornflour	1½ oz. butter, melted and slightly cooled
3 large eggs	

Oven temperature: fairly hot (375 °F, mark 5)

Grease and base-line a 9-inch or 8-inch straight-sided sandwich tin or a 7-inch square cake tin.

Sift together the flour and cornflour. Place the eggs in a large basin over a saucepan of hot water, whisk for a few seconds, add the sugar and continue whisking over the heat until the mixture is very pale in colour and the whisk will make a figure of eight trail. Remove from the heat and whisk for a few seconds longer.

Using a metal spoon, carefully fold in half the sifted flour, then fold in the melted butter (cooled until it just flows) alternately with the the remaining flour. Turn the mixture into the prepared tin and bake towards the top of the oven for 30 minutes, or until well risen and just firm to the touch. Turn out carefully and leave to cool on a wire rack.

Note: For a deeper sponge, use an 8-inch sandwich tin, lined with a band of greaseproof paper, coming 2 inches above the edge of the tin.

Chestnut Gâteau

Reasonably quick and easy to decorate

3 eggs	4 oz. almonds, chopped and toasted
3 oz. caster sugar	¼ pint double cream
3 oz. plain flour, sifted	Candied chestnut spread (in a tube)
1 tbsp. warm water	
Apricot jam	

Oven temperature: fairly hot (375 °F, mark 5)

Grease and line a straight-sided Swiss roll tin, measuring 12 by 8 inches.

Whisk the eggs and sugar until thick enough to leave a trail. Fold in the flour with a metal spoon, along with the warm water. Turn the mixture into the prepared tin and bake above the oven centre for 12–15 minutes, until well-risen and golden-brown. Turn on to a rack and remove the paper.

When cold, cut across into three oblongs. Sandwich together in layers with apricot jam. Coat the sides with jam and press in the chopped nuts. Decorate the top with piped whipped cream and lines of chestnut spread, piped straight from the tube.

Galette Jalousie

(*See picture above*)

'Jalousie' in this instance means Venetian blind or shutter. You'll see why when the cake is baked

8 oz. puff pastry	Beaten egg white
Beaten egg	to glaze
½ lb. jam or apple purée	Caster sugar

Oven temperature: hot (425 °F, mark 7)

Roll out the pastry into a strip 18 by 4 inches. Cut into two portions, one 2 inches shorter than the other. Roll out the smaller piece to the same size as the larger. Place this piece on a dampened baking sheet. Brush a border ½ inch wide at each side of the strip with beaten egg. Spread the jam or purée over the centre of the pastry. Fold the thicker strip of pastry in half lengthwise. Using a sharp knife, cut across the fold at intervals to within ½ inch of the edge. Unfold the pastry and lift it carefully on to the portion on the baking sheet. Press the edges well together and 'knock up' with a knife. Bake in the centre of the oven for about 20 minutes. Remove from the oven, brush with egg white, dredge with caster sugar and return to the oven for a further 5 minutes to frost the top.

Gâteau à l'orange

This soft, rich filling is improved if the cake is chilled before serving

4 eggs, separated	4 tbsps. orange juice
4 oz. caster sugar	3½ oz. plain flour
Grated rind of 1 orange	

For the Filling and Decoration

4½ oz. butter	4 tbsps. orange juice
5 oz. caster sugar	1 tbsp. orange liqueur
1 egg and 1 yolk	1 oz. ground almonds,
Grated rind of 1 orange	lightly toasted

Oven temperature: moderate (350 °F, mark 4)

Grease and base-line a 9-inch straight-sided sandwich tin.

Place the egg yolks and sugar for the cake mixture in a basin and whisk until pale and thick. Beat in the orange rind and juice. Fold in the flour and finally the stiffly-beaten egg whites. Turn the mixture into the prepared tin and bake above the oven centre until well risen and firm to the touch. Turn out and cool on a wire rack.

Meanwhile, prepare the filling. Put 1½ oz. butter in a bowl with the caster sugar, egg, egg yolk, orange rind and juice and liqueur. Place over a pan of hot water and whisk until smooth and thick. Leave until completely cold.

Split the cake and sandwich together with a little of the filling. Cream the remaining butter, beat into the rest of the filling and use the thickened mixture to cover the top and sides of the cake. Press the ground almonds into the sides of the cake to decorate.

Grape Delight: p. 67

'Good Housekeeping's' Christmas Cake

Favourite from 'way back'

8 oz. stoned raisins	8 oz. plain flour
8 oz. sultanas	1 level tsp. mixed spice
8 oz. currants	A pinch of salt
4 oz. chopped mixed peel	8 oz. butter
	6 oz. soft brown sugar
4 oz. ground almonds	4 large eggs
4 oz. glacé cherries, quartered	1½ tbsps. brandy

Oven temperature: cool (300 °F, mark 1–2)

Grease and line an 8-inch round cake tin.

Check the raisins to make sure all stones are removed; cut large ones in half. Clean the sultanas and currants. Mix the raisins, sultanas, currents, peel, almonds and cherries together. Sift together the flour, spice and salt. Cream the butter until soft, add the sugar and beat until light and fluffy. Beat in the eggs one at a time. Fold in the dry ingredients, adding the fruit and brandy last. Turn the mixture into the prepared tin. Place in a larger tin or line the outside with brown paper. Bake in the lower part of the oven for 3½–3¾ hours. Cool on a wire rack, store, and finally decorate as desired.

Note. If wished, baste with a little more brandy before storing.

Two-Tier Wedding Cake

Outstandingly good basic fruit cake mixture

3 lb. 9 oz. currants	2 lb. 5 oz. plain flour
1 lb. 5 oz. sultanas	3 level tsps. ground cinnamon
1 lb. 5 oz. stoned raisins	2 level tsps. ground mace
1 lb. glacé cherries	2 lb. butter
10 oz. mixed chopped peel	2 lb. soft brown sugar
10 oz. nibbed almonds	16 eggs, beaten
Grated rind of 1 lemon	6 tbsps. brandy

Grease and line an 11-inch square cake tin and a 7-inch one, using double greaseproof paper. Tie a double band of brown paper round the outside (or put each tin in another slightly larger tin). Stand the tins on a layer of newspaper or brown paper during the baking.

Wash and thoroughly dry the fruit (unless it is pre-washed). Chop the raisins; quarter the cherries; skin, blanch and chop the almonds, if you bought whole ones; grate the lemon rind.

Sift together the flour and spices and add the lemon rind. Cream the butter and gradually beat in the sugar until light and fluffy. (It is often easier to cream larger quantities with the hand instead of using a wooden spoon.) Beat in the eggs a little at a time; if the mixture shows signs of curdling, beat in 1–2 tbsps. of the flour. Fold in the rest of the flour alternately with the fruit, nuts and brandy.

Long, slow cooking gives a dark colour to the cake, but if you wish you can add a few drops of ready-prepared gravy browning or some home-made caramel.

Spoon the mixture into the prepared tins, making it slightly deeper in the larger tin than in the smaller one. Level the surface and with the back of a spoon hollow out the centre slightly, to ensure a level top. At this stage the mixture may be left overnight; cover lightly with a cloth and leave in a cool place, but not a refrigerator.

Bake on the lowest shelf of a cool oven (300 °F, mark 1–2). The larger cake will take about 7½ hours and the other about 3¼ hours. Look at each half-way through its cooking time – if either cake seems to be browning too quickly, cover the top with a double thickness of greaseproof paper. With large cakes it is often wise to reduce the oven to very cool (275 °F, mark ½) after two-thirds of the time. Take the idiosyncrasies of your own oven into account.

Cool the cake in the tin for a short time before turning it on to a wire rack. When it is cold, prick at intervals with a fine skewer or clean hat-pin and spoon more brandy over the whole surface. Wrap completely in greaseproof paper and then in kitchen foil. Store for at least a month – preferably 2–3 months – in a cool, dry place.

When you come to do the icing, you will need 2 silver cake-boards, one 13–14 inches square, the other 8–9 inches square. You will require about 4½ lb. almond paste, ready-made weight (roughly 1½ lb. for the small tier and

193

Glazed Apple Flan: p. 65

3 lb. for the large one). This should be applied 1–2 weeks before the royal icing is added, 3–4 weeks before the wedding. For the royal icing you need approx. 5 lb. icing sugar and 10 egg whites (or equivalent in dried albumen). Put on the first coat 10–14 days before the wedding, and the second one 48 hours later. After another 48 hours you can begin the actual decoration, but if you need sugar flowers, plaques, etc., you can be making these meantime. Be sure to buy any pillars, silver leaves, and so on in good time, and to order a plated stand for the cake, if you require one.

A Good Housekeeping Institute leaflet, *Planning the Cake* (price 10p) advises on planning the design, choosing the tin sizes, icing and decorating, etc.

Layered 'Fork' Cake

So light you have to eat it with a fork

4 oz. butter	2 level tsps. baking
7 oz. caster sugar	powder
Vanilla essence	¼ level tsp. salt
Almond essence	4 fl. oz. milk
5 oz. plain flour	3 egg whites
1 oz. cornflour	

For the Frosting

1 egg white	A pinch of cream of
6 oz. caster sugar	tartar
A pinch of salt	

For the Filling

2 oz. shelled walnuts,	1 oz. sultanas
chopped	1 oz. chopped peel

Oven temperature: fairly hot (375 °F, mark 5)

Grease and base-line a pair of 7-inch straight-sided sandwich tins.

Cream the butter, add the sugar and beat thoroughly. Add ½ tsp. each of vanilla and almond essence. Sift together the flour, cornflour, baking powder and salt. Stir into the creamed mixture, alternately with the milk. Whisk the egg whites till stiff, then fold into the mixture. Divide the mixture between the tins and bake towards the top of the oven for about 30 minutes, until just firm to the touch. Turn out and cool on a wire rack.

Frosting: Put all the ingredients into a bowl and whisk lightly. Place the bowl over hot water and continue whisking until the mixture thickens sufficiently to hold 'peaks'.

Filling: Quickly add enough frosting to the fruit and nuts to bind together. Sandwich the 2 halves with the filling, then immediately cover the cake with the remaining frosting.

Light Fruit Cake

Fruity and moist, this can replace the richer fruit cake mixture traditional to Christmas

8 oz. sultanas	8 oz. butter or
2 oz. currants	margarine
2 oz. seedless raisins	9 oz. caster sugar
2 oz. glacé cherries,	5 eggs
quartered	10 oz. plain flour
2 oz. chopped mixed	2 oz. self-raising flour
peel	Milk if needed

Oven temperature: cool (300 °F, mark 1–2)

Grease and line an 8-inch round cake tin.

Wash and dry the fruit and combine with the cherries and peel. Cream the butter and sugar until light and fluffy. Add the eggs a little at a time, beating thoroughly. Lightly fold in the flours and fruit, adding a little milk if necessary to mix to a stiff dropping consistency. Turn the mixture into the prepared tin and bake in the lower part of the oven for about 2½ hours, until well risen and firm to the touch. Cool on a wire rack.

Note: This cake will store for a couple of weeks. Prettily frosted and finished, it's perfect for children's birthdays or, for that matter, any anniversary.

Nut Crumb Torte

Typically Continental use of hazelnuts

6 large eggs, 4 of	4 oz. hazelnuts, finely
them separated	chopped
6 oz. caster sugar	4 tbsps. raspberry jam
2 oz. dried white	Chocolate vermicelli
breadcrumbs	2 oz. chocolate dots

For the Crème au Beurre

3 oz. caster sugar	2 egg yolks, beaten
4 tbsps. water	4–6 oz. unsalted butter

Oven temperature: moderate (350 °F, mark 4)

Grease 2 sandwich tins, 10 inches in diameter and 1½ inches deep, and line so that the paper extends 1 inch above the rim.

Place 2 whole eggs and 4 yolks in a bowl with the sugar. Whisk together until thick. Stiffly whisk the 4 egg whites and fold in the creamed eggs. Lightly fold in the breadcrumbs and hazelnuts. Divide the mixture between the tins and bake in the centre of the oven for about 30 minutes. Cool and remove paper.

Sandwich the cakes with raspberry jam and completely mask with Crème au Beurre. Press the vermicelli on to the sides. Transfer the cake to a serving plate. Melt the chocolate dots in a small basin over a pan of warm water and drizzle over cake in a 'web' pattern. Leave in a cool place.

Note. This cake keeps for several days in an airtight tin.

Crème au Beurre: Slowly dissolve the sugar in the water in a saucepan; bring to the boil and boil to 225 °F. Slowly pour the syrup in a thin stream into the egg yolks, whisking all the time. Whisk until cold. Gradually beat into the well-creamed butter.

Orange Coffee Cake

Serve warm with coffee for a morning party, or cold in the ordinary way

2 oz. butter	2 level tsps. baking
5 oz. caster sugar	powder
1 egg	½ level tsp. salt
⅛ pint milk	1½ level tsps. grated
⅛ pint orange juice	orange rind
6 oz. plain flour	

For the Crumb Topping

3½ oz. sugar	1½ level tsps. grated
1½ oz. plain flour	orange rind
½ level tsp. ground	2 oz. butter
cinnamon	

Oven temperature: fairly hot (375 °F, mark 5)

Grease and line the base of an 8-inch square cake tin.

Cream the butter and sugar until light and fluffy and beat in the egg. Stir in the milk and orange juice, then the sifted flour, baking powder and salt. Add the orange rind. Turn the mixture into the tin and smooth level. Sprinkle evenly with the crumb mixture (made by mixing together the sugar, flour, cinnamon and rind and lightly rubbing in the butter). Bake in the centre of the oven for about 30 minutes, or until a skewer comes out clean.

Orange Log

More attractive to some palates than the well-known chocolate log

3 eggs	1 tbsp. warm water
6 oz. caster sugar	Grated rind of 1 orange
6 oz. plain flour	

For the Filling and Icing

¼ lb. apricot jam	1 tbsp. orange juice
4 oz. butter	Orange colouring
8 oz. icing sugar, sifted	

Oven temperature: hot (425 °F, mark 7)

Well grease and line a Swiss roll tin measuring 12 by 9 inches.

Put the eggs and caster sugar together in a large bowl over a pan of hot water and whisk until the beater leaves a trail. Remove the bowl from the heat. Sift half the flour over the egg mixture and fold in, using a metal spoon. Repeat with the remainder of the flour, and lastly fold in the water and orange rind. Turn mixture into tin. Bake above oven centre about 10 minutes, till golden-brown and firm.

Have ready a sheet of non-stick paper. Turn the cake out on to the paper. Quickly trim off the edges and spread the surface with warmed jam. Roll up with the aid of the paper, making the first turn firm, then rolling lightly. Cool on a wire rack.

Cream together the butter and icing sugar. Add the orange juice and a few drops of orange colouring and beat well. Spread evenly over the cake, mark with a fork handle and decorate.

Raspberry Surprise Cake

Showy variation on the sponge sandwich theme

3 large eggs	2 tbsps. water
3 oz. caster sugar	2 tbsps. sherry
3 oz. plain flour	½ pint whipping cream
2 tsps. glycerine	An 8-oz. pkt. of frozen
2 level tbsps. sugar	(or fresh) raspberries
for syrup	Icing sugar

Oven temperature: fairly hot (375 °F, mark 5)

Grease and flour a 3½-pint fluted ring mould.

Whisk together the eggs and sugar over a bowl of hot (not boiling) water, until the mixture is thick and pale in colour. Remove from heat and continue whisking till cold. Re-sift half the sifted flour over the egg mixture and fold in quickly and lightly. Repeat with the remaining flour and the glycerine.

Turn into the mould and bake above the oven centre for about 30 minutes. Turn out and cool on a wire rack.

Prepare a thin syrup by boiling the 2 level tbsps. sugar and the water together and adding the sherry. Split the cake in half and moisten the cut surface with the sherry syrup. Stiffly whisk the cream and spoon over the sponge halves. Embed the raspberries in the sponge base cream, top with the lid and dust with icing sugar. (Allow frozen raspberries to thaw out in the cream.) Once the cake is filled, serve and eat within the same day.

Simnel Cake

Some people serve this on Mothering Sunday, some at Easter-time

1½ lb. almond paste	6 oz. butter or
12 oz. currants	margarine
4 oz. sultanas	6 oz. caster sugar
3 oz. mixed candied	3 eggs, beaten
peel, chopped	Milk to mix
8 oz. plain flour	Apricot jam or beaten
A pinch of salt	egg to use under
1 level tsp. ground	almond paste topping
cinnamon	Glacé icing (optional)
1 level tsp. ground	Decorations as desired
nutmeg	

Oven temperature: warm (325 °F, mark 3)

Line a 7-inch round cake tin.

Divide the almond paste into 3 portions; take one piece and roll it out to a round the size of the cake tin.

Using the remaining ingredients and following the method given for Christmas Cake, make up the mixture. Put half of it into the prepared tin, smooth and cover with the round of almond paste. Put the remaining cake mixture on top. Bake in the centre of the oven for

about 1 hour, lower the heat to cool (300 °F, mark 1–2) and bake for 3 hours, until the cake is golden-brown, firm to the touch and no longer 'sings'. Allow to cool in the tin.

Take another third of the almond paste and roll out to a round the size of the tin; make small balls from the remaining third – eleven is the traditional number. Brush the top of the cake with apricot jam or beaten egg, cover with the round of paste and place the small balls round the edge. Brush the paste with any remaining egg or jam and brown under grill.

The top of the cake can then be coated with glacé icing, made by mixing 3 tbsps. sifted icing sugar with a little cold water until it will coat the back of the spoon. Decorate with a model chicken or a few coloured sugar eggs.

Note. If you buy almond paste, make sure it has a high almond content, otherwise it tends to become too soft during the cooking, and the line of almond paste filling disappears.

Sticky Gingerbread Ring

Homely cake in a new shape

6 oz butter	1 level tsp. mixed spice
½ pint golden syrup	2 large eggs
2 oz. caster sugar	¼ pint milk
10 oz. plain flour	2 oz. flaked almonds
1 level tsp.	4 oz. drained stem
bicarbonate of soda	ginger, chopped
2 level tsps. ground	Golden syrup to glaze
ginger	Icing sugar for dusting

Oven temperature: moderate (350 °F, mark 4)

Grease and flour a 4-pint ring mould tin.

In a saucepan warm together the butter, syrup and sugar until the butter has melted. Sift together the flour, soda, ginger and mixed spice. Beat together the eggs and milk. Make a well in the centre of the flour, add the milk mixture and gradually beat in the flour. Add the syrup mixture a little at a time, beating well. Stir in the almonds and stem ginger. Pour the batter into the ring mould tin. Bake in the centre of the oven for about 1 hour. Unmould, cool on a wire rack and store wrapped in kitchen foil. Serve brushed with warm syrup and dusted with icing sugar.

Streusel Madeira

(See picture above)

The delightful Continental topping makes this cake

6 oz. butter	3 eggs
2 oz. blended white vegetable fat	3 oz. plain flour
	5 oz. self-raising flour
6 oz. caster sugar	Milk

For the Streusel

1 oz. butter	1 oz. ground almonds
2 oz. fresh white breadcrumbs	½ level tsp. ground cinnamon
2 oz. sultanas	½ level tsp. mixed spice
2 oz. seedless raisins	Grated rind and juice
1 oz. nibbed (chopped) almonds	of 1 small lemon

Oven temperature: moderate (350 °F, mark 4)

Grease and line an 8-inch round cake tin, preferably loose-based, or a ring mould tin.

Cream together the fats and sugar until light and fluffy. Gradually beat in the eggs a little at a time. Lightly beat in the sifted flours, with a little milk if necessary. Turn the mixture into the prepared tin and bake just below the centre of the oven for 15 minutes. Spoon the Streusel mixture over the cake mixture, top lightly with foil and continue to bake for about 1 hour in a warm oven (325 °F, mark 3).

Cool in the tin for ½ hour before carefully lifting out the cake and cooling on a wire rack. Store in an airtight container.

Streusel: Melt the butter, add the crumbs and fry, turning frequently until evenly browned. Add the fruit, almonds, cinnamon, mixed spice, lemon rind and juice and mix well.

Bateaux de Miel

Not only honey, but also almonds and coffee, form the cargo of these boats

2 oz. Pâte Sucrée	3 tsps. thick honey
4 oz. butter	2 tsps. coffee essence
4 oz. caster sugar	Coffee glacé icing
4 oz. ground almonds	

Oven temperature: fairly hot (375 °F, mark 5)

Have ready 6 4½-inch boat-shaped patty tins.

Roll out the pâte sucrée and use to line the patty tins, pressing the pastry into shape. Bake 'blind' without beans towards the top of the oven, for 5–7 minutes, until tinged brown. Cool on a wire rack.

Cream together the butter and sugar until light and fluffy. Beat the almonds, honey and essence. Divide between the pastry boats, piling the mixture up to a peak and smoothing the surface. Chill. When the filling is firm, coat with coffee glacé icing based on 4 oz. icing sugar. Decorate with a wavy line of stiffer glacé icing, piped with a plain icing nozzle. (Makes 6.)

Pâte Sucrée

4 oz. plain flour	2 oz. butter at normal
A pinch of salt	room temperature
2 oz. caster sugar	2 egg yolks

Sift together the flour and salt on to a pastry board, or better still, a marble slab. Make a well in the centre and into it put the sugar, butter and egg yolks. Using the finger-tips of one hand, pinch and work the sugar, butter and egg yolks together until well blended. Gradually work in all the flour and knead lightly until smooth. Put the paste in a cool place for at least 1 hour to relax.

Note: Pâte sucrée may be made a day ahead and left in a plastic bag in the refrigerator or a cool place. With this amount you could make up two batches of 'boats'.

Bateaux aux Fruits

Perhaps the prettiest of all the 'boat' pastries

2 oz. pâte sucrée	A 14-oz. can of fruit
Apricot glaze	Blanched pistachio nuts

Prepare pastry boats as for Bateaux de Miel. Brush the inside of the pastry boats with some hot apricot glaze. Drain the fruit – apricot halves, pineapple pieces, or cherries (which should be stoned before use). Arrange the chosen fruit attractively in the pastry boats, brush with more apricot glaze and decorate with pistachio nuts. (Makes 6.)

Apricot Glaze: Gently heat ½ lb. apricot jam with 2 tbsps. water, sieve, re-boil to required consistency.

Congress Tarts

Characterized by the neat pastry crosses

4 oz. shortcrust pastry	2 oz. ground almonds
Raspberry jam	Grated rind and juice of ½ a lemon
2 oz. butter	1 egg, separated
2 oz. caster sugar	

Oven temperature: hot (425 °F, mark 7)

Have ready 12 patty tins.

Roll out the pastry and use to line the patty tins. Put a little jam in the base of each. Cream the butter and sugar until light and fluffy. Add the ground almonds, lemon rind and juice, then the egg yolk. Mix well. Stiffly beat the egg white, fold into the mixture and divide this between the pastry cases. Roll out the pastry trimmings and use to make a pastry cross on the top of each tart. Bake in the centre of the oven for 10 minutes, reduce the heat to moderate (350 °F, mark 4) and cook for a further 25 minutes. Cool on a wire rack. (Makes 12.)

As a variant, line the tins with pastry and place a little jam in the base of each as above. Cream together 2 oz. butter and 2 oz. caster sugar, beat in 1 egg, then fold in 2 oz. desiccated coconut and 1 oz. self-raising flour. Fill the cases with this mixture and sprinkle the tops with desiccated coconut. Bake in a fairly hot oven (375 °F, mark 5) for about 25–30 minutes – do not over-cook.

Cream Horns

A trifle difficult to eat? Well worth it!

8 oz. puff pastry (made weight)	5 fl. oz. double cream
1 egg, beaten	2½ fl. oz. single cream
Raspberry jam	Icing sugar to dredge

Oven temperature: hot (425 °F, mark 7)

Roll out the pastry to a strip 26 inches by 4–4½ inches. Brush with beaten egg glaze. Cut 8 half-inch ribbons from the pastry with a sharp knife. Wind each round a cream horn tin, glazed side uppermost; start at the tip, overlapping ⅛ inch, and finish neatly on the underside. The pastry should not overlap the metal rim. Place on a damp baking sheet, join-side down. Bake near the top of the oven for 8–10 minutes. Cool for a few minutes. Carefully twist each tin, holding the pastry lightly in the other hand, to ease it off the case. When cold, fill the tip of each horn with a little jam. Whip together the two creams, and fill the horns. Dust with icing sugar. (Makes 8 horns.)

Palmiers

Fluffy cream filling with crisp flaked pastry

8 oz. puff pastry (made weight)	5 fl. oz. double cream
Caster sugar	2½ fl. oz. single cream
	Vanilla sugar

Oven temperature: hot (425 °F, mark 7)

Roll out the pastry to a rectangle 12 by 10 inches. Dredge with caster sugar. Fold the long sides half-way towards the centre. Dredge with sugar and repeat, folding right to the centre. Dredge with sugar and fold in halves lengthwise, hiding the first folds; press lightly and evenly. Cut into 12 equal-sized slices. Place the palmiers on a baking tray, cut side down, open the tip of each and flatten the whole palmier slightly with a round-bladed knife. Bake towards the top of the oven for 8 minutes. Turn over and bake for a further 4 minutes, cool.

Whip together the 2 creams with a little vanilla-flavoured sugar, till lightly peaked. Sandwich the palmiers together with the cream just before serving. (Makes 6 pairs.)

Strawberry Almond Tartlets

Even the pastry is different in this recipe

4 oz. butter	6 oz. plain flour
2 oz. caster sugar	2 oz. ground almonds
1 egg yolk	

For the Filling

8 Petit-suisse cheeses	1 lb. strawberries, hulled
2 level tsps. caster sugar	3 tbsps. red-currant jelly

Oven temperature: fairly hot (375 °F, mark 5)

Have ready 8 loose-based 4-inch fluted French pastry tins.

Cream together the butter and sugar. Beat in the egg yolk, then work in the flour and ground almonds. Chill in the refrigerator or in a cold place until of a manageable consistency —about 1 hour. Divide into 8 pieces, roll out thinly on a lightly floured surface and use to line the tins. Bake 'blind' towards the top of the oven for about 15 minutes, until light golden-brown. Cool on a wire rack.

Cream the cheese and sugar and spread over each pastry case. Top with over-lapping sliced berries and glaze with warmed jelly. (Makes 9.)

Note. The unfilled pastry cases may be stored for a couple of days in an airtight tin.

Tartelettes aux Fruits

Another exquisite French creation

4 oz. pâte sucrée	¼ pint cherry juice
½ pint crème pâtissière	1 level tsp. arrowroot
A 15-oz. can of black cherries	5 fl. oz. double cream
	2½ fl. oz. single cream

Oven temperature: fairly hot (375 °F, mark 5)

Have ready 6 4½-inch shallow patty tins.

Line the tins with the pastry and bake 'blind' towards the top of the oven for 15–20 minutes. Cool on a rack. Before serving, spread a layer of crème patissière over the base of each tart. Drain the cherries (reserving the juice) and stone them. Thicken ¼ pint of the juice with the arrowroot in the usual way, and leave to cool. Whip the two creams together and pipe stars round the edge of the pastry cases. Arrange cherries in the centre, glaze with thickened juice.

Crème Pâtissière

Often known in this country as Confectioner's Custard

2 egg yolks	½ pint milk
2 oz. caster sugar	1 egg white
¾ oz. plain flour	Vanilla essence
½ oz. cornflour	

Cream the egg yolks and sugar together until really thick and pale in colour. Beat in the flour and cornflour and a little cold milk to make a smooth paste. Heat the rest of the milk in a saucepan until almost boiling and pour on to the egg mixture, stirring well all the time. Return the mixture to the saucepan and stir over a low heat till it boils. Whisk the egg white until stiff. Remove the custard mixture from the heat and fold in the egg white. Again return the pan to the heat, add essence to taste and cook for a further 2–3 minutes. Leave to become cold, then use as required for filling pastries, etc.

Butterscotch Brownies

Chewy fudge squares with a brown sugar flavour

2 oz. blended vegetable fat or butter	1 level tsp. baking powder
7 oz. light, soft brown sugar	½ level tsp. salt
1 egg	Vanilla essence
3½ oz. plain flour	1½ oz. shelled walnuts, coarsely chopped

Oven temperature: moderate (350 °F, mark 4)

Grease a shallow cake tin measuring about 8 inches square and 2 inches deep.

Melt the fat over a low heat, remove from the heat and blend in the sugar. Cool, then stir in the egg. Sift together the flour, baking powder and salt and stir into the ingredients in the pan. Mix in ½ tsp. essence and the walnuts. Turn the mixture into the tin and bake in the centre of the oven for about 30 minutes. Cool in the baking tin and cut into squares. Store in an airtight tin for a few days to keep soft. (Makes about 2 doz.)

Cherry Almond Pinwheels

Best eaten fresh

6 oz. self-raising flour	1½ oz. blended white vegetable fat
1 oz. caster sugar	1 egg
1½ oz. butter	

For the Filling

2 oz. ground almonds	2 pieces of stem ginger, chopped
2 oz. glacé cherries, quartered	1 egg yolk
2 oz. soft brown sugar	

Oven temperature: fairly hot (400 °F, mark 6)

Have ready some baking sheets.

Mix the flour and sugar in a bowl. Rub in the fats. Add the egg and mix well until the mixture binds together. Turn on to a floured surface and knead lightly, then roll into a rectangle ⅛ inch thick.

In a bowl mix together the ground almonds, cherries, brown sugar and ginger. Drop in the egg yolk and mix well. Spread the mixture over the rectangle of pastry. Brush one long edge (farthest away from you) with water and roll up away from you, then cut into ¼-inch slices. Place well apart, cut side uppermost, on the baking sheets. Bake in the oven centre for about 20 minutes. Cool on a wire rack. (Makes about 30.)

Chocolate Top Hats

Simple but eye-catching

2 oz. self-raising flour	2 oz. caster sugar
1 oz. cocoa	1 egg, beaten
2 oz. butter	1 tbsp. water
	Icing sugar

For the Butter Cream

2 oz. butter	4 oz. icing sugar, sifted

Oven temperature, fairly hot (375 °F, mark 5)

Place 10 paper cases in patty tins.

Sift the flour and cocoa powder on to a plate. Cream the butter and sugar until light and fluffy; add the egg, beating well. Fold in the flour, then add the water and mix well. Divide the mixture between the paper cases and bake in the centre of the oven for 15–20 minutes, until well risen and firm to the touch. Cool on a wire rack. When cold, cut a round from each, using a pointed knife. Pipe a star of butter cream into each bun, dust the tops with sugar and replace. (Makes 10.)

Butter Cream: Cream together the butter and sugar. Place in a piping bag fitted with a star vegetable nozzle.

Dutch Macaroons

(See picture on p. 203)

There's an artfully casual air about these cakes

4 oz. ground almonds	12 oz. icing sugar, sifted
3 egg whites	Vanilla essence

Oven temperature: cool (300 °F, mark 2)

Line 2–3 baking sheets with rice paper.

Beat together the almonds and egg whites until of an 'oily' consistency. Gradually add the sugar and ¼ tsp. vanilla essence and beat until smooth. Spoon or pipe the mixture (using a ½-inch vegetable nozzle) on to the lined baking sheets – the macaroons should measure about 2 inches across. Allow them to 'crust' for 3–4 hours at room temperature. Before baking, make a light cut across each macaroon just through the crust, using a sharp knife. Bake in the centre of the oven for about 25 minutes, until risen and lightly coloured. Trim the rice paper and cool the macaroons on a wire rack. They may be stored in an airtight container. (Makes about 16.)

Éclairs

These always give a party air to the tea-table

2½ oz. choux paste (see below)	Chocolate or coffee glacé icing or 2 oz. melted chocolate
Whipped cream or flavoured custard	

Oven temperature: fairly hot (400 °F, mark 6)

Put the choux paste into a forcing bag fitted with a plain round pipe of ½ inch diameter. Force in fingers 3½–4 inches long on to a baking tray, keeping the lengths very even and cutting the pastry off with a wet knife against the edge of the pipe. Bake towards the top of the oven for about 35 minutes, until well risen and of a golden-brown colour. Remove from the tin,

Raspberry Coffee Vacherin;
Gooseberry Chartreuse;
Refrigerator Cheese Cake;
Dressed Pineapple: pp. 85, 179

For over 100 years, we at Rayner's have
helped to make good cakes and sweets better,
and all the time we've been keeping up with
the demands made by each generation for new
and different cakes and sweets. Today, we
offer you fifteen different flavours, but
although our range has increased considerably
beyond our traditional Vanilla, the result
is still the same: better cakes, better sweets.

For every cake or sweet you can think of, Rayner's have thought of a Flavouring Essence.

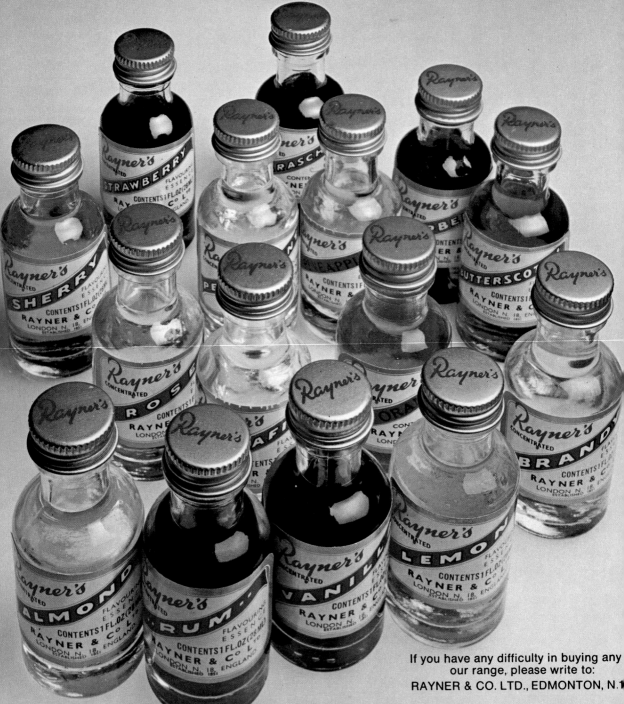

If you have any difficulty in buying any
our range, please write to:
RAYNER & CO. LTD., EDMONTON, N.1

slit down the sides with a sharp-pointed knife to allow the steam to escape and leave on a rack to cool. When the éclairs are cold, fill with whipped cream or custard, then ice the tops or dip them in melted chocolate. (Makes 10–12.)

Note. If you make 'bite-size' éclairs you will get about 2 dozen from this amount of pastry.

Choux Paste

2 oz. butter	2½ oz. plain flour,
¼ pint milk and	sifted
water mixed	2 eggs, beaten

Melt the butter in the liquid and bring to the boil. Remove from the heat and quickly tip in the flour all at once. Beat until a smooth paste is formed and then cook gently, stirring all the time, until the paste begins to leave the sides of the pan and form a ball in the centre. Remove from the heat again and allow to cool slightly. Beat in the eggs gradually, adding just enough to give a smooth, glossy mixture of piping consistency. Cool, then use as required.

Jap Cakes

Mouth-watering almond plus coffee flavour

3 egg whites	Coffee butter cream
8 oz. caster sugar	Coffee glacé icing
8 oz. ground almonds	Roasted hazelnuts to
Almond essence	decorate

Oven temperature: cool (300 °F, mark 1–2)

Line a Swiss roll tin, 9 by 13 inches, with non-stick vegetable parchment.

Whisk the egg whites very stiffly, then fold in the sugar, ground almonds and a few drops of almond essence. Mix thoroughly, then spread this mixture over the lined tin. Bake in the centre of the oven for about 25 minutes. Remove from the oven and, using a 2-inch plain cutter, mark into rounds. Return to the oven and bake for a further 30-35 minutes. Allow to cool slightly, then remove the rounds from the tin and cool on a rack. Rub the trimmings through a metal sieve. Pair the rounds with coffee butter icing. Spread the sides with butter icing and roll them in the sieved crumbs. Lastly spread the top with the remaining butter icing. Place a small drop of glacé icing in the centre and top with a nut. (Makes 8.)

Meringues

Crisp yet melting – sheer perfection!

2 egg whites	2 oz. caster sugar
2 oz. granulated	¼ pint double cream,
sugar	whipped

Oven temperature: very cool (250 °F, mark ¼)

Line a baking tray with a sheet of greaseproof paper and rub a trace of olive oil over the surface, or line it with non-stick vegetable parchment.

Whisk the egg whites very stiffly, add granulated sugar and whisk again until the mixture regains its former stiffness. Lastly, fold in the caster sugar very lightly, using a metal spoon. Pipe through a forcing bag (or put in spoonfuls) on to the baking sheet and bake near the bottom of the oven for 2–2½ hours, or until the meringues are firm, dry and crisp but still white; if they begin to brown, prop the oven door open a little. When they are cool, sandwich them together with whipped cream. (Makes 12–16 meringue shells.)

Note. If preferred, use 4 oz. caster sugar, adding it in two portions, as above.

Variations

1. Tint the mixture pink or pale green by adding 1–2 drops of red or green colouring with the sugar.

2. To make coffee meringues, add 1 tsp. coffee essence to each egg white when the sugar is folded in.

3. For chocolate meringues, add 1 level tsp. cocoa to each egg white, with the caster sugar.

4. Add finely chopped nuts, melted chocolate or a little liqueur to the meringue filling.

Afghans

Delicious crispy chocolate drop-cookies

6 oz. butter	2 oz. cornflakes, crushed
4 oz. caster sugar	Vanilla essence to taste
5 oz. plain flour	A little cooking
2 level tbsps. cocoa	chocolate, melted

Oven temperature: moderate (350 °F, mark 4)

Grease 2 baking trays.

Cream the butter and sugar until soft and creamy. Gradually work in the flour and cocoa, sifted together, and the cornflakes. Add a few drops of vanilla essence. Place the mixture in small heaps on the baking trays and bake in the centre of the oven for 15–20 minutes. Cool on a rack, then top each with a little melted chocolate. (Makes about 2 dozen.)

Almond Melt-aways

Excellent with tea or coffee

4 oz. butter	2 oz. ground almonds
2 oz. caster sugar	Raspberry jam
1 egg yolk	Glacé icing
4 oz. plain flour	Flaked almonds

Oven temperature: fairly hot (375 °F, mark 5)

For this recipe you will need a square tin $7\frac{1}{2}$ by $7\frac{1}{2}$ by $1\frac{1}{8}$ inches.

In a bowl cream together the butter and sugar. Beat in egg yolk, then work in the flour and ground almonds. Chill in the refrigerator, or in a cold place, until the dough is of a manageable consistency – about 1 hour. Divide the mixture and roll half out to line the base of the greased and floured tin. Spread nearly to the edge with jam. Cover with the second rolled out portion. (If rolling out the almond dough is difficult on an ordinary surface, roll between 2 sheets of greaseproof paper.) Bake in the centre of the oven for 20 minutes, until golden-brown. While it is still in the tin, drizzle glacé icing over the top, then scatter it with flaked almonds. Return the tin to the oven for a further 15–20 minutes. Cool a little, and mark into fingers or squares in the tin. Ease out when nearly cold.

If you omit the icing and flaked almonds you've got the basis for a pudding: just serve the warm squares topped with vanilla ice-cream.

Brandy Snaps

Tantalizing combination of crisp biscuit and luscious filling

2 oz. butter or margarine	2 oz. plain flour
3 oz. caster sugar	$\frac{1}{2}$ level tsp. ground ginger
2 oz. golden syrup, or approx. 1 rounded tbsp.	1 tsp. brandy (optional) Whipped cream

Oven temperature: moderate (350 °F, mark 4)

Grease the handles of several wooden spoons and several baking trays.

Place the butter, sugar and golden syrup in a saucepan and heat slowly until the butter is melted. Take off the heat and stir in the sifted flour and ginger and the brandy (if used). Place teaspoonfuls of the mixture on the baking trays, spacing them 6 inches apart to give plenty of room for spreading. Bake in the top part of the oven for 8–10 minutes, until golden-brown. Allow to cool for 1–2 minutes, then loosen with a palette knife and roll them round the spoon handles, with the upper surface of each brandy snap on the outside. When the biscuits have hardened, slip them off gently. (If the biscuits cool too much while still on the tray and become too brittle to roll, return the tray to the oven for a moment to soften them.) Cool on a rack. Fill the brandy snaps with whipped cream just before serving. (Makes about 15 brandy snaps).

Note. If you have not got enough baking trays you can let surplus mixture wait and bake the brandy snaps in batches until all the mixture is cooked.

Anzac Biscuits

A crunchy, munchy cookie

4 oz. butter	8 oz. caster sugar
1 level tbsp. golden syrup	3 oz. desiccated coconut
1 level tsp. bicarbonate of soda	4 oz. rolled oats
2 tbsps. water	1 oz. halved walnuts, chopped
3 oz. plain flour	

Oven temperature: moderate (350 °F, mark 4)

Grease 2 baking sheets.

Melt the butter with the syrup in a saucepan, then cool for a short time. Add the soda, blended with the water. In a bowl stir together the remaining ingredients. Gradually stir in the contents of the saucepan, blending well. Roll the mixture into walnut-sized balls and place on the baking sheets, allowing room for spreading. Bake in the centre of the oven for 12–15 minutes. Cool slightly before removing from the sheets. (Makes about 30.)

Choco Mints

Lots of eye appeal

4 oz. butter	½ oz. cocoa
4 level tbsps. icing sugar, sifted	4 level tbsps. custard powder
3½ oz. self-raising flour	

For the Peppermint Filling

2 oz. butter	Peppermint essence
4 oz. icing sugar	Green colouring

Oven temperature: moderate (350 °F, mark 4)

Grease 1–2 baking sheets.

Cream the butter and sugar until light and fluffy. Sift together the flour, cocoa and custard powder and add a little at a time to the creamed mixture, stirring thoroughly. Turn the mixture on to a lightly floured surface. Knead, then roll out to ⅛ inch in thickness. Cut into rounds with a 1½-inch fluted cutter, place on the baking sheet and bake in the centre of the oven for 20–25 minutes. Cool on a wire rack.

Make the filling by creaming together the butter and the sifted sugar, adding essence to taste and tinting a pale green. Using a star vegetable nozzle, pipe a star of filling on to half the biscuits. Sandwich together with the remainder. (Makes about 16.)

Coconut Curls

Almost see-through, toffee-like wafers

1 oz. long-shred coconut	4 oz. caster sugar
1 oz. angelica	1 level tsp. flour
3½ oz. butter	1 tbsp. top of the milk

Oven temperature: moderate (350 °F, mark 4)

Line 2 baking sheets with non-stick paper.

Roughly chop the coconut and angelica. Melt the butter in a small pan, add the sugar and boil for 1 minute, stirring. Take off the heat and stir in the remaining ingredients. Cool a little, then drop in small heaps, well apart, on the baking sheets. Bake for about 10 minutes, until golden. When they are firming a little, lift with a palette knife and cool over a rolling pin. They'll store well in an airtight tin for up to a week. (Makes about 16.)

Fun to serve with summer cold sweets.

Florentines

(See picture above)

Luscious favourite for special tea-times

3½ oz. butter or margarine	1 oz. glacé cherries, chopped
4 oz. caster sugar	1 oz. mixed peel, chopped
4 oz. nuts (walnuts and almonds mixed if possible), chopped	1 level tbsp. whipped cream
1 oz. sultanas, chopped	¾ oz. plain flour
	4 oz. plain chocolate

Oven temperature: moderate (350 °F, mark 4)

Line some baking trays with non-stick vegetable parchment or rice paper.

Melt the butter, add the sugar and dissolve, then boil gently for 1 minute. Add all the other ingredients except the chocolate and mix well. Cool slightly. Drop the mixture in small, well-shaped heaps on to the baking trays 5 inches apart and bake for about 10 minutes in the centre of the oven, until golden-brown.

Remove and cool; peel off any rice paper if used, then spread the backs of the biscuits with melted chocolate and mark wavy lines across with a fork. Leave to harden before serving. (Makes about 18.)

Note. May be stored in an airtight tin without the chocolate coating.

Gingernuts (Ginger Snaps)

Even more delicious when home-produced

4 oz. self-raising flour	1 level tsp. ground cinnamon
½ level tsp. bicarbonate of soda	2 level tsps. caster sugar
1–2 level tsps. ground ginger	2 oz. butter
	3 oz. golden syrup

Oven temperature: fairly hot (375 °F, mark 5)

Grease 2 baking trays.

Sift together the dry ingredients. Melt the fat and stir in the syrup; stir into dry ingredients and mix well. Roll the mixture into small balls, place well apart on the baking trays and flatten slightly. Bake in the centre of the oven for 15–20 minutes. Cool for a few minutes before lifting carefully on to a rack. (Makes about 2 dozen.)

Note. Use the smaller amount of ginger if you like a subtler taste.

Grantham Gingerbreads

Unusual hollow effect

9 oz. self-raising flour	4 oz. butter or margarine
1 level tsp. ground ginger	12 oz. caster sugar
	1 egg, beaten

Oven temperature: cool (300 °F, mark 1–2)

Grease 2 baking trays.

Sift the flour and ginger together. Cream the butter and sugar and beat in the egg gradually. Stir in the flour and ginger until a fairly firm dough is obtained. Roll into small balls about the size of a walnut and put on the baking trays. Bake towards the top of the oven for 40–45 minutes, until crisp, hollow and very lightly browned. Cool on a rack. (Makes about 2½ dozen.)

Hazelnut Bars

(See picture on right)

Luxury biscuits

4 oz. hazelnuts	4 oz. icing sugar
8 oz. plain flour	1 egg white
6 oz. butter	½ tbsp. coffee essence

Oven temperature: fairly hot (375 °F, mark 5)

Have ready some ungreased baking sheets.

Place the hazelnuts in a tin and roast until beginning to brown; place in a paper bag and rub to remove the skins. Chop the nuts. Sift the flour into a mound on a working surface, make a well in the centre and add the butter, cut in small pieces, and the icing sugar. Work the butter and icing sugar together. When pale and creamy, gradually work in the flour, using the fingertips. Knead in the hazelnuts and work to a smooth dough. Divide the dough into two parts. Roll out lightly on a floured board to about ⅛–¼ inch thick. (The dough needs careful handling.) With a knife mark lightly in a criss-cross fashion. Brush over with a little egg white and coffee essence mixed together. Cut into fingers about 3 by 1½ inches and lift carefully on to the baking sheets. Bake in the centre of the oven for about 15 minutes, until lightly coloured. Cool on a wire rack and store until required in an airtight container. (Makes about 32.)

Honey Coffee Nutties

For the sweet-toothed

4 oz. butter	2 level tbsp. thick honey
2½ oz. caster sugar	
3 oz. ground hazelnuts	Coffee glacé icing
	Browned whole hazelnuts to decorate
5 oz. plain flour, sifted	

Oven temperature: moderate (350 °F, mark 4)

Grease 2 baking sheets.

Cream the butter and sugar until light and fluffy. Gradually stir in the nuts and flour alternately. Leave the mixture in a cool place for about 1 hour, until firm but not hard. Roll out on a floured surface to about ⅛ inch in thickness. Cut out 24 rounds, using a 2½-inch plain cutter. Lift carefully on to the baking sheets and bake in the centre of the oven for 20–30 minutes. Cool on a wire rack.

To serve, sandwich together in pairs with honey; ice the centres with coffee glacé icing, top with the whole hazelnuts and leave to set. (Makes 12 biscuits.)

Hungarian Chocolate Biscuits

Easy to make, and should be eaten really fresh

4 oz. butter	1 level tbsp. cocoa
2 oz. caster sugar	A pinch of salt
Vanilla essence	Nibbed almonds
4 oz. plain flour	

Oven temperature: moderate 350 °F, mark 4)

Grease 2 baking sheets.

Cream the butter and sugar and add a few drops of essence. Fold in the flour, previously sifted with the cocoa and salt. Form into small balls, roll in the nibbed almonds and place on the baking sheets. Flatten with a fork dipped in water and bake in the centre of the oven for 10–20 minutes. Cool on a wire rack. If liked, sandwich in pairs with peppermint butter cream. (Makes about 2 doz.)

Lemon-Glazed Meltaways

True to their name

8 oz. butter	8 oz. plain flour
2 oz. icing sugar, sifted	Apricot jam, sieved
Grated rind of 1 lemon	Icing sugar and lemon juice to glaze tops

Oven temperature: warm (325 °F, mark 3)

Grease 2–3 baking trays.

Cream the butter until soft, add the sifted icing sugar and beat well. Stir in the lemon rind and flour. When the mixture is well blended, put it into a nylon forcing bag fitted with a large star vegetable nozzle. Pipe about 20 rosettes and 20 shell shapes on to the baking trays and chill for ½ hour. Bake in the centre

of the oven or just below for about 25 minutes, or until slightly coloured; remove from the oven. Brush each cookie with a little jam and then with a soft glaze made by blending about 2 level tbsps. icing sugar to a coating consistency with lemon juice. Return them to the oven for 5 minutes, remove and cool on a rack. (Makes 3–3½ dozen.)

Linzer Kisses

From Hungary, a plainer biscuit with an interesting speckly appearance and a glazed finish

5 oz. butter	¼ level tsp. ground cloves
5 oz. caster sugar	
2 egg yolks	5 oz. ground almonds
Grated rind of ½ a lemon	4 oz. chocolate, grated
	Blanched almonds
5 oz. plain flour	Egg white to glaze
¼ level tsp. ground cinnamon	A little caster sugar to dredge

Oven temperature: moderate (350 °F, mark 4)

Lightly grease 1–2 baking trays.

Beat the butter until soft, then add the sugar and cream the mixture until fluffy. Add the egg yolks and lemon rind and continue to beat. Sift the flour with the cinnamon and cloves, then stir into the mixture. Add the ground almonds and chocolate. Mix thoroughly, then roll the pastry out on a floured board till it is ¼ inch thick. Cut with a 2-inch plain cutter and put the biscuits on a baking sheet. Press half a blanched almond on to the top of each biscuit and brush the tops with egg white. Bake in the centre of the oven for 12–15 minutes, then sprinkle the biscuits with caster sugar as soon as they are removed from the oven. Cool on a wire rack before storing it an airtight tin. (Makes about 20.)

Nig-Nogs

These crisp, buttery cookies are good stand-bys

3 oz. plain flour	3 oz. butter or margarine
½ level tsp. bicarbonate of soda	1 tbsp. milk
3 oz. caster sugar	1 level tbsp. golden syrup
3 oz. rolled oats	

Oven temperature: cool (300 °F, mark 2)

Grease 1–2 baking trays.

Sift the flour and bicarbonate of soda and stir in the sugar and oats. Heat the butter, milk and syrup together until melted, pour on to the first mixture and mix well. Roll into small balls and place at least 4 inches apart on the baking trays – they must be well spaced, as they spread while baking.

Flatten slightly and bake towards the top of the oven for 25–30 minutes. Cool on the trays for 2–3 minutes before lifting on to a rack. (Makes about 1½ dozen.)

Raisin Nut Cookies

Pleasantly filling, spicy, and well flavoured

2 oz. butter	1½ oz. walnut halves,
2 oz. blended white	chopped
vegetable fat	6 oz. plain flour
5 oz. light soft brown	½ level tsp. bicarbonate
sugar	1 level tsp. powdered
1 whole egg	cinnamon
1 egg yolk	½ level tsp. powdered
2 oz. seedless raisins	cloves

Oven temperature: fairly hot (375 °F, mark 5)

Grease 2 baking trays.

Cream the butter and vegetable fat, then add the sugar and beat until light and fluffy. Gradually beat in the whole egg and the yolk, then stir in the raisins and walnuts. Sift together and fold in the dry ingredients. Place the mixture in teaspoonfuls on the baking trays about 2 inches apart. Bake in the centre of the oven or just above for 20–25 minutes. Cool on a wire rack. (Makes about 2 dozen.)

Note. These cookies will store in an airtight tin or in foil for up to 1 week.

Rich Flapjacks

Simplicity itself

3 oz. butter	4 oz. rolled oats
3 oz. Demerara sugar	

Oven temperature: hot (425 °F, mark 7)

Grease a shallow 7-inch square tin.

Cream the butter. Mix together the sugar and oats. Gradually work all together until thoroughly blended. Press evenly into the prepared tin, using a round-bladed knife. Bake for about 15 minutes in the centre of the oven. Allow to cool slightly in the tin. Mark into fingers with a sharp knife and loosen round the edges when firm, then break into fingers. Store in an airtight tin. (Makes 12 pieces.)

Shortbread Fans

Pretty shape for an old favourite

4 oz. butter	Caster sugar for
2 oz. caster sugar	dredging
6 oz. plain flour	

Oven temperature: cool (300 °F, mark 1–2)

Have ready some baking sheets.

Cream together the butter and sugar. Work in the flour and knead lightly to form a ball. Roll out carefully on a lightly floured surface – the mixture will be crumbly and needs knitting together between rollings. Stamp out 9 large fluted rounds, using a 4-inch cutter. Place on the baking sheets and cut each into quarters with a sharp knife. Open up and separate the 'fans', to allow for spreading. Bake in the centre of the oven, or just below for about 20 minutes until just lightly tinged with colour. Cool on a wire rack. Store in an airtight container. To serve, dredge with caster sugar. (Makes about 3 doz.)

9
Savouries, Snacks, Impromptu Meals

Salted Almonds

Simplest of nibbles to offer with a drink, but perennially welcome

Just shake some blanched whole almonds in a little butter in a frying pan until they are an even golden colour. Drain them on crumpled kitchen paper and sprinkle with plenty of salt.

Anchovy Roll-ups

Good thirst-builders

Divide the anchovies from a 2-oz. can between 4 oz. lean ham (5 slices); roll up the drained fillets tightly in the ham slices and cut each roll in four. Serve on cocktail sticks. (Makes 20.)

Bacon, Date and Cheese

Pleasant hot titbits

Rind some bacon rashers and cut each into two; stone some dates. Stuff each date with a strip of cheese and wrap a piece of bacon round. Grill for 8–10 minutes and serve on cocktail sticks.

Cheese Balls

Piquant, interesting

12 oz. cream cheese	1 level tbsp. curry
4 oz. coarse-cut coconut	powder
	Parsley

Roll the cheese into small balls and chill them. Blend the coconut and curry powder, brown under a moderately hot grill and cool. Roll the balls in the coconut mixture and chill again before serving. Serve spiked on cocktail sticks, or as desired. Sprinkle with chopped parsley.

Cocktail Stick 'Cheeseries'

(See picture on p. 209)

Arrange a variety of morsels on cocktail sticks and skewer these into a small cheese or whole apples

Here are some examples:

A chunk of pineapple, a Maraschino cherry and a piece of Cheddar cheese.

Strips of blanched green pepper interspersed with chunks of cheese.

Cheddar cheese with celery or a cocktail onion.

Stoned prunes, with cheese placed in the hole.

A tiny sausage, a piece of Cheddar cheese and a cocktail onion.

Green grapes, split, seeded and filled with cream cheese.

A sausage, split in half lengthways, filled with a slice of cheese and with a slice of cucumber wrapped round one end of the sausage.

Stuffed Grapes

Succulent mouthfuls you can prepare in advance

Slit and seed ½ lb. big black juicy grapes. Beat 3 oz. Danish Blue cheese till smooth. Star-pipe the cheese into the slits in the grapes and serve on cocktail sticks. (Makes about 30.)

Sweet and Salty

Something a bit newer

Rind and halve 8 oz. thinly sliced streaky rashers and drain the contents of a 7½-oz. bottle of Maraschino cherries. Wrap each half-rasher round a cherry, mount on skewers and grill till crisp. Serve on cocktail sticks. (About 40.)

Spiced Fish Dip

Almost a party piece on its own

In advance, cut some plaice fillets into strips 1½ by ½ inch. (A small packet of frozen fillets makes about 30 pieces.) Dip in flour, then in beaten egg, then in cornflake crumbs. Deep-fry in oil until golden, and drain well. Serve with a piquant dip of 3 tbsps. mayonnaise mixed with 3 tsps. tomato ketchup, ½ tsp. chilli sauce and a dash of Worcestershire sauce.

Savoury-Topped Biscuits

For the hostess-in-a-hurry

You'll get enough for 20 toppings for buttery Ritz crackers (or fillings for bite-sized pieces of celery) by creaming together 8 oz. cream cheese, 2 level tsps. curry powder and 1 tsp. lemon juice.

Savoury Butters for Canapés

These 'anchor' the toppings and prevent the bases from becoming soggy; they can also be piped on top of canapés or small savouries for decoration. Make them at least a few hours beforehand and leave in a cool place to become firm before you use them.

With 4 oz. butter, use one of the following flavouring ingredients:

Anchovy Butter: 6 anchovies, mashed with a fork. (Or flavour and colour with anchovy sauce, cayenne and red colouring.)

Blue Cheese Butter: 2 oz. soft blue cheese.

Chutney Butter: 4 tbsps. smooth-textured chutney and a good squeeze of lemon juice.

Curry Butter: 2 level tsps. curry powder.

Devilled Butter: As for curry butter, but include some cayenne pepper.

Golden Butter: Sieved yolks of 2 hard-boiled eggs.

Green Butter: 2 oz. chopped watercress.

Ham Butter: 4 oz. minced cooked ham and a little mustard.

Horseradish Butter: 2 tbsps. horseradish sauce.

Lobster Butter: 2 oz. lobster coral.

Maître d'Hôtel (Parsley) Butter: 2 tbsps. finely chopped parsley and a squeeze of lemon juice, with salt and cayenne pepper.

Onion Butter: 2 level tbsps. finely grated onion.

Pimiento Butter: 2 level tbsps. sieved canned pimiento.

Sardine Butter: 4 sardines, mashed with a fork.

Tomato Butter: 2 tbsps. tomato ketchup (or 2 tsps. tomato paste and 1 level tsp. sugar).

Cream Cheese Spreads for Canapés

These, too, can also be used for decorating canapés and small savouries. Use 3 oz. softened cream cheese and blend with one of the following flavourings:

Chive Spread: 1 level tbsp. finely chopped chives.

Guava Spread: 1½ mashed canned guavas and ½ level tsp. salt.

Ham Spread: 1 oz. finely chopped or minced ham.

Pimiento Spread: 1–1½ level tbsps. sieved canned pimiento.

Tuna Spread: 2–3 level tbsps. finely mashed tuna fish mixed with 1 tsp. vinegar or 1 tbsp. mayonnaise.

Toppings for Canapés

Put one or more of the following toppings on the base, after spreading with a savoury butter or cheese spread:

Anchovies

Crab-meat

Prawns

Shrimps

Sardines, mashed with seasoning

Smoked salmon, thinly sliced

Flaked cooked fish or very small whole fish

Thin slices of cold meat, rolled or chopped

Liver sausage, cut with a fluted cutter

Pâté de foie or pâté de foie gras

Hard-boiled eggs, sliced, quartered or chopped

Slices or segments of Danish Blue or Gruyère cheese

Cream cheese, flavoured to taste

Small leaves of lettuce or watercress

Asparagus tips

Gammon and Onion Pizza;
Cheese and Spinach Quiche;
Seafood Quiche: pp. 136, 154

Celery, chopped or celery sprigs
Mushrooms, cooked
Rings or segments of tomato (preferably skinned)
Thin slices of cucumber, flat or in cones
Cooked beetroot, diced or sliced
Segments of fruit, such as pineapple
Stuffed olives, sliced or halved
Pickled onions, sliced
Cocktail onions
Green peas, cooked
Whole or chopped nuts

The canapés can be decorated with piped savoury butter or any simple savoury garnish. For a more formal occasion, canapés may be finished with a thin coating of aspic jelly – in which case they should be served fairly quickly, so that the base does not become soggy.

Quick Canapés

Slice a loaf thinly lengthwise, spread or pipe with savoury filling and coat with aspic jelly, just on the point of setting. Pipe with savoury butter and cut into fingers.

Cheese Mushroom Bouchées

(*See picture below*)

Traditional-style savouries

6 oz. flaky pastry	4 oz. cooked
$\frac{1}{3}$ pint cheese	mushrooms, chopped
sauce	A little grated cheese

Oven temperature: very hot ($450\,°F$, mark 8)

Roll out the pastry about $\frac{1}{4}$ inch thick, stamp out rounds with a small fluted cutter and mark the centre of each with a smaller cutter. Put on a baking tin and bake for about 15 minutes; remove the tops and fill with the sauce, mixed with the mushrooms. Sprinkle with cheese and brown in a hot oven or under the grill.

Cheese Puffs

Delicious hot canapés

2 egg whites	4 oz. grated cheese
$\frac{1}{4}$ level tsp. baking	Small toast canapés
powder	Watercress
Salt and pepper	

Whisk the egg whites stiffly and whisk in the baking powder and seasonings. Fold in the cheese and pile on to the canapés. Cook under a moderately hot grill until golden and puffy, and serve hot, garnished with watercress.

Creamed Kippers

All drinks go well with the homely kipper in this gourmet guise

Grill and skin 8 oz. kipper fillets and mash with $\frac{1}{2}$ level tsp. paprika, 4 tbsps. double cream, $\frac{1}{2}$ tsp. lemon juice and some pepper. Spread the mixture on 1-inch squares of fresh crisp toast. Decorate with thinly sliced radish or gherkin. (Makes about 20.)

Ham and Cranberry Roulades

A new twist to the ham roll

8 slices of ham	An 8-oz. can of whole-
Made mustard	berry cranberry
9 oz. cream cheese	sauce
Salt	8 large, soft rolls
Freshly ground pepper	Butter

Spread the slices of ham with a little mustard. Season the cream cheese with salt and pepper, beat till soft and fold in the cranberry sauce.

209

*Globe Artichokes; Courgettes;
French Beans; Asparagus:
pp. 120, 157, 158*

Divide between the ham slices, spreading evenly, and roll up. Cut the rolls lengthwise almost through, leaving a 'hinge'. Butter the cut surface and insert a ham roll in each. Wrap in plastic film until required, if you make them in advance.

Beef Champignons

Store-cupboard special for the unexpected supper guest

An 8-oz. can of butter beans	A 10½-oz. can of condensed mushroom soup
A 12-oz. can of corned beef	
A small can of mushrooms	Potato crisps for topping

Oven temperature: fairly hot (375 °F, mark 5)

In a casserole layer the drained beans, beef, cut in pieces, and the mushrooms. Spoon the soup over, and top with a layer of crisps. Place in the oven for 20 minutes, or until heated through. (Serves 4.)

Burger Stroganoff

Grown-up presentation of a children's favourite

2 small onions, chopped	2 5-oz. cartons of soured cream
2 oz. butter	8 tbsps. stock, approx.
4 oz. button mushrooms, sliced	8 frozen or canned beefburgers
1 level tsp. concentrated tomato paste	Fat for frying

First make the Stroganoff sauce. Sauté the onions in the butter until soft but not coloured, stir in the mushrooms and cook for a further 5 minutes. Stir in the tomato paste and soured cream, with the stock; heat through. Meanwhile cut the beefburgers into strips and fry until brown, then pour off the surplus fat. Season the sauce, pour over the beefburgers and bubble gently for a few minutes. (Serves 4.)

Mushroom and Bacon Savoury

Couldn't be simpler, nor more appetizing

Oven temperature: cool (300 °F, mark 2)

For each person make up a foil-wrapped parcel of 2 oz. crisply-fried bacon, cut into small pieces, with 4 oz. washed but unpeeled button mushrooms, well seasoned and dotted with butter. Cook on a baking sheet for about 20 minutes. This makes a grand individual supper savoury, or an accompaniment to foil-baked cod steaks.

Macaroni Cheese Soufflé

(See picture below)
Short-cut to an imposing supper savoury

A 15-oz. can of macaroni cheese	3 large eggs, separated
	Salt and pepper

Oven temperature: moderate (350 °F, mark 4)

Place the macaroni in a saucepan and heat gently, stirring, for 5 minutes, until quite thick. Remove from the heat, beat in the egg yolks and add seasoning to taste. Whisk the egg whites until stiff, fold into the macaroni, then turn the mixture into a greased 2-pint soufflé dish. Bake for 30 minutes, or until it is well risen and the centre is just firm to the touch. Serve at once. (Serves 4.)

Canadian Fish Balls

Canned salmon in disguise

A 4-portion pkt. of instant potato	Salt and pepper
	Ground mace
A pkt. of parsley sauce mix	Beaten egg
	Golden crumbs
¼ pint milk	Fat for frying
A 7¾-oz. can of salmon	

Make up the potato; make up the sauce with

the milk and combine with the potato. Drain and flake the salmon and stir in. Season with salt, pepper and a little mace and leave to cool. Shape into 12 balls, coat with beaten egg and then with crumbs. Fry in hot fat until golden, turning them frequently. Drain well and serve immediately. (4 servings.)

Prawn Celeste

Has a luxury taste, and looks its best served in natural scallop shells

A 7½-oz. can of button mushrooms, drained	A 6-oz. can of cream A 6-oz. can of prawns
2 oz. butter	1–2 tsps. sherry
2 oz. flour	Chopped parsley
½ pint milk	Fried bread cubes

Lightly cook the mushrooms in the butter for 2–3 minutes. Stir in the flour, cook for 2 minutes and gradually add the milk and cream. Bring to the boil, stirring constantly until the sauce has thickened. Season to taste. Rinse the prawns in cold water, then add to the sauce, with the sherry. Re-heat, sprinkle in the parsley and serve with the fried bread cubes. (Serves 4.)

Prawn Risotto

Use 'jumbo' prawns and you won't lose them in the rice

1 level tbsp. dried onion flakes (or 1 large onion, chopped)	A 7-oz. can of prawns 3 large eggs
2 oz. butter	2 oz. button
6 oz. long-grain rice	mushrooms, sautéed
¼ level tsp. dried basil	2 tbsps. chopped
¾ pint stock	parsley
	Salt and pepper

Soak the onion flakes in a little water for several minutes, then drain. Melt the butter in a saucepan, add the onion and fry gently for 3 minutes. Stir in the washed rice and cook, stirring occasionally, for several minutes, until the rice appears opaque. Add the basil, stock and prawn liquor, bring to the boil, cover and simmer for 25 minutes, or until the rice is cooked and the liquid absorbed. Meanwhile hard-boil and quarter the eggs. When the rice is cooked stir in the prawns, egg, mushrooms

and half the parsley. Check the seasoning. Turn the mixture into a serving dish and garnish with the remaining parsley, and if liked, some whole prawns. (Serves 4.)

Tuna and Corn Fricassee

Tailor-made for a teenage party

8 oz. long-grain rice	2 7-oz. cans of tuna fish,
Salt	drained and flaked
A 10½-oz. can of condensed cream of chicken soup	Lemon juice 1 oz. butter 2 level tbsps. crisp
4 tbsps. milk	fried onion
A 7-oz. can of sweet corn kernels	Hard-boiled egg Parsley sprigs to
A 4-oz. can of pimiento, sliced	garnish

Cook the rice in salted water in the usual way. Meanwhile blend the soup with the milk. Add the drained corn, pimiento and tuna and heat gently. Season to taste with a squeeze of lemon juice. Drain the rice and stir in the butter and onions; use to make a border round a serving dish. Spoon the tuna mixture into the centre. Garnish with sliced hard-boiled egg and parsley sprigs and serve hot. (Serves 4.)

As an accompaniment, serve canned, drained, whole round tomatoes heated with a little butter. Peppery watercress sprigs make pleasant munchers.

Note. Crisp fried onions can be purchased in cans or packets – a handy ingredient for a quick garnish and good in sandwich fillings.

Scalloped Tuna Macaroni

Easily assembled fish snack

A 15¼-oz. can of macaroni with cheese sauce	A 7½-oz. can of tuna fish 2 oz. cheese, grated 1 tbsp. crumbled
Mixed herbs	cornflakes

Oven temperature: moderate (350 °F, mark 4)

Put the macaroni into a 1-pint ovenproof dish and add a sprinkling of herbs. Top with the drained and flaked fish and cover with the mixed grated cheese and cornflake crumbs. Cover with foil and bake for 20 minutes, then remove the foil and cook for a further 12 minutes. (Serves 4.)

Devilled Gammon with Pineapple

Hot, sweet and succulent

2 gammon rashers ($\frac{1}{2}$–$\frac{3}{4}$ inch thick) and about 12 oz. each)	6 oz. light, soft brown sugar
4 level tbsps. dry mustard	An 8$\frac{1}{2}$-oz. can of pineapple rings (4 rings)
	8 Maraschino cherries

Trim the rind from the gammon rashers and snip the fat at intervals. Mix together the mustard, sugar and 4 tbsps. pineapple juice. Lay the gammon on the grill rack, spread evenly with some of the sugar mixture and cook under a medium grill for 15 minutes, basting every 5 minutes with the pan drippings. Turn the gammon, spread with the remaining sugar mixture and cook for a further 15 minutes. Place 2 pineapple rings and 2 cherries on each rasher; baste, and cook for a further 5 minutes. If the fat shows signs of over-browning, cover the area with a piece of kitchen foil.

Note. If the gammon tends to be salt, leave it to soak in cold water for about 1 hour prior to cooking, then pat it dry.

Scotch Eggs

A substantial – and versatile – snack

4 eggs, hard-boiled	1 egg, beaten
2 level tsps. seasoned flour	Dry bread-crumbs
Worcestershire sauce	Deep fat
$\frac{1}{2}$ lb. sausage-meat or skinless sausages	Parsley
	Tomato sauce or green salad

Dust the eggs with the seasoned flour. Add a few drops of Worcestershire sauce to the sausage-meat and divide it into 4 equal portions. Form each quarter into a flat cake and work it round an egg, making it as even as possible, to keep the egg a good shape, and making sure there are no cracks in the sausage-meat. Brush with beaten egg and toss in bread-crumbs. Heat the fat until it will brown a cube of bread in 40–50 seconds. (As the sausage-meat is raw, it is essential that the frying should not be hurried unduly, so the fat must not be too hot.) Fry the eggs for about 7–8 minutes. When they are golden-brown on the outside, remove them from the fat and drain on crumpled kitchen paper.

Cut the eggs in half lengthways, garnish each half with a small piece of parsley and serve hot with tomato sauce or cold with salad.

Sausage en Casserole

Sausage-meat dressed up

1 lb. pork sausage-meat	A 10$\frac{1}{2}$-oz. can of condensed cream of mushroom soup
Flour	A small pkt. of frozen green beans
Lard	
An 8-oz. can of Italian tomatoes	

Oven temperature: moderate (350 °F, mark 4)

Shape the sausage-meat into about 16 balls, using a little flour. Lightly brown them in a little lard, then drain off the surplus fat and arrange the balls in a shallow casserole. Pour over them the tomatoes and soup, cover and cook in the oven for 15 minutes. Remove from the oven, stir and cook for a further 15 minutes. Remove again and stir in the green beans. Cook for a further 15 minutes. (Serves 4.)

Quickie Hot-Pot

Proves the value of a well-stocked food cupboard

A 15$\frac{1}{2}$-oz. can of stewed steak	A 19-oz. can of new potatoes, drained
A 10$\frac{1}{2}$-oz. can of sliced carrots, drained	1 oz. butter, melted
	Salt and pepper
A 9$\frac{1}{2}$-oz. can of sliced green beans, drained	Parsley to garnish, if available

Oven temperature: fairly hot (375 °F, mark 5)

Layer the stewed steak and gravy, the carrots and the beans into a shallow 2$\frac{1}{2}$-pint dish. Coat the potatoes evenly with the melted butter and place them on top of the casserole. Season with salt and pepper and cook in the oven until the potatoes are lightly browned. Garnish with parsley. (Serves 4.)

10
Cold and Hot Drinks

SOFT DRINKS
Apple Mint Cocktail

Fresh and thirst-quenching

1 pint non-alcoholic cider or apple juice
¼ pint orange juice
¼ pint pineapple juice
Crushed ice
Small sprigs of mint

Mix the fruit juices together and shake with crushed ice, or chill. Serve in glasses, with a small mint sprig to garnish. (Makes 1½ pints approx.)

Grape and Lemon Juice Cocktail

Good blend of flavours

½ pint grape juice (canned or bottled)
Lemon juice
Caster sugar
1 pint ginger ale, chilled

Mix the grape juice and 3–4 tbsps. lemon juice and chill. Frost the rims of some cocktail glasses by dipping them first into a saucer of lemon juice and then into the sugar. Add the ginger ale to the fruit juice just before serving. (Makes 1½ pints, approx.)

Jungle Juice

(*See picture below*)

Interesting offering for soft-drink fanciers

1 can of Florida frozen orange juice
2 tbsps. Ribena
¼ pint orange and passion fruit drink
½ pint water
1 pint sparkling lemonade
Juice of 1 lemon
Thinly sliced cucumber to garnish

Blend all the ingredients together, stirring until the frozen orange juice has melted. Serve with a garnish of thinly sliced cucumber. (Makes about 9 goblets.)

Quick Quencher

Nice after summer exertion

2 pints ginger beer, chilled
¾ pint bottled lime juice, chilled
Ice cubes
Fresh mint sprigs to garnish

Just before the drink is required, combine the ginger beer and lime juice, then add the ice cubes and mint sprigs to garnish. (Makes 10 glasses.)

Spicy Fruit Punch

An all-round 'soft' winner

1 pint fresh or canned orange juice
½ pint canned pineapple juice
Juice and rind of 1 lemon
½ level tsp. ground nutmeg
6 cloves
½ level tsp. ground mixed spice
1 pint water
4–6 oz. sugar
6 splits of Canada Dry ginger ale, chilled
Crushed ice
Lemon or orange peel twist to garnish

Mix the fruit juices, lemon rind and spices in a large jug. Put the water and sugar into a saucepan and heat gently to dissolve the sugar; cool

213

and add to the other ingredients in the jug. Chill. Strain the liquid and add the ginger ale and some crushed ice before serving. Garnish with peel. (Makes 20 glasses.)

Note. Fresh, canned or frozen (reconstituted) orange juice may be used.

LONG DRINKS
Everyman's Bubbly
Slightly sparkling and very refreshing drink

1 bottle of Graves or Sauternes   2 pints soda water

Chill both ingredients and combine just before serving. (Makes 3½ pints, approx.)

Gin Ricky
A long drink to set you up

1 wineglass gin	A dash of Grenadine
2 tsps. lemon or lime juice	Ice chips
	Soda water

Mix together the gin, lemon juice and grenadine, pour the mixture over the ice chips in a tall glass and fill up with soda water. (Makes 1 drink.)

Pride of Oporto
Popular and quite potent

2 lemons	4 tbsps. Curaçao
1 bottle of tawny port	1 siphon soda water

Squeeze the juice of 1 lemon into a bowl and add the port and Curaçao. Slice the second lemon, float it on top and leave for 20 minutes. Fill glasses two-thirds full and top up with chilled soda water. (Makes 3½ pints, approx.)

Rum Cooler
Tastes dreamy in Barbados when the sun's going down

Put ice in the cocktail shaker, and for each drink add the juice of 1 fresh lime, 4 dashes of Grenadine, 2 fl. oz. of Mount Gay rum. Shake short and sharply, strain into a tall slender tumbler, add a cube of ice, a splash of soda water and lime juice.

Sangria
Don't overdo the sugar or the drink won't be so refreshing

1 bottle of Portuguese or Spanish red wine, chilled	1 liqueur-glassful of brandy (optional)
1 pint fizzy lemonade, chilled	Slices of apple and orange
A slice of lemon	Caster sugar

Chill the wine in the bottle and chill an equal amount of bottled lemonade. Before serving mix together the wine and lemonade in a large bowl and add a slice of lemon and the brandy. Add slices of apple and orange and caster sugar to taste. (Makes 2½ pints, approx.)

Vermouth Fizz
A long drink for hazy-lazy days

6 cubes of ice	½ wineglass apricot brandy
1 bottle of French (white dry) Vermouth, well chilled	A 26-fl.-oz. bottle of sparkling lemonade
½ wineglass Maraschino	Orange and lemon slices to decorate

Put the ice in a jug. Pour in the French vermouth, Maraschino and apricot brandy, and just before serving add the sparkling lemonade. Serve with a float of orange and lemon slices. Sweeter-tooths can add a little sugar syrup to suit their taste. (Makes 6 goblets.)

Vin Blanc Cassis
To sip in the sun

4 parts dry white wine (Chablis or similar)   1 part Crème de Cassis

Thoroughly chill the wine before adding it to the crème de cassis: serve in claret glasses. This French refresher makes a good mid-morning drink or apéritif.

CUPS AND COLD PUNCHES
Fruit Cups
If well made, these are ideal for summer parties

Slices of lemon peel, cucumber peel or sprigs of

borage or mint add subtle distinction to fruit cups. To fruit juice or mixed juices, add bits of apple, orange, grapes, cherries or soft fruits.

You can buy non-alcoholic 'wines' – unfermented grape juice – still or sparkling, in red, white and rosé. Rose-hip syrup and blackcurrant syrup like Ribena are good mixers; so are the syrups from canned fruits. If the cup doesn't have to be a temperance drink, lace it with gin or an *eau de vie* to match the fruit juice, allowing approximately 3 oz. to the pint.

Wine Cups

The variety is infinite – but temper imagination with discretion

White wine : Add to white *ordinaire* half as much soda water, plenty of ice cubes, any diced fruits or small fruits and slices of lemon and cucumber with the skin left on. Sugar to taste, and lace with brandy, white port, sweet sherry or a liqueur, again to taste.

For a rosy cup : Use a rough red wine and red or tawny port.

Fruit wines, like those in the Merrydown range, make good cups.

Cider Cups

Less expensive than wine-based mixtures, but really good

To chilled sweet sparkling cider add half as much soda water, some wedges of red apples with the skin left on and curls of lemon zest. Lace it with Calvados, 2 oz. to the pint.

For a temperance cup, leave out the Calvados and use apple juice instead of cider – Shloer, a non-alcoholic cider, is one with a slight sparkle.

June Cup

Essence of Summer

1 bottle of Beaujolais, chilled	2 bottles of fizzy lemonade (1-pint size), chilled
4 tsps. brandy	
A few strawberries	

Pour the Beaujolais and brandy over the sliced berries and leave in a cool place for at least ½ hour. Just before serving, add the lemonade. (Makes 3½ pints, approx.)

Lemon Cider Cup

Refreshing acid tang

3 lemons	1 quart cider, chilled
4 oz. caster sugar	1 split of soda water, chilled
1 cinnamon stick	
1 pint boiling water	

Peel 2 lemons very finely, free of any white pith. Place the peel, juice, sugar and cinnamon stick in a jug, pour on the boiling water and stir until the sugar is dissolved. Allow to cool and strain into a bowl. Just before serving, add the cider and soda water. Decorate with the remaining lemon, thinly sliced. (Makes 12 glasses.)

White Wine Cup

Fruity and clean-tasting

Fresh fruit in season	1 bottle of medium-dry white wine
1 level tbsp. sugar	
4 tbsps. Kirsch or Maraschino	1 bottle of sparkling hock

Slice the fruit (strawberries, peaches, apricots, etc.) and place in the bottom of a bowl. Sprinkle with sugar, pour on the liqueur and leave for ½ hour. Pour on the still white wine and chill for a further ½ hour. Add the sparkling wine, and serve at once. (Makes 12 glasses.)

Planter's Punch

Not, repeat not, for teetotal friends

2 lb. sugar dissolved in ½ pint fresh lemon juice	½ pint brandy
	3 pints water
	A block of ice
½ pint Barbados rum	Nutmeg

Chill the ingredients and pour into the bowl over the ice. Grate a little nutmeg over the punch. (Makes about 5 pints.)

COCKTAILS
Alfonso

Rosy and not-so-potent version of the Champagne cocktail, called after its inventor.

A lump of sugar	A lump of ice
2 dashes of Angostura bitters	Champagne, well-chilled
1 fl. oz. Dubonnet	

Put the first 4 ingredients into a glass and top with champagne. (Makes 1 drink.)

Aperitifo

With a pleasant kick

1 bottle of dry Italian Vermouth	6 tbsps. Grand Marnier Ice cubes
2 splits of tonic water	

Chill the Vermouth and tonic water. Pour them, with the Grand Marnier, over the ice; stir well. (Makes 10 glasses.)

Bloody Mary

Poor Mary Tudor – she never tasted it!

1 part vodka	A dash of Worcestershire sauce
2 parts tomato juice	
A squeeze of lemon juice	Cracked ice

Shake all the ingredients with the cracked ice. (Makes 1 cocktail.)

Brandy Cocktail

For your more extravagant parties

1 part brandy	Crushed ice
1 part French Vermouth	Lemon rind curls
	Maraschino cherries

Shake the brandy and vermouth with some crushed ice in a shaker. Pour into glasses and serve each with a curl of lemon rind and a cherry.

Champagne Cocktail

Champange still suggests luxury and gaiety

4 dashes of Angostura bitters	Juice of a ¼ lemon
1 small sugar lump	Champagne, chilled
	Lemon slice to decorate

Pour the bitters over the sugar lump and put into a glass. Add the strained lemon juice and fill up with champagne. Float a wafer-thin slice of lemon on top. (Makes 1 cocktail.)

Dubonnet Cocktail

Smooth perfection

Equal quantities of Dubonnet and gin	Orange peel

Shake the Dubonnet and gin together, strain, and squeeze a piece of orange peel over the top.

216

Gin and Vermouth

Vary the proportions to individual taste

Shake together equal quantities of Italian or French vermouth and dry gin, strain and serve.

Manhattan Cocktail

This is comparatively speaking a very old cocktail, named after the district of New York, and still one of the best known.

Broken ice	3 tbsps. rye whisky
1–2 dashes of Angostura bitters	3 tbsps. Italian vermouth
2–3 dashes of Curaçao	A cherry and a piece of lemon peel to garnish

Fill a glass half-full of broken ice and add the other ingredients. Stir up well, strain into a cocktail glass, add a cherry and squeeze a piece of lemon peel on top. (Makes 1 cocktail.)

If a dry Manhattan is required, use French vermouth instead of Italian. For a medium cocktail use half each of French and Italian.

Dry Martini

Classic cocktail . . .

2 parts French vermouth	Cracked ice
1 part dry gin	Stuffed olives or lemon rind curls

Shake the vermouth and gin together with some cracked ice in a shaker. Pour into glasses and float a stuffed olive or a curl of lemon rind on top of each.

The proportions of a Martini are a matter of personal taste; some people prefer 2 parts of gin to 1 of vermouth, others equal parts of gin and vermouth.

Sweet Martini

. . . and its cousin

2 parts Italian vermouth	A few drops of orange bitters per cocktail
1 part dry gin	One maraschino cherry for each cocktail
Cracked ice	

Shake all the ingredients thoroughly together in a shaker and strain into glasses. Serve with a cherry in each glass.

Dressed Avocado Pears: p. 63

Old-Fashioned

Whisky-based

1 lump of sugar	1–2 ice cubes
1–2 dashes of Angostura or orange bitters	Whisky A half-slice of orange

Put into a glass the sugar and a little water to dissolve it (or use sugar syrup). Add the bitters and ice cubes, top up with whisky and float the orange slice on top. (Makes 1 cocktail.)

Pink Gin

Fairly potent

Put 2–3 drops of Angostura bitters into a cocktail glass and turn the glass so that the bitters run round the inside. Fill up with dry gin. (Makes 1 cocktail.)

White Lady Cocktail

The lady has something of a punch

½ a shaker of broken ice	½ gill (2½ fl. oz.) Cointreau
½ gill (2½ fl. oz.) lemon juice	1 gill (5 fl. oz.) gin

Place all the ingredients in the shaker and shake well. Strain into cocktail glasses. (Makes 4 cocktails.)

THE HOT DRINK PARADE

Punch and posset, mull and negus, toddy and grog. Whatever you call them they are all warmer-uppers worthy of the name: pretty, partyish – and potent

Punch

The generous bowl is the essence of punch, the ritual of mixing ingredients under the noses of the guests a great part of the pleasure. It doesn't matter what the bowl is so long as it is heat-resistant and large enough. It does matter that you have a long ladle or spoon for stirring with and ladling from. If facilities don't allow for the whole concoction to be brewed in full view, at least the final flourish can be made with your circle of friends around you. A hot-plate or other table heater that will safely take the punch bowl is all that's needed for keeping the potion hot. Only basic rule is don't ever *boil* your hot drinks – the magic of your alchemy will disappear if you do. If you haven't regulation punch cups, serve it in little mugs – anything with a handle and strong enough to withstand the heat.

If it's a real punch you're making, it's a bit of party ploy to chat about its origin. Punch was, in fact, introduced to England from India in the seventeenth century, when thirsty traders out there needed a drink to recompense them for their spoiled wines. Some say its name is from the Hindustani word *panch*, meaning five, since it had five ingredients – spirit, water, spice, sugar and citrus juice. But then it's just as likely the name itself is a contraction of puncheon, the large casks from which sailors on the East India run were served with their grog rations. Those five ingredients, though, are still the heart of a good punch today.

Punches can be hot or cold – according to climate and taste. Quantities per head? Half a pint of good punch is enough for most people and too much for others. Your own arithmetic, plus the scaling up or down of ingredients to taste, is a matter for a small rehearsal.

Apples and oranges with their skins on can be quartered into the bowl for hot mixes; slices of melon rind or cucumber skin give a special lift to cold ones.

Rum Punch

This can be an amusing party piece if you have a good but sturdy old punch bowl

Stick a dozen cloves into each of 6 oranges and bake them until the rind browns. Mix them in a warmed punch bowl with 6 level tbsps. brown sugar and 1 bottle of rum, and set alight. Pour in 3 pints of cider or fruit juice, stir and serve.

Spiced Cider Punch

Cheaper than a spirit-based punch, but good

1 quart cider	Juice of ½ a lemon
½–1 level tbsp. sugar	¼ level tsp. powdered cinnamon, ginger and grated nutmeg, combined
Juice and thinly pared rind of 2 oranges	

217

Chilled Soups for Summer Entertaining: p. 118

Heat the cider with the other ingredients but do not boil. Strain and serve very hot. (Makes 2¼ pints approx. – more if brandy is used – see below.)

For a stronger drink: Add ½ pint brandy to the hot brew.

For a lighter drink: Replace the cider by a non-alcoholic type cider.

Woodpecker Punch

(*See picture above*)

Another real cockle-warmer

1 flagon of Bulmer's Woodpecker Cider	12 cloves
	1 orange
1 miniature bottle of rum	1 cinnamon stick
	1 lemon, quartered

Pour the cider and rum into a saucepan. Stick the cloves into the orange and add to the pan, with the cinnamon and lemon. Bring to the boil, reduce the heat, cover, and simmer for 15 minutes. Serve hot. (Makes 2 pints.)

Mulls

These are basically sugared-and-spiced wines (or beers or ciders), diluted with water and served piping hot. They can be spiked with fortified wines, liqueurs or spirits. The ritual of presentation is as for punch.

Two of the most pleasant wine mulls for winter enjoyment are also among the simplest – they are the *glühwein* of Austria and the *vin chaud* of France.

Red Wine Mull

This concoction is sometimes given the Pickwickian name of 'negus'

Gently heat 1 bottle of red table wine in a pan and pour in an equal quantity of boiling water in which you've first dissolved 1 heaped tbsp. sugar. Stir in a few cloves, some lemon slices and grated nutmeg. Add, if you like, a measure of brandy.

White Wine Mull

Deceptively innocent-looking

To 1 bottle dry white wine add 1 wineglass of brandy, the juice of 1 lemon and 6 dessertsps. honey, before heating gently.

Glühwein

(*See picture above*)
For evening relaxation after sport or work

6 lumps of sugar	1 bottle of red wine
2 slices of lemon	A small piece of
2 slices of orange	cinnamon stick
2 cloves	

Put all the ingredients into a saucepan and slowly bring almost to boiling point. Remove from the heat, strain and serve at once. (Makes 1¼ pints approx.)

Note. Best made with a lightish red wine – claret rather than Burgundy type.

CLAN HOTELS LTD.

DRUMOSSIE HOTEL
PERTH ROAD INVERNESS

Telephone: 0463 36451

M   Mrs. Marshall. B.M.A.

West Park.

INSHES.

V.A.T. Reg. No. 266 0409 66   30-5- 19 78

| 25 | 5 | To Ladies Benevolent Luncheon. | £66.00 |

Vin Chaud

Very hard to beat

8 lumps of sugar	A small piece of
2 bottles of full-	cinnamon stick
bodied red wine	6–8 tbsps. brandy
¾ pint water	Lemon slices

Put the sugar, wine, water and cinnamon into a saucepan and as the mixture warms, add the brandy. Slowly heat almost to boiling point, but on no account let it boil. Strain and serve at once, with a lemon float in each glass or tankard. (Makes 3 pints approx.)

The proportion of brandy in this recipe is very much a matter of personal taste, but if you reduce the brandy, then use less water.

Note. Use an earthy Rhône wine, a Tuscan red, a Portuguese Dao or Vila Real.

Mulled Ale

For really cold days mulled ale is a fun starter to a party where the main drink will be beer

Heat – but don't boil – a good-strength ale with sugar and spices to taste, and add just before serving it hot a couple of fluid ounces of rum or whisky, gin or vodka for each pint. Experiment in advance to decided what sort of ale, how much sugar and what spices combine to please you best. A fairly standard mix is to add for each pint of ale 1 level tbsp. brown sugar, 1 level tsp. grated nutmeg and 4 cloves.

Spiced Ale

Spirit is not essential in this brew

Using mild rather than heavily hopped beer, heat it with grated nutmeg or ground cinnamon and brown sugar to taste, plus a twist of lemon rind. Lastly, add a measure of brandy.

Lamb's Wool

Sieved cooked apple makes the froth that gives the drink its name

This is a sort of beer mull. To make it, bake 8 medium-sized cooking apples in the oven; mash them, add 2 pints old ale and push through a sieve. Add ground ginger, nutmeg and sugar – all to taste. Heat gently and serve hot. Brown ale does very nicely for this drink.

Hot Toddies (and Grogs)

These cold-night comforters can be made by the glass

Measure-guidance for beginners: 2 fl. oz. rum, 1 fl. oz. Florida orange juice (straight from the can), 1 level tsp. caster sugar, 2 cloves. Top up with hot water, stir and give each tall glass an orange-slice float and a sprinkle of grated nutmeg.

Variation: Use lemon juice instead of orange, fill up with hot, freshly brewed Indian tea and garnish with a twist of lemon peel.

Possets

Mulls with a difference

These are mulls made with sweetened and spiced milk curdled with ale, and often used to be served as a Christmas drink. The frothy result looks a bit like Lamb's Wool. Eggs were sometimes used instead of milk and the whole sometimes laced with spirit. Here is a characteristic recipe:

Huckle-My-Buff

Worth making for the name alone

These amounts make enough for 6 glasses. Heat 1 pint draught beer with 6 well-beaten eggs and 2 oz. sugar. Remove from the heat and add a further 1 pint beer, a generous amount of grated nutmeg, and brandy to taste.

TEA AND COFFEE FOR A PARTY

If you must have hot tea, it should be freshly made, and there are advantages in using a couple of ordinary pots in relays rather than one outsize pot.

Iced tea and coffee are convenient because they can be made in advance. Iced tea with a slice of lemon but no milk is probably the most civilized accompaniment for curries, and is good with almost any buffet fare. Tea or coffee for cold drinks is best made a good deal stronger than for hot drinks, and should be strained off the leaves (or grounds) immediately it has infused. Serve it thoroughly chilled. It is usually pre-sweetened.

Sugar Syrup

Sugar syrup, made in advance, is much the most convenient sweetener for cold drinks, including tea or coffee. Simply dissolve 1 lb. sugar in 1 pint water, bring it gently to the boil for 5 minutes. Chill.

Iced Tea

For the sophisticated palate

Make China tea in the usual way and strain it over the back of a spoon into some glasses which have been half-filled with crushed ice. Sweeten to taste and slice a lemon to each glass. Re-chill before serving. As a variation add a sprig of mint.

Iced Coffee

More than mere drink

Make some strong coffee, using 4 heaped tbsps. coffee to $1\frac{1}{2}$ pints water. While it is still hot, sweeten to taste. Cool and chill. Pour into glasses, add a cube of ice and top with whipped cream.

Christmas Night Coffee

For a small circle of friends round the fire, with the lights dimmed

Pour each guest a cup of black coffee and let people add their own 'float' of 1 or 2 tsps. Cognac. Then they must put a cube of sugar in a teaspoon, fill the spoon with Cognac, warm it over the coffee and light the liquor in the spoon. As it burns, the spoon should be lowered gently into the coffee and held barely below the surface of the liquid, so that the whole of the top surface is ignited. Swish the spoon gently back and forth in the cup until the flame dies down. Then drink!

Irish Coffee

(*See top picture*)

Ah . . . . h . . . . . h!

Place 1 tbsp. whiskey in a small warmed goblet. Add sugar to taste and fill to within $\frac{1}{2}$–1 inch of the top of the glass with strong black coffee. Pour over this a $\frac{1}{4}$- or $\frac{1}{2}$-inch layer of double cream. You drink the coffee through the cream.

Turkish Coffee

(*See lower picture*)
How to make the real thing

A copper coffee pot with a long handle and without a lid should be used, if possible, and the brew is served in very small coffee cups.

The coffee should be ground very finely, almost to a powder; no chicory is added. For 2 small cups use the following quantities:

Boil 2 cupfuls of water in the coffee pot. Add 3 lumps of sugar. Add 2 level tsps. of coffee to the boiling water and sugar. Stir until the mixture comes to the boil and is frothy. Remove from the heat to allow the froth to subside, then replace on the heat and bring to the boil again. Repeat the operation 4 times in all. Pour a little coffee into each cup, dividing the froth equally between the cups.

11
Those Little Extras

GARNISHES, TOPPINGS

Suitable decorations add good looks as well as flavour to food and drinks – but they must be very fresh, and preferably quite simple and comparatively small. The garnish for any particular dish should be decided on beforehand. Colours should be chosen to tone with both the food and the serving dish – two, or at most three, colours are sufficient. Sometimes ingredients which are an integral part of the recipe can also add decorative value.

Vegetable and Salad Garnishes

One of the easiest ways to a party finish

Turned Mushrooms have a nicely tailored look. You need to use large button mushrooms and 'turn' them with a small, sharp-pointed knife, by making a series of cuts from the top of the cap to the base at intervals. Then repeat in the opposite direction to remove each narrow 'fillet'. Sauté the mushrooms in butter.

Baby Turnips can be 'turned' to pretty effect in the same way.

Carrot Curls look crisp on open sandwiches, and in salads (or served as cocktail nibblers). Just scrape raw carrots and slice them lengthwise and paper thin, using a vegetable peeler. Roll up, fasten with a toothpick and put them in iced water until they curl. Serve on or off the picks.

Celery Curls: Cut celery into strips about $\frac{1}{2}$ inch wide and 2 inches long and then slit one or both ends in narrow strips almost to the centre. Leave the pieces in iced water for an hour or so, until the fringed strips curl.

Pickle Fans always stay fresh, and suit hot or cold dishes. Make lengthwise cuts almost to the end of each gherkin, from the 'flower' end. Spread carefully to form a little open fan.

Lattice Potatoes, which are deep-fried, require the use of a crinkle cutter. Choose largish old potatoes, peel them and then, using the cutter, cut a slice off one end. Now rotate the surface and cut against the serrations, so leaving the slice with little lattice holes. (You can use this cutter to make crinkly 'sticks' of any raw root vegetables before cooking them as desired.)

Radish Roses for salads and open sandwiches or to garnish cold meat platters are always popular. Cut off a narrow slice from the root end of each radish, then cut thin 'petals' from stem to root. Put into iced water until the cuts open to form petals.

Water Lilies: Make 4–8 small deep cuts, crossing in the centre of the radish at the root end, and leave to open out as before.

Orange or Lemon Garnishes

Truly versatile

Citrus Twists look cool on an iced drink or on top of a chiffon dessert. Using a sharp-edged potato peeler start to remove a strip of peel from the narrow end of a lemon, orange or grapefruit. Work in a continuous spiral, removing only the coloured part of the peel. Let the peel twist naturally as a garnish.

Orange and Lemon Slices, deftly twisted, suit fish and chicken dishes and may be used wherever these flavours are present in a recipe. Slit the slice through the rind to the centre of the slice, then twist in opposite directions. A double twist with 2 slices gives more emphasis. Nestle an olive or a tiny sprig of parsley into the twist – or a well-drained Maraschino cherry, for a sweet dish.

Croûtons

Classic finishing touch for soups, hot entrées

Basically, croûtons are small, fancy-shaped pieces of bread, which have been fried, baked,

or toasted. Cut the slices of white bread
$\frac{1}{4}$–$\frac{1}{2}$ inch thick, remove the crusts and then
either cut the bread into $\frac{1}{4}$–$\frac{1}{2}$ inch cubes and fry
them, or leave the slices whole and bake or
grill them before cutting up.

Fried: Fry them quickly in hot lard or oil
until crisp and golden, and drain well. A small
amount of mixed herbs may be added to the
pan.

Toasted: Put under a hot grill and take care
not to let them become too brown; cut up with
a sharp knife.

Baked: Spread out on a baking sheet and put
in the oven if you have it on for some other
dish; take out as soon as they are golden-
brown and cut up as above.

When croûtons are used as a garnish for
minced meat, etc., it is usual to cut them into
triangles, crescents etc., and to make them
somewhat larger than the kind used as an
accompaniment for soup.

Cheese Triangles

For soups or savouries

Well butter 6 slices of crustless bread and
arrange close together on a baking sheet.
Sprinkle 1 oz. finely grated cheese over. Bake
in a moderate oven (350 °F, mark 4) for about
40 minutes. Overlap round the dish, or float
on puréed soups.

Fleurons

*Small fancy-shaped pieces of pastry to lend interest to
entrées, ragoûts, mince and so on.*

Roll out some puff, flaky, or rough puff pastry
to $\frac{1}{4}$ inch in thickness, then stamp it into shapes
with small fancy cutters, or cut with a sharp
knife into squares, triangles or diamonds. To
make crescents, which are a traditional shape,
use a small round cutter; place it about $\frac{1}{2}$ inch
on to the edge of the pastry for the first cut,
then move the cutter a further $\frac{1}{2}$ inch inwards
and cut again, thus making one crescent. Continue the length of the pastry, moving the
cutter $\frac{1}{2}$ inch each time.

Place the fleurons on a baking sheet, brush
the tops lightly with beaten egg and bake in a
very hot oven (450 °F, mark 8) until well
risen, golden-brown and firm underneath –
7–10 minutes. Use at once, while crisp.

Buttered Crumbs

Topping you can store

Melt 1 oz. butter and add 1 pint fine white
breadcrumbs and let them absorb the fat, fork-
ing the mixture several times. Spread out on
baking sheets and dry in a very cool oven
(lowest setting). When ready, they are cream-
coloured and dry. Stored in a screw-top jar or
polythene bag in a cool place, they will keep
fresh for 2 months.

Use dry for coating rissoles, etc.; toss them
with butter or grated cheese for other toppings.

Crunchy Topper

For casseroles

Fry 2 oz. fresh white breadcrumbs in 1$\frac{1}{2}$ oz.
butter until golden-brown. Sift together 8 oz.
self-raising flour, 1 level tsp. salt, pepper and
$\frac{1}{4}$ level tsp. dried onion powder. Stir in 3 tbsps.
cooking oil and enough milk to give a soft
dough. Drop tablespoonfuls of the dough into
buttered crumbs and roll into balls in the
crumbs. Arrange on top of the casserole about
50 minutes before serving. Bake uncovered in
a fairly hot oven. (375 °F, mark 5).

Egg and Sugar Glazes

To give sweet pies an extra touch of glamour

Brush uncooked pastry with lightly beaten egg
white and dredge heavily with white or brown
sugar before baking. Unglazed pastry: for the
last few minutes of baking, drizzle it with
glacé icing and return to the oven.

ACCOMPANIMENTS
Melba Toast

Serve instead of rolls

Cut stale bread into very thin slices, lay these
on a baking sheet and dry off in the bottom of
a very slow oven. Before serving, brown them
lightly in a moderate oven or under a very
slow grill. Air on a rack, and serve at once.

Bacon Rolls

Good with bland meats and poultry

Choose streaky bacon. Cut each rasher in half,
then 'spread' it with a knife on a board, roll up

and string 2 or 3 together on a skewer. Grill for about 2 minutes on each side.

Use bacon rolls as an accompaniment to roast chicken, or to garnish made-up dishes. For an unusual variation, wrap the bacon round some cooked stoned prunes and grill.

Fried Crumbs

Classic accompaniment for game birds

Melt 1 oz. butter in a frying-pan. Stir in 4 oz. fresh white breadcrumbs until blended and fry until the crumbs are evenly browned.

Boiled Rice

Traditonal with curries, excellent with many other savoury dishes

Rice sold in unbranded packs or loose should be washed before it is cooked. Put it in a strainer and rinse it under the cold tap until all the loose starch (white powder) is washed off – it is this loose starch which prevents rice drying out into separate grains when cooked.

The 1–2–1 Method: For 3–4 servings place 1 cup of long-grain rice in a saucepan with 2 cups water and 1 level tsp. salt. Bring quickly to the boil, stir well and cover with a tight-fitting lid. Reduce the heat and simmer gently for 14–15 minutes. Remove from the heat and before serving separate out the grains gently, using a fork. (The rice will not need draining.)

If a drier effect is required, leave the rice covered for 5–10 minutes after it has been cooked. The grains should then be tender, but dry and quite separate.

Here are some points to remember when using the 1–2–1 method:

Don't increase the amount of water or the finished rice will be soggy.

Don't uncover the rice while it is cooking or the steam will escape and the cooking time will be increased.

Don't stir the rice after it has come to the boil – it breaks up the grains and makes them soggy.

When the rice is cooked, don't leave it longer than 10 minutes before serving, or the grains will stick together.

Ordinary Method: Allow $1\frac{1}{2}$–2 oz. long-grain per person. Half-fill a large pan with water (about 6 pints to 6 oz. rice) bring to the boil and add 1 level tsp. salt. Add the rice and continue to boil rapidly, uncovered, until the rice is just soft – 15–20 minutes. Drain the rice in a sieve and rinse by pouring hot water through it, then return it to the pan with a knob of butter; cover with a tea towel or lid and leave on a very low heat to dry out for 5–10 minutes, shaking the pan from time to time. Alternatively, spread the drained rice on a shallow baking tray or ovenproof dish lined with greaseproof paper, cover with a tea towel or greaseproof paper and place in a very low oven to dry out.

Tomato Chutney

(See picture overleaf)

More of a relish, with a judicious blend of flavours

6 lb. red tomatoes	1 level tsp. mixed spice
1 lb. onions or shallots, skinned	A pinch of cayenne pepper
1 clove of garlic, skinned and crushed	$\frac{1}{2}$ oz. salt
12 oz. Demerara sugar	$\frac{1}{2}$ pint white distilled vinegar
2 level tsps. paprika	$\frac{1}{2}$ lb. stoned raisins, halved

Skin the tomatoes and slice roughly. Mince or finely chop the onions or shallots. In a saucepan cook together the tomatoes, onions or shallots, and garlic until a thick purée is obtained. Add the remaining ingedients. Continue to cook until reduced, with no loose liquid visible.

Pot and cover with vinegar-proof skin or use jars with ground stoppers. (Yield about 4 lbs.)

Drunken Pineapple

Four good flavours combined to make a mouth-watering accompaniment for cold poultry and sliced roast meat.

A 1 lb. 13 oz. can of pineapple cubes or pieces	A 2-inch stick of cinnamon
3 cloves	$\frac{1}{4}$ pint brandy or Kirsch

Drain the juice from the pineapple and put it into a saucepan. Add the cloves and cinnamon and simmer. Add the pineapple and simmer for a further 10 minutes. Remove from the heat and add the brandy or Kirsch. Cool. Pack the drained fruit into a wide-necked bottle, and pour syrup over to cover completely. Seal and store in a cool place.

Note. This doubles also as a delicious sweet.

Preserved Melon

The sort of thing you can't easily find in the shops – ideal with boiled ham, turkey or cold roast chicken

½ level tsp. powdered alum	4 fl. oz. vinegar
1 pint water	1 stick of cinnamon
1½ lb. prepared melon, cubed	1 level tsp. cloves
	4 oz. cherries (see below)
12 fl. oz. boiling water	12 oz. sugar

Dissolve the alum in the water and bring to the boil. Add the cubed melon and cook for 5 minutes. Drain.

In a pan combine the remaining ingredients. When the sugar has dissolved, add the melon and cook for a further 10 minutes. Leave overnight in a bowl, covered.

Drain off the syrup. Bring the syrup to the boil and boil for 5 minutes. Add the melon and return to the boil. Reduce the heat and simmer for 20 minutes. Bottle and seal as for a pickle.

Note. Use bottled Maraschino cherries; fresh, drained or canned cherries can be substituted.

Spiced Orange Rings

(See picture below)

Try these with cold roast duck, roast pork or glazed gammon

8 medium-sized thin-skinned oranges	½ pint white distilled vinegar
1½ pints water	¼ oz. whole cloves
1½ lb. granulated sugar	1½ sticks of cinnamon
	6 blades of mace

Wipe the oranges, cut into ¼-inch slices and discard the pips.

Place the sliced oranges in a pan, cover with water, cover the pan and simmer the contents for about 40 minutes, or until the peel is soft. Make a syrup by dissolving the sugar in the vinegar, add the spices and boil for 3–4 minutes.

Drain the oranges, place in a shallow pan and cover with vinegar syrup. Simmer covered for 30–40 minutes, until the orange slices look clear. Remove from heat and leave in the syrup for 24 hours.

Drain the orange rings and pack into jars. Stand these on a tray and cover the fruit with the syrup. Do not seal at once. Keep topping up with syrup for the next 3–4 days. Cover as for jam. Mature if possible for at least 6 weeks.

PETITS FOURS AND SWEETMEATS
Chocolate Fruit Balls

Richly delicious and not difficult to make

4 oz. nuts, chopped	Grated rind of 1 orange
4 oz. seedless raisins	¾ tsp. almond essence
4 oz. sultanas	8 oz. plain chocolate

Mix the nuts, raisins and sultanas and put through a mincing machine or chop very finely. Add the orange rind and almond essence and form into small balls. Set aside to dry for 24 hours. The next day, grate the chocolate and put it into a small pan. Melt over a gentle heat, then stand it over a saucepan of boiling water so that it does not solidify too rapidly. Dip each ball in the melted chocolate, drop on to a well-greased baking sheet and allow to set in a cold place. (Makes 1¼ lb. approx.)

Chocolate Rum Truffles

Creamy-smooth, rich

¼ lb. plain chocolate
10 oz. icing sugar, sifted
¼ lb. unsalted butter
Rum
Chocolate vermicelli

Melt the chocolate, stirring, then cream it with the icing sugar and butter and flavour with rum. Form into small balls and roll in chocolate vermicelli. Put into paper sweet cases and allow to harden for a few hours before serving. (Makes 1 lb. approx.)

Variations

Add Grand Marnier for a subtle orange flavour, or cherry brandy and chopped glacé cherries.

Note. Store these truffles for up to a week in a cool place, but not in the refrigerator.

Mocha Truffles

Favourite combination of flavours

8 oz. plain chocolate
4 level tbsps. sweet-ened condensed milk
Coffee essence
Cocoa powder to coat

Break the chocolate into small pieces and melt it in a basin standing in a pan of boiling water. Stir in the condensed milk and a few drops of coffee essence. Remove from the pan, mix thoroughly and allow to cool slightly. Form the mixture into small balls, roll in cocoa and leave until set. (Makes ½ lb. approx.)

Coconut Kisses

Simple, good and of a pastel prettiness

1 lb. granulated sugar
4 oz. powdered glucose
¼ pint water
6 oz. desiccated coconut
Colouring (optional)

Put the sugar, glucose and water into a pan and heat gently until the sugar has dissolved, then boil to 240 °F (soft ball stage). Remove from the heat and stir in the coconut; if you wish, add also a little pink or green colouring. Form the mixture into small rocky heaps and leave on waxed paper to cool and harden. (Makes 1½ lb. approx.)

Marzipan Bon-Bons

(See picture below)

Good way of using almond paste trimmings

Sharpen some almond paste with grated lemon rind and juice before rolling into little balls. Insert half a glacé cherry into each; or leave plain and decorate with almond spears later. Make a clear syrup using the proportion of ¼ pint water to 1 lb. granulated sugar. Heat in a pan to 312 °F or hard crack stage. Hold each marzipan ball on a skewer and dip carefully in toffee glaze to crown the tops. Add almond spears now. Leave to harden on waxed paper. Serve in paper cases.

Peanut Brittle

(See picture above)

Homespun but very popular

14 oz. granulated sugar
6 oz. soft brown sugar
6 oz. corn syrup
¼ pint water
2 oz. butter
¼ level tsp. bicarbonate of soda
12 oz. unsalted peanuts, chopped

Butter a tin measuring 12 by 4 inches.

Dissolve the sugars, syrup and water over a low heat in a 4-pint heavy-based saucepan. Add the butter and bring to the boil; boil very gently to 300 °F (hard crack stage). Add the bicarbonate of soda and slightly warmed nuts. Pour slowly into the tin and mark into bars when almost set. (Makes 2 lb. approx.)

Note: Golden syrup may replace the corn syrup.

Peppermint Creams

Very acceptable to round off a dinner

These are smoother and creamier if made from fondant. As a short cut, use Hartley Smith fondant mix and flavour it with oil of peppermint. Roll it out on waxed paper to about $\frac{1}{4}$ inch in thickness and stamp in 1-inch rounds. Each is topped with a crystallized violet and left to dry on the paper. They can be stored in an airtight container when dry.

Rich Chocolate Cups

Your mouth will water even when you read the recipe!

A little couverture chocolate	4 oz. icing sugar, sifted
4 oz. plain chocolate, grated	Rum to flavour and mix
	Chopped pistachio nuts

Dissolve the couverture chocolate and brush it over the inside of some small tinfoil cases, then let them dry. Mix the grated chocolate and icing sugar in a basin, with sufficient rum to form a stiff paste. Fill the cases with this mix-ture, then cover them with more melted coating chocolate. When nearly set, sprinkle with a little finely chopped pistachio nut. (Makes $\frac{1}{2}$ lb. approx.)

Stuffed Dates and Plums

Set your more responsible youngsters to making these – but limit the number of 'samples'

Choose good quality dessert plums. Remove the stones and fill the cavities with coloured marzipan; roll the dates in caster sugar and put them into paper cases.

French plums may be used in the same way, or you can soak some really good, plump prunes, stone them and treat as above.

Uncooked Chocolate Fudge

No problems about sugar-boiling temperatures

$\frac{1}{2}$ lb. plain chocolate	1 lb. caster sugar
$\frac{1}{4}$ lb. butter	1 tsp. vanilla essence
1 egg	2 oz. walnuts, finely
2 level tbsps. condensed milk	chopped

Grease a tin about 7 inches square.

Melt the chocolate and butter together over hot water. Mix the egg, condensed milk, sugar and vanilla essence together, then blend in the chocolate and butter. Stir in the nuts and turn the mixture into the greased tin. Chill in the refrigerator for several hours. Cut into squares. (Makes $1\frac{3}{4}$ lb. approx.)

Note. This quickly-made fudge is at its best for eating a day or so after making.

PART FOUR

1
Catering for Crowds

Catering for larger numbers strikes panic in every female breast – and not without cause. Anyone who's been faced with a W.I. annual tea, Cricket Club get-together, or a daughter's wedding breakfast will know how daunting the prospect can be. But don't be intimidated. Like the nettle, once you come to grips with the problem, it can be handled in a (fairly) painless way. The secret lies in cold calculation. Reduce your guests to mere mouths to be fed, and work out their eating capacity in advance. It is difficult of course to assess exactly how much humans are capable of consuming in any given circumstance, both as regards food and the even less predictable drink. However, we've set out below a catering guide based on the elusive 'average' man – but you know your friends better than we do, and must adapt where you think fit.

GENERAL CALCULATIONS (Per head)

Cocktail party: 4 or 5 small savouries and 3 or 4 drinks.

Fork buffet: 1 starter, 1 main dish, 1 sweet, 3 or 4 drinks.

Wedding reception: 4–6 savouries, 1–2 sweet foods, 3–4 drinks.

Adult tea-party: 3–4 savoury items, 2 small cakes or slices of cake, 2 cups of tea.

Teenage party: 1 main dish, plenty of crusty bread, butter, cheese, 1 sweet dish, 4–6 drinks (coffee and cold soft drinks in variety).

Children's party (for the under-tens): 4–6 savoury items, including potato crisps, cheesy biscuits, baby sausages; 1–2 sweet items, of which ice cream is certainly one; and 2 cold drinks (milk and fruit squash).

SANDWICH FILLINGS

Each filling is sufficient for 12 rounds, using a 2-lb. loaf and 6 oz. butter, or about 12 small bridge rolls split in half and topped with the filling.

8 eggs, hard-boiled and mashed, or scrambled

14–16 oz. cold meat, sliced or minced and seasoned

2 7-oz. cans of salmon (mashed, seasoned and suitably garnished)

4 4¾-oz. cans of sardines (as above)

2 7-oz. cans of tuna (as above)

12 oz. Cheddar or other hard cheese, finely grated and softened with butter or mayonnaise

6–8 oz. cream or cottage cheese, seasoned or with chopped chives added

4 bananas, mashed, with a little lemon juice, and chopped walnuts or dates added to taste.

Note. An even and economical way to spread butter on bread is to start at the corners and spread inwards – not to slap a large lump in the middle and try to work it to the corners.

227

APPROXIMATE QUANTITIES FOR BUFFET PARTIES

	1 PORTION	24–26 PORTIONS	NOTES
Soup: cream, clear or iced	⅓ pint	1 gallon	Serve, garnished, in mugs or cups
Fish cocktail: shrimp, prawn, tuna or crab	1 oz.	1½ lb. fish 2–3 lettuces 1½ pints sauce	In stemmed glasses, garnished with a shrimp or prawn
Meat with bone	5 oz.	7–8 lb.	Cold roasts or barbecue chops
boneless	3–4 oz.	5–6½ lb.	Casseroles, meat balls, sausages, barbecue steaks
Poultry: turkey	3–4 oz. (boneless)	16 lb. (dressed)	
chicken	1 joint (5–8 oz.)	6 2½–3 lb. birds (dressed)	Serve hot or cold
Delicatessen: ham or tongue	3–4 oz.	5–6½ lb.	Halve the amounts if making stuffed cornets
pâté for wine-and-pâté party	3–4 oz.	5–6½ lb.	Halve the amounts if pâté is starter course
Salad vegetables lettuce	⅙	3–4	Dress at last minute
cucumber	1 in.	2 cucumbers	
tomatoes	1–2	3 lb.	
white cabbage	1 oz.	1½ lb.	For winter salads
boiled potatoes	2 oz.	3 lb.	For potato salads
Rice or pasta	1½ oz. (uncooked)	2 lb.	Can be cooked a day ahead, reheated in 5 mins. in boiling water
Cheese (for wine-and-cheese party)	3 oz.	4½–5 lb. of at least 4 types	You'll need more if you serve a cheese dip too
Cheese (for biscuits)	1–1½ oz.	1½–2 lb. cheese plus 1 lb. butter 2 lb. biscuits	Allow the larger amounts for an assorted cheese board

SAVOURIES, SWEETS

	INGREDIENTS	PORTIONS	NOTES
Sausage rolls	1½ lb. shortcrust or flaky pastry 2 lb. sausage meat	25–30 medium or 50 small rolls	Pastry based on 1½ lb. flour, ¾–1 lb. fat
Bouchées	1 lb. puff pastry 1 pint thick white sauce 10 oz. prepared filling	50 bouchées	Pastry based on 1 lb. flour, ¾ lb. butter Fillings: chopped ham, chicken, egg, mushrooms, shrimps
Cheese straws	½ lb. cheese pastry	100 cheese straws	½ lb. flour, ¼ lb. fat, ¼ lb. cheese
Meringues	6 egg whites 12 oz. caster sugar ¾ pint whipped cream	50 (small) meringue halves	2 halves per head with cream 1 half with fruit and cream; or ice-cream
Jelly	2½ quarts	25	

Savouries, Sweets, continued

	INGREDIENTS	PORTIONS	NOTES
Trifle	4 pints custard 25 sponge fingers 1 large can fruit	25	Decorate with cream, glacé cherries, chopped nuts, angelica
Fruit salad	6½ lb. fruit 3–4 pints sugar syrup 1½ pints cream	25	Can be prepared a day ahead and left submerged in syrup but bananas should be added just before serving

QUANTITIES FOR PARTY DRINKS

Rough guide only, as drinking habits vary vastly.

Buffet Parties

Allow for each, 1 to 2 shorts and 3 to 6 longer drinks plus coffee. Reckon a half-bottle of wine per person.

Dinner Parties

One bottle of table wine is sufficient for 4 people.

Drop-in-for-Drinks

Reckon on 3 to 5 short drinks each and 4 to 6 small savouries besides the usual olives and nuts.

Drinks by the Bottle

Sherry and port and straight vermouths give roughly 12–16 glasses. In single nips for cocktails, vermouths, and spirits give just over 30 a bottle. Reckon 16–20 drinks of spirit from a bottle when serving them with soda, tonic or other minerals. Liqueurs served in proper glasses – 30 portions. A split bottle of soda or tonic gives 2–3 drinks. A 1-pint can of tomato juice gives 4–6 drinks. Dilute a bottle of fruit cordial with 7 pints water for 20–25 drinks.

APPROXIMATE COFFEE AND TEA QUANTITIES

	1 SERVING	24–26 SERVINGS		NOTES
Coffee ground, hot	⅓ pint	9–10 oz. coffee 6 pints water	3 pints milk 1 lb. sugar	If you make the coffee in advance strain it after infusion. Reheat without boiling. Serve sugar separately
ground, iced	⅓ pint	12 oz. coffee 6 pints water	3 pints milk sugar to taste	Make coffee (half sweetened, half not), strain and chill. Mix with chilled milk. Serve in glasses
instant, hot	⅓ pint	2–3 oz. coffee 6 pints water	2 pints milk 1 lb. sugar	Make coffee in jugs as required. Serve sugar separately
instant, iced	⅓ pint	3 oz. coffee 2 pints water	6 pints milk sugar to taste	Make black coffee (half sweetened, half not) and chill. Mix with chilled creamy milk. Serve in glasses
Tea Indian, hot	⅓ pint	2 oz. tea 8 pints water	1½ pints milk 1 lb. sugar	It is better to make tea in several pots rather than one outsize one
Indian, iced	⅓ pint	3 oz. tea 7 pints water	2 pints milk sugar to taste	Strain tea immediately it has infused. Sweeten half of it. Chill. Serve in glasses with chilled creamy milk
China	⅓ pint	2 oz. tea 9 pints water	2–3 lemons 1 lb. sugar	Infuse China tea for 2 or 3 minutes only. Put a thin lemon slice in each cup before pouring. Serve sugar separately

Food Taboos

Since one of the pleasures of entertaining is to see your guests enjoying their food, it is as well to be prepared for the rare occasion when you entertain someone who, by reason of health, religion or ethical principles, is unable to eat certain foods.

Anyone you know fairly well who follows a very strict diet (religious or other) would probably warn you beforehand, but in the case of business entertaining you might be taken unawares. If in any doubt, provide a choice of dishes. Always see that you serve plenty of salad or vegetables in case someone turns out to be a vegetarian, and have cheese available as an alternative to the sweet.

These short notes give some basic guidance: for further information, consult specialist books. We give here brief details on some useful ones which were available at the time of going to press.

Jewish Guests: In most cases it is enough to avoid serving pork, ham, bacon or shellfish, but as some Jewish people follow fairly strict dietary laws, to be on the safe side it is best to avoid a meat dish, a soup made with meat stock or a savoury containing aspic jelly. This still leaves a wide choice of vegetable soups, hors d'oeuvre or fruit to start with, and fish, salads, eggs or vegetarian dishes as a main course. Desserts present no problem if you have not served meat (strict Jews will not eat meat and dairy products at the same meal), but remember to avoid dishes made with gelatine. You can use butter, vegetable oil, Kosher margarine or cooking fat (not lard) in the preparation of the meal.

There are various Jewish cookery books which give guidance on the choice of foods and some interesting recipes. The following are good: *Jewish Cookery*, by Leah W. Leonard (André Deutsch); *The Jewish Home*, by Evelyn Rose (Vallentine, Mitchell).

Muslims (Moslems, Mohammedans): Strict Muslims avoid pork, shellfish, etc., and are not permitted to take alcohol. It is therefore best to avoid serving anything cooked in alcohol, including desserts made with a liqueur. However, since the dietary laws are not always slavishly followed, don't register surprise if a Muslim guest takes a glass of wine. *A Book of Middle Eastern Food*, by Claudia Roden (Nelson), has an excellent chapter on Muslim dietary customs.

Buddhists: It is best to avoid all meats, as most Buddhists are vegetarian.

Hindus: The cow is sacred to Hindus, so don't serve beef in any form (including soup).

Vegetarians: Generally speaking, vegetarians do not eat any meat, poultry, or fish. Vegans (a very strict vegetarian sect) will not even eat eggs, milk, or any food of animal origin. Good handbooks are: *Vegetarian Cuisine*, by Isabel James (from The Vegetarian Society of London, 53 Marloes Road, London, w8 6oD); *Simply Delicious*, by Rose Elliot (The White Eagle Publishing Trust, New Lands, Liss, Hants.; also available from the Vegetarian Society).

Diabetics: You'll find that most diabetics manage their own diet discreetly and without fuss: in fact, you probably won't know you're entertaining one, but if you *are* aware that one of your guests is a diabetic, remember that carbohydrates and sugar are the things they'll want to keep to a minimum, so serve consommé rather than a thickened cream soup, and a straightforward roast or grilled meat with vegetables for the main course, with cheese as an alternative to dessert.

Other Health Hazards: People with ulcers won't eat curry or highly spiced foods. Many people are allergic to oysters and other shellfish, so these should never be served without an alternative choice, and never in disguise and unannounced, so to speak, unless you're sure you are on safe ground.

'How Do I Serve it?'

Some of the most delicious things are difficult to eat tidily, but you can at least present your guests with the right equipment or prepare the food as helpfully as possible. If you are in doubt about the best things to provide, here's a brief check list for the foods that cause most doubt.

Artichokes, Globe. Although the outer leaves are eaten in the fingers, a small knife and fork are necessary for the 'choke'. Provide individual small plates or bowls for the discarded leaves. Finger bowls are a help here, too. (Incidentally, even if you haven't special bowls, you might be able to gather together enough matching glass dishes to serve the purpose.)

Asparagus: If served as a separate course, asparagus is eaten in the fingers, each spear being dipped in melted butter, sauce or dressing, which is poured on the side of the plate. It helps if, when you cook the asparagus, you leave part of the firm stalk to serve as a 'handle'. Lay a small knife and fork to be used to retrieve any of the tips which may break off. Finger bowls are a help, but if you haven't got these, provide thick table napkins.

Avocado: Serve these on a small plate, with a teaspoon. It's quite in order to use your left hand to steady the avocado.

Corn on the Cob: It is easier to eat this vegetable tidily with special holders to spear into each end of the cob, instead of grasping it in the fingers. Whether or not you provide holders, a small knife and fork should also be laid – the knife to spread the butter, and a fork to help with the last bits. It's very difficult to eat this vegetable elegantly, and almost impossible if your teeth are not your own.

Melon: Your guests will find it much easier to eat melon if it's been pre-cut into bite-size pieces and arranged back on the skin. Provide a fruit knife and fork, which is also the best equipment if you have not pre-cut the melon. For the little Charentais or Ogen melons which are served cut in halves, provide a teaspoon.

Chicken in a Basket: Fingers only, so have plenty of thick paper napkins, and finger bowls if you can manage it (or disposable plastic gloves, Corner House fashion).

Gulls' and Quails' Eggs: Serve hard-boiled and in their shells, for your guests to peel the eggs themselves, dip them in salt or celery salt and eat in the fingers.

Pasta: Lay a spoon, fork and knife, and serve the pasta in a soup plate. The skilful will twist the strands round the fork in the bowl of the spoon, Italian style, others will use the knife and fork and then the spoon to get up the difficult bits. It doesn't matter which.

Lobster: It's probably more sensible to serve lobster as a salad or in some other way in which the flesh is taken out of the shell. If you serve lobster halves, crack the claws and provide a fish knife and fork.

Mediterranean Prawns: People will find it much easier to pull the shell off the prawn in the fingers, and then eat the flesh with the aid of a small fish fork, but you should lay both fish knife and fork, to meet all preferences.

Mussels (Moules Marinière): These are best eaten from a bowl or soup plate, with a fork to get the mussel out of the shell (while you hold the shell in your fingers) and a spoon for the liquor. A discard plate is essential, and finger bowls are a help.

Oysters: A small fork is all that is necessary.

Prawn or Lobster Cocktail: Put a teaspoon on the plate which holds the fish cocktail – this is the easiest implement with which to eat it.

Bouillabaisse: Serve this thick peasant fish soup with crusty bread, a spoon and a fork to facilitate breaking up the large bits of fish. Alternatively, you can pour the liquor off and serve it in a bowl, and then present the fish to be eaten with a fish knife and fork and bread.

French Onion Soup: A soup spoon is usually all that is needed for this soup.

Foods in Season

In the deep mid-winter, when you're thoroughly fed up with a diet of greens, 'tops' and battered old carrots, it's only natural to race over to the frozen or canned food counter, and come back with some golden sweet corn or delectable baby peas to relieve the monotony. But it isn't natural or economical to make this a habit all year round.

FRUIT

Apples, Bananas, Grapes, Grapefruit, Pears, Pineapple, Melons, Oranges: all year round
Apricots: May–August; December–February
Avocados: October–April
Blackberries: July–October
Black-currants: June–August
Cherries: June–August
Chestnuts: December–February
Cranberries: November–January
Damsons: August–October
Figs: September–December
Gooseberries: July–September
Mandarins: November–February; December–March
Nectarines: July–October
Peaches: January–October
Plums: December–October
Raspberries: May–August
Strawberries: January–August
Rhubarb (not strictly a fruit): December–June

GAME AND WILD BIRDS

Black Game: August 20–December 12
Duck (wild): August 1–March 1
Grouse: August 12–December 12
Hare: August 1–February 28
Partridge: September 1–February 8
Pheasant: October 1–February 1
Plover: October 1–March 15
Ptarmigan: August 12–December 12
Quail: All year
Rabbit: September 1–April 30
Snipe: October 1–March 1
Teal: October–February

Venison: July 1–February 28
Widgeon: October–February
Woodock: August 1–March 1
Wood Pigeon: August 1–March 15

FISH AND SHELLFISH

Cod: All year	Plaice: All year
Dab: All year	Salmon: Feb.–Aug.
Halibut: All year	Sole: All year
Herrings: All year	Trout: March–August
Mackerel: All year	Turbot: All year
Crab: All year	Prawns: All year
Lobster: All year	Scallops: Nov.–March
Oysters: Sept.–April	Shrimps: All year

POULTRY

Capon: All year	Goose: Sept.–Feb.
Chicken: All year	Guinea Fowl: All year
Poussin: All year	Pigeon: All year
Duck: March–Sept.	Turkey: Sept.–March

VEGETABLES, SALADS

Aubergines, Beetroot, Cabbage, Carrots, Onions, Potatoes, Turnips, Mushrooms, Spinach: all the year round.
Artichokes, Globe: March–November
    Jerusalem: March–July
Asparagus: September–June
Beans, French, February–March
    Broad: April–July
    Runner: June–September
Broccoli: October–April
Brussels Sprouts: September–March
Cauliflower: June to March
Celery: August to February, April–May
Celeriac: September–March
Courgettes: June–September
Leeks: September–April
Parsnips: September–April
Peas: May–October
New Potatoes: May–September
Lettuce (round), Endive, Cucumber, Watercress, Capsicums (peppers), Tomatoes, Radish: all the year round. Webb and Cos Lettuce: available during summer months

Wine Guide

Cooking With Wine

Cooking with wine or spirits means a lot more than brandy in the Christmas pudding or sherry in a trifle. Wine can give flavour and 'body' to innumerable sweet and savoury dishes, and is a 'must' for classics like Boeuf Bourguignonne, Chicken Marengo, Lobster Newburg, Zabaglione, and Crêpes Suzette. It's not an extravagance, either. Quite apart from the fact that you can use left-overs, it's an economical way of making cheap cuts of meat and fish moist and tender. That's why wine's used as a marinade, and why it so often gets added to stews and casseroles. But it's best not to get carried away by enthusiasm. You can kill a dish with kindness, and too much alcohol can smother rather than encourage existing flavours. More than one wine-based dish in any menu is a mistake, too, and a wine-based main course plus perhaps sherry in the soup or brandy in the trifle, gives a better balance.

Unless you're making an extra-special sauce, it's not worth wasting an expensive wine. Almost anything will do – even yesterday's sparkling wine that's lost all its sparkle. As well as red and white wines and the fortified wines, spirits and liqueurs are frequently used in cooking. Beer, ale, and cider are used less frequently, but even flat beer can be used up as long as it's not actually stale. So can the remains of any not-too-sweet sparkling cider, though still cider is always preferable.

There are no rigid do's and don'ts, though generally it's best to use dry wines for savoury dishes and to keep sweet or fruity wines or liqueurs for desserts. Full-bodied red wines like Burgundies and clarets, fortified wines like port, sherry, Madeira and Marsala, and also brown ale feel most at home in rich 'dark-meat' dishes like beef casserole and steak and kidney pie, with game and in spicy sauces for spaghetti. Light, dry white wines, vermouth and cider go best with poultry, veal and fish dishes. Sherry, port, and Madeira usually go in soups, as well as in some beef and ham dishes. Cider, too, teams up happily with ham. With-out cooking, wine gets added to consommé, aspic jelly, trifles, and other chilled sweets, to give them a delicious lift. French vermouth is the perfect choice for any dish calling for white wine and herbs. The notes below give more details – and if you're worried your guests may slide under the table as course succeeds course – rest assured: most of the alcoholic content gets driven off during the cooking, and it's only the flavour that stays to get mellower and mellower.

Here are the general methods of using wine in cooking:

1. *In a Marinade:* Combined with bay leaf, peppercorns, lemon rind, herbs, etc., and used to flavour meat, poultry or fish prior to cooking. Meat and poultry are best left for several hours in the marinade; put in a cool place, or in a covered container in the refrigerator, and turn the meat or poultry over once or twice. Fish gains a fine flavour after being left for an hour in a marinade based on sherry, French vermouth, or dry white wine.

Fresh raspberries or strawberries may be sugared, then marinaded for an hour or so in vodka or Champagne; a good cider may be used in the same way. Peaches, too, may be marinaded, but will probably not need sugar.

2. *In Stews, Casseroles, and Braises* – and for a *court-bouillon* – wine is added at the start of the cooking, usually in the proportion of half wine to half stock.

3. *In Frying or Grilling,* to make a glaze. Cook the food completely – plain or marinaded – then add the wine to the juices in the pan and heat rapidly for a few minutes. Pour over the hot food and serve.

4. *In Sauce-making:* The wine and any other liquor is reduced considerably and then added to a basic sauce, or it may be simply thickened with egg yolk and cream.

5. *In Flambé dishes:* Gently heat some brandy or other spirit in a ladle, spoon or tiny pan, ignite with a match, then pour the whole over the hot food and let the flame spread by

agitating the pan. When the flames have died down a delicious concentrated essence is left.

6. *To Flavour without cooking:* Add sherry, port, or Madeira to a clear soup before serving, stirring in a spoonful at a time and tasting for flavour.

Port used in moderation gives a subtle taste to aspic jelly.

White or red wine and a touch of brandy add sophistication to home-made jellies.

Trifle-sponges are enriched by being soaked in sherry and fruit juices; sherry is appropriate, too, in a chilled sweet soufflé.

Marsala is good with egg dishes and is the classic wine in Italian zabaglione.

White port may be used in custard sauces, trifles, fruit salad, and whipped cream.

A BRIEF GUIDE TO THE WORLD'S WINES

France

A. Bordeaux

The Bordeaux region is the most prodigious producer of fine wines in the world. The châteaux or properties run into many hundreds, and there is a vast variety in the character of the wine.

Claret (Red Bordeaux) – the red wine of the region.

Four principal districts are:

THE MEDOC, where the notable parishes or communes are Margaux, Saint Julien, Pauillac, and Saint-Estèphe. These are names worth asking about when you want a claret of delicacy and finesse for a special dinner party.

SAINT-ÉMILION, where the wines are full and fragrant.

POMEROL adjoins Saint-Émilion: the wines are noted for their distinctive bouquet.

GRAVES south of the Médoc, though best known in Britain for its white wines, produces some memorable red ones. The first claret known in this country, seven centuries ago, is likely to have come from *Château Haut-Brion* – one of the big four among the lordly clarets.

White Bordeaux

There are two main styles of this wine – Graves and Sauternes. GRAVES is a wine that comes in many tastes, from the quite dry to the very sweet. A good choice for beginners, if taken chilled with poultry or fish.

SAUTERNES are naturally sweet wines of quality. Among them, *Château D'Yquem* is the great one, the finest dessert wine. *Barsac* and *Monbazillac* are good-natured sweet wines that cost much less.

From *Entre-Deux-Mers* come medium-sweet white wines of that name (and also inexpensive red wines.)

B. Burgundy

This region produces an abundance of red and white wines, some of them ranking with the greatest in the world.

RED BURGUNDIES. Most of the great wines are grown in the area known as the Côte de Nuits, from Dijon in the north down to Nuits-Saint-Georges. These wines are full-bodied, with a superb bouquet, and at their best when they are really well matured. The commune of *Vosne-Romanée* produces some of the superlative ones. Most of the villages and towns in this area have annexed the names of their most famous vineyards. Among them are the wines of *Gevrey-Chambertin, Chambolle-Musigny, Vougeot, Nuits-Saint-Georges*, and *Vosne-Romanée*.

From *Aloxe-Corton*, just south of the Côte de Nuits, comes the delicate and beautiful wine of that name. In the area between Beaune and Chagny – known as the Côte de Beaune – the red wines are elegant and round, though less full-bodied than those from the more northerly vineyards. Names synonymous with good Burgundy and worth remembering are *Pommard, Volnay*, and of course *Beaune* itself.

BEAUJOLAIS. This most popular of red wines comes from the hilly district between Mâcon and Lyons. These wines are fruity and light, usually best drunk when they're young – after one or two years in the bottle. Remember the names of *Juliénas, Fleurie, Chenas, Moulin-à-Vent*, for instance, when you want a 'better' Beaujolais, for these are village names and the wine has indeed come from there. It may cost a shilling or two more, but it is well worth it.

WHITE BURGUNDIES. The best ones are not produced in large quantities. *Chablis* is the best known white Burgundy, and when indeed it comes from the place by which it is named, north-west of Dijon, it can be superb – bone-dry, very clear and light and perfect to drink with shellfish.

The other white Burgundies, which notably come from south-west of Beaune, are full, fruity, pale golden, and dry. The vineyard of *Montrachet* produces the finest of all white Burgundies and *Bâtard-Montrachet* is a great one too. *Puligny-Montrachet* and *Chassagne-Montrachet* are well-favoured wines that come from the area. *Pouilly-Fuissé*, *Meursault*, and white *Mâcon* can be wonderful wines – or just pleasant table wines that come in the more reasonable price ranges. There are also more white *Beaujolais* available here now – and very pleasant too.

C. Loire
A wide variety of red, white and rosé wines are grown down the length of this great river.
Muscadet is very dry and fresh, a white wine that is pleasant with shellfish.
Pouilly Fumé is a white wine of elegance and distinctive bouquet, not as dry as Muscadet.
Sancerre wines are light and fruity and when well chilled are delightful for summer drinking.
Anjou is a rather sweet rosé wine: *Vouvray* a medium-dry sparkling wine or a good rather sweet still wine.

D. Rhône
From this part of France – below Lyons and extending down almost to Avignon – come the very robust and full-bodied red wines of *Hermitage* and *Châteauneuf-du-Pape*. Also the young medium-dry rosé wines of *Tavel* and *Lirac*.

E. La Champagne
This is the region of France where the grapes are grown for Champagne.

Unlike most of the other great wines of France, Champagne is not known by the names of the vineyards, but by the names of the numerous houses which make the wine. Vintage Champagne is of a year selected as of outstanding quality, non-vintage a blend from different years.

Note. Other sparkling French white wines, made by the Champagne method (*la méthode champenoise*) come from Burgundy, the Rhône and the Loire, and are certainly worth trying.

They usually cost much less than Champagne, but are excellent celebration drinks.

F. Alsace
The delicate wines from this beautiful part of France are sold under the name of the grapes from which they are made, these are:
Sylvaner: Agreeable, light, dryish.
Riesling: Distinguished, delicate, and sometimes full-bodied.
Traminer and *Gewürztraminer:* Much more full-bodied and fruity, the latter being especially spicy.
Muscat d'Alsace: A dry, spicy table wine, not to be confused with the rather cloying dessert wine usually associated with the Muscat grape. All of these wines drink very well with fish and light poultry dishes.

Germany
A. Hock
This is the name generally used in English-speaking countries for the white wines of the Rhineland: it is a corruption of the name of the village of Hochheim. The wine is made notably from the *Riesling* grape, from the *Sylvaner* or the *Scheurebe* which comes from the crossing of the vine stocks of the other two.

Names on labels are very important when you're buying hocks – if you don't study them you can be very disappointed or surprised, for the wines can range from a light and dryish type to the full sweetness of a dessert wine. *Liebfraumilch*, for instance, is one of the most popular hocks in this country. It derives its name from the Church of Our Lady at Worms, but none of the wine comes from there nowadays. It is in fact an invented name for any blend of German table wine, and that is why it is important to enquire of your reputable wine merchant about the best kind of Liebfraumilch. As with Beaujolais, the extra shilling or so can make all the difference to your enjoyment.

The important wine districts of the Rhineland are:
The Palatinate. The sunny, southernmost part, where the wines mature early and are round, mellow and sweet: good with spicy foods.

Important localities are *Deidesheim, Forst, Wachenheim,* and *Bad Dürkheim.*

Rheingau. Where the aristocratic hocks come from – slower in maturing, achieving delicate elegance and bouquet. The finest – and most expensive – are bottled on the estates where they are grown, e.g. *Schloss Vollrads, Schloss Hochheim, Schloss Johannisberg.*

Rheinhessen. The hocks from this area – which falls geographically between the Palatinate and Rheingau – are never quite as sweet as the former, but have some of the maturing quality of the latter.

Niersteiner and *Nachenheimer* are the finest, full of scent and flavour.

Nahe. The wines from this area, which are comparatively little known in Britain, are often said to be reminiscent of both the Rhine and the Moselle. *Kreuznacher* and *Schloss Bockelheim* are distinguished examples.

B. Moselle

The white wines of the Moselle, which is a tributary of the Rhine, are less grand than the hocks, but their fragrance is ineffable. They have a green delicacy and are best drunk when they are young. At table they are at their best with simple fish dishes or with plain grilled veal or lamb. Some of the Moselle wines make leisurely apéritifs for a sunny evening. Among the finest – and names to look out for – can be those from *Wehlen, Piesport,* and *Berncastel.*

Glossary: Both hocks and moselles are the better enjoyed for knowing even more about the terms of reference that appear on the bottle. For instance:

Spätlese: Wine made from late-gathered grapes.

Auslese: From the specially selected late-gathered ripest grapes.

Beerenauslese: Wine made from grapes which have been left on the vine until they have shrivelled to wrinkled berries, full of sugar.

Trockenbeerenauslese. From the choicest grapes left on the vine longest of all, until they're like raisins.

Following the order in which they are listed above, each of the wines bearing such labels will be richer, mellower, sweeter than the last; the last two indeed are natural liqueurs and are usually very highly priced. Hocks with these appellations can be very perfumed and even heavy; Moselles keep more sweetness of taste and smell.

C. Franconian

These white wines – which come in flat, oval green flasks, unlike the classic hock and Moselle bottles – are produced on the banks of the Main. They are very robust, less fragrant than Rhine wines. The most famous is *Steinwein* from Wurzburg.

Italy

A. Red Wines

Chianti, the most famous Italian wine, is made near Florence, in the heart of Tuscany. Wine from a now-extended area is entitled to be called *Chianti Classico,* and being bottled there, carries a black cock on its label. This wine is of a vivid crimson colour, sunny aroma, and robust flavour. There are also pleasant white chiantis.

Valpolicella is called the claret of the Veronese: at its best it is ruby-red, dry, and fresh. It is pleasant when young, but is also worth keeping to mature.

Barolo is a full-bodied but not heavy wine from villages near Alba; it is rather reminiscent of red Burgundy.

Barbera is a pleasant wine of Piedmont, of a rich garnet colour and with an almost smoky bouquet.

B. White Wines

Soave di Verona is one of Italy's best dry white wines – drunk in Venice with scampi.

Frascati wines are full bodied and honey-coloured, and can be dry, medium or sweet.

Orvieto is pale gold, fragrant and in its most popular form fairly sweet and full-bodied, but there is also a refreshing dry type.

Lacryma Christi made on the slopes of Vesuvius, is rather sweet, golden in colour – nice after dinner in sunny Italy.

Spain

Spain means Jerez, that is sherry – see later, under *Fortified Wines.*

However, good table wines, both red and white, come from the *Rioja* district. Their labels usually add a type name – claret, Burgundy, Sauternes or Chablis – which give a rough clue to their character.

Portugal

From the homeland of port wine (see *Fortified Wines*, later in this section) come honest table wines, some of them very reasonably priced.

Dao wines, red and white, have fullness and smoothness. They are gaining deserved popularity here, for they're very good value.

Vila Real table wines (from the Douro) red and white, are both very dry.

Vinhos Verdes are wines with a slight natural sparkle – called 'green' because of their extreme youth, but in fact white or red – pleasant when taken well-chilled as a before-dinner apéritif or drunk with fish.

The best known of the Portuguese rosés in this country, *Mateus*, also has a slight sparkle and can be served in the same way as the *vinho verde*. Both are imported in bottle and therefore rather more expensive.

Yugoslavia

Lutomer hock-style wines, from the district of that name, are excellent value. They carry the Riesling label – this type of grape has been growing in that part of the world for about a thousand years.

Zilavka is a white Burgundy-style wine, from inland of Dubrovnik.

Cabernet Brda, a soft red wine, comes from the Trieste region.

Ranina Radgona is a sweet, quite full-bodied white wine.

Hungary

Tokays, which are all estate-bottled, include the following kinds:

Tokay Aszu, the most renowned wine, delicate, sweet, and golden – a dessert wine.

Tokay Szamarodni, which also is pale golden, ranges from medium-dry to sweet.

Cheaper wines from Hungary are *Balatoni Riesling* and *Balatoni Furmint*, white with a touch of sweetness. *Bikaver* is a very dry red wine, otherwise known as Bull's Blood.

Other European Wines

AUSTRIA: From the Wachau district come: *Schlück*, a fresh, dry white wine, and *Trifalter*, rather more fragrant and sweet; both are good value, lower-priced table wines.

SWITZERLAND produces reasonable white wines, made from the Riesling grape, in the *Valais* region; the best-known of the red wines, *Dôle*, also comes from there.

GREECE: Largely for holiday reasons, more people have acquired a taste for the national resin-wine, *Retsina*. This and one or two red table wines, are available in Britain at reasonable prices.

Non-European Wines

AUSTRALIAN table wines are in the styles of Burgundy, the Rhône, Sauternes, and hock. A splendid list of Australian wines is available from the Australian Wine Centre in London; it is always up-to-date and the people there really know about the wines of their country.

SOUTH AFRICA supplies us with hock types, drier than those from Europe.

SOUTH AMERICA produces much red and white wine. Chile is sending more and more of her wines, reasonably priced ones, too, to Britain, notably a Cabernet red and a German-style white, fairly full, called *Steinwein*.

CALIFORNIAN wines are not widely available in Britain, though there are some Rieslings and, among the finer wines, a red, *Beaulieu's Special Reserve Cabernet*.

Sparkling Wines

Champagne is of its own quality and price, but there are other kinds of sparkling wines much in demand.

GERMAN sparkling wine is usually made by the blending of good hocks and Moselles and is called *Sekt*, often with a trade name attached.

ITALY'S sparkling wines are the famous sweet, white *Asti Spumante* and a red wine of *Valpolicella*.

FRANCE produces, in addition to the white sparkling wines already mentioned in the French section, some pink and red *Sparkling Burgundy* and *Muscatel*.

BRITAIN'S sparkling wine is *Moussec*, which is fermented and matured in England from French grape juice.

Fortified Wines

Wine is 'fortified' by the addition of spirit, usually brandy, which gives it a greater alcoholic strength.

PORT is made from grapes grown in the upper valley of the Douro river in Portugal. It is fortified with brandy at the time of the vintage. There are many types of port – red, white, and tawny in colour, and differing in style, strength, age, and sweetness. Vintage port, which is red, is the great dessert wine; it is shipped from Oporto about two years after the vintage, bottled in England and may then be left to mature for ten or even twenty years.

Wood ports are blends of wines of different years and ages which are matured in cask; they may be ruby, tawny, crusted or vintage character. Ruby is generally a blend of young wines, tawny a blend of older ones. White port, which can be sweet or dry, is now increasingly popular and dry white port makes a pleasant apéritif if chilled.

SHERRY, the glory of Spain, is made from white grapes grown in the Jerez district. It is usually, but not always, fortified with brandy. Sherry is a blend of wines, matured by what is called the Solera system, to ensure a continuing supply of wines of the same style and quality. Sherries initially divide themselves into two main categories:

FINO, which will be a dry sherry, and OLOROSO, which will be a full one.

Finos as they come to us are pale straw-coloured, dry and quite delicate. *Manzanilla* is a fino from near the sea, which accounts for its slightly sharp or salty flavour. *Amontillados* are strictly speaking finos which acquire body and colour with age and are blended as medium-dry wines. *Palo Cortado*, quite a rarity, is a wine mid-way between a fino and an amontillado. all of these wines make fine apéritifs, and many people prefer them lightly chilled.

OLOROSO is the basis of all sweet sherries. They are the wines usually sold as 'cream' sherry or 'golden' sherry. *Amoroso* is a sort of rich oloroso and usually slightly darker.

The darkness of a sherry is a clue to its sweetness. The darkest and sweetest of all is East India Brown, very rich in taste and essentially a dessert wine.

We get, too, some good South African sherries, made by the *solera* system, and only an expert could tell the difference between some of these and the less expensive Spanish ones.

MADEIRA, made and matured on the island of Madeira, is fortified by the addition of cane spirit. The wines are then blended and left for some years to mature. There are four basic types of Madeira, named after the grapes from which they are made. They are: *Sercial*, dry and pale: *Verdelho*, medium-dry, darker in colour: *Bual*, which is medium-sweet: and *Malmsey*, a rich, dark brown dessert wine that is slightly nutty.

MARSALA, the famous wine of Sicily, is made from a blend of local wines, brandy, and unfermented grape juice. Marsalas can be dry or sweet. This wine's particular distinction is in its use for two classic Italian dishes – *Scallopine alla Marsala* and the luscious sweet, *Zabaglione*.

Vermouths and Patent Apéritifs

The patent or brand-name appetizers are either wine-based or spirit-based. Vermouths are flavoured-and-fortified wines. In the broadest sense, there are two main kinds, still tending to be known as 'French' (dry) and 'Italian' (sweet), although nowadays both are made more in Italy than in France. Turin is, in fact, the capital city of vermouth.

French Vermouths
The most famous bone-dry white vermouth of France is *Noilly Prat*. It is with this or a similar dry vermouth, plus dry gin, that the dry martini cocktail is made.
Chambéry. A subtle regional vermouth from Haute Savoie. Nice to drink 'straight', slightly chilled.
Chamberyzette. A variant that is pink and perfumed with wild strawberries.

Italian Vermouths
These can be dry white, sweet white or sweet red. The reds (*rosso*) are used in a Manhattan cocktail, mixed with American whiskey. The sweeter version of white vermouth (*bianco*) is

nicest taken iced or with a dilution of soda and a twist of lemon, but can also be laced with gin or vodka. *Cinzano*, *Martini*, and *Gancia* are among the major Italian vermouth producers.

Other Wine-based Apéritifs

These are descended, like the vermouths, from concoctions of medicinal herbs, spices, and wine, but they also have quinine as an ingredient.

From France we get the following, all of them best served iced, with a twist of lemon peel:

Dubonnet: White or red.
St. Raphael: White or red.
Lillet: White.
Byrrh: Red.
From Italy comes Carpano's *Punt e Mes*, red and bitter-sweet.

SPIRIT-BASED APÉRITIFS include the following:

Campari: An Italian bitters, rosy-pink when served with ice and soda – and a twist of lemon.
Amer Picon: The French equivalent of Campari, very bitter and black to look at, too. English people like it with a measure of Grenadine, ice, and a dash of soda.
Suze: Very bitter, bright yellow, no stronger than the wine-based apéritifs, it is made basically from the root of the gentian and is rather a good restorative, drunk straight with a little ice.
Fernet Branca; Underberg. Two ferocious-looking and tasting medicinal bitters, recommended for hangovers.
Angostura is the best known of the 'bitters', used in drips only as for 'pink' gin and in many cocktails and other mixed drinks.

ANIS drinks – *Pernod*, *Pastis*, *Ricard*, and *Ouso* – should be taken well diluted with water, for they are very potent, though they taste sweetly harmless.

Choosing and Looking after Cheeses

You're either a cheese person or you aren't – and Orientals most emphatically aren't; they think cheese smells of corpses and decay, and wouldn't touch it with a chopstick. Come to that, some of it does, but the most powerful stench doesn't deter the cheese-lover.

Connoisseurs frown upon storing cheese in fridges, and ideally a cool, airy larder is the best place. But so long as the cheese goes into the least cold part, and *never* gets below freezing point, a fridge is the simplest solution for most people. Most cheeses manage quite happily when they're well-wrapped (individually, please!) in polythene or aluminium foil, and kept on the top shelf of the fridge. Pre-packaged cheeses, once they're opened, must be taken out of their original packs and wrapped in this way, too. Alternatively, the butter or egg compartments inside the fridge door are good storing places, if they're big enough. But only ever take out as much cheese as you are likely to need for a particular meal, because abrupt and frequent temperature changes can be disastrous. And above all, take it out several hours before you're going to eat it, so it can 'breathe' and develop its full flavour (not to mention bouquet!) like a good wine. However well-wrapped, cheese left out in a high temperature will come to grief. Firm and semi-firm cheeses will sweat all their fats away, and soft-ripened cheeses will first spread, then run, and finally harden and dry.

Basically, the more moisture a cheese has, the shorter its life. Hard, firm cheeses like Cheddar and Parmesan can last for months, but soft, runny cheeses like Camembert and Brie blossom briefly and die. The only way of making sure they don't spoil is to buy them in small quantities, to eat up at their best. Cottage and cream cheeses are as perishable as milk, and must be kept in the fridge or eaten promptly. And a word of warning for both your cheeses and other foods: keep mild cheeses away from strong-smelling foods – and strong cheeses from mild foods.

When you're using cheese in cookery, remember that the less actual cooking cheese has, the better. Over-heating tends to make it tough and indigestible; always heat it gently and for a short time only.

BRITISH CHEESES

Blue Vinney (Blue Dorset): White as chalk, with bright blue veins. A very strong table cheese of crumbly texture. It does not keep well.

Caerphilly: White, soft but firm, with a mild, milky flavour. Ripens quickly and needs to be eaten when it is about 10 days old. It is not a good cooking cheese. Originally Welsh, but now made in Devon, Somerset, Wiltshire, and Dorset as well.

Cheddar: One of the most versatile cheeses – excellent for table use and for cooking. At its best, nutty and sharp-flavoured, but unfortunately much Cheddar sold nowadays is mild, tasteless and rubbery – true mousetrap. Good Cheddars improve in flavour and texture with age. If you want the best, buy carefully from specialist cheese shops. Although it is traditionally English, there are first-class Canadian Cheddars available, and less exciting New Zealand and Australian varieties.

Cheshire: Another cheese which is good for both table use and cooking. It keeps in good condition for about 3–4 months. Available in three distinct varieties, probably the best known being Red Cheshire, coloured with a vegetable dye. This is mild but salty, with a rich texture. The white variety is mellow but less mild, the fullest-flavoured Cheshire is Blue-Red.

Derby: White, with a good tangy taste. Occasionally made with sage to give a special flavour. More solid than Cheshire, but flakier than Cheddar. Not at its best until 6 months old. Goes well with pineapple and in salads. Is also a good cooking cheese.

240

Prawn Pyramid; Salmon Trout or Grilse with Sauce Verte: pp. 123, 149

Double Gloucester: A distinctive pale vermilion-coloured table cheese, with a close, crumbly texture, and mild flavour. Should mature for at least 3 months and keeps well. Single Gloucester, which was pale yellow in colour, is no longer made commercially.

Dunlop: A Scottish cheese made originally in Dunlop, Ayrshire, but now fairly general throughout Scotland. It is not unlike Cheddar, but moister and of a closer texture.

Ilchester: Cheddar cheese ground and mixed with beer to a soft spreadable texture. Pleasant tangy taste. A good special-occasion table cheese rather than an everyday standby.

Lancashire: Rather similar to white Cheshire. Very soft and spreadable when young, but hardens with age. Mild, slightly acid flavour and splendid for Welsh Rarebit. Thought by some to be the best English cooking cheese.

Leicester: Even-textured, red-brown cheese, with a rich, tangy flavour. Popular dessert cheese, with excellent keeping qualities. Can be used in cooking.

Stilton: This dessert cheese is at its best eaten with bread, biscuits, and celery, and accompanied by port or a full-bodied red wine. To some people Stilton is the King of Cheeses and for them eating it is something of a ritual. In appearance Stilton is distinctive, light in colour with blue veining (there are some white Stiltons). In texture it is crumbly and it tastes sharp. Its flavour develops with age (ripening time 4–6 months). Stilton made with summer milk and eaten at Christmas is best. Buy a whole or half Stilton for perfection, but if you can't cope with so much cheese, buy it carefully, avoiding pieces with a stale-looking, brownish edge. Keep at room temperature.

Wensleydale: This mild, flaky cheese with a crisp, lingering flavour is a good cheese-board choice. Better for eating than cooking, though it is good for cheese dips. Only the white variety is available now, though at one time you could buy a superior blue-veined quality.

Soft Cheeses

The soft cheeses made in England are of the 'unripened' type. At one time there were various regional ones, known by such names as Cambridge, Slipcote, Smearcase and York.

Nowadays, they are usually known simply as cream cheese and cottage (or curd) cheese.

Cream Cheese: This term denotes cheese made from the cream of the milk, and there are two kinds: Double Cream Cheese is made from creamy milk with a high fat content (45–50 per cent), which is warmed, then left to go sour naturally, or soured by the addition of a 'starter'. It is then put to drain in muslin, and when solid is seasoned or flavoured and shaped into cakes. Single Cream Cheese is produced from creamy milk with 25–30 per cent fat content. It is made by a similar method to that used for the double type, but a cheese-making rennet is usually used to aid souring and obtain a good curd – this gives a more 'cheesy' flavour. These cream cheeses are made in small quantities, as they keep for 2–3 days only. Delicious either plain or flavoured with herbs or curry powder for spreads and a basis for dips.

Cottage or Curd Cheese: Made from skimmed milk by a similar method to that used for cream cheese. Rather tasteless, but good with salads, mixed with chopped fresh herbs, or flavoured for cocktail snacks, also in cheesecake.

Commercially-produced Soft Cheeses are mainly sold in packets and cartons, under brand names of the large dairy concerns, though some are sold loose, by weight. They are similar to Cream Cheese in taste and uses and can be used as an ingredient in desserts like cheesecake.

'Boursin' is a full-fat soft cheese, flavoured with *fines herbes*, garlic, or pepper, and is tastier than most packet cream cheeses. Essentially a table cheese, and a good choice for a cheese board.

Processed Cheeses

Firm Types: Manufactured to resemble in taste a number of the well-known and popular cheeses such as Gruyere, Cheddar, and Cheshire. Packaged in foil in individual wedges or cubes. Economical, dependable, but rather lacking in character.

Creamy Types: Made in a similar way to the firm cheeses, but with the addition of butter as well as emulsifying salts. The finished cheese is of a soft creamy texture and pale in colour; it often has an added flavouring such as chopped ham, shrimps, celery, herbs, garlic, etc., and it

Crab-and-Sweetcorn Soup;
Jade Spinach; Fried Beef and
Green Peppers; Almond
Chicken; Sweet–sour Fish;
Rice: pp. 119, 159, 141, 131, 152, 223

is usually sold in small portions (often individual size).

FOREIGN CHEESES

Supplies available in this country vary from time to time and from one locality to another; only the very largest shops can afford to stock a really comprehensive range, but the following kinds can all be obtained in one or other of the better grocers, provision shops, delicatessens, and supermarkets.

Alpestra (Alpin): Hard, dry cheese made in the French Alps.

Bel Paese: Soft, creamy, and rich, with a very mild flavour and somewhat rubbery texture, but nonetheless agreeable. A pleasant table cheese, can be used for cooking and is a good substitute for Mozzarella. Made in Italy.

Bondon: Small, cylindrical, whole-milk cheese from Normandy. When ripe has a fairly pungent flavour.

Bresse Bleu: French imitation of Gorgonzola; creamy-textured and strong-flavoured. Packed rather nicely in a round carton, which is convenient for keeping and serving; on the whole less satisfactory than Gorganzola at its best.

Brick: American; usually made in shape of a brick; semi-soft, with small holes; rather less sharp in flavour than Cheddar.

Brie: French, soft paste cheese; it has a reddish-brown 'mouldy' crust with white tracings and a pale yellow curd. Flavour is sharp and distinctive. It should be smooth and creamy, almost runny – avoid Brie which looks chalky. You can buy it in convenient-sized wedges though it is sometimes easier to select Brie in good condition when it is cut from a big flat round cheese. Don't attempt to keep it for more than a day or two. Excellent choice for a cheese-board. Best eaten with bread, accompanied by celery or radishes.

Cacciocavallo: Italian: name due to the fact that the roundish cheeses are strung together in pairs and dried suspended over a pole, as though astride a horse. If eaten fresh, the cheese has a tangy taste and firm, yet soft texture; if kept, it becomes hard and is then grated and used in cooking.

Camembert: A wonderful cheese if eaten in prime condition. Pale yellow, smooth and soft, tastes slightly bitter; its distinctive flavour strengthens as it ripens. It can be bought in one-portion wedges or as a whole small round cheese. Only buy it from shops with a good cheese counter – it can be horrid if it's dry. Like Brie, is essentially a table cheese to eat with fresh bread and crisp salad, accompanied by a full-bodied red wine.

Danish Blue: There are two types: Danablu, which is milk-white with a network of blue/green veins. Sharp, thirst-provoking, and very buttery. Mycella, which is yellow with green rather than blue veins. Milder and more aromatic, smooth and creamy.

Both are table cheeses and not for cooking. Delicious for cocktail titbits.

Demi-Sel: French cheese, pale in colour, mild in flavour; smooth, creamy, and buttery. Made from double or single cream and dried sufficiently to be cut with a knife. It will not keep. Demi-Sel is good for salads, cheesecake, and sandwiches, especially if flavoured with herbs.

Edam: Dutch cheese, with bright red rind and yellow inside. Mild but distinctive flavour. Very smooth, soft, even texture. It is not a very exciting cheese, but a good standby. Is best eaten in wafer-thin slices. Can be used for cooking, but has a tendency to go rubbery.

Emmenthal: Swiss (valley) cheese with a hard golden-brown rind and very smooth texture. Ivory yellow in colour, pitted with irregular holes. Strong, distinctive flavour, which is excellent for cooking. Very popular for Fondues and the French toasted cheese-and-ham sandwich called Croque Monsieur. Good, too, with salads. There is also a Danish Emmenthal.

Fontainebleau: French; creamy cheese, which is sometimes eaten with strawberries.

Fromage de Monsieur: French; white cheese, sold in small wooden boxes or loose – weighing 5–6 oz. Brie/Camembert type, but milder.

Gervais: French; cream cheese sold packed in boxes of 6 small portions.

Gorgonzola: Italian; semi-hard with creamy texture. It is blue-veined and normally has a strong flavour. However, there are mild varieties of Gorgonzola, the Dolcelatte, made from a sweet milk, being much milder in flavour than the ordinary type; between the two comes the kind known as creamy Gorgonzola. Another good cheese for a cheese-board, but buy carefully and avoid over-blue, stale-looking pieces.

Gouda: Dutch; pale in colour, darkening as it matures. Flavour improved with ageing. It is similar to Edam, but has a yellow rind. Like Edam, it is best eaten in thin slices. Goes well with crispbread or on pumpernickel. Tends to go rubbery when cooked.

Gruyère: Swiss (Alpine); similar to Emmenthal. Rind is slightly oily; holes are smaller and more even. More salty and pungent than Emmenthal, and considered by some to be superior. Excellent for cooking when a good flavour is needed. Used in cheese Fondues. Gruyère looks waxy, and can be dry, so buy it fresh. French Gruyère also available.

Havarti: Danish; semi-hard, small, irregular hole-pocked. Light golden-brown colour, mild, and creamy. Good for open sandwiches, cocktail bits with pineapple or grapes on a stick.

Kümmelkäse: German; caraway-flavoured; good with cocktails.

Limburger: Belgian or German; strong 'ripe' flavour and smell.

Marc de Raisin: French; pale creamy curd with a crust of grape skins and pips replacing the ordinary rind. Looks more exciting than it tastes – its flavour is bland, and it is not good for cooking.

Mozzarella: Italian; pale-coloured egg-shaped cheese, when fresh, very soft milk cheese dripping with buttermilk. Should be made from buffalo milk, but nowadays it's more often made from cow's milk. Should be eaten fresh; once the buttermilk has drained away, the cheese dries out and becomes stodgy. Although you can buy it fresh in the U.K., it is only available from specialist Continental shops. It is uninteresting to eat raw, but is splendid for pizzas, lasagnes and other Italian dishes. Bel Paese can be used as a substitute.

Munster: Alsatian; semi-hard cheese, which is good for both cooking and table use; not unlike Pont L'Évêque in flavour.

Mysost: Norwegian; whey cheese, principally made from goats' milk. Hard and dark brown, with a sweetish flavour.

Neufchâtel: French; whole-milk cheese; soft, dark yellow, similar to Bondon.

Parmesan: Italian; excellent flavour. Very dry, leaving a granular effect on the palate. Semi-fat cheese with slow melting rate. Matures for 2–3 years. Ideal for cooking and serving grated with soup and pasta dishes. It can be bought ready grated, but is often a little tasteles this way.

Petit Suisse: French; full-cream cheese, very mild, with little bite. Smooth and creamy, delicious with strawberries and a little sugar.

Pommel: French; a brand of double-cream cheese, similar to Petit Suisse.

Pont L'Évêque: French; semi-hard cheese, sold in small square boxes; delicious mild flavour somewhere between that of a Brie and a Camembert. It's not easy to find this cheese in first-class condition in this country.

Port de Salut: French; creamy yellow curd, golden rind. Mild flavour; requires warmth to mature. Inclined to be rubbery. Table cheese – flavour not strong enough for use in cooking.

Ricotta: Italian; a soft cheese made from ewes' milk. Unsalted, creamy flavour. Must be eaten fresh. Delicious when pounded up and used for gnocchi and ravioli. Used widely in sweet dishes, with fruit. Demi-Sel or Primula cheese can be substituted for Ricotta, which you may not be able to find in fresh condition.

Roquefort: French; white with blue veins; made from ewes' milk. This delicious cheese has a sharp, pungent flavour and a soft, creamy, crumbly texture. A little salty for some people's taste. Very good for salads, mixed with the dressing or used for stuffing raw tomatoes.

Samsoe: Danish; firm-textured, with regular holes, golden in colour; mild and sweet in flavour. Danbo is a small, square-shaped version; Fynbo, Elbo, and Tybo are other variants fairly similar in type. Molbo has a richer, more fruity flavour; Maribo is also more full flavoured. Ideal for sandwiches and cooking.

Smoked Cheese: Austrian; brown skin, pale curd, sold in small rounds or 'sausages'. Mild and smoky, with a very smooth and soft texture. Table cheese – excellent with wine.

Herbs and Spices

These romantic ingredients (unromantically used in the past to disguise food that wasn't fresh) are swinging back into favour. Refrigeration, the very discovery that made them almost redundant for one purpose, has made them essential again with food that's 'too fresh'. Battery-bred poultry, for instance, lacks flavour more because it's been quick-frozen than because of the method of production.

HERBS

Obviously, fresh herbs are best. They're not difficult to grow in gardens, and chives, mint, parsley, thyme, and sage will even grow happily in window-boxes – though the mint goes on the rampage if you let it. Dried herbs are second-best, but a very good second-best when used properly. Generally speaking, they're far stronger-flavoured and more concentrated, and you will usually need only half the amount as compared with fresh herbs – e.g., if a recipe calls for 1 tsp. fresh thyme, you will use only $\frac{1}{2}$ tsp. dried thyme. Take particular care with the more pungent ones such as rosemary, thyme, sage.

For drying your own, pick the fresh herbs on a dry morning, just before they begin to flower. Dry them as quickly as possible in a warm, dry place (several hours), or even in a slow oven (about 1 hour). Rub off the crisp, dry leaves and store in airtight jars away from direct light. This, alas, rules out most of the pretty glass herb jars around, because unless they're made of dark smoked glass, light will damage the flavour and fragrance of their contents almost as much as air, damp or extreme heat.

Bought dried herbs should be kept in the containers in which they come, unless these are obviously unsuitable. Store as above – they will keep for up to 6 months.

Especially for dressings or sauces, dried herbs can be coaxed to truer flavour by marinading them in a little stock, lemon juice, wine, vinegar or milk – whichever suits the recipe – for anything from 10 minutes to 1 hour before using. Alternatively, simmer the herbs in a little hot butter before adding to a sauce – or, if you're making an omelette, add the dried herbs to the beaten eggs and allow to stand for a while before cooking. Whether fresh or dried, delicate herbs should only be added to stews and soups towards the end of the cooking, so they don't have time to lose their flavour. Even the stronger herbs, such as savory and tarragon, like being added towards the end, too, to give a more distinctive flavour.

A Bouquet Garni is simply a combination of herbs, either tied together, or when dried, put in a muslin bag, so that they can easily be fished out before serving. The combination is really up to you. At its simplest, it can be a sprig of thyme, some stalks of parsley, and a bay leaf. For long, slow meat stews, more aromatic bouquets are often used, with mixtures like chervil, basil, tarragon, rosemary, and dried celery seed. Here is a typical recipe:

Bouquet Garni (Fresh Herbs)

2 sprigs of parsley	1 sprig of thyme
2 sprigs of chervil	$\frac{1}{2}$ a bay leaf
1 sprig of marjoram	

Tie together with cotton, or tie in a small square of muslin. Use in stocks, casseroles, stews and sauces, removing before the dish is served.

Notes. Dried herbs may also be combined (usually with some spices) to make a bouquet garni – tie them in a square of muslin. A usual mixture is a small bay leaf, a pinch of mixed herbs, a pinch of dried parsley, 6 peppercorns and 1 clove.

Ready-prepared bouquets garnis made from dried herbs may be bought in sachets resembling tea-bags.

Fines Herbes again consist simply of a combination of herbs – though finely chopped this time. But in practice, the combination is usually parsley, chervil, tarragon, and chives, and it's most commonly used in omelettes. When the herbs are fresh, the omelette can be made really green with them, but with dried ones, ½ level teaspoonful of the mixture is plenty for a four-egg omelette.

Mixed Herbs are usually a combination of dried parsley, tarragon, chives, thyme, and chervil.

See the chart overleaf for herbs and their uses.

SPICES

Most spices come from faraway places, so the nearest any of us get to 'fresh' is grating our own nutmeg, or grinding our own curry powders. This last is well worth the pestle-and-mortar performance, because ready-mixed curry powders are second-rate rather than second-best. If that sounds too dedicated, a sensible compromise is to buy the separate ready-ground spices and combine them into curry powder yourself, because then you can be sure the ingredients aren't 'padded out'.

For a *meat curry* (but do vary this according to what you are cooking and your personal taste), try: 1 level dessertspoonful of coriander seed; 2 level dessertspoonfuls of turmeric; ½ level teaspoonful each of cinnamon and mace; 1 level dessertspoonful of cumin seed; ½ level tablespoonful of cardamom seed; ½ level teaspoonful each of grated ginger, cayenne pepper, and chili powder; 1 clove, ground; a suspicion of allspice (pimento), black pepper and nutmeg – plus some dried chillies if you like your curry very hot.

For a *fish curry*, try: 2 level dessertspoonfuls of coriander seed; 1 level dessertspoonful turmeric; 1 level teaspoonful of black pepper; 1 level teaspoonful of cumin seed; ½ level tea-spoonful each of cayenne pepper and ground ginger.

Best way to use both these curry mixtures is to cook a chopped onion and some crushed garlic in plenty of melted butter until soft and golden, and then add the spices, cooking for at least another 5 minutes before the meat or fish is added. For the curry powder quantities we've described, allow 1–1½ lb. of meat, and 1½–2 lb. of fish.

The chart which follows gives details of spices, with many more uses to supplement the usual example of cloves in an apple pie!

Sodium Glutamate (Monosodium Glutamate)

This is extracted from a cereal source and is sold in powder or crystal form. It has a slightly sweet-salty flavour, and when added to foods such as meat, poultry or fish, it intensifies or enhances the natural flavour. It has been increasingly added to manufactured meat, fish and other savoury products, and is present in many Chinese foods. If taken to excess it can cause an unpleasant but usually short-lived sensation or condition which has been given the name of Kwok's disease. In any case it is not a good idea to add sodium glutamate to too many savoury dishes, as it tends to make everything taste rather similar. However, it is a useful standby for improving the flavour of soups, etc., that might otherwise be a little lacking in taste and character. It is available for domestic use as a powder, sold under such names as 'Ac'cent', and occurs as an ingredient in some special seasonings such as 'seafood spice' and 'barbecue spice'.

HERBS

NAME	CHARACTERISTICS	USED PARTICULARLY FOR	OTHER DISHES
Balm	Fragrant leaves, with Lemon scent and flavour	Punches, fruit drinks	Soups, sauces, stuffings
Basil	Pungent, sweet; has a flavour of cloves and orange peel, with a minty after-taste. Use sparingly. Cooking enhances its flavour; does not lose pungency when dried	Tomatoes	Cold rice salads; lamb's liver, lamb chops; basil butter
Bay	Very mild and sweet but distinctive flavour, sometimes called musky. Leaves may be used straight from the tree, or dried. Use sparingly	Included in *bouquets garnis* Meat and fish casseroles; marinades for poultry and game. Remove before serving dish	Bolognese sauce; soups, stews; soused herrings. Infuse in milk to be used for sauces. Sweet dishes, especially milk puddings
Borage	Both leaves and blue flowers are used; they give a faint cucumber flavour	To flavour claret cup and iced drinks; the flowers make a pretty garnish	Salads
Capers	Pickled flower-buds of the caper bush	Sauce served with boiled mutton and some fish	Mayonnaise, salads
Chervil	Delicate, sweet taste, fragrant aroma. Used similarly to parsley. May be used generously	Sauces, such as parsley, Hollandaise; for salads. Important ingredient of *fines herbes*	Omelettes, especially cheese. Sauces for fish, poultry. Sprinkle on buttered vegetable
Chives	Member of the onion family, the tender, narrow leaves being used. They are delicately flavoured, best used when freshly cut	Flavouring salads and dressings; used chopped or minced	As garnish for soups and other savoury dishes
Dill	Two forms of the same plant — weed and seed. Mild, aromatic, slightly sweet caraway flavour. Use fairly generously. More pungent when dried	Seed in pickles; cucumber and soured cream, in lemon butter; weed with grilled or poached fish, e.g., salmon, halibut	Seed in potato salad, cucumber sandwiches, cole slaw, bread rolls, apple pie, and with veal, pork. Pleasant on new potatoes
Fenne	Seeds: sweet, with flavour resembling aniseed or liquorice. Use fairly generously, but remember it is more pungent when dried.	Boiled fish, oily fish — counteracts the richness; tie the seeds in muslin; sauces; salad dressings	With roast pork; with apples in any form. In Scandinavian countries it is used fresh as garnish
Garlic	Bulb of a plant of the onion family; each bulb is really a collection of smaller ones, called 'cloves'. Will keep for months in a dry place; not impaired when some cloves are removed. Has a powerful acrid taste; use sparingly. Available also powdered and as garlic salt	Soups, stews, re-heated savoury dishes, curries, sauces, gravies	Salad dressings — mere suggestion only — it is often sufficient to rub the bowl round, with a cut clove

HERBS

NAME	CHARACTERISTICS	USED PARTICULARLY FOR	OTHER DISHES
Horse-radish	Plant with a pungent, acrid-flavoured root, which is grated for use	Flavouring sauce or cream to serve with roast beef and with smoked or freshwater fish	Include in sandwiches. Use to flavour salad dressing
Lemon Thyme	Aromatic plant with a lemon flavour	Flavouring stuffings, (especially for veal), salads, fish dishes	Sometimes used as a substitute for true lemon flavour
Marjoram	Spicy, slightly bitter, nutmeg flavour. Can replace basil in meat dishes. Use rather sparingly; more pungent when dried	Sprinkled over meat — roast, stewed, grilled, fried — and in meat soups	In stuffing for meat, poultry, and fish, with buttered vegetables
Mint	One of the most widely grown herbs; about 14 varieties (e.g. spearmint, curly, pennyroyal). Less pungent when dried	Mint sauce to serve with lamb; flavouring for new potatoes and peas. Mint jelly is a popular alternative to sauce	Other vegetables, tomatoes, pea soup, scrambled eggs. Garnish for wine and fruit cups
Oregano	Wild marjoram, used widely in Italian cookery	Interchangeable with marjoram as flavouring for meats, sausages, soups	In salads
Parsley	Mild, pleasant flavour. Very widely employed, and may be used quite generously	Essential ingredient of *fines herbes*. Sauces for boiled ham and bacon, fish, chicken; soups. Garnish	Mashed and new potatoes; egg dishes; rissoles; stuffings. Parsley, butter
Rosemary	Pungent, aromatic, sweet. Use with care. Less pungent when dried	Roast lamb (sprinkle over before cooking), lamb stews; when simmering meat and poultry	With veal chops or steaks; in creamy soups. May also be used in scones and in some sweet dishes
Sage	Bold flavour, slightly bitter: use sparingly. Good with rich, oily meats — said to aid digestion	Pork (including sausages) and stuffings for pork, veal, duck; in Italian and French Provençal dishes	Minced meat, fish dishes; spinach, beans, aubergines. Delicious with cream cheese as a sandwich spread
Savory	Two varieties — summer and winter. Distinctive but pleasant pungent, peppery flavour. Use with care. Keeps flavour when dried	Omelettes	Eggs, tomato sauce, veal, turkey, fish (use with marjoram and/or thyme). Summer variety, in conserves and syrups
Sorrel	Wild plant with strongly acid flavour. Use sparingly, when young and fresh	Lettuce and other salads and some sauces	May be cooked like spinach, or mixed with it. Can be used to make a soup
Tarragon	Two culinary types — French and Russian. Strong aromatic flavour; use sparingly. Less flavour when dried	One of the *fines herbes*. Used in sauces such as Hollandaise, Bearnaise, Tartare; wine vinegar; marinades; with egg dishes	With fish and shellfish; salads; chicken dishes such fricassees; meat stews
Thyme	Strong, pungent, aromatic, rather clove-like. Many varieties. Use sparingly. More aromatic when dried	Meat — beef, lamb, veal — rub it in before roasting	Soups, stuffings and forcemeat for mutton and chicken; with hare. Use with wine-cooked dishes

S P I C E S ,   E T C .

NAME	DESCRIPTION	USES, ETC.
Allspice (also called Pimento and Jamaican pepper)	Small dried berries resembling smooth peppercorns. Aroma recalls that of cloves, cinnamon and nutmeg	Whole: for meat, broths, pickling Ground: fruit cakes, pies, relishes, and preserves. Delicious with tomatoes, carrots
Aniseed	Small seeds of the Anise plant, which contain a volatile oil with a warm, sweet, aromatic taste and odour	The extracted oil is used to flavour sweets, liqueurs, and cordials (and has certain medicinal uses)
Caraway Seed	Small, brown and hard; curved in shape, tapering at the ends	In rye bread and other baked loaves and cakes; in cheeses; scattered over pork dishes, soups, meats, and stews
Cardamom Seed	Member of the ginger family. Available with or without the pod and whole or ground. Use seed sparingly	Use to flavour apple and pumpkin pies and curries
Cassia	The inner bark of a type of cinnamon tree; resembles cinnamon; but is coarser and less expensive	Can be used in same ways as cinnamon
Cayenne	Prepared from the smallest, hottest chillies, which vary in colour from red to yellow. A very hot, pungent pepper	Use (with restraint) to flavour meats and sauces, eggs, fish, and vegetables in curries
Celery Seeds	Ground aromatic seeds of a plant related to vegetable celery	In stews and other meat dishes, fish dishes, salads, pickling spice
Chillies (*powdered*)	The whole chilli pepper, crushed or ground. Hot, nippy flavour. (Not to be confused with chilli powder)	Use (with discretion) in tomato, meat and spaghetti dishes
Cinnamon	Pungent, sweet spice, available as bark (rolled in slender 'sticks') or ground	Ground cinnamon: used widely in baking, for cakes, buns and biscuits, and in pies Stick form is used in sugar syrups for preserves, in pickling vinegars and in beef stews
Clove	Available whole or ground. Distinctive pungent aroma	Whole: used to stud ham and pork, when pickling fruits, in spicy sweet syrups, in stews, and meat gravy Ground: used in baked goods, desserts, chocolate mixtures. Cloves enhance sweet vegetables, beets, sweet potatoes, baked onions
Coriander Seed	Mild, delicately flavoured; available whole or ground. Used in every curry powder formula	A baking spice, used as flavouring for buns, pastries, biscuits, and cakes
Cumin Seed	In appearance and aroma similar to caraway. Available whole and ground. One of the chief ingredients in chilli and curry powder	Add to pork and cheese dishes
Fenugreek	A leguminous plant resembling celery in flavour	The ground seeds are used in curry powder and chutneys
Ginger (Crystallized and preserved gingers are made from fresh roots and are confections rather than spices)	Available whole, cracked or ground. Requires about 30 minutes' cooking to release all the flavour	Ground: in baked goods; rubbed into meats, poultry, and fish; in ginger ale Whole or cracked: in syrups and pickling vinegar

SPICES, ETC.

NAME	DESCRIPTION	USES, ETC.
Juniper Berries	The fruit of the Juniper tree – small, dark purple-blue berries	Used to flavour gin, in stuffing for game and with pork and mutton.
Mace	The membrane or aril surrounding the nutmeg seed. Used ground or in 'blade' form	Ground: in Pound Cake, cherry pie, in fish sauces and in sausage-making Blade: in pickling and preserving
Mustard	Three kinds of mustard seed – white, black, and brown. The black and brown seeds contain the oil which gives the piquant flavour. White seeds have less flavour, but keep better	Use to flavour sauces, pickles, meat, and cheese dishes, and as a condiment to accompany beef, ham, bacon, etc.
Nutmeg	The pit or seed of the nutmeg fruit, with a sweet and delicate flavour. Available ground and whole (for grating as required)	In baked goods, puddings, sauces, vegetables, and beverages. Try nutmeg in chicken soup or veal fricasee; mixed with butter for corn or spinach
Paprika	Bright red powder. There are two varieties, with a sweet mild flavour or with a slight bite	A 'garnish' spice – used to give an appetizing appearance to salads, fish, meat, chicken, soup, eggs
Pepper (See also Cayenne and Paprika)	Most widely-used spice. It promotes the appetite and digestive processes. *White:* Berries are picked when fully ripe and the kernels are ground *Black:* The unripe berries are cured (dried) until dark brown or black. Available whole or ground. Stronger and more aromatic than white. *Coralline* is made from a mild variety of red pepper, finely ground	General seasoning agent. Used in manufacture of food products, especially in curing meats and seasoning sausages

Generally used for decorating |
Peppercorns	Unground pepper seeds – retain their flavour better than ground pepper	Used in *bouquet garni* and pickles
Poppy Seeds	Small deep-blue seeds of a type of poppy, with a mild but distinctive flavour	Sprinkled on top of bread and cakes as a decoration, and used as a flavouring in Continental pastries
Saffron	A yellow powder with aromatic, slightly bitter taste; made from the flower stigmas of a type of crocus	Used for flavouring and colouring buns, cakes and rice. Very expensive but normally only a pinch is needed
Turmeric	Dried and ground roots of a plant of the ginger family. Yellow-orange colour; aromatic, slightly bitter flavour	An essential ingredient of curry powder and also used in pickles

Spice Mixtures, Flavoured Salts, etc.

NAME	DESCRIPTION	USES, ETC.
Barbecue Spice	Blend of onion, salt, monosodium glutamate, garlic, and tri-calcium-phosphate	Use to sprinkle on grilled or barbecued foods — steaks, hamburgers, kebabs, cutlets, poultry. Add to marinades
Seafood Spice	Blend of herbs and spices with onion and tri-calciumphosphate	Sprinkle on fish during frying and grilling or add to sauces used to coat fish fillets or steaks
Chilli Powder (not to be confused with powdered chillis)	Blend of spices, with chilli pepper as basic ingredient, plus ground cumin seed, ground oregano, powdered garlic, and usually salt. Other seasonings may be added, e.g. ground cloves, ground allspice	Basic seasoning for chilli con carne. Good in shellfish and oyster cocktail sauces, with hard-boiled and scrambled eggs, minced meat or hamburgers
Curry Powder	Rich golden powder, a blend of many spices — cayenne, coriander, turmeric, cumin, ginger, mace, clove, cardomon, fenugreek, and pepper. Very distinctive flavour; the degree of 'heat' depends on the blend	For curries made with eggs, fish, shrimps, poultry, meat, vegetables; French dressing, mayonnaise, soups, salted nuts
Curry Paste	Same spices and uses as curry powder, but mixed to a thick paste with either clarified butter or vinegar	
Celery Salt	Table salt plus ground celery seed	Imparts a celery flavour to many dishes — soups, stews, salads, meat, and poultry dishes. (Reduce ordinary salt proportionately.)
Garlic Salt	Table salt plus powdered garlic	Use discreetly to improve the flavour of meat dishes, salads, and sauces. (Reduce ordinary salt proportionately.)
Savoury Seasoning Salt	Consists of salt, monosodium glutamate, sugar, herbs, onion, garlic, spices, tri-calcium phosphate	Used to heighten the flavour of sauces, soups, stews, salad dressings, marinades, omelettes, etc. (Reduce ordinary salt proportionately.)
Seasoned Pepper	Mixture of black pepper, spices and sugar	For flavouring and garnishing savoury dishes, and as a condiment

Store-Cupboard Notes

Ignoring family jokes about stocking up for a siege, kit out your store-cupboard with basic ingredients that will see you through Unexpected-Guest crises – and also save you extra trips to the shops when your memory fails.

If you're lucky enough to have an old-fashioned walk-in larder, this is the ideal place for dry foods and cans, which like dry, cool and ventilated surroundings. Otherwise, a kitchen cupboard with good interior fittings can pack away masses in a minimum of space. But however tempting it is when you're in a hurry to grab the first can or packet that comes to hand, it's vital to use your stocks in strict rotation.

Dry Stores

Packaged dry ingredients can be kept quite safely in their original packets – but once they've been opened, it's best to transfer the contents to a storage jar with a well-fitting lid. Really air-tight lids are also essential for strong smelling foods like coffee, herbs and spices that otherwise lose their aroma, and for things like salt and baking powder, that absorb moisture and can become caked. Cereal products like flour and semolina keep well, but if you live in the country, watch out for possible insect infestation. Wholemeal flour and oatmeal won't last indefinitely, because their high fat content results in rancidity after a while. The same is true of nuts, which shouldn't be kept too long. Dried fruits especially need cool, dry storage, because they're liable to ferment in damp conditions – and to shrink in warm ones.

Preserves

A mould growth on the top of jam or marmalade can be carefully scooped off, but what's left should be used up as soon as possible. Syrups and honey crystallize if kept too long. They can still be used for sweetening, or if they haven't gone too rock-solid, you can reconvert them to liquid by standing in hot water.

Canned Goods

Fish and meat, with the exception of fish in tomato sauce, are safe to keep for several years – though no one's likely to want to. Canned ham, too, is an exception; this shouldn't be stored more than six months, and definitely prefers to be kept in a fridge. If one stray oddment gets tucked away and 'discovered' long after, check that the can hasn't rusted and perforated, because there's always this danger. Use canned fruit within a year, because although the food value stays the same, the colour deteriorates in a discouraging way. Condensed milk begins to discolour after six to nine months. Dried full-cream milk keeps for a few weeks after opening, but then tends to become rancid. Long Life milk is a minor miracle: unopened, it keeps well for a year in a cool larder, and Long Life cream for six months.

Bulk or Not?

A word of caution: bulk buying often *sounds* more economical than it is. Unless you've plenty of storage space, you'll curse the day you first thought of it. And even if you have got almost unlimited space, remember you're going to need unlimited smaller containers, too, to house perishable bulk goods once their giant packs have been opened. Desperate eating sprees, and a family bored to tears with something that's 'got to be used up', have made bulk-buying a dirty word in many a well-meaning kitchen. So unless your cupboards, supplies of containers – and your family – are large, it's wisest to organize a bulk-buying project with friends or neighbours, so that nobody gets swamped with a surplus, and everyone benefits from the lower prices.

However, when you are shopping for a large party, it pays to get catering-size packs of such perishable things as ice-cream, fruit juices and fruit salad. Other foods you might need for less formal occasions or for children's parties are large jars of instant coffee, catering-size cans of soup, tins of biscuits, and big bags of frozen peas.

Home Freezing for the Cook-Hostess

The how-to-freeze and how-to-thaw information is all set out in the charts which follow, along with notes on *what* you can freeze and how long you can keep it. We have concentrated on the foods most likely to help in entertaining.

For best flavour and texture results, turn your freezer to the lowest possible setting twenty-four hours beforehand; once the food has frozen, turn the freezer back to 'normal' setting. Speed of freezing is all-important, so always put foods into the coldest part of the cabinet, redistributing them when frozen.

FOOD AND MAXIMUM STORAGE TIME	PREPARATION	FREEZING	THAWING AND SERVING
Apples, cooking 6–8 months	(*a*) Purée: A useful way to preserve a glut of really ripe fruit. Prepare and cook in minimum amount liquid, with sugar – ¼ lb. to every 1 lb. fruit. (*N.B.* Add only a very little sugar when apple purée is used as a meat accompaniment. The addition of lemon juice prevents discoloration)	Pack into waxed cartons, seal and freeze	Thaw in refrigerator, allowing 6–8 hours per lb. of fruit or 3–6 hours at room temperature. Use for sauces, pie fillings, cold sweets, and baby foods. For a sauce, heat slowly in a saucepan from frozen, or in a covered dish in the oven
9–12 months	(*b*) Sliced or in wedges. Prepare and slice, blanch for 2 minutes in boiling water; drain and cool.	Either pack apple slices with 4 oz. sugar per lb. of fruit or in 20 per cent sugar syrup solution (4 oz. sugar to 16 fl. oz.)	Thaw as above, allowing 6–8 hours per lb. Use for pies, flans, and cold sweets
Asparagus up to 12 months	Grade stalks, cut in even lengths. Blanch in boiling water for 2–4 minutes.	Pack into suitable containers	Place direct from freezer into boiling salted water, cover and simmer until tender
Avocado Pear 6–8 months	Purée: Halve, removing pulp, and mash. Add 1 tsp. lemon juice per pear, and either salt and pepper or sugar	Place in waxed containers, and cover with polythene sheeting before sealing to prevent discoloration	Thaw as for apple purée; do not heat
Biscuits 6 months	Prepare in the usual way. Rich mixtures are the most satisfactory	Either baked or non-baked. Pack carefully. Wrap rolls of uncooked dough, or pipe soft mixtures into shapes, freeze and pack when firm in polythene bags. When cooked mixtures are cold, pack carefully	Thaw uncooked rolls of dough slightly, slice off required number of biscuits and bake. Very thin baked biscuits can be eaten without thawing, otherwise thaw for about 30 minutes in wrappings

FOOD AND MAXIMUM STORAGE TIME	PREPARATION	FREEZING	THAWING AND SERVING
Biscuit pie crust 2 months	Not easy to handle unfilled unless crust is pre-baked. Shape in a sandwich tin or pie plate lined with foil or waxed paper. Add filling if suitable	Freeze until firm, then remove from tin in the foil wrapping and pack in rigid container to prevent damage	To serve cold : thaw at room temperature for approx. 6 hours if filled
Bread 4 weeks	Freshly baked bread, both bought and home-made, can be frozen. Crisp, crusty bread stores well up to 1 week, then the crust begins to 'shell off'	Bought bread may be satisfactorily frozen in the original waxed wrapper for up to 1 week; for longer periods, seal in foil or polythene. Home-made bread : freeze in foil or polythene bags	Leave to thaw in the sealed polythene bag or wrapper at room temperature, or remove from bag and crisp in hot oven, if so wished. Sliced bought bread can be toasted from frozen state
Yeast doughs (uncooked) : 2–8 weeks, depending on type; risen : 2–3 weeks; unrisen, plain white; up to 8 weeks; enriched white up to 5 weeks	Freeze dough in quantities you are most likely to use. Better results are obtained if the proportion of yeast is increased, e.g. increase $\frac{1}{2}$ oz. yeast to $\frac{3}{4}$ oz.	Place dough in lightly greased polythene bags and seal, excluding as much air as possible, but leave a little space in case of chance rising	Dough takes about 3–4 hours to defrost at room temperature, or overnight in the refrigerator. Leave in loosely sealed polythene bag
Butter (commercially produced) Salted : 6 months Unsalted : 9–12 months	Always buy fresh stock. Both salted and unsalted butters freeze well. Farm butter must be made from pasteurized cream	Overwrap in foil, in $\frac{1}{2}$-lb. quantities	Allow to thaw in body of of refrigerator
Cakes, Fatless Including sponge flans, Swiss rolls, and layer cakes : 6 months	Bake in usual way. Leave until cold on a wire rack. Swiss rolls are best rolled up in cornflour, not sugar, if to be frozen without a filling. Do not spread or layer with jam before freezing	Wrap plain cake layers separately, or wrap them together with a double thickness of Saran or waxed paper between layers. If wished place in cardboard boxes for additional protection. Freeze frosted cakes (whole or cut) unwrapped until the frosting has set, then wrap, seal and pack in boxes to protect icing	Iced cakes : unwrap before thawing, then the wrapping will not stick to the frosting when thawing. Cream cakes : may be sliced while frozen, for a better shape and quick thawing. Plain cakes : leave in package and thaw at room temperature.
Cakes, made with Fat Up to 4 months. (Frosted cakes lose quality after 2 months; since ageing improves fruit cakes, they may be kept longer)	Omit essences, which tend to develop 'off' flavours; most spices, particularly ginger, are fine. Bake cakes in usual way and cool	See Cakes, Fatless	See Cakes, Fatless. Un-iced layer cakes and small cakes thaw in about $\frac{1}{2}$–1 hour at room temperature, while frosted layer cakes take up to 3 hours

FOOD AND MAXIMUM STORAGE TIME	PREPARATION	FREEZING	THAWING AND SERVING
Cakes, etc.: Scones and Teabreads 6 months	Bake in usual way	Freeze in polythene bag in convenient numbers for serving	Tea scones can be thawed in the oven. Girdle scones should be thawed in their wrappings for about 1 hour, drop scones for 30 minutes, or in a mod. oven, covered with foil, for 10 minutes—or toast from frozen. Teabreads : thaw at room temperature 2–3 hours
Cakes etc.: Danish Pastries: Unbaked, in bulk : 6 weeks Unbaked shaped : 2–3 weeks Baked : 2–3 weeks	Freezing without icing is best	See Yeast doughs. Freeze for 2 hours before packing. Store in airtight polythene bags or foil	Thaw shaped raw pastries for 1 hour at room temperature. Bake in hot oven (425 °F, mark 7) for 20 minutes, cool, ice, top with nuts. Baked : thaw for 20 minutes (or in hot oven for 5 minutes)
Cream Up to 12 months : ideally about 4 months	Use pasteurized only with a 40 per cent butter fat content, or more (i.e. double cream) Whipped cream may be piped into rosettes on waxed paper	Always transfer cream into suitable container, e.g. waxed cartons, leaving sufficient headspace for expansion. Freeze rosettes unwrapped ; when firm, pack in a single layer in foil	Thaw in refrigerator, allowing 8 hours, or 1–2 hours at room temperature Put rosettes in position as decoration before thawing, or they cannot be handled
Eggs Whole : 9 months	Break eggs into containers and inspect. For every 6 eggs add 1 level tsps. salt for savoury dishes or 1 level tbsp. sugar for sweet dishes ; mix lightly to combine	Pack in watertight container. Label must state number of eggs and whether salted or sugared Plastic ice cube trays are useful : store the cubes in plastic bag	Thaw unopened and use immediately, as required. The whole eggs may be used for omelettes, cakes, etc.
Separated : 9 months	Prepare as above, but whites do not need the addition of salt or sugar	As above	Use yolks in custard, flan pastry, mayonnaise, lemon curd, whites for meringues or icings
Fish, Cooked Pies, fish cakes, croquettes, kedgeree, mousse, paellas : 2 months	Prepare according to your recipe instructions, but be sure fish is absolutely fresh. Hard-boiled eggs should be added to the kedgeree before heating	Freeze in foil-lined containers and remove from containers when hard, then pack in sealed bags	Either slow-thaw in refrigerator or put straight into moderate oven to heat

FOOD AND MAXIMUM STORAGE TIME	PREPARATION	FREEZING	THAWING AND SERVING
Meat, Raw (leave unstuffed) Beef: 1 year Lamb: 9 months Veal: 9 months Pork: 4 months Freshly minced meat: 2–3 months Offal: 6 weeks Cured and smoked meats: 1 month	Use good quality fresh meat which has been well-hung. Removing bones will save space. Butcher in quantities suitable to the size of the family. If bones are left in, wrap sharp ends well to avoid puncturing the packaging material. Place a double thickness of Cellophane between individual chops or steaks *N.B.* Frequent turnover of meat will ensure a consistently high quality	Package carefully in heavy-quality polythene bags. Group in similar types, and overwrap with mutton cloth, stockinette, thin plastic or newspaper, to protect against puncturing and loss of quality	All meats may be cooked from frozen, especially for an emergency, but large joints need skilful attention to avoid the meat being over-cooked on outside and raw at centre. Thawing in the refrigerator is the most satisfactory way, keeping wrappings on. Allow about 6 hours per lb. Cook joints straight from the freezer by the slow method Small items like chops, steaks can be cooked frozen, but use gentle heat. Partial thawing is necessary before egg-and-crumb-coating, etc.
Meat, Cooked Dishes Casseroles, stews, curries, etc.: 2 months	Prepare as desired, see that the meat is cooked but not over-cooked, to adjust for re-heating. Do not season too heavily – check at point of serving. Have enough liquid or sauce to immerse solid meat completely. Don't add potato, rice or spaghetti, as they acquire a warmed-up flavour – best added at point of serving ; same applies to garlic	When mixture is quite cold, transfer to waxed cartons, inner-line cartons with polythene bags for dishes with a strong smell or colour. Or use foil dishes, or freeze in foil-lined cook-ware	Re-heat food from a waxed carton or polythene bag in a saucepan or casserole dish. Pre-shaped foil wrapped mixtures can be re-heated in the original dish. Re-heat food in special foil dishes. In each case from cold, always covered. In the oven, if casserole is very deep, allow at least 1 hour for heating through in a fairly hot oven (400 °F, mark 6) then reduce heat to moderate (350 °F, mark 4) for a further 40 minutes. In a pan, heat gently until thawed and simmer until thoroughly heated
Meat, Roast: 2–4 weeks	Joints can be roasted and frozen for serving cold – don't over-cook. Re-heated whole joints are not very satisfactory. Re-heated left-over frozen cooked meat tends to be dry	Best results are achieved from slicing the whole cooked and thawed joint, just prior to serving. Small pieces can be sliced and packed between double thickness of Cellophane if required to serve cold, or put in foil containers and covered with gravy, if to be served hot	Allow plenty of thawing-out – about 4 hours per lb. at room temperatures, or double the time in the refrigerator, in the wrapping. Sliced meat requires less time

FOOD AND MAXIMUM STORAGE TIME	PREPARATION	FREEZING	THAWING AND SERVING
Meat Loaves, Pâtés: 1 month	Follow regular recipe. Package in the usual way, after cooling rapidly. Keep for minimum time		Thaw, preferably, overnight, or for at least 6–8 hours in the refrigerator
Poultry and Game Chicken: 12 months Duck: 6 months Goose: 6 months Turkey: 6 months Giblets: 2 months Venison: 12 months	Use fresh birds only: prepare and draw in the usual way. Do not stuff before freezing. Cover protruding bones with grease-proof paper or foil. Hang game desired time before freezing	Pack trussed bird inside polythene bag and exclude as much air as possible before sealing. Freeze giblets separately. If wished, freeze in joints, wrap individually, and then overwrap.	Thaw in wrapping, preferably in refrigerator. Thaw a small bird overnight; birds up to 4 lb. up to 12 hours; 4–12 lb. up to 24 hours; over 12 lb. 48–72 hours; joints 6 hours
Pastry, Uncooked Shortcrust: 3 months	Freezing in blocks is impractical – they take so long to thaw, so roll out to size required. Pie shells should be frozen solid unwrapped to avoid damage. Use foil plates or take frozen shell out of dish after freezing but before wrapping. Suitable-sized discs of pastry can also be stacked, with waxed paper between, then over-wrapped. Use for bases or tops.	Stack pastry shapes with 2 pieces of Saran or waxed paper between layers, so if needs be one piece can be removed without thawing the whole batch. Place the stack on a piece of cardboard, wrap and seal	To use pastry, thaw at room temperature, fit into pie plate and proceed as recipe directs. Place shaped unbaked pie shells in the oven from the the freezer (ovenproof glass should first stand for 10 minutes at room temperature); add about 5 minutes on to normal time. Prick shell with a fork after 5 minutes' baking.
Flaky and puff: 3 months	Weigh off blocks of paste to fit the type of dishes usually made. Or shape vol-au-vent cases	Wrap and freeze in the usual way	Thaw before rolling out and use as required
Choux: 1 month	Freeze in bulk in a rigid container (disadvantage – has to be thawed before use), or after shaping. Choux cases, e.g. éclairs, may be baked, filled and iced before freezing	Freeze on baking sheet until firm, transfer to polythene bag or cook in the usual way before freezing. If already baked, freeze until firm, then pack in boxes	Place shaped (piped) choux pastry on baking sheet straight into fairly hot oven (400 °F, mark 6). Refresh cooked cases in the oven if wished: cool. Thaw filled éclairs at room temperature
Pastry, Cooked Puff, flan, cheese, flaky, shortcrust: 2 months	Prepare as usual. Empty cases, etc., freeze fairly satisfactorily, although there may be a change in texture. Do not overbake	Wrap carefully (see uncooked pastry). Very fragile	No need to thaw – can be warmed through from frozen in a fairly hot oven (400 °F, mark 6)
	To freeze pies, prepare as recipe directs, using a pie plate or an aluminium foil dish. Cool completely before freezing – avoid meringue toppings, cream pies and custard mixtures. Brush pastry case with egg white or oil before filling	Protect the tops of pies with an inverted paper plate or aluminium pie plate, then wrap and seal	Thaw flans with unbaked fillings unwrapped in fridge 1–1½ hours. Unwrap baked fruit pies, heat in fairly hot oven (375 °F, mark 5) about 30 minutes, or thaw at room temperature about 1 hour if to be served cold

FOOD AND MAXIMUM STORAGE TIME	PREPARATION	FREEZING	THAWING AND SERVING
Pastry Pies, Uncooked Double-crust	Prepare pastry and filling accordingly. Do not slit top crust of fruit pies before freezing. See pastries (cooked) for fillings to avoid	Protect as for cooked pies	Unwrap unbaked fruit pies and place while still frozen in a hot oven (425 °F, mark 7) for 40–60 minutes, according to type and size. First slit tops of double-crust pies
Top Crust	Prepare pie in the usual way, cut fruit into fairly small pieces, toss with sugar and cover with pastry. Do not slit the crust. Use ovenproof glass or foil dishes	Wrap in foil or plastic film	Unwrap and bake from frozen state (ovenproof glass should first stand for 10 minutes at room temperature) ; add a little more on to usual cooking time
Mushrooms (must be very fresh) 1–2 months	Wash in cold water, trim and slice. Sauté in butter, drain and allow to cool thoroughly.	Pack in polythene bags	Very useful for casseroles, etc., as they can be used straight from the freezer
Fruit, Soft Raspberries, strawberries, blackberries, gooseberries, bilberries, etc.: 10–12 months	Wipe with kitchen paper ; don't wash unless absolutely necessary. Avoid excessive handling, to prevent bruising	Spread out on tray and freeze individually, or in dry sugar – use 4 oz. caster sugar per lb. fruit. Turn fruit in sugar, leave until juice begins to run ; pack in waxed cardboard or plastic containers	Thaw at room temperature, allowing 2–4 hours per lb. of fruit, or in refrigerator for 6–8 hours ; as a decoration, do not completely thaw
Fruit, Stone Plums, cherries – black ones are best – apricots, etc. : 10–12 months	Wipe, halve and stone ; place fruit in 40 per cent cold syrup solution (8 oz. sugar 12 fl. oz. water), allowing ½ pint per lb. fruit	As above	Re-heat plums from frozen state, to prevent discoloration
Herbs Thyme, sage, rosemary, parsley: 2–3 months	Wash and dry herbs. These can be chopped before freezing, or crumbled when frozen. Prepare bouquet garni if required	Wrap in small bundles and place in moisture-proof bags. Make individual foil-wrapped packs of chopped herbs, say 1 tbsp.	If kept accessible, frozen herbs are as useful as dried, for they can be popped into stews, etc, while still frozen
Ice-Cream 3 months	Either home-made or bought ice-creams and sorbets can be stored in the freezer	Bought ice-cream should be re-wrapped in moisture-proof bags before storing. Home-made ones should be frozen in moulds or waxed containers	Put in freezing compartment of fridge at 20 °F (−7 °C) for 6–8 hours, to soften a little. Some 'soft' bought ice-cream can be used from freezer
Butter Cream, Apricot Glaze 2 months	Make butter cream as usual. For apricot glaze – mix 4 oz. jam, ⅛ pint water, 1 tbsp. lemon juice ; boil for 5 minutes, strain	Freeze butter cream unwrapped, then transfer to polythene bag. Apricot glaze is best packed in tubs	Remove wrapping from butter cream before thawing at room tempeature. Re-heat apricot glaze from frozen

At-a-Glance Chart

When you're cooking for your family, measures and oven temperatures probably get guessed – and successfully at that. But when guests are coming, misgivings can creep in, and a better-safe-than-sorry attitude sends some of us scurrying to the basic beginners' charts. So that no one has to scurry too far, we've included our most useful quick reference charts, to give you reassuring confirmation of what you've probably been doing for years.

ROASTING TIMES
Beef

Cook top-quality joints at 425 °F (mark 7) for 15–20 minutes plus 15–20 minutes over depending on degree of rareness. For less good quality joints cook at 375 °F (mark 5) for 25 minutes per lb. (boned and rolled 30 minutes). Cheap roasting cuts are best cooked at 325–350 °F (mark 3–4) for 40 minutes per lb.

Lamb

Cook joints with bone at 350 °F (mark 4) for 27 minutes per lb. plus 27 minutes over.

Pork

Cook at 375 °F (mark 5) for 30 minutes per lb. plus 30 minutes over.

Veal

Cook at 425 °F (mark 7) for 25 minutes per lb. plus 25 minutes over. Baste or cover with bacon rashers.

Bacon

Cook for 20 minutes per lb. plus 20 minutes over. Simmer soaked joint for half calculated cooking time. Remove rind. Put joint in roasting tin, spread with 2 tbsps. extra dripping. Cook in the oven at 350 °F (mark 4) for the rest of the time. 20 minutes before end prick fat with fork, raise to 425 °F (mark 7).

Turkey

See full notes on pages 102 and 103.

Chicken/Capon

Cook at 375 ° F (mark 5) for 20 minutes per lb. plus 20 minutes over, vary times slightly depending on ratio of bone and tightness of trussing.

Goose

Cook at 400 °F (mark 6) for 15 minutes per lb. plus 15 minutes over. Baste once. Cover bird with double thickness of greaseproof paper, remove if necessary at the end to brown bird.

Duck

Cook for 25–30 minutes per lb., starting at 375 °F (mark 5) for $\frac{1}{2}$ hour and reducing to 325 °F (mark 3) for the remainder of the time.

Venison

Cook for 30 minutes per lb. plus 30 minutes over. Cook in flour and water paste at 450 °F (mark 8) for 10 minutes, then reduce to 375 °F (mark 5), for the remainder of the time.

Game

Start at 450 °F (mark 8) for first 10 minutes, reduce to 400 °F (mark 6) for rest of time. Young pheasants take 30–40 minutes, older ones 40–60 minutes. Do not roast very old birds. Use a double tin or baste frequently.

BASIC QUANTITIES

Note. Use level spoonfuls for all Good Housekeeping recipes.

Scones

$\frac{1}{2}$ lb. plain flour, 4 level tsps. baking powder (or $\frac{1}{2}$ lb. self-raising flour plus 1 level tsp. baking powder), $\frac{1}{2}$ level tsp. salt, $1\frac{1}{2}$–2 oz. margarine or butter, $\frac{1}{4}$ pint milk. Makes 8–12.

Batter for Pancakes or Yorkshire Pudding

¼ lb. plain flour, 1 egg, ½ pint milk or milk and water, ¼ level tsp. salt.

Shortcrust Pastry

½ lb. plain flour, pinch salt, 2 oz. margarine, 2 oz. white fat, 4 tbsps. water, approx.

Rich Shortcrust (Flan) Pastry

½ lb. plain flour, 5 oz. butter or margarine, or a mixture of both, 1–2 egg yolks, 4–6 tsps. water, 2 level tsps. caster sugar.

Crumble Topping

¼ lb. plain/self-raising flour, 2 oz. margarine or butter, 1–2 oz. sugar.

Crumb Crust

8 oz. digestive biscuits, 3 oz. butter, melted, 2 oz. sugar.

Meringues

As a topping: to each egg white allow 1–1½ oz. caster sugar. As shells: to each egg white allow 2–3 oz. caster sugar.

Victoria Sandwich

4 oz. self-raising flour, 4 oz. margarine or butter, 4 oz. caster sugar, 2 large eggs.

Glacé Icing

½ lb. icing sugar, approx. 2 tbsps. warm water or any fruit juice.

Butter Cream

2 oz. butter, 2–3 oz. icing sugar.

Royal Icing

½ lb. icing sugar, 1 white of egg, 1 tsp. lemon juice, ½ tsp. glycerine (optional).

Custards

Cup (pouring) – 2–3 eggs, 1 pint milk, 1 oz. sugar. Baked – 2–3 eggs or 2 whole eggs and 1 yolk, 1 pint milk, 1 oz. sugar.

FRYING TEMPERATURES

(oil or fat for deep frying)
If you have no thermometer, judge the heat by the time taken to brown a 1-inch cube of bread

Doughnuts, fritters, onions, uncooked fish
350–360 °F   60 seconds

Croquettes, cooked food
360–380 °F   40 seconds

Potato chips, crisps, straws
370–390 °F   20 seconds

LIQUID TEMPERATURES

Water, milk, etc.

Boiling	212 °F
Simmering	approx. 205 °F
Tepid, lukewarm blood heat	approx. 98 °F
Freezing point	32 °F

HANDY MEASURES

		Approx.	
Almonds, ground	1 oz. = 3¾	level tbsps.	
Breadcrumbs, fresh	1 oz. = 7	,,	,,
dried	1 oz. = 3¼	,,	,,
Butter, lard, etc.	1 oz. = 2	,,	,,
Cheese, cheddar grated	1 oz. = 3	,,	,,
Chocolate, grated	1 oz. = 3¼	,,	,,
Cocoa	1 oz. = 2¾	,,	,,
Coconut, desiccated	1 oz. = 5	,,	,,
Coffee, instant	1 oz. = 6½	,,	,,
ground	1 oz. = 4	,,	,,
Cornflour, custard powder	1 oz. = 2½	,,	,,
Curry powder	1 oz. = 5	,,	,,
Flour, unsifted	1 oz. = 3	,,	,,
Gelatine, powdered	1 oz. = 2½	,,	,,
Ginger, ground	1 oz. = 4½	,,	,,
Mustard, dry	1 oz. = 3½	,,	,,
Rice, uncooked	1 oz. = 1½	,,	,,
Sugar, granulated, caster	1 oz. = 2	,,	,,
icing	1 oz. = 2½	,,	,,
Syrup, unheated	1 oz. = 1	,,	,,
Yeast, granulated	1 oz. = 1½	,,	,,

Index

Index

Index

Index